MEXICO

Author
Author Andrew Coe was born into a family of Mexican scholars and visited all the major archeological sites as a child. Based in New York, he has travelled the world extensively and now works as a freelance author specializing in Mexican popular culture.

Photographer
Currently based in Mexico, photographer Kal Muller has experienced, photographed and written about many of the most interesting and isolated places of the world. He has produced a number of books, and his photographs and articles have appeared in *National Geographic*, *Geo* and many other prestigious magazines.

MEXICO

— ⊘ —

Andrew Coe
Photography by Kal Muller

PASSPORT BOOKS
a division of *NTC Publishing Group*
Lincolnwood, Illinois USA

Published by Passport Books in conjunction with
The Guidebook Company Ltd

This edition first published in 1993 by Passport Books,
a division of NTC Publishing Group, 4255 W Touhy Avenue,
Lincolnwood (Chicago), Illinois 606-46-1975, USA
originally published by The Guidebook Company Ltd.

Library of Congress Catalog Card Number: 92-60496

Grateful acknowledgement is made to the following authors and publishers for permissions granted:

International Publishers Co for
Insurgent Mexico by John Reed © 1969 International Publishers Co

Penguin Books UK for
The Conquest of New Spain Bernal Díaz, translated by J M Cohen © 1978 J M Cohen

Grove Press Inc, New York and Penguin Books UK for
The Labyrinth of Solitude by Octavio Paz, translated by Lysander Kemp, Yara Milos and Rachel Phillips Belash ©
1961, 1972, 1990 Grove Press Inc

Jonathan Cape and Harper & Row Publishers
Under the Volcano by Malcolm Lowry © 1947 Malcolm Lowry

Eland Books for
A Visit to Don Otavio by Sybille Bedford © 1953 Sybille Bedford

Farrar Straus Giroux, New York for
The Hydra Head by Carlos Fuentes, translated from the Spanish by Margaret Sayers Peden © 1978 Farrar Straus
Giroux

Jonathan Cape and Viking Penguin, a division of Penguin Books USA for
So Far From God by Patrick Marnham © 1985 Patrick Marnham

University of Oklahoma Press for
'Legend of the Suns' from *Pre-Columbian Literatures of Mexico* by Miguel León-Portilla, translated by Grace
Lobanov and Miguel León-Portilla © 1969 University of Oklahoma Press

Editor: David Clive Price
Series Editor: Anna Claridge
Illustrations Editor: Caroline Robertson
Design: Teresa Ho
Map Design: Bai Yiliang

Photography by Kal Muller
Additional illustrations courtesy of Andy Coe 67, 69; Archivo Nacional 48, 143

Production by Twin Age Limited, Hong Kong
Printed in Hong Kong by Sing Cheong Printing Co Ltd

Contents

Charro in a bell tower, Jalisco

(following pages) Village horse race, Michoacán

Introduction

Mexico lives on top of a volcano, literally. The Volcanic Cordillera stretches across central Mexico and clasps the capital in a broad valley surrounded by volcanoes and rocked by occasional earthquakes. Mexico also lives under the threat of other kinds of eruption: explosions of human rage and frustration caused by the tension between ancient and modern, Indian and white, rich and poor, urban and rural. However, there are positive sides to living on a volcano. Mexican culture is rich, like the volcanic soil from which it springs, indeed one of the most vibrant in the world, producing Nobel-Prize-winning writers and the makers of beautiful traditional crafts. Life on a volcano also breeds a tough people—Mexicans are proud, passionate, stoic and driven. Their friendliness, hospitality and work ethic puts many other nations to shame. These qualities make every visit to Mexico a worthwhile and fascinating experience.

The tourist industry divides the country into what it calls 'Resort Mexico', 'Colonial Mexico' and 'Archeological Mexico'. This over-simplification ignores many areas of Mexico and in a sense short-changes visitors. In the north, Mexico would seem to consist only of a string of wild border towns running from Tijuana to Matamoros. Baja California, on the other hand, is a long, rocky peninsula filled with natural wonders, like whale-spawning grounds, and surrounded by beautiful waters perfect for sport fishing and surfing. Inland, northern Mexico is cowboy country—Chihuahua and Durango are the 'last frontier'—and is also the home of the corporate and industrial powerhouse of Monterrey. The Pacific Coast is lined with sun-drenched resorts like Puerto Vallarta and Acapulco, both spectacularly set against the coastal mountains. Northern Mexico's dry plateau ends at a fertile plain called the Bajío, where the Spanish discovered some of the richest silver mines in the world. Around the mines they built cities like Zacatecas and Guanajuato, which contain jewels of colonial architecture. The states of Jalisco and Michoacán, just to the west, are centers of Mexican cultural traditions like *charrerías* (Mexican rodeos) and of the manufacture of beautiful craft objects. South of the Bajío lie the valleys of the central highlands, which hold the three industrial centers of Mexico City, Puebla and Toluca.

As a capital, Mexico City has enormous problems like pollution and overcrowding, but it nevertheless possesses beautiful colonial buildings, stunning museums and the most exciting urban culture in Mexico. Nearby are the magnificent remains of the pre-Columbian cities of Teotihuacán and Tula. The states of Oaxaca and Chiapas along the southern Pacific coast are also heavily Indian and many of their villages have been barely touched by modern life. The ruins of Monte Albán, near the charming colonial city of Oaxaca, are one of the most stunningly situated in Mexico, and the ancient Mayan city of Palenque in Chiapas is considered the most beautiful site in Mesoamerica. The Yucatán

Peninsula, which divides the Gulf from the blue waters of the Caribbean, contains elegant Mayan cities, traditional Indian villages, and some of the most modern resorts in Mexico—like the fantasy that is Cancún.

History

MEXICO THROUGH THE CONQUEST

The history of pre-Conquest Mexico is marked by periods of slow but steady development, sudden bursts of cultural expansion and then cataclysmic collapse causing migration to other lands. The first humans probably entered the New World over 20,000 years ago, via a land bridge in the Bering Straits between Siberia and Alaska. Middens of extinct animal bones, including mammoths and early horses, found near Mexico City and Puebla indicate that hunter-gatherers had populated Mexico by 10,000 BC. The first signs of settled culture—semi-permanent dwellings, ceramic vessels and nascent agriculture—appeared around 5000 BC throughout central and southern Mexico. Signs of the earliest domesticated corn, which was the staple on which all Mesoamerican civilizations were built, have been found in caves in the Tehuacán Valley and its cultivation is believed to be 5,000 years old.

Mexico's first civilization, the Olmec, arose on the coastal plain of Veracruz around 1200 BC, and has left evidence of large ceremonial centers, a complicated hierarchical society, a writing system and an elaborate cosmology. The Olmecs produced massive pieces of monumental art, such as stone colossal heads weighing many tons, which remain remarkable today. Until they disappeared around the birth of Christ, the Olmecs' influence was felt throughout Mesoamerica. Perhaps spurred by their example, other groups began to show signs of 'development'—including the Zapotecs, who began their hill-top capital of Monte Albán around 500 BC. The great Mesoamerican florescence that archeologists call the Classic era began around AD 150 in the Valley of Mexico. At this time construction commenced on a city called Teotihuacán, whose population has been estimated at 200,000 at its peak. Teotihuacán was the first city in the New World that was supported largely on long-distance trade (with places as far away as Guatemala), rather than on agriculture and tribute from surrounding communities. The worship of its gods, including the Rain God and the Feathered Serpent, followed the trade routes, and later cultures made pilgrimages to Teotihuacán's magnificent Pyramids of the Sun and Moon. The city itself was destroyed and burned around AD 700, perhaps by invaders from the north.

In about AD 300, another culture—the Maya—began to develop outwards from the Mayan heartland in Guatemala's Petén jungle. On both the Yucatán Peninsula and along

Goddess Coatlicue ('Skirt of Serpents')

*Mosaic funeral mask from Teotihuacán,
Mexico City Anthropology Museum*

the Usumacinta River in Chiapas, the Mayas built fierce city-states whose achievements are frozen in reliefs, murals and ceramics that are among the jewels of Mesoamerican art. The Mayas had a highly developed hieroglyphic writing system, which has only recently been translated, and a sophisticated calendar more accurate than our own.

The other important Classic-era cultures included the Totonacs of Veracruz and the Zapotec kingdoms of Oaxaca, but by AD 900, for reasons unknown, almost all of these civilizations had collapsed, abandoning their cities to barbarian tribes and the jungle. One of these new tribes was the Tolteca-Chichimeca, which late in the tenth century founded the city of Tula, north of Mexico City. The Toltecs, who were known as great artists, craftsmen and warriors, extended their influence throughout Mesoamerica via trade and warfare. A Toltec prince, expelled in a factional struggle, may have conquered the late Maya capital of Chichén Itzá in far away Yucatán. In the mid-12th century, because of drought and internal disputes, the Toltec state collapsed, and many of the survivors migrated to the rich lakeshores of the Valley of Mexico to build new city-states.

Around AD 1300, more wanderers, a ragged group of barbarians who called themselves the Aztecs, arrived in the area. The Aztecs worshipped their terrible god, Huitzilipochtli, who needed a regular diet of human sacrifices to win the sun's daily battle with the night. Their practices repelled the other tribes; nevertheless, they were fast learners and fierce warriors—and they flourished. Within 150 years, through a combination of Machiavellian politics and brute force, they were the rulers of the

Valley of Mexico and had begun to expand their empire throughout central Mexico. The Aztecs were just reaching their peak, when a new emperor, Motecuhzoma II, ascended the throne. Motecuhzoma was a new type for the Aztecs; he was not a warrior but an intellectual, and a deeply superstitious one at that. When he heard that bearded, white-skinned men had been seen off the coast of Veracruz, he feared that they were heralds of the Toltec prince who had headed toward Yucatán centuries before, now worshipped as a deity but returning to reclaim his throne. In 1519, in fact, the Spanish soldier, Hernán Cortés, landed in Veracruz; his aims were to conquer Mesoamerica for his king, convert the heathen Indians to Christianity and, most importantly, capture vast treasures of gold.

He was aided in his plans by his own skill in forging alliances with Indian states anxious to topple the oppressive Aztec empire, and by Motecuhzoma's indecision as to Cortés' identity: by the time he decided the Spaniard was merely human, it was too late. After numerous setbacks and much loss of life, Cortés and his allies were able to capture Cuauhtémoc, the last Aztec emperor (Motecuhzoma was stoned to death by his own people), as well as Tenochtitlán, their capital. Assisted by epidemics of European diseases that travelled faster than any army, the Spaniards had conquered most of what we call Mexico within 25 years of their arrival, bringing to an end the long history of Indian Mesoamerica.

The Palace at the Maya site of Palenque, Chiapas

Colonial Mexico

Much of the history of Colonial Mexico is the history of the Spanish Crown exerting ever greater control on its colony, and in so doing extracting more money for its coffers. After the Conquest, Mexico was reorganized and rebuilt on Spanish lines, and the seat of the viceregal government—the *Virreynato*— was Mexico City, constructed on the foundations of Tenochtitlán. The first subjects to be reined in were not the Indians, who were mostly too demoralized and sick from epidemics to rebel, but the conquistadors. These had discovered that the stories of Mexican gold were just fables and that the real wealth lay in land and Indian slaves: Cortés quickly became the largest *hacienda* ('estate') owner in Mexico. The Spanish Crown saw the conquistadors' power and wealth as a threat to royal interests and sent administrators from Spain with new rules to whittle away their property. This mistrust—later repeated with rich *criollos* (Mexicans of pure Spanish blood), who were seen as greedy and polluted by the lax tropical environment—led to constant tension between Spain and its colony. Along with the Spanish administrators came priests and missionaries, who were spurred by the Inquisition and saw in the millions of pagan Indians a chance to win glory in the eyes of God. Some of the missionaries, notably Bartolomé de las Casas in Chiapas, decried the conquistadors' treatment of the Indians; their pressure eventually led to the abolition of Indian slavery, although abuses certainly continued. However, as the centuries passed, the idealists were confined to the hinterlands—such as the mountains of northern Mexico—while the church fathers in the cities turned their attention to amassing power, money and land. By 1800, the Church was the largest landowner and money-lender in Mexico.

The economy of the new colony had in fact taken off around 1550, after the discovery of rich silver mines in places like Taxco. Within a century Mexico was producing most of the world's silver, and wealthy cities sprang up around the mines in Guanajuato and Zacatecas. Every three to five years a Spanish fleet took the silver to the royal treasury in Spain, returning with luxury goods for the new classes of wealthy. Colonial culture flowered, particularly in the realms of religious architecture, painting and literature. However, beneath the Spanish and *criollo* élite, there was less to celebrate: the lower classes were ranked by an elaborate racial classification (white, Indian, black, and various mixtures of the three) that determined where they could live, what they could own and what trades they could practice. By the early 19th century, resentment against the arbitrary and money-hungry Spanish government had reached such a point that some kind of crisis was inevitable. It happened in 1808, and at first in a far country; Napoleon invaded Spain and deposed the Spanish monarch.

Independence to Revolution

Mexico's fight for independence, called the Insurgency, began in 1810 in the Bajío region north of Mexico City and quickly spread throughout central Mexico. Its leaders were *criollo* priests, officers and landowners, whose liberal land-reform policies brought them a huge army of followers from the Indian and *mestizo* poor. They were opposed by the Church and by conservative aristocrats who feared the vengeance of the masses. This liberal-conservative split was the most important factor in Mexican politics for most of the century. The Insurgency raged for over a decade, but the deciding factor was Spain's inability to support its troops. When the royalist commander, Agustín de Itúrbide, went over to the rebel side, the colonial government collapsed. Chaos, both political and economic, was the watchword for the next 30 years as Mexico struggled to restructure itself. Between 1822 and 1855, there were over 25 presidents and many more administrations. The country was actually ruled by *caudillos* ('chiefs'), the most powerful of whom was the corrupt and ruthless General Santa Anna, who dropped in and out of the presidency every few years. In 1846, when United States President James K Polk realized how weak Mexico was, he decided to annex not only Texas, which was filled with US settlers, but also New Mexico, Arizona and California—more than half of Mexico's land mass. Using a flimsy pretext, the US army invaded, captured Mexico City and forced the government to sign a treaty ceding all these territories to the United States—and, in 1848, gold was discovered in California.

After such a fiasco, the liberal faction led by Benito Juárez, a stern Zapotec Indian who believed in the rule of law above all, was able to gain power. The liberals passed a series of laws that greatly restricted the Church's power and forced it to sell most of its property. The conservatives, however, were outraged at such a move; they immediately took up arms and plunged Mexico into full civil war. In 1861, Juárez emerged victorious, but foreign forces had already seen a further opportunity in Mexico's chaos. Using the excuse that property of their citizens had been destroyed during battle without reimbursement, the French under Napoleon III landed troops in Mexico in 1862. After some stunning early defeats, they were able to capture Mexico City in 1863; Napoleon III then offered a naïve Austrian archduke the crown to the Mexican Empire. Maximilian and his Empress Carlota did not realize that their empire was surrounded by Juárez' troops waiting to pounce, which they did in 1867, when the French withdrew to face the threat of Bismarck in Europe. Maximilian was captured and executed in Querétaro; his wife lapsed into madness on her return to Europe. However, after Juárez' death in 1872, his erstwhile liberal ally, the military leader Porfírio Díaz, declared his intention to topple Juárez' successor. Díaz' government ruled from 1876 to 1911, introducing remarkable changes to Mexico. Foreign investment in industrial projects like mines, railroads and oil fields was encouraged, and huge public works projects sprang up everywhere. All the major cities and ports were renovated, Mexico's budget was balanced and its debt was paid for the first time ever. But there was a dark side to this boom—increasingly severe political and economic repression.

A Wise General

It was while Villa was in Chihuahua City, two weeks before the advance on Torreón, that the artillery corps of his army decided to present him with a gold medal for personal heroism in the field.

Four regimental bands grouped in one wedged in the crowd. The people of the capital were massed in solid thousands on the Plaza de Armas before the palace.

'¡Ya viene!' 'Here he comes!' '¡Viva Villa!' '¡Viva Madero!' 'Villa, the Friend of the Poor!'

The roar began at the back of the crowd and swept like fire in heavy growing crescendo until it seemed to toss thousands of hats above their heads. The band in the courtyard struck up the Mexican national air, and Villa came walking down the street.

He was dressed in an old plain khaki uniform, with several buttons lacking. He hadn't recently shaved, wore no hat, and his hair had not been brushed. He walked a little pigeon-toed, humped over, with his hands in his trousers pockets. As he entered the aisle between the rigid lines of soldiers he seemed slightly embarrassed, and grinned and nodded to a compadre here and there in the ranks.

At the foot of the grand staircase, Governor Chao and Secretary of State Terrazzas joined him in full-dress uniform. The band threw off all restraint, and, as Villa entered the audience chamber, at a signal from someone in the balcony of the palace, the great throng in the Plaza de Armas uncovered, and all the brilliant crowd of officers in the room saluted stiffly.

It was Napoleonic!

Villa hesitated for a minute, pulling his mustache and looking very uncomfortable, finally gravitated toward the throne, which he tested by shaking the arms, and then sat down, with the Governor on his right and the Secretary of State on his left.

Señor Bauche Alcalde stepped forward, raised his right hand to the exact position which Cicero took when denouncing Catiline, and pronounced a short discourse, indicting Villa for personal bravery on the field on six counts, which he mentioned in florid detail. He was followed by the Chief of Artillery, who said: 'The army adores you. We will follow you wherever you lead. You can be what you desire in Mexico.' Then three other officers spoke in the high-flung, extravagant periods necessary to Mexican oratory. They called him 'The Friend of the Poor', 'The Invincible General', 'The Inspirer of Courage and Patriotism', 'The Hope of the Indian Republic'. And through it all Villa slouched on the throne, his mouth hanging open, his little shrewd eyes playing around the room. Once or twice he yawned, but for the most part he seemed to be speculating, with some intense interior amusement, like a small boy in church, what it was all about.

Finally, with an impressive gesture, Colonel Servín stepped forward with the small pasteboard box which held the medal. General Chao nudged Villa, who stood up. The officers applauded violently; the crowd outside cheered; the band in the court burst into a triumphant march.

Villa put out both his hands eagerly, like a child for a new toy. He could hardly wait to open the box and see what was inside. An expectant hush fell upon everyone, even the crowd in the square. Villa looked at the medal, scratching his head, and in a reverent silence, said clearly: 'This is a hell of a little thing to give a man for all that heroism you are talking about!' And the bubble of Empire was pricked then and there with a great shout of laughter.

John Reed, Insurgent Mexico, 1914

In the early 20th century, unrest began to spread; liberal politicians campaigned from the United States and there was a growing number of revolts and strikes, all of which Díaz brutally squashed. In 1910, the liberal leader Francisco I Madero called on the people to take up arms against Díaz; peasants, mostly from northern Mexico, spontaneously formed armies and attacked the federal troops. Within six months Díaz had to resign and flee the country. Madero became president—but even then Mexico was thrown into renewed chaos. In 1913, Madero's treacherous military leader, Victoriano Huerta, arrested the president and later had both him and the vice-president assassinated. This crime shocked Mexico; the peasant armies appeared again, this time determined to kill Huerta. In 1914, Huerta was forced to resign, but the Revolution continued because none of the rebels could agree on a president. It took six more years of fighting and untold suffering throughout Mexico for one of the armed groups, led by Venustiano Carranza, Pancho Villa and Emiliano Zapata, to gain the upper hand. Carranza became president but he too was assassinated in 1920. It was left to his successor, Alvaro Obregón, to move Mexico finally out of the shadow of war.

MODERN MEXICO

The main legacies of the Revolution were the desire for stability and the acknowledgement of the importance of land reform, which was in turn a demand made by Zapata and other peasant revolutionaries. Plutarco Calles, Mexico's strong-man president from 1924 to 1934, made the first great strides in achieving these goals. Between 1924 and 1928, over eight million acres of land were redistributed, and in 1929 Calles organized the National Revolutionary Party, the precursor of today's Institutional Revolutionary Party (PRI). The goal of this party (and PRI today) was to encompass the interests of all major sectors of Mexican society from trade unionists to generals, reconcile them, and thereby ensure an orderly succession. The key to this concept is the rule that presidents can only govern for one six-year term, so that power will be shared rather than concentrated among a few. However, the opportunities for corruption in such a system are great, and Calles and his followers availed themselves of these freely. Calles was also a rabid anti-cleric, and his repressive policies led to the Cristero rebellion, in which Catholic militants blew up trains and police stations while soldiers retaliated by killing priests and burning churches.

Calles controlled a string of puppet presidents and he clearly thought he had another such when Lázaro Cárdenas was 'elected' in 1934. However, this ex-governor of Michoacán had the army on his side—Calles was soon on a plane to the United States. Cárdenas turned out to be the most beloved president in modern Mexico and his memory is still venerated. He distributed 49 million acres of land to the peasants, more than twice as much as all the previous presidents combined; he spent more on education than any

(above left) Modern Mexico City; (above right) Ciudad Satélite shopping center; (below) Satélite Towers, sculpture by Luis Barragan

other administration; and in 1938, he nationalized foreign oil holdings, mostly American, a move that did much to lift national pride.

During the decades that followed, the new oil wealth and an industrial boom spurred by World War II led to rapid development throughout Mexico. Ambitious public works projects blossomed, and by the 1960s it seemed as if Mexico might become a Second or even a First World nation. Then came the crisis of 1968: international student unrest had spread to Mexico, and students marched daily in the streets calling for the toppling, not only of the conservative President Díaz Ordáz, but of the entire system as well. Díaz Ordáz, who was anxious to avoid embarrassment at the upcoming '68 Olympics in Mexico City, gave permission for violent counter-measures, which resulted in the massacre of hundreds of students in the capital's plaza of Tlatelolco. In the following decade, the left went into hiding, while presidents Echeverría and López Portillo broke all records for blatant corruption. The police chief of Mexico City, Arturo 'Negro' Durazo, became known as one of the biggest drug dealers in the Western hemisphere. Millions of poor Mexicans moved to huge slums in Mexico City, straining municipal services to breaking point.

In 1982, President Miguel de la Madrid inherited empty coffers and a collapsed economy. Little wonder that the 1980s became known as 'the Crisis Decade'—in 1985, Mexico City was hit by a massive earthquake that killed tens of thousands, and then the government completely mishandled the disaster relief, which almost lost PRI the 1988 elections (some say that they did lose). Since then, President Carlos Salinas de Gortari has worked assiduously to prop up not only the economy but also the faltering PRI machine. However, he is finding it difficult to reform the party to international democratic standards while it continues to tolerate electoral abuses. Only time will tell whether Mexico will once again revert to chaos or find some new course for stability and prosperity.

Geography

Mexico is appropriately shaped like a cornucopia whose wider end is the border it shares with the United States, and whose narrowest part is the Isthmus of Tehuantepec. Beyond the isthmus, the country's land mass swells north to the Yucatán Peninsula. Mexico's diverse array of climatic zones—from snowfields to deserts to jungle—supports one of the largest numbers of plant and animal species of any country in the world; efforts have just begun to try to preserve them. Northwest Mexico and the long rocky peninsula of Baja California are arid desert environments. From the US border, two mountain ranges run south along the coast. The Sierra Madre Occidental, an extension of the Rockies, rises in steep, dry slopes along the Pacific. The lusher Sierra Madre Oriental is separated from the Gulf of Mexico by a broad coastal plain. Between these ranges lies a wide, thinly-populated plateau covered with barren desert and grasslands. This plateau ends about 300 miles north of Mexico City in a fertile plain called the Bajío, from which the Santiago and Panuco rivers drain to the west and east respectively. To the south lies the Volcanic Cordillera, also called the Central Highlands, a belt of huge, snow-capped volcanoes, lakes and fertile valleys that runs across Mexico from Veracruz to Colima. The most important valley here is the Valley of Mexico, the site of Mexico City; to the east lies the Valley of Puebla, and to the west is the Valley of Toluca.

The great valley of the Rio Balsas is situated on the southern slopes of the cordillera, and just beyond rises the Sierra Madre del Sur, a coastal range that runs from Michoacán to Oaxaca. The only blip on the otherwise flat and steamy plain along the Gulf of Mexico is a small volcanic range in Veracruz called the Tuxtlas. The Isthmus of Tehuantepec, Mexico's narrowest point, is a forest-covered region of rolling hills and flat flood plains. To the east rise Chiapas's highlands, which look like a choppy green sea from the air. The highlands slope down to the Lacandon rain forest in the east, one of the last untouched regions of Mexico. The flat limestone shelf of the Yucatán Peninsula bulges to the north, and the forest covering gradually becomes drier and more scrubby as you approach the north coast. Some geologists believe that millions of years ago, northeastern Yucatán was hit by a huge meteorite, in whose sun-darkened aftermath the dinosaurs became extinct.

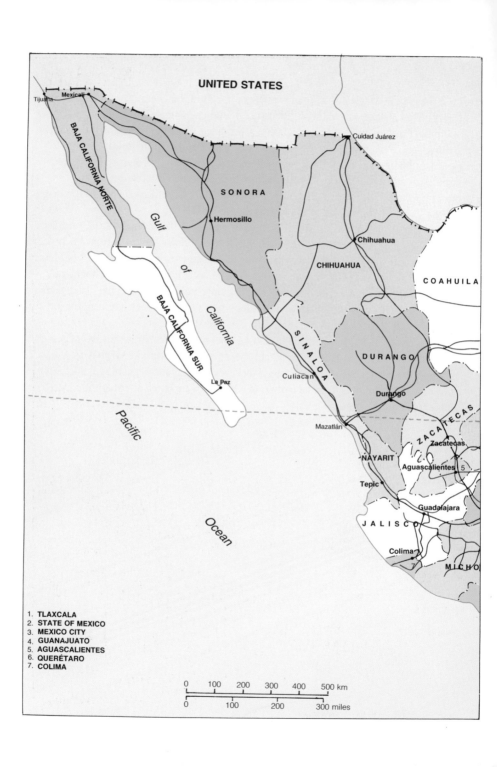

UNITED STATES

Tijuana Mexicali

BAJA CALIFORNIA NORTE

SONORA

Hermosillo

Cuidad Juárez

Chihuahua

CHIHUAHUA

COAHUILA

Gulf

of

California

BAJA CALIFORNIA SUR

La Paz

SINALOA

Culiacán

DURANGO

Durango

Pacific

Mazatlán

ZACATECAS

Zacatecas

NAYARIT

Aguascalientes 5

Tepic

Ocean

Guadalajara

JALISCO

Colima

MICHO

1. TLAXCALA
2. STATE OF MEXICO
3. MEXICO CITY
4. GUANAJUATO
5. AGUASCALIENTES
6. QUERÉTARO
7. COLIMA

| 0 | 100 | 200 | 300 | 400 | 500 km |

| 0 | 100 | 200 | 300 miles |

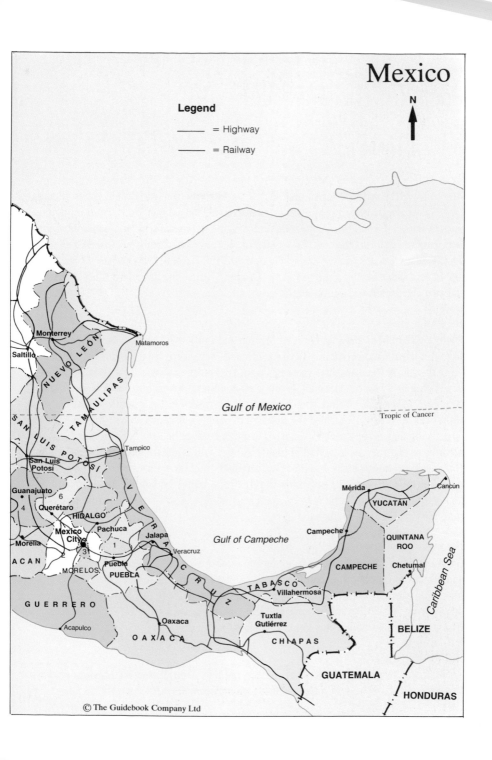

Mexico

Legend
——— = Highway
——— = Railway

N

Monterrey
Matamoros
Saltillo
NUEVO LEÓN
TAMAULIPAS
SAN LUIS POTOSÍ
Gulf of Mexico
Tropic of Cancer
Tampico
San Luis Potosí
Guanajuato
6
4   Querétaro
HIDALGO
Pachuca
Mexico City
Morelia
Jalapa
Veracruz
Puebla
MORELOS
PUEBLA
ACAN
GUERRERO
Acapulco
Oaxaca
OAXACA
V E R A C R U Z
Gulf of Campeche
Mérida
Cancún
YUCATÁN
Campeche
QUINTANA ROO
CAMPECHE
Chetumal
Caribbean Sea
TABASCO
Villahermosa
Tuxtla Gutiérrez
CHIAPAS
BELIZE
GUATEMALA
HONDURAS

© The Guidebook Company Ltd

Facts for the Traveller

Getting There

BY AIR

Mexico is well served by international flights, particularly from the United States. Mexico City, Guadalajara, Monterrey and all the major resorts have direct flights from numerous cities in the US. From Eurasia, the only direct flights to Mexico City originate in Amsterdam, London, Madrid, Moscow, Paris and Tokyo. Latin American cities with flights to the capital are Buenos Aires, Caracas, Guatemala City, Havana, Lima, Panama City, San José (Costa Rica), Santiago and Sao Paulo. Within Mexico, the national airlines of Aeromexico and Mexicana connect almost every city and resort.

BY CAR

There are 24 border crossings between Mexico and California, Arizona, New Mexico and Texas; Tijuana, Ciudad Juárez, Nuevo Laredo and Matamoros have the highest volume. From the south, there are three crossings from Guatemala, all near Tapachula, and one from Belize just west of Chetumal. If you want to bring your car into Mexico, you must buy Mexican insurance before you cross the border (difficult in the south). Mexican authorities have recently tackled the problem of people selling US-bought cars in Mexico by insisting that either their American car insurance policy be valid for at least two months, or that they leave a bond as high as 50 per cent of the car's entire assessed value at the border. However, this has provoked an outcry and the policy will likely be eased. If you are only driving your car within the 'free zone' along the border, these regulations do not apply. Automobile permits are good for 180 days; if you forget to get an extension, the penalties can be huge.

BY BUS

Greyhound has a service to the US border towns of Brownsville, Laredo, El Paso, Nogales and San Isidro (just south of San Diego). From there you must cross the border and travel into Mexico on one of the many Mexican bus lines. From the south, there is a bus service from Belize City to Chetumal and from Guatemala City to the Mexican border, where you can take a mini-bus to the Tapachula bus station.

BY TRAIN

There is no direct connection between the US rail line, Amtrak, and the Mexican railway. However, Amtrak's Sunset Limited, which runs between New Orleans and San Diego, passes near to border towns with Mexican railway terminals at El Paso, Texas (Ciudad Juárez) and Yuma, Arizona (Mexicali). Mexicali, Nogales, Ciudad Juárez, Ojinaga, Piedras Negras, Nuevo Laredo, Reynosa and Matamoros have terminals for Mexican passenger trains, which either run directly to Mexico City or connect with a line that goes further into Mexico.

Visas

United States and Canadian residents need a passport, birth certificate, voter's registration card or Green Card to enter Mexico. If you are visiting a border town for a short stay and do not plan to travel further into Mexico, you only need some proof of residency to pass through US customs on the way back. Except for the French, who need a visa, all citizens of Western European countries only need a passport to enter Mexico. Citizens of the former Eastern Bloc nations need a visa. On arrival at Mexican immigration, you must present a filled-out tourist card (available at the larger border crossings, on planes and with most travel agents, always *free*) to the officer. These are normally stamped for a 30-day stay. If you need more time, ask for longer, although this is not always granted. You can get extensions at the Secretaría de Gobernación, Dirreción General de Servicios Migratorios office (first floor) at 19 Calle Albañiles, Colonia 20 de Noviembre in Mexico City, or at international airports. Do not lose your tourist card, because this causes problems when you are trying to leave the country. There is a departure tax of US$12 on international flights, and US$7.6 on domestic flights.

Customs

You are allowed to bring into Mexico three litres of alcohol, one carton of cigarettes (or 50 cigars or one kilogram of tobacco), US$80 worth of gifts, 12 rolls of film and—for personal use only—electronic gadgetry like a portable computer, camera, radio or television. At customs in international airports, you are asked to push a button, and if the light turns red (not often), your luggage is cursorily searched. At smaller border crossings, the search depends on the whim of the customs agents. Bear in mind that on entering the United States, the importation of endangered species products, ie tortoise shell and black coral, is prohibited.

Climate

Mexico is a year-round destination, although some seasons are definitely more pleasant than others. Most tourists visit during the dry season, between late October and May. At the end of the dry season in April and May, much of Mexico is dry, dusty and burnt-over looking. The summer rainy season may signify the mere 2.5 centimetres (one inch) that falls in Mexicali every year, or the daily indundations in Chiapas and along the Veracruz coast. Mexico is prettiest in late October and November, when the rains have ended and the vegetation is still green (and there are the fewest tourists). Baja California and coastal Sonora are essentially deserts with hot summers (max over 42C, 105F), cool winters (night-time min 4C, 40F) and little rain. During the summer, inland northern Mexico is the hottest place in the country—Mexicali reaches 47C (116F)—but it cools off as you head to higher elevations. It is also the coldest place in Mexico during the winter; in the mountains of Chihuahua the temperature often falls below freezing, and there are occasional snowfalls. The Gulf Coast is wet and steamy during the rainy season and more pleasant in the winter, although *nortes*, storms from the United States, can inundate the area with cold rain. The Pacific Coast is generally dry and hot year round, except for pockets like Acapulco, which get afternoon rains May through September. Late summer and early fall are also the cyclone and hurricane seasons for the Pacific and Gulf Coasts, and there is a chance that your visit could be washed out.

The Central Highlands are dry and mild during the winter—daytime temperatures usually hover around 20C (68F) with occasional cold snaps—and the hottest weather usually comes in April and May, before the rainy season. Mexico City is flooded by daily downpours (that also wash the pollution from the air) during the rainy season—even the money becomes damp and clammy. Chiapas' highlands are hot and dry in the winter but cooler and wetter, particularly on the northern slopes, during the rainy season; the Pacific Coast near Guatemala is hot and steamy year round. Winters are warm and dry in Yucatán, although a *norte* occasionally passes through, and the steamy summers are punctuated by afternoon downpours.

Clothing

Mexicans prefer to dress more formally than Americans or Europeans. Outside of resort areas like Acapulco and Cancún, where attitudes are much more relaxed, men wear long pants and, for business, suits or jackets and ties. Many of the better restaurants in the big cities will require you to wear at least a jacket, if not a tie, for dinner. In the steamy city of Mérida, men eschew jackets for the traditional *guayabera* shirt. Women also dress

The churrigueresque entry and façade of the Ocotlán Sanctuary, one of Mexico's architectural gems

more modestly than their northern counterparts; slacks are acceptable but short-shorts, mini-skirts and belly-exposing outfits are thought fit only for prostitutes. Foreign women so dressed will expose themselves to the full onslaught of Mexican *machismo*. Mexicans take these customs particularly seriously in regard to religion: unacceptably dressed tourists will not be allowed into churches. In the Indian towns of Chiapas, tourists may be physically attacked if they offend the local mores. Remember that you are a guest in Mexico.

Health

Health is a major concern of visitors to Mexico. By following a few rules, you can avoid the most common trip-ruining ailments. On first arriving in Mexico City (altitude 2,278 metres, or 7,493 feet) and other elevated cities, like Zacatecas, go slowly for the first day or two, and restrict your alcohol intake until you become acclimatized to the height. The tap water in most Mexican towns and cities, including Mexico City, is impure. You can avoid stomach problems by drinking and brushing your teeth with bottled *agua purificada* ('purified water'), which is available in supermarkets, discount stores, hotel gift shops and some pharmacies throughout Mexico. Many big resort-type hotels have their own water purification systems that produce safe tap water. If there is no other water available, the water from the hot water tap is usually heated long enough to kill the germs. Most of the better restaurants also purify their water, but if you have any doubts drink soda or mineral water (*agua mineral*) without ice (*sin hielo*). Contaminated water also affects the food you eat, because it is washed in it. Raw unpeeled vegetables, salads, fruits you have not peeled yourself, and all food from street stands and cheap restaurants should be avoided. You can also get many diseases from unpasteurized milk and ice cream. The symptoms of the most common intestinal complaint, Montezuma's Revenge or *La Turista*, are cramps and diarrhea (locals, particularly children, actually suffer from this more than tourists). If you have a mild case, stop eating and keep up your water (or apple juice) intake, perhaps with a little sugar and salt added, until it is over. In more severe cases or if you have to travel, medication should be added to the fluid regimen. Yoghurt is now considered counter-productive. Avoid over-medication; use drugs like Pepto-Bismol or Imodium unless the cramps become acute, when Lomotil-type medications are recommended. For anything worse, you should see a doctor as soon as possible.

English-speaking doctors are found in all the resorts and major cities; ask at the desk of any large hotel. Mexican pharmacies are well-stocked with drugs, many manufactured by American and European firms, and most do not require a prescription. The combination of Mexico City's altitude and severe pollution may lead to lung problems for those with chronic respiratory disorders. High ozone and pollutant levels can irritate the air-ways and open the way for bacteria to infect the lungs with bronchitis and other diseases. If you are susceptible to these disorders, consult your doctor before leaving and travel with a supply of antibiotics. Visitors planning to travel into the hinterlands should be inoculated for typhoid and, if travelling rough along the Gulf Coast, bring along anti-malarial tablets. Cholera has recently spread to Mexico from South America, but so far it has been confined to small communities outside the resorts and metropolitan areas. The Aids epidemic has hit Mexico's big cities; condoms are widely available.

Money

Mexico's currency is the peso, which has the same symbol ($) as the US dollar. In the late 1970s, there were 22 to the US dollar. The peso went into free fall after the privatiza-tion of the banks and the collapse of the Mexican economy in the early 1980s; it was only reined in by the government of President Salinas de Gortari. Currently, the rate has stabilized at around 3,070 to the dollar (unfortunately for tourists, inflation has erased many of the savings caused by the peso's instability). The Mexican government is now considering wiping out the last two digits as a means of restoring the currency's honor. Pesos are issued in notes of 2,000, 5,000, 10,000, 20,000, 50,000 and 100,000 and coins of 5,000, 1,000, 500 and 100. There are still some smaller coins in circulation, but they are so worthless that people tape them together to make a jury-rigged coin of a higher denomination!

Transportation

BY AIR
The two main national airlines—Mexicana and Aeromexico—serve the following Mexi-can destinations: Acapulco, Aguascalientes, Campeche, Cancún, Chetumal, Chihuahua, Chichén Itzá, Ciudad del Carmen, Ciudad Juárez, Ciudad Obregón, Cozumel, Culiacán, Durango, Guadalajara, Guaymas, Hermosillo, Huatulco, Ixtapa/Zihuatenejo, La Paz, León, Los Cabos, Los Mochís, Manzanillo, Mazatlán, Mérida, Mexicali, Mexico City, Minatitlán, Monterrey, Nuevo Laredo, Oaxaca, Puerto Escondido, Puerto Vallarta, Rey-nosa, San Luis Potosí, Támpico, Tapachula, Tijuana, Torréon, Tuxtla Gutiérrez, Veracruz, Villahermosa and Zacatecas. Mexico City and, to a lesser extent, Guadalajara are the main hubs. There are also numerous smaller regional airlines.

By car

Travelling by car in Mexico has its pleasures and its perils. A car allows you to delve into many of the country's nooks and crannies to see marvels you would otherwise be unable to reach. Driving through rural areas from the dry hills of Baja California to the jungle of Yucatán is a joy; the cities are something else. Rental cars are expensive, but you can generally save money if you make the reservation outside Mexico. Remember that the cost of the insurance and a 15 per cent tourist tax are added to the basic rental rates. Gasoline is less expensive than in the United States and is sold in unleaded ('*Magna Sin*'), leaded ('*Nova*') and diesel form. All new cars sold in Mexico must use unleaded, but not all gas stations sell this fuel; look for the green *Magna Sin* sign. Check that the pump is set at zero before they start filling and that you receive the correct change after paying. Due to the pollution, authorities have restricted the days that you can drive in Mexico City; they are based on the last number of your license plate (foreign plates are not exempt). On Monday the forbidden final numbers are five or six, Tuesday seven or eight, Wednesday three or four, Thursday one or two, and Friday nine or zero. If you are caught, your vehicle will be impounded and you will have to pay a heavy fine.

A book could be written about the perils of the Mexican highway. The roads are overcrowded, potholed, narrow and with no shoulders. Mexican drivers usually enter a road first and look second. Instead of lights and stop signs, Mexican use *topes*, speed bumps, which come in the following varieties: metal bumps, single ridge, washboard, washboard between two ridges, and the dreaded reverse *tope*, which is actually an invisible ditch that scrapes the bottom off your car. Many Mexican policemen supplement their salaries through traffic fines, and tourists are considered easy pickings. If you are in such a shake-down situation, you have two alternatives: the one most commonly practiced by Mexicans is to *politely* say that you had no idea you were breaking a (non-existent) regulation but you are in a great hurry, is there not some way you could pay a fine right there? Then you agree on a price (not showing them your wallet) and make the pay-off. If the idea of paying a bribe offends you and you have a good command of Spanish, take down the policeman's name and number and ask to be taken to the nearest police station, where you can register a complaint (if of course the charge was unjustified). In car accidents, the Mexican practice is to lock up both parties until all claims are settled, even if you have insurance— some people prefer to leave the accident scene first.

Driving at night is also not advisable, because those are the hours that *bandidos* roam the roads, particularly in rural Oaxaca and Guerrero, and you may also encounter farm animals or drunks wandering from their nap on the pavement. When parking in big cities, never leave the car on the street overnight, unless you want your luggage, battery or your entire car stolen. Hotel parking lots with 24-hour guards are the safest. Mexico's roads are patrolled by the *Angeles Verdes* ('Green Angels'), a free government traveller's

(above) Statue of Bishop Vasco de Quiroga in Pátzcuaro, Michoacán;
(below) Michoacán woodcrafter's art

aid service that cruises along nearly every Mexican road of any size, at least twice a day. They can perform minor repairs and first aid; they can also call for assistance if necessary.

BY BUS

Buses reach nearly every community in Mexico and are generally an inexpensive, fast and reliable way to travel. There are first-, second- and local-class buses; in most cities, all the lines are collected in one central bus station, while in others each line has a separate terminal— sometimes many blocks apart. The distinctions between first and second class are not always clear. First class has reserved seats and is usually newer, cleaner, air conditioned (sometimes), makes less stops and no unscheduled pick-ups; second class is slower, less expensive and slightly dirtier. The toilets are kept locked, and you have to ask the driver for the key. On long-distance trips there are two drivers; one drives while the other sleeps on a mattress in the luggage compartment. There has been a rash of robberies on late night buses; travel during the day time if possible. A new luxury bus service is now offered by lines like ETN between Mexico City, the Bajío region and Guadalajara. Seats may be more than twice as expensive as regular first class, but the buses feature leg rests, complimentary sodas, uniformed attendants and video monitors that usually show the latest Stallone movies. Mexican bus stations are often jammed around the holidays; arrive early and be prepared to queue.

BY TRAIN

Travelling on the state-run train service, Ferrocarriles Nacionales de Mexico, can be an exercise in frustration. The antiquated rolling stock is slow and frequently breaks down, while buying tickets is sometimes a bureaucratic nightmare. The Copper Canyon train and the luxury-sleeper services from Guadalajara and Monterrey to Mexico City are happy exceptions. Sleeping accommodations include curtained berths, small private rooms and larger rooms with a private bathroom. Tickets for these should be purchased as far in advance as possible. The best non-sleeper tickets are special first class, with comfortable reclining seats. Thieves frequently work the regular first-class and second-class carriages, particularly at night. The Mérida-Mexico City train has a reputation for running days late.

Communications

Nearly every town and city has a post office, and the bright red mailboxes are widespread. Postal service is slow; letters to the United States often take three weeks. Corruption scandals regularly rock the agency; you should never send anything valuable by mail, although books and documents are generally considered safe. For fast and reliable package service within Mexico, try one of the long-distance bus lines. International packages should be sent via an overseas courier service like DHL or Federal Express.

Mexico's telephone company, Télmex, long had a reputation for terrible and overpriced service—witness the cellular phone explosion in Mexico City—but it was recently purchased by a consortium of national and foreign investors; better service is now promised. Many hotels impose exorbitant surcharges on operator-assisted calls; try to self-dial as much as possible. The Mexican government also charges high taxes on all international calls. Regular pay phones need small denomination coins or *fichas*, while LADA telephones (preferable for long distance) let you use larger denominations. Since the 1985 earthquake, most pay phones in Mexico City have been free for local calls. US long-distance companies, including Sprint, now have service to and from Mexico, which brings down rates significantly. The long-distance prefixes are 91 for calls within Mexico, 95 for the US and Canada, and 98 for the rest of the world; then dial the country code (if needed), city code and number. Telegraph service from Telegrafos Nacionales is also available.

Mexico is saturated with newspapers, because the price of newsprint is state-subsidized, the government buys most of the advertising space, and owning a newspaper can confer great political power (whether they have a significant readership or not is a matter of debate). The *Mexico City News*, the main English-language paper, is distributed in all tourist areas and has good coverage of US events, but very little local coverage. American papers and magazines like the *New York Times*, *USA Today*, the *Wall Street Journal*, *Time* and *Newsweek* are available in Sanborn's, in gift shops in the more expensive hotels, and in some newsstands in Guadalajara and Mexico City. Most big tourist hotels have US television beamed via satellite. The largest national Spanish dailies include *El Excelsior* (middle of the road), *El Universal* (more conservative), *Novedades* (*USA Today*-style), *El Financiero* (business), *La Prensa* (a lurid tabloid—the most popular) and *La Jornada* (the left-wing bible). The most respected regional dailies are *El Norte* from Monterrey and Mérida's *El Diario de Yucatán*. The magazines *Proceso*, *Epoca*, *Este Pais* and *Siempre* are the best for in-depth political reporting. The best English-language book store in Mexico City is the American Book Store at 25 Calle Madero near the Alameda; also try Librería Británica at 125 Calle Serápio Rendón and any Sanborn's branch.

Time, Measurements and Electricity

Most of Mexico is on the equivalent of US Central Standard Time (six hours behind Greenwich Mean Time), except for the states of Sonora, Sinaloa, Nayarit and Baja

California Sur, which are on Mountain Standard Time (seven hours behind GMT) and Baja California Norte, which is on Pacific Time (eight hours behind GMT).

Mexico adheres to the metric system. It also runs on 110 volt AC current with two-pin rectangular plugs, as in the United States. Electrical cords with different-sized prongs will not fit in Mexican plugs, so bring an adapter. Power failures and brown-outs are not uncommon.

Holidays

The most important religious holidays in Mexico are: December 10–12, when the Festival of Our Lady of Guadalupe is celebrated throughout the country; Christmas, which begins at least a week before December 25 and continues until the Day of the Three Kings, the traditional time of gift-giving, in early January; and the weeks leading up to Easter, first with Carnival (Veracruz' is the most famous), then with re-enactments of the Passion, and finally Easter itself. Mexico's most unique religious holiday is the Day of the Dead, the night between November 1 and 2, when Mexicans honor their ancestors by constructing elaborate altars and holding all-night vigils in the graveyards. The Day of the Dead is celebrated throughout Mexico, but the rituals practiced around Lake Patzcuaro, in Cuernavaca, and in Xochimilco, south of Mexico City, are particularly famous.

Masked fiesta in Uruapán, Michoacán

LEGAL NATIONAL HOLIDAYS

January 1	New Year
February 5	Constitution Day
March 21	Benito Juárez Birthday
May 1	Labor Day
September 16	Independence Day
November 20	Revolution Day
December 25	Christmas

Many local saints and historical events are also celebrated in cities and towns across Mexico. Here is a partial listing of regional celebrations:

Aguascalientes, Fair of St Mark	April 25
Chiapa de Corzo, Festival of St Sebastián	January 20
Cholula, Festival of Our Lady of Remedies	September 8
Cuernavaca, Flower Festival	May 2
Cuernavaca, Festival of the Virgin Mary's Birth	September 15
Guadalajara, Procession of Our Lady of Zapopan	October 12
Oaxaca, Guelaguetza Folk Festival	last two Mondays in July
Oaxaca, Festival of Our Lady of Solitude	December 18
Patzcuaro, Festival of Our Lady of Health	December 8
Puebla, Commemoration of Victory Over the French	May 5
San Andrés Chamula, Festival of St Andrew	November 29
San Felipe (Guanajuato), Festival of St Michael	September 28
San Miguel de Allende, Festival of St Michael	September 28

Tourist Information

In Mexico City, the Department of Tourism main offices are located at 172 Avda Masaryk, near Reforma. Abroad, there are Mexican Government Tourism Offices in New York (405 Park Avenue, Suite 1402, New York, NY 10022), Washington DC (1911 Pennsylvania Avenue, Washington, DC 20006), Chicago (70 Lake Street, Suite 1413, Chicago, IL 60601), Houston (2707 North Loop West, Suite 450, Houston, TX 77008), Los Angeles (10100 Santa Mónica Boulevard, Suite 224, Los Angeles, CA 90067), Toronto (2 Bloor Street West, Suite 1801, Toronto, Ontario H3B 3M9), London (60/61 Trafalgar Square, London WC2N 5DS), Madrid (126 Calle Velazquez, Madrid 28006), Paris (4 rue Notre-Dame Des Victoires, 75002 Paris), Frankfurt (26 Wiesenhüttenplatz, D6000 Frankfurt Am Main 1), Rome (3 Via Barberini, 00187 Rome) and Tokyo (2-15-1 Chiyoda-ku, Tokyo 100).

Eating and Drinking

FOOD

Mexican cuisine is one of the finest in the world. Unfortunately, authentic dishes are becoming harder to find because of the influence of fast food, tourists' food prejudices and the levelling of regional differences by modern urban culture. Corn was the staff of life for all the great Mesoamerican civilizations. It was usually ground and made into tortillas, *tamales* and other breads, or mixed into drinks, flavored gruels and stews. Chilli peppers and salt were the essential seasonings, and a meal without them was considered fasting. The Aztecs, who lived in the middle of an incredibly rich lake environment, ate a wide variety of plant and animal foods, including beans, squash, tomatos, manioc, ducks, fish, frogs, flies, amaranth, chocolate, cactus fruit, dried algae, mushrooms, fat hairless dogs and, yes, human meat, usually in a stew with tomatoes and chillies! Cooking fat was unknown, as were sweets, except for a few dishes flavored with honey. Motecuhzoma's meals usually included over a hundred dishes (as a deity, he ate alone), and perishable delicacies, like fresh fish from the Gulf, were raced to him by teams of runners. The Mayas of southern Mexico had a similar diet but added tropical gourmet items like iguana and monkey meat (for the élite, at least). *Tamales*, corn meal wrapped in corn husks and steamed, were a Maya specialty, and they also invented the *pibil*, a stone-lined oven in which food was sealed and baked until tender.

When the conquistadors arrived, they were forced to live on the local cuisine, some of which they found tasty, but the lack of fat and oil was unbearable. After the Conquest, they imported pigs, cattle, sheep, barrels full of wine, cheese, olive oil, herrings, European spices and sugar, in order to reconstruct their Spanish diet. Nevertheless, the intermingling of cuisines was inevitable; the Spanish royalty were soon sipping chocolate drinks and Yucatecan Indians cooked pork in their *pibils*. The next great influence on Mexican cuisine began when Napoleon's troops invaded in 1862; French cooking was the height of fashion under Porfirio Díaz. In this century, it is American food that has transfixed Mexican diets, although they are beginning to relish Italian pastas as well.

Each of Mexico's regions has a distinctive cuisine, and a trip dedicated to sampling their dishes can be rewarding and delectable. Central Mexico has the most clearly Aztec and Spanish food. *Mole* sauces, which were invented in Puebla and are made from ground chilli, chocolate and spices, are delicious on chicken and other meats. The Mexican national dish, *chiles en nogada*, is a perfect example of the Aztec-Spanish blend; these are breaded peppers (Aztec) stuffed with ground meat and pine nuts, covered with a sweet walnut-cream sauce (Spanish) and topped with pomegranate seeds and parsley. Michoacan is famous for its sweets, like *chongos*, a sugary curd made from rennet. The states of Jalisco, Colima and Nayarit to the northwest are known for their *carnitas* (roast meats) and *pozole*, a stew made from hominy and tripe and other meats. In Oaxaca and Chiapas, they add to their *moles* more sugar and spices like cloves and cinnamon; *tamales* are also their specialty. The Gulf states are famous for their seafood, like *veracruzana*-style fish with tomatos, chillies, olives and capers, and this is where the Caribbean influence is felt the strongest as well. Yucatán has the most distinctive regional cuisine; the warming *achiote* powder is the favorite seasoning; the fiery, mouth-watering *habanero* chilli accompanies every meal; and many dishes are still cooked to perfect tenderness in the *pibil* ovens. In the North, they serve cowboy food: corn tortillas are replaced by wider flour tortillas, and the regional specialties are 'cowboy-style' bean stew, steak, *chorizo* sausage and roast goat.

GUIDE TO A MEXICAN MENU

HUEVOS	EGGS
Fritos	Fried
Revueltos	Scrambled
Rancheros	Fried, with a chilli and tomato sauce
Mexicanos	Scrambled with chillies, onions and tomatoes
Machacado con	Scrambled with beef jerky

TORTILLAS	
Chilaquiles	Casserole of tortillas, sometimes with chicken, in a green chilli sauce
Enchiladas	Soft tortillas filled and covered with red or green chilli sauce
Tacos	Tortillas with meat
Chalupas	Tortilla boats, usually with a meat and bean filling
Tostadas	Fried and garnished tortillas
Quesadillas	Tortilla turnovers filled with cheese and fried
Quesadillas con huitalcoche	Quesadillas with corn fungus
Panuchos	Tortillas stuffed with beans and fried
Gorditas	Fat tortillas with a bean filling and a topping
Burritos	Filled flour tortillas

ANTOJITOS OR BOTANAS	APPETIZERS
Carnitas	Pieces of browned pork
Guacamole	Avocado blended with onions, chillies, coriander and lime juice

Fleshly Delights

For each meal his servants prepared him more than thirty dishes cooked in their native style, which they put over small earthenware braziers to prevent them from getting cold. They cooked more than three hundred plates of the food the great Montezuma was going to eat, and more than a thousand more for the guard. I have heard that they used to cook him the flesh of young boys. But as he had such a variety of dishes, made of so many different ingredients, we could not tell whether a dish was of human flesh or anything else, since every day they cooked fowls, turkeys, pheasants, local partridges, quail, tame and wild duck, venison, wild boar, marsh birds, pigeons, hares and rabbits, also many other kinds of birds and beasts native to their country, so numerous that I cannot quickly name them all. I know for certain, however, that after our Captain spoke against the sacrifice of human beings and the eating of their flesh, Montezuma ordered that it should no longer be served to him.

When he began his meal they placed in front of him a sort of wooden screen, richly decorated with gold, so that no one should see him eat. Then the four women retired, and four great chieftains, all old men, stood beside him. He talked with them every now and then and asked them questions, and as a great favour he would sometimes offer one of them a dish of whatever tasted best. They say that these were his closest relations and advisers and judges of lawsuits, and if he gave them anything to eat they ate it standing, with deep reverence and without looking in his face.

Montezuma's food was served on Cholula ware, some red and some black. While he was dining, the guards in the adjoining rooms did not dare to speak or make a noise above a whisper. His servants brought him some of every kind of fruit that grew in the country, but he ate very little of it. Sometimes they brought him in cups of pure gold a drink made from the cocoa-plant, which they said he took before visiting his wives. We did not take much notice of this at the time, though I saw them bring in a good fifty large jugs of this chocolate, all frothed up, of which he would drink a little. They always served it with great reverence. Sometimes some little humpbacked dwarfs would be present at his meals, whose bodies seemed almost to be broken in the middle. These were his jesters. There were other Indians who told him jokes and must have been his clowns, and others who sang and danced, for Montezuma was very fond of music and entertainment and would reward his entertainers with the leavings of food and chocolate. The same four women removed the tablecloths and again most reverently brought him water for his hands. Then Montezuma would talk to these four old chieftains about matters that interested him, and they would take their leave with great ceremony. He stayed behind to rest.

One thing I had forgotten to say is that two more very handsome women served Montezuma when he was at table with maize-cakes kneaded with eggs and other nourishing ingredients. These maize-cakes were very white, and were brought in on plates covered with clean napkins. They brought him a different kind of bread also, in a long ball kneaded with other kinds of nourishing food, and pachol cake, as they call it in that country, which is a kind of wafer. They also placed on the table three tubes, much painted and gilded, in which they put liquidambar mixed with some herbs which are called tobacco. When Montezuma had finished his dinner, and the singing and dancing were over and the cloths had been removed, he would inhale the smoke from one of these tubes. He took very little of it, and then fell asleep.

Bernal Díaz, *The Conquest of New Spain*,
translated by J M Cohen

Tamales	Corn meal and meat steamed in a corn husk
Ensalada de nopalitas	Nopal cactus salad
Queso fundido	Melted cheese served with tortillas
Seviche	Marinated raw fish with chillies and onions
Frijoles charros	Beans in broth
Frijoles refritos	Refried beans
Cebollitas asadas	Roast spring onions with lime

SOPAS	SOUPS
Caldo de pollo	Chicken soup
Sopa de lima	Lime soup with chicken and tortillas
Caldo de queso	Cheese broth
Caldo tlalpeno	Vegetable soup with chicken and chick peas
Sopa de elote	Corn soup
Menudo Norteño	Tripe stew
Pozole	Hominy stew with tripe or pork
Caldo de pescado	Fish stew

POLLO	CHICKEN
Pollo con mole poblano o verde	With brown or green *mole*
Pollo en pipián rojo	In a red sesame seed sauce
Pollo pibil	Baked in a pibil oven with *achiote* seasoning
Pollo en escabeche	With onions, chillies and vinegar
Pechuga de pollo	Chicken breasts
Pollo Norteño	Marinated and grilled

CARNE	MEAT
Carne asada a la Tampiqueña	Roast meat with assorted appetizers, including *quesadillas* and *guacamole*
Puntas de filete a la Mexicana	Beef with tomatoes and onions
Albóndigas	Meatballs
Chorizo	Spicy sausage
Puerco en mole verde	Pork in green *mole* sauce
Loma de puerco en adobo	Pork in a rich red chilli sauce
Chiles rellenos de picadillo	Chilles stuffed with pork
Cochinita pibil	Pork baked in a *pibil* oven
Carne con chile colorado	Meat in red chilli sauce

Lengua	Tongue
Cabrito	Roast baby goat

MARISCOS	SEAFOOD
Pescado relleno	Stuffed fish
Pescado al mojo de ajo	Fried fish with garlic
Huachinango	Red snapper
Camarones	Shrimp
Langosta	Lobster
Jaibas rellenas	Stuffed crab
Ostiones	Oysters

POSTRES	DESSERTS
Flan	Egg custard
Pay de queso	Cheese pie
Pay de nuez	Pecan pie
Crepas con cajeta	Crepes with sweet goat's milk syrup
Arroz con leche	Rice pudding
Buñuelos	Sweet fritters
Pastel	Cake
Guayabas	Guava in syrup
Helado	Ice cream

DRINK

As with food, the political and cultural history of Mexico can be traced through what people drank. Chocolate was the favorite non-alcoholic beverage for the pre-Columbian Indians, and the main alcoholic drink was *pulque*, the sour, mildly fermented juice of the maguey cactus. Despite their blood-thirsty practices, the Aztecs were remarkably puritanical; drunkenness was savagely punished, and only senior citizens were allowed to imbibe *pulque* freely. After the Conquest, the Indians turned to *pulque* to forget their troubles and alcoholism was widespread. The Spanish, who preferred wine and *aguardiente* (firewater), discovered that the juice of the agave cactus (related to maguey) could be distilled into a clear liquor that packed a hefty punch; mezcal was born. The Spanish settlers later imported grape vines, but wine production was forbidden because vineyard owners back in Spain complained about the competition. One of the reasons that Miguel Hidalgo started the Insurgency was that colonial authorities had destroyed his vines. In the late 19th century, Porfirio Díaz encouraged the importation of German beer-making technology, and many excellent breweries sprang up across the country.

Today, *pulque* production, which is confined to the central highlands, has fallen off sharply, and the *pulquerias* that remain are generally dirty and dangerous. This is a shame because scientists have discovered that *pulque* has many nutritive properties. The liquors of choice are *tequila*, produced only in Jalisco, and *mezcal*, which is made in northern Mexico, Oaxaca and Chiapas (check to see that the *mezcal* bottle says '100% agave'; if not it is just flavored alcohol). The most common ways of drinking these liquors is straight with a beer, with a chaser of *sangrita* (blood orange juice, tomato juice and chilli powder) or in a cocktail like a margarita. Mexican breweries produce many excellent beers. The main national brands are Superior, Dos Equis, Carta Blanca, Corona, Tecate, Bohemia and Negra Modelo, and you can also buy good regional brands like León and Montejo in Yucatán, or Pacífica from Mazatlán. Mexico's wine industry has been struggling ever since the royal ban on vineyards during colonial days. The most

Pottery on sale in the Plaza Vasco de Quiroga, Pátzcuaro

renowned vineyards are now just inland from Baja's Pacific coast, near the towns of Tecate and Ensenada (Bodegas de Santo Tomás here is one of the best). Vineyards are also starting production in Zacatecas and Querétaro. The majority of pressings from Mexican grapes go toward making brandy; Domecq is the major brand. Interesting non-alcoholic drinks include *café de olla* (coffee with brown sugar, cinnamon and anise seeds), *horchata* (a sweet rice drink), *aguas de jamaica* (water-flavored with hibiscus flowers) and *tamarindo* (tamarind-flavored water).

Crafts

Visitors interested in crafts will find an overflowing bounty in Mexico. Almost every major city and resort has a state- or federal government-operated crafts store that usually has the lowest prices and highest-quality merchandise. Craft items available in Mexico include silver and gold jewelry, ceramics, textiles (from clothes to blankets and rugs), leather, lacquerware, musical instruments, hammocks, baskets, hats, toys, onyx, masks, furniture, copperware, tiles and copies of pre-Columbian artefacts. The principal crafts manufacturing centers are Indian towns in the highlands (with the exception of Yucatán). Michoacan is perhaps the richest crafts center; here you can buy wooden furniture, clothing, guitars, green pineapple-shaped pots, wooden masks, lacquerware and copper. Oaxaca is known for its blankets and rugs, wooden animal carvings, green and black pottery, and baskets. The most important silver jewelry manufacturing town in the world is Taxco, where literally hundreds of dealers offer incredible bargains. For textiles, the place to go is the Chiapas highlands; San Cristóbal de las Casas attracts Indian weavers from throughout the state and Guatemala. Yucatán is known for its traditional *huipiles* (blouses) and excellent hammocks.

Mexico City

Introduction

It is easy to be maddened by Mexico City, which sits in the center of the Valley of Mexico like a giant octopus extending its tentacles in all directions. It is the second largest population center in the world after Tokyo-Yokohama, and by the end of the millenium it may be the largest. It preserves a rich and marvelous pre-Hispanic and colonial heritage in hundreds of old buildings and some of the finest museums in the world. Mexico City is the cultural capital of Latin America and produces an incredible variety of art and entertainment, both high and low, from Day of the Dead decorations to soap operas to street slang to literature by Nobel Prize-winning authors. On the other hand, Mexico City is the most polluted major city in the world, mainly as a result of vehicle emissions, and the smog is both sickening its inhabitants and eating away at its colonial buildings with acidic grime. On the political front, the capital has a monopoly on people (more than a quarter of the Mexican population), corruption, money and power, sapping the resources of the provinces and creating vast economic inequities. Nevertheless, there are few cities on earth more vibrant and exciting than Mexico City. Once you go, you will keep coming back.

Getting There

All roads in Mexico eventually lead to Mexico City. The main highways into the capital are Mexico 95 from Cuernavaca, Mexico 15 from Toluca, Mexico 57 from Querétaro, Mexico 85 from Pachuca and Mexico 150 from Puebla. Bus lines arrive from the provinces into one of four bus stations named after the points of the compass. Mexico City's railway station lies at the junction of all the main train lines, originating at Mexicali, Guadalajara, Ciudad Juárez, Piedras Negras, Veracruz, Mérida, Oaxaca and Uruapan. The capital's Benito Juárez International Airport is served by direct flights from nearly every city in Mexico, as well as international flights from Amsterdam, Atlanta, Buenos Aires, Caracas, Charlotte (North Carolina), Chicago, Cincinnati, Cleveland, Dallas, Denver, Guatemala City, Havana, Houston, Lima, London, Los Angeles, Madrid, Memphis, Miami, Moscow, New York, Orlando, Panama City, Paris, Philadelphia, Rio de Janeiro, San Antonio, San Diego, San Francisco, San Jose (California), San José (Costa Rica), San Juan (Puerto Rico), Santiago (Chile), Sao Paulo, Tokyo, Toronto and Tucson.

History

It is hard to believe (and a Mexican politician might deny it) that M_ always the most important place in Mesoamerica. Nevertheless, it did until the 14th century. Millions of years ago, a volcanic eruption blocked of Mexico's streams from flowing to the sea; the valley became what is technic, known as a closed hydrographic system, or a basin, and wide shallow lakes formed at the bottom. During the Pleistocene era, herds of now extinct mammals gathered around the lush lakeshore and attracted the arrows and knives of early hunters. Many lively ceramic figurines and utensils have been found in Formative-era (1200 BC–AD 150) tombs from the lakeside settlements at Tlatilco, Zacatenco and Cuicuilco. The most important of these sites is Cuicuilco, just south of UNAM, which was buried under a lava flow from the Xictli volcano around AD 100. The highlight is a four-tiered circular pyramid that was topped with altars and incense burners dedicated to the Fire God. During the Early Classic era, the great city of Teotihuacán rose in the northeastern corner of the valley to become the dominant force in Mesoamerica. When factional conflicts and droughts led to the collapse of the Toltec empire and the abandonment of Tula in the 12th century, the Toltecs moved into the Valley of Mexico and settled on the hill of Chapultepec and in Culhuacán. They were followed by other migrating tribes, like the Chichimeca, Acolhua, Otomi and Tepanecs, who divided the land around the lake into city-states. They intermarried with the Toltecs and gradually began to profess themselves the true heirs of that fallen empire.

Around AD 1300 a ragged group of wanderers entered the valley carrying an image of their blood-thirsty god, Huitzilipochtli, the God of the Sun and of War. They called themselves the Aztecs and had left their now-mythical island home of Aztlán about AD 1111 on the orders of Huitzilipochtli; speaking through his priests, he had foreseen that they would conquer 'all peoples of the universe'. The other residents of the valley saw them as savages and evicted them from their first home at Chapultépec. The Culhuas hired them as mercenaries and gave them a snake-infested strip of volcanic rock as home. The Aztecs surprised the Culhuas by thriving; they ate all the snakes, were brutally efficient as mercenaries and began to intermarry with the local aristocratic lineages. One day, Huitzilipochtli decreed that a noble virgin be sacrificed to become his godly consort. The Aztecs asked a Culhua ruler to give them one of his daughters to be their sovereign, took her back to their settlement, sacrificed her and invited the ruler to a feast at which an Aztec priest dressed in her flayed skin.

The Culhuas, appalled and frightened by the Aztecs' crime, took up arms and drove them from their settlement into the marshes of the lake. As the Aztecs shivered through a long night among the reeds, Huitzilipochtli spoke again and told them that they would

(above) Mexican revolutionaries, 1911; (below) victim of revolutionary violence, Mexico City

find a new home nearby, on an island where an eagle seated on a nopal cactus was eating a serpent. This eagle is now the symbol of Mexico and is enshrined on the national flag. The Aztecs named their settlement Tenochtitlán ('Place of the Cactus') and began to prosper by growing food on *chinampas*, artificially constructed platforms, and by hunting and fishing on the rich network of lakes. Tenochtitlán's location proved crucial to its subsequent growth, because far more goods could be transported by canoe than via the only land-based beast of burden, the human back. When the town became too crowded, a group of traders settled on an island to the north, which they named Tlatelolco. Those that remained in Tenochtitlán, who called themselves the Mexica (from which the name 'Mexico' derives), were dominated by warriors; they hired themselves out as mercenaries to the Tepanecs, who were trying to conquer the valley.

The Tepanec ruler, Tezozómoc, was a ruthless Machiavellian who delighted in playing factions off each other and taught the Aztecs many lessons in imperial politics. Tezozomoc's successor, his inept and unpopular son Maxlatzin, hated the Aztecs and was afraid of their newfound status. He decided to destroy them, but the Aztec king, Itzcoatl, and his minister of state, Tlacaelel, resolved to fight rather than flee. They convinced the Texcocans, Tlaxcalans and Huexotzingans to form an alliance, besieging, then capturing Azcapotzalco, the Tepanec capital. Thereafter, the valley was ruled by a triple alliance of the Aztecs, the Texcocans and the Tacubans. The Aztecs quickly emerged as the dominant partner and captured the remaining towns around the lake, including Coyoacán and Xochimilco. Tlacaelel became the power behind the Aztec throne and forged the new political and economic structure of the empire. He rewrote Aztec history to trace Aztec lineage directly back to the glorious Toltecs, constantly emphasizing that Huitzilipochtli needed the hearts of his enemies.

Between 1440 and 1468, Tlacaelel's brother, Motecuhzoma I, reigned, and his armies expanded the realm as far as Oaxaca and the Huasteca of northern Veracruz. During this period the first Flowery Wars were fought; these were arranged battles with the nearby but never conquered states of Chalco, Huexotzingo and Tlaxcala, whose sole purpose was to provide captives for ritual sacrifice. In 1487, the militaristic Aztec king, Ahuitzotl, celebrated the completion of the Great Temple (Templo Mayor) with the sacrifice of as many as 20,000 captives in a five-day festival. Ahuitzotl was succeeded in 1502 by a very different type of ruler, the philosopher-king Motecuhzoma II. Although he continued the Aztec expansion, Motecuhzoma II emphasized the consolidation of lands already conquered into the vast system of tribute flowing into Tenochtitlán. By this time the Aztec capital was a wonder of the New World, with a population over 200,000 and a vast network of canals filled with canoes and lined with whitewashed stone palaces, all heading toward the magnificent hub of the Great Temple. Tlatelolco to the north held the great markets that were the largest in Mesoamerica. Motecuhzoma's fatal flaw was that he was deeply superstitious and had a corps of magicians and soothsayers working for him. He was especially fearful of bad omens, and they started coming fast and furious—a comet, a mysterious fire in the Great Temple and, in 1518, news of a mountain that moved on the water and was populated by white-skinned and bearded men (probably Juan de Grijalva's expedition).

When Cortés appeared off the Tabasco coast in 1519, Motecuhzoma had spies waiting on the shore, and they sent detailed reports to the capital. These descriptions led to one conclusion for Motecuhzoma: here was the legendary Toltec ruler, Quetzalcoatl, returned from the East to herald the downfall of the Aztec empire. By the time he realized that the Spaniards were mere mortals, the conquistadors had penetrated deep into Aztec territory. Cortés' arrival in the Valley of Mexico caused great alarm among the Aztec population, 'as if they had eaten hallucinating mushrooms, or seen some dreadful vision'. Motecuhzoma met the Spanish with expressions of welcome and quartered them in a palace while he secretly planned to kill them.

However, Cortés made the first move; he heard that six of his soldiers had been killed by Aztec troops in Veracruz and took Motecuhzoma hostage. Militant members of the Aztec nobility stood outside waiting to slaughter the Spanish, while their ruler vacillated about giving the order to attack. His delay seemed justified when a punitive expedition from Cuba, led by Pánfilo Narváez, landed in Veracruz to arrest Cortés. Cortés left Motecuhzoma in the custody of 80 soldiers under Pedro de Alvarado and quick-marched to the coast. Before he left, he rashly smashed the most important Aztec idols, further antagonizing the Indians. The Narváez expedition proved a boon to Cortés, because after his troops defeated them, many of the gold-hungry soldiers joined his forces. Meanwhile, Alvarado led his men into an Aztec festival and, fearing it presaged an uprising, systematically slaughtered dozens of priests. When Cortés returned, the Aztecs cut off all food and water to the Spanish troops and replaced Motecuhzoma with his more militant brother, Cuitlahuac. Fighting began, and the conquistadors forced Motecuhzoma onto a battlement to plead with his people to lay down their arms. He was answered by a shower of stones that killed him. Cortés decided that it was time to flee and told his troops that they could take whatever gold and jewels they could carry. On July 10, 1520, known as the *Noche Triste* ('Sad Night'), the Spanish escaped along a causeway; the Aztecs discovered their flight and destroyed the bridges. With the enemy at their heels and weighed down with booty, most of the conquistadors drowned in the canals, and only Cortés and a fraction of his men survived. However, the Aztecs lost the chance to complete their victory by neglecting to hunt down and kill the fleeing Spaniards.

For almost a year, the conquistadors rested on the coast, welcomed reinforcements drawn by news of gold and conquered the city-states in the area that still paid tribute to the Aztecs. The populations that resisted were enslaved and marked with a brand on their faces. The Aztecs knew that war was coming, but their population was weakened by a smallpox epidemic that killed Cuitlahuac. On June 1, 1521, backed by Tlaxcalán troops, the Spaniards attacked the vastly larger Aztec force along the three major causeways and with war brigantines on the water. The Aztecs won the first battles but wasted time and energy in capturing the enemy alive (for sacrificial purposes) rather than killing them immediately. Cortés himself was about to be sacrificed when his troops saved him. The Spaniards changed tactics and cut off the food and water supplies to Tenochtitlán. Then they slowly tightened the circle around the capital, destroying the Aztec buildings as they advanced. The Aztecs finally realized that defeat was inevitable, and their last ruler, Cuauhtemoc, was captured as he tried to escape. During the days that followed, Tenochtitlán was abandoned and then sacked and burned by the Spanish and their Tlaxcalan allies, who also celebrated with human sacrifices when the Spanish were out of the way. The fleeing Aztecs spread smallpox and other European diseases to the rest of Mexico, beginning the next cycle of conquest.

Cortés established the first Spanish government in the more pleasant city of Coyoacan to the south. In 1522, he ordered the razing of the Aztec palaces and temples around the Great Plaza and began to rebuild Tenochtitlán, renamed 'Mexico', as the capital of New Spain. His architects kept the quadrangular Aztec plan and, perhaps unwittingly, designed the first true Renaissance city, with broad avenues and plazas and no confining city walls. The Spanish lived in the center around the Great Plaza and the Indian neighborhoods lay in the outskirts on the other side of a canal. This division of races was considered crucial to Spanish plans for the evangelization and colonization of the natives. The first new buildings were fort-like palaces and churches built on the Aztec foundations and from Aztec stones, including the Palacio Real, the Palacio de Cortés (now the Palacio Nacional) and the Cathedral. As the colonial era advanced, the old conquistador élite was replaced by a generation of *criollo* (Mexican-born) mining and merchant barons whose tastes ran to elegant Renaissance palaces. The vast wealth of New Spain allowed the Church and the colonial government to build ornate edifices in both the churrigueresque (Mexican baroque) and the more restrained classical style.

Meanwhile, tens of thousands of Indians, *mestizos* and blacks were drawn to the capital and found that their lives were strictly controlled by a complicated system of racial classification. Inequalities between the races exploded in a series of riots, the most violent of which was the Tumult of 1692, when the Palacio Real and other government buildings were torched. Mexico City was also devastated by a series of floods; in 1608, engineers began a centuries-long project of draining the lakes through a canal to the north.

By the beginning of the 19th century, Mexico City, the seat of the colonial government, had come to symbolize everything that was wrong with New Spain. For the next century it was the target of provincial armies' rage and of the imperial designs of foreign

invaders. After Independence, all emblems of Spanish power were erased from city buildings and the equestrian statue of Charles IV was removed from the Great Plaza, now
called the Zócalo. The political and economic chaos that followed led to great destitu-
tion; thousands became *léperos*, homeless vagabonds terrorizing the city streets. In 1847,
an American invading army led by General Winfield Scott arrived at the outskirts of the
capital. After victories at Contreras and Churubusco to the south, Scott's troops defeated
the Mexicans at Molino del Rey in a bloody battle during which 2,000 Mexicans and 700
Americans died. Scott advanced to the last Mexican position, the castle on Chapultépec
Hill, and stormed it on September 13. The last defenders were young military cadets,
some of whom threw themselves from the ramparts rather than surrender. They are
enshrined in the Mexican national pantheon as the Child Heroes (*Niños Héroes*) of
Chapultepec. At the end of the 1850s, Benito Juárez' anti-clerical policies caused many
churches and convents to be converted into offices, hotels and private homes. The great
city planning project of the Emperor Maximilian was the Paseo de la Reforma (originally
named the Avenue of the Empire), which ran from the Alameda, the upper class's favorite promenade, to the Imperial Palace in Chapultépec. Public works construction
reached a fever pitch under the rule of Porfirio Díaz. Electric lighting arrived in 1880,
mule-drawn omnibuses were replaced by electric trolleys and the first planned *colonias*
('neighborhoods') were built along Reforma.

By the time of the 1910 Centennial of Independence gala, Mexico City shone with a
French-style Porfiriato gloss, exemplified by the white marble monument to Juárez at the
south side of the Alameda. The outbreak of the Revolution immediately afterward was
proof that a gulf had opened between the capital's Europeanized élite and the provincial
poor and middle class. The revolutionary armies of Zapata, Villa and Carranza inflicted
years of violence and starvation on the city, not just to topple the government but to
punish the citizens for representing everything they hated. In the 1920s, the new political leaders—many of whom were from the North—preferred more relaxed American-
style mansions to the old palaces. Mexico City was flooded with European refugees
during World War II, bringing a new cosmopolitan atmosphere, and an economic boom
led workers to abandon the siesta for *el lunch*. The 1950s were a decade of highway
construction, including the Periférico, Insurgentes Sur and the northern extension of
Reforma, which expanded the city and destroyed many old neighborhoods. At the same
time millions of rural poor began to move to Mexico City to work in the many industries, beginning the population explosion that continues unabated today. The government encouraged urban pride with great public works projects like University City, the
Ciudad Tlatelolco housing project and the Anthropology Museum.

The culmination of these was to be the 1968 Olympics. The year leading up to the
Olympics was marked by ever-growing demonstrations of left-wing students, who were

met by increasingly violent police and soldiers. The conservative President Díaz Ordáz decided to squash the protest before it embarrassed him in front of a world audience. On October 2, he ordered soldiers to open fire on a night meeting in Tlatelolco's plaza; hundreds of students and bystanders were systematically massacred. This tragedy and the political repression that followed left scars on the national psyche that have yet to heal. In the 1970s, planners began to realize that the city's expansion was out of control. The first Metro line opened in 1969 (and now covers most of the city) but it hardly dented the geometric growth of vehicular traffic. A new phenomenon—smog—blankets the ground every morning and causes serious health problems for children and old people. New immigrants from rural poverty have settled in vast slums like Netzahualcoyotl, which spread across the dry salt-poisoned bed of Lake Texcoco. Experts estimate that the total population for the Federal District and the adjacent metropolitan areas in the State of Mexico is over 20 million. The pressure on the water supply is so great that the water table has dropped and caused the city to sink; many old buildings, including the Cathedral, teeter crookedly.

At 7.19 am on September 19, 1985, an earthquake measuring 8.1 on the Richter scale killed tens of thousands, left many more homeless and destroyed dozens of poorly built modern buildings downtown. The government's slow response so enraged the residents that they finally began to turn their city around. Citizens' groups calling for political and ecological change almost toppled the government in 1988 and have continued to put pressure on the local and national administrations. In response, President Salinas de Gortari has recently begun to take drastic steps to heal Mexico City's ravaged environment, but so far these have not lowered the levels of any major pollutants. Now the middle and upper classes have begun leaving the capital for healthier lives in the provinces, but the flood of rural poor entering the Valley of Mexico persists.

Getting Around

Mexico City is enormous, and you should set aside at least a week to see it properly. It is also necessary to plan how to get around, because the sights are so widely spread apart. All the major hotels have English-speaking tour guides, who can show you around in their big American cars. An inexpensive alternative are the ubiquitous taxis, but the drivers (often moonlighting from other jobs) do not always know the city well. The cheapest above-ground way to travel is by bus; unfortunately they are slow, crowded and often carry pickpockets. Mini-buses, called *combis*, ply the same routes as buses for slightly more money and are more comfortable and faster. Fares for taxis, buses and *combis* are set by the government—do not let anyone tell you differently—although late

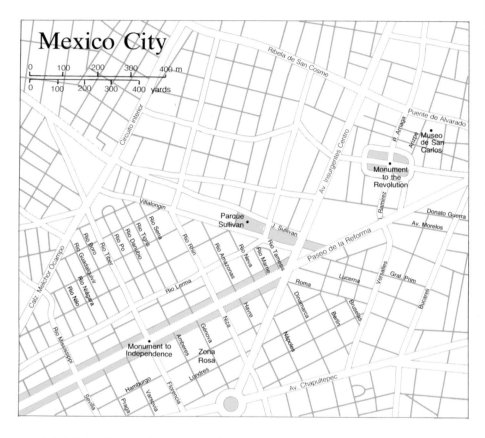

at night it is hard to avoid paying more for a taxi. Every visitor should also try Mexico City's Metro system, with nine lines covering most of the city. The tickets are cheap (the price is heavily subsidized by the government), the stations are clean and the trains run quietly on rubber wheels. During rush hours the crush can be oppressive; this is also prime time for pickpockets, so watch your bags and wallets and beware of anyone deliberately blocking your way. Mexico City is so large and has so many streets (almost 45,000) that street names are often duplicated. If you are trying to find an out-of-the-way address, you must know the name of the *colonia* ('neighborhood') as well.

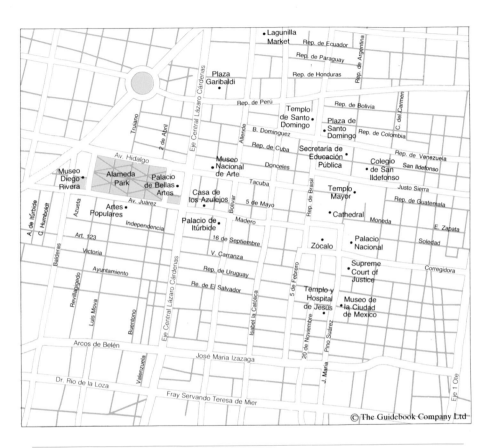

© The Guidebook Company Ltd

The Historic Center

THE ZÓCALO

The heart of Mexico and the main stage for the nation's political theater is the broad plaza of the **Zócalo**; an enormous Mexican flag flies from the pole in the center. During the Aztec era this was the Plaza Mayor ('Great Plaza') of Tenochtitlán. Nearly every day it is filled with official celebrations or with protesters rallying to change (or topple) the government. The city's main market was located here during the Colonial era, but it was moved because of congestion and the expansion of the population. To the north stands the massive **Cathedral** (begun 16th century), the most important in Mexico, with a relatively austere classical façade (1813) and two massive towers. Much of the interior's glory is obscured by metal scaffolding holding up the arches. The subsidence of the ground—you will notice that the floor slants up to the altar—and damage from the 1985 earthquake have caused the building to show signs of collapse. Visitors may be barred during Cathedral services. The nave is lined with 13 chapels and the gilt **Altar de los Reyes** (1718–25) at the end is a churrigueresque masterpiece. A stairway near the west entrance leads down into the **crypt**, where many of Mexico City's bishops are buried. The **Sagrario Metropolitano** (18th century) next to the Cathedral is a Latin-cross-shaped church with an ornate churrigueresque façade and a less interesting classical interior.

The east side of the Zócalo is bordered by the massive, three-story **Palacio Nacional**, which contains the offices of the president, the National Archives and the Secretariat of the Treasury. Every September 15, in Mexico's most important national festival, the president appears on a balcony of the palace and recites the **Grito de Dolores**, the speech that Miguel Hidalgo used in 1810 to ignite the Insurgency, to an audience of hundreds of thousands gathered in the plaza. Motecuhzoma II's royal palace originally stood on this spot, and the current edifice has gone through numerous expansions and restorations, most recently in the 1920s. The central entrance leads into a large courtyard, the staircase of which is decorated with Diego Rivera's most magnificent **mural** (1929–35), depicting Mexico's history from the Indians until the modern industrial state, and including cameos by Frida Kahlo and 'Carlos Marx'.

The south side of the Zócalo is lined with city government offices, while on the west stand two good hotels, the Majestic and the Gran Hotel (visit the Art Nouveau atrium), with many hat and jewelry stores along a colonnade. At the northwest corner of the Zócalo stands the **Monte Nacional de Piedad**, the flagship of the government-run chain of pawn shops found throughout Mexico; another of Motecuhzoma II's palaces stood on this spot. On the Aztec foundations Cortés built a fort-like one-story palace, which later became the seat of the colonial government and then an aristocrat's palace with added additional stories. The interior contains a **museum** on the pawn shop's history as well as many rooms where jewelry, furniture, computers, books, paintings, cameras, medical instruments and so on are sold; it is fun to browse in, but bargains are hard to find.

North of the Zócalo

If the Zócalo is the center of modern Mexico City, then the **Templo Mayor**, a half block to the north of the Palacio Nacional and east of the Cathedral, was the heart of the Aztec universe. Just below street level you can see remains of the temple that was razed to obliterate the Aztec religion and to provide building stones for the Spanish palaces. The entrance (Tues–Sun, 9–5.30) is just to the south of the ruins, and the ticket gets you into the excellent **museum** as well. The ruins themselves are confusing, because they expose later temples superimposed on older ones (they were apparently expanded every 52 years). Huge serpent decorations, a **chac mool** and other sculptures are visible around the site. The museum, one of the best organized in Mexico, is devoted to Aztec culture and history, with a number of stunning artefacts. The highlight is the **monument of the Goddess Coyolxauhqui**, which was found at the foot of the temple by construction workers and caused archeologists to realize that they had found the Templo Mayor. The stone depicts a woman with a severed head and limbs, as if she has just fallen from a great height. According to Aztec legend, the Goddess Coatlicue, already mother of 400 sons and one daughter, Coyolxauhqui, became pregnant from a ball of feathers. Her offspring were scandalized, and Coyolxauhqui encouraged her brothers to slay their mother. The unborn child, the God Huitzilipochtli, heard of this plotting, armed himself with a shield and a mystical weapon called the Serpent of Fire, and leaped forth from the womb to kill Coyolxauhqui and most of her brothers. The goddess's body was thrown down the holy Coatepec Mountain and broke into many pieces. Every dawn Huitzilipochtli, the Sun God, relived this deed, killing the stars so the day might be born, and the Aztec priests fortified him by feeding him the hearts of sacrificial victims.

The **Museo Nacional de las Culturas**, a block southeast of the Templo Mayor on Calle Moneda, contains collections of ceramics, textiles and artisanry from cultures around the world. It is housed in the Casa de Moneda, the only mint in Mexico from the Conquest to Independence. One block north, the **Colegio de San Ildefonso** (begun late 16th century), a Jesuit school and later the National Preparatory School, is now a cultural center. During the early 1920s, a group of Mexican artists were given the building's walls to make their first attempts at building a national form of mural painting. Murals by Diego Rivera ('The Creation'), José Clemente Orozco ('The Eviction') and David Siquieros, among others, decorate the corridors and stairways. The 17th-century convent building of the **Secretaría de Educación Pública**, just west of the Colegio on Calle Argentina between San Ildefonso and Venezuela, contains two stories and 1,585 square meters (1,896 square yards) of magnificent Diego Rivera murals (1923–28) around one of the courtyards. These represent scenes from Mexican culture and history, including the Day of the Dead and the life of Zapata as well as overtly left-wing political statements. Unfortunately, most of the murals will be closed for restoration until late 1993 at the earliest.

The **Palace of the Inquisition**, until 1820 the center of incarceration, trials and torture for the crime of heresy, and now the Museum of Medicine, stands across Calle Venezuela at the corner of Calle Brasil. The **Plaza de Santo Domingo** to the west has been a center of the printing trade for centuries. Outdoor printing presses are set up under the portals on the west side and the printers tout their wares to passers-by. Public scribes also keep their desks here and type up love letters for the illiterate or documents for people doing business in the neighborhood's many government offices. The **Templo y Convento de Santo Domingo** (rebuilt 18th century) at the plaza's north end was built by

Plaza Mexico, the world's largest bullring

the Dominicans, with a baroque façade, many fine colonial paintings and two gilt retables inside the Latin-cross-shaped interior. The **Hostería Santo Domingo**, a block west of
the plaza on Calle Belisario Domínguez, is Mexico City's oldest restaurant and one of the
finest for traditional dishes. One of Mexico City's oldest wrestling and boxing arenas, the
Arena Coliseo, stands nearby on Calle Perú between Calles Chile and Allende.

SOUTH OF THE ZÓCALO

The **Supreme Court of Justice** (1935–41), just south of the Palacio Nacional on Avda
Pino Suarez, contains at the top of the staircase four violent, visionary murals by José
Clemente Orozco entitled 'The Social Movement of Work', 'Justice' (two panels) and
'National Riches'. The **Museo de la Ciudad de Mexico** two blocks south on Pino Suárez
is housed in the mansion of the Counts of Santiago Calimaya (begun 1536, frequently
rebuilt). The façade is notable for the cannon-shaped gargoyles along the roof. The museum inside contains good exhibitions, with many dioramas, on the history and cultures
of the Valley of Mexico, from the first inhabitants to the Revolution. Across Avda Pino
Suárez, the fort-like **Templo y Hospital de Jesús** (begun 1524) is built on the supposed
site of Cortés' and Motecuhzoma's first meeting (November 8, 1519) and was founded by

Cortés himself. The hospital, still in operation, was one of the first in the New World, and the austere interior of the church is decorated with José Clemente Orozco's black vision of the Apocalypse (1942–44). Cortés' bones are buried with little fanfare behind the altar—passions still run high about him almost 500 years after his death. The **Pino Suárez Metro Station** three blocks south contains the remains, now restored, of an Aztec pyramid dedicated to Quetzalcoatl. Eight blocks to the east on Avda San Pablo, in a run-down neighborhood, is the **Mercado de la Merced**, a four-block-long building where huge amounts of meat, produce, Ninja Turtle *piñatas* and housewares are sold every day. During the Day of the Dead celebrations, the vendors construct elaborate shrines to their ancestors.

Around the Alameda

In 1592, Don Luis de Velasco, the Virrey, ordered the construction of an **alameda**, a tree-lined walk, to 'ornament the city and give recreation to its citizens'. Today, the **Alameda Park**, seven blocks east of the Zócalo, still conforms with the Virrey's orders; every day it is filled with families, courting couples, balloon vendors, snake-oil salesman and so on. On weekends, there are concerts by top Mexican entertainers in the park's west end. The Alameda is also filled with fountains and sculptures, the most prominent of which is the white marble **Monument to Benito Juárez**, built for Porfírio Díaz' Centennial of the Revolution celebration, on the south side of the park. Across the street stands the **Museo de Artes Populares y Industria** , 44 Avda Juárez, a huge and excellent government crafts store in the ex-church of Corpus Christi (1720–24). A wall inside is covered with a mural by Miguel Covarrubias, the artist and writer, depicting the 'Map of Mexican Popular Arts'. Another good crafts store, **FONART**, occupies a building a block west of the Alameda on Avda Juárez. A block north stands the **Museo Diego Rivera**, which stages temporary exhibitions. The highlight of this museum is Rivera's huge mural, 'Dream of a Sunday Afternoon in the Central Alameda', which shows the park filled with a cast of characters including a victim of the Inquisition, Benito Juárez, Rivera himself as a school-boy, Frida Kahlo, Porfírio Díaz, Emiliano Zapata, peasant revolutionaries and many more. The mural was originally housed in the Hotel del Prado, which was destroyed in the 1985 earthquake. Between FONART and the Alameda, a square now filled with a permanent encampment of political protesters marks where the Prado used to be. At the eastern end of the park stands the wedding cake-like edifice of the **Palacio de Bellas Artes** (1904–1934). General Porfírio Díaz commissioned Bellas Artes (as it is familiarly known) to be a theater to rival in splendor the Paris Opera. The white marble façade is decorated with neo-classical details depicting serpents, eagles and other Mexican motifs as well as sculptural groupings with themes like 'Apollo and the Muses'. Construction was stopped by the Revolution in 1916, with only the exterior completed; in 1930, work began again, and the interior was completed in the Art Deco style. The theater in Bellas Artes is now used for concerts and weekly Ballet Folklorica dance performances. The first floor contains temporary exhibition spaces, while the second and third floors have arresting paintings by Orozco (*Catharsis*), Rivera (*Universal Man and the Machine*), Siquieros and Rufino Tamayo. The 46-story **Torre Latinoamericano** skyscraper, east across the Eje Central Lázaro Cárdenas, was built in 1956, and its innovative design survived the 1957 and 1985 earthquakes with little damage. Pollution permitting, the observation platform on the top floor has a great view of the surrounding city.

Avda Francisco Madero heads east from the Torre to the Zócalo. The **Templo de San Francisco** (begun 1524) next to the Torre, now sunken below street level, is one of the oldest colonial structures in the city and has a pollution-darkened churrigueresque façade. Across the street stands the 16th-century **Casa de los Azulejos** ('House of Tiles'), built by the Count of the Valley of Orizaba in the style of Puebla, with beautiful blue tiles covering the façade. The Sanborn's restaurant and department store chain now occupies the interior; the main dining room—traditionally a spot for politicians' power breakfasts—is located in the beautiful courtyard, and the main staircase above it is decorated with a mural by Orozco titled 'Omniscience'. A block and a half east on Madero, the **Palacio de Iturbide** (1779), Mexico City's finest baroque mansion and now a branch of Banamex, possesses an ornate façade covered with reliefs and coats of arms. The interior courtyard is a copy of the one in the Royal Palace in Palermo, and excellent temporary exhibitions (free) are displayed here. **Calle Tacuba**, parallel to Madero and two blocks north, also runs from the Alameda to the Zócalo.

The ornate **Post Office Building** (1902–07), across the street from Bellas Artes, was ordered by Porfirio Díaz to show the level of progress reached by Mexico under his administration. The building contains details in almost every style known to the architects at that time. Next door stands the **Palacio de Minería** (1797–1813), until 1860 the government school of mines, which was built in the neo-classical style by architects who wanted to put an end to the extravagances of the baroque; the interior is now used for conventions and expositions. Manuel Tolsá, the designer of this edifice, also sculpted the **Equestrian Statue of Charles IV** (1803) that faces the Palacio across the Calle Tacuba. Nicknamed *El Caballito* ('The Little Horse') by locals, this bronze presided over the center of the Zócalo until Independence. The **Museo Nacional de Arte** behind the statue occupies the old Secretariat of Communications building (1904–11). The collection is made up of Mexican painting and sculpture since the Conquest, being particularly strong on the 19th and early 20th century. Among the highlights is a room devoted to the 19th-century landscapes of the Valley of Mexico by José María Velasco, depicting a beautiful pre-industrial setting. It is also interesting to see how, in the early 20th century, Mexican artists shrugged off the influence of European styles like Impressionism and forged their own distinctly Mexican art.

Five blocks north of Bellas Artes on Eje Central Lázaro Cárdenas, you come to the heart of traditional Mexican music, the **Plaza Garibaldi**. During the day this is usually empty, but at night the plaza is filled with bands of *mariachis* in their Mexican cowboy costumes, practicing and soliciting work from passers-by who need entertainment for a party. The buildings around the plaza are occupied by bars, nightclubs and *pulquerías*, some sedate, others wild (watch out for thieves and pickpockets). The surrounding streets are filled with burlesque shows, and there is also one family-oriented theater, the **Teatro Blanquita**, which presents top Mexican entertainers. In the **Mercado de Lagunilla**, three blocks further north and then east, vendors sell antiques and an incredible variety of other wares; Sunday mornings are the most popular times to visit.

Reforma and Chapultepec

The Emperor Maximilian's pride and joy, the eight-lane **Paseo de la Reforma**, runs southwest from the Alameda to Chapultepec park and is lined with statues of 19th-century Mexican politicians and generals. Although a few old mansions still stand along Reforma, most of the buildings here are glass skyscrapers containing expensive hotels and corporate headquarters. Avda Juárez crosses Reforma and ends at the **Monument to the Revolution**, a large dome held up by four huge columns. This structure was begun in 1910 by Porfirio Díaz as part of a new legislative palace, but construction was stopped by the Revolution; it was transformed into a monument in the 1930s. The tops of the columns contain sculptural groups depicting Independence, Reform, Labor Laws and Agricultural Laws. The monument contains the remains of Pancho Villa and Presidents Carranza, Madero, Calles and Cárdenas. The basement of the monument is a **Museum of the Revolution**. Two blocks north on Calle Arizpe stands the **Museo de San Carlos**, in a colonial mansion (begun 1795) that contains the collection (mostly 17th- and 18th-century European paintings) of the Academy of San Carlos, the first art academy in the New World.

Returning to Reforma, the first traffic circle contains a **statue to Christopher Columbus** and is frequently the target of pro-Indian demonstrations; these originate at the **monument to Cuauhtemoc**, in the next traffic circle a few blocks down. **Avenida Insurgentes**, the major north–south artery and the city's longest avenue, crosses Reforma at the latter circle; the **Parque Sullivan** a half block north is the site of a popular open air art show and sale on Sunday mornings. Beyond Insurgentes the neighborhood south of

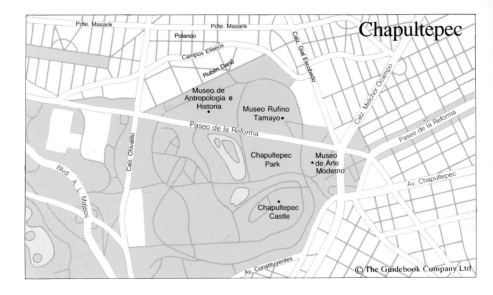

Reforma is known as the **Zona Rosa** ('Pink Zone'), Mexico City's flashy shopping and nightlife district, and many expensive hotels and excellent restaurants are also found here. This neighborhood is bounded by Reforma, Insurgentes, Avda Chapultepec and Calle Sevilla. Calles Hamburgo and Londres are the Zona Rosa's main streets; Calle Amberes contains many upscale crafts and jewelry stores and art galleries, while Calle Genova is lined with boutiques aimed at the teenage market. Across Reforma, the massive **United States Embassy** occupies the block between Calles Rio Sena and Rio Danubio. A block west stands the **Monument to Independence** (1909), a 20-metre (65-foot) column topped with the golden 'Angel of Independence', one of Mexico City's most beloved sculptures. The next traffic circle contains the healthy but distinctly unathletic statue of *Diana the Huntress.*

Three blocks further on, Reforma arrives at the massive **Chapultepec Park**, which has been a site for recreation since Aztec days, when Motecuhzoma built a palace here and an aqueduct carried water from the springs to Tenochtitlán. Inside the main park gates, to the south of Reforma, stands a **monument to the Child Heroes** (the cadets who threw themselves from Chapultepec Castle rather than surrender to the Americans) and the **Museo de Arte Moderno** (Tues–Sun, 11–6), which contains rooms devoted to the great Mexican artists of this century as well as temporary exhibitions.

A walkway winds up Chapultepec Hill ('Grasshopper Hill' in Nahuatl) to **Chapultepec Castle**. This 19th-century structure was a military college during the US invasion,

(*above*) The History of Theater in Mexico, *a mosaic by Diego Rivera on the façade of the Teatro Insurgentes; (below) painted house, southern Mexico City*

and in 1864 became the palace of the Emperor Maximilian and the Empress Carlota. The castle is now the **Museo Nacional de Historia** (daily 9–5); it contains exhibitions, many with unique artefacts, from Mexican history since the Conquest, as well as murals by Siquieros and others. Across Reforma, north of the Museo de Arte Moderno, stands the **Museo Rufino Tamayo**, with a permanent collection of that artist's work as well as temporary exhibitions of 20th-century art. A short walk to the west leads to Mexico's largest and most celebrated museum, the **Museo Nacional de Antropología** (Tues–Sat, 9–7; Sun, 10–6), in a stunning building designed by Pedro Ramírez Vasquez; it was completed in 1964. The interior patio is shaded by a huge rectangular roof held up only by a carved column in the center, which also spouts water from the top. A day or even two should be set aside to see the museum properly; a museum guidebook is also recommended, because the labelling is scanty. At the entrance there is a good bookstore, a theater and a hall for temporary exhibitions; a cafeteria occupies the basement. The first floor is devoted to the archeology of pre-Hispanic cultures, including introductory exhibitions (Rooms 1 and 2), early settlements in the Valley of Mexico (Room 3), pre-Classic cultures (Room 4), Teotihuacán (Room 5), Toltec (Room 6), Aztec (Room 7), Oaxaca (Room 8), Olmec and Totonac (Room 9), Maya (Room 10) and Northern Mexico (Rooms 11 and 12). Many of the greatest artefacts found in Mexico are included in these displays. Even though other cultures, like the Maya, had greater achievements, the Aztecs occupy the largest and most central room (the highlight is the famous **Solar Calendar Stone**); the Nobel Prize-winning poet, Octavio Paz, believes that this is intended as a subtle justification of Mexico City's hegemony over the rest of the country. The second floor of the museum is devoted to the ethnography of present-day Indian tribes, including the Purepechans, Otomís, Totonacs, Nahuas, Mixtecs, Huastecs and Mayans. Chapultepec Park also contains a zoo, **museums of technology and natural history** and **Los Pinos**, the official residence of the president of Mexico.

The North

Reforma heads north from the Alameda to **Ciudad Tlatelolco**, an enormous housing project that begins just after the **monument to Cuitlahuac**, the penultimate Aztec king. Many of Tlatelolco's apartment buildings were severely damaged or destroyed by the 1985 earthquake and remain empty. During the Aztec era, Tlatelolco was the largest market of the empire, and trading expeditions set out from here to the furthest reaches of Mesoamerica. The remains of the market and a pyramid, now called the **Plaza de las Tres Culturas**, lie one block west of the Cuitlahuac traffic circle.

After the Conquest, a church was built here in 1524 and replaced in the early 17th century with the **Iglesia de Santiago**, which has an austere, single-vaulted interior and a huge fresco of St Christopher over the side door. The third 'culture'—modern Mexico—is represented by the headquarters of the Secretariat of Foreign Relations along one side of the plaza.

Reforma continues north and turns into Calz de Guadalupe, which ends at the **Villa de Guadalupe**, Mexico's holiest shrine, in the northern part of the city. In 1531, a Christianized Indian named Juan Diego had a vision on the hill of Tepeyac of the Virgin Mary, dressed in the clothes of an Indian. She told him to go to Bishop Zumarraga and tell him to build a shrine to her on the hill. Juan Diego was too scared to obey until she gave him a bouquet of roses, which were out of season, and told him to take them to the bishop as proof. When Juan Diego opened his cloak to show the bishop the roses, the bishop saw that a beautiful dark-skinned image of the Virgin had appeared on the cloak's lining. The shrine to the Virgin of Guadalupe was quickly built, and her image became central to the Spanish campaign to convert the Indians. Juan Diego was recently canonized by Pope John Paul II. The current **basilica** is a huge and ugly concrete building (completed 1976) designed to hold over 20,000 people. The original cloak hangs behind bulletproof glass above the altar; it may be seen by stepping on a conveyor belt behind the altar and passing under it. Enthusiastic researchers have discovered that the image becomes younger and purer looking with the passing years and that her eyes actually contain the tiny silhouettes of the Apostles, as if they were caught by a camera. Pilgrims frequently approach the shrine on their knees, and some have walked from towns hundreds of miles away; on major religious holidays, particularly December 11–12, the shrine is jammed with tens of thousands of people.

A covered **market** next door is filled with hundreds of vendors selling all manner of religious artefacts, from jewelry to life-size sculptures of saints. The original basilica, the **Iglesia de Guadalupe** (1704–25), stands on the hill behind the new building and is now a religious museum, with many votive offerings and a collection of church treasures; these include a stupendous solid silver altarpiece. A path winds up the hill past some smaller shrines to a look-out with a fine view over the (polluted) city.

The South

Avenida Insurgentes, which is lined with upscale restaurants and nightclubs south of Reforma, is the main artery to Mexico City's southern suburbs. At the corner of Calle Filadelfia stands the skeleton of the 50-story **Hotel Mexico** (recently renamed the 'World Trade Center'), which has remained unfinished since the owner ran out of money; a popular restaurant and nightclub is open on the top floor. In front of this edifice is the

Lucha Libre

Mexico is no longer a rural and agricultural nation. Its population lives predominantly in cities, and its tastes have changed accordingly. Traditional entertainments like bullfights and *charrerías* (Mexican rodeos) are now supported mainly by tourist dollars. Today, the top spectator sports are European football and *lucha libre* ('free fighting'), the name for Mexican professional wrestling. The latter bears only a passing resemblance to US pro wrestling (both are fixed). In its themes and passions, *lucha libre* is an authentic and unaffected reflection of Mexican urban culture at its liveliest.

Wrestling arenas that seat from a few hundred to 15,000 are scattered through Mexican cities from Tijuana to Chetumal; Mexico City has at least a dozen. Tickets, which go on sale the morning of the show, can cost from US$1 for a cheap seat in the rafters to over US$30 for a front row seat at a big Mexico City arena. The crowd—mostly families, dating couples and pals out for a good time—is in the mood for laughter and excitement. The most famous wrestling fan in the country is Doña Virginia Aguilera, a 92-year-old great-grandmother who is a fixture at the Arena Coliseo in Mexico City.

When the lights dim and the wrestlers jog down to the raised ring at the center of the arena, the first unique element of *lucha libre* becomes apparent: most of them wear masks. These are fabric masks that cover the entire head and are decorated with the wrestlers' insignia. Ever since the era of the silver-masked El Santo, the most popular Mexican wrestler ever, *lucha libre* has been in the throes of what one wrestler calls '*mascararitis*'. The excitement and mystery of masked wrestlers is heightened by the possibility that the mask will be torn off during the match and the audience will be able to glimpse the wrestler's real face before he hides it in his hands. In Mexico, masks—which have been important since ancient times—are objects of obsession. According to Octavio Paz, Mexicans in their daily lives wear masks of stoicism and reserve in order to protect themselves from the vicissitudes of existence—those who 'open themselves up' are considered cowards and weaklings. The most dramatic *lucha libre* bouts are 'mask versus mask' matches, in which the loser forfeits his mask forever and is forced to reveal his face and true identity to the spellbound crowd.

The match takes place between wrestlers divided into teams of 'good' and 'bad'. This distinction is made on purely Mexican terms (in the US, 'good' is often the most 'American', whereas 'bad' is the most 'foreign'). 'Good' wrestlers

continues

Blue Panther demonstrating a complicated move on one of the Villanos

are called *téchnicos* or *científicos* and are usually clean-cut, well-built, modest and kind to children; they are every parents' dream of a devoted son and good citizen. They fight hard but fair, always following the 'scientific' rules of wrestling. 'Bad' wrestlers, called *rudos*, are mean, swaggering brutes, often with pot bellies and unkempt hair. Between holds they scream obscenities at the audience. They represent the bar-room bullies, the corrupt cops and officials who terrorize poor and lower-middle-class neighborhoods; they humiliate and rob you and then walk away with a cruel laugh.

Each *lucha libre* match is an epic battle between these two Mexican types. There are usually two or three wrestlers to a side, and a match is the best of two rounds out of three. *Lucha libre* action is fast, furious and, you might even say, churrigueresque in its complexity; every moment is filled with dazzling combinations of moves. Although wrestlers are always anticipating and playing with the audience's expectations, the usual progression of a match is: the *téchnicos* win the first round through skill, the *rudos* are victorious in the second via cheating and double-teaming, and the final round is up for grabs. The finale is often the 'suicide dive', in which a wrestler leaps from the top of a corner post onto his opponent outside the ring and both crash into the first rows of the seats unconscious. The first to crawl back into the ring is the winner.

Women wrestlers, confined for years to the provinces, have recently fought their way into the big Mexico City arenas. Mexico is one of the world's most sexist nations, and it is amusing to see the gender role confusion caused by the sight of a battling woman. A *macho rudo* lingers in the ring after his match, milking the audience for a last few catcalls, when a woman wrestler next on the card leaps into the ring and decides he has overstayed his welcome. She hits him on the back, and he wheels round, fists ready, to face a...woman! Her fists are cocked too, and she gestures him, come on, let's fight. He looks at the audience for help; he wants to hit her, but...a woman! Finally, he throws up his hands in disgust and flees the ring.

Of equal importance to the battle in the ring is the give and take between wrestlers and audience. If the crowd is not reacting sufficiently, a *rudo* will hurl a few choice obscenities at them to warm them up. Frequently, the *rudo* and a *borracho* ('drunk') in the audience will engage in a duel of insults, all unprintable, each trying to top the other (the *rudo* usually wins, it being his job). Others in the audience spend the entire evening hurling catcalls at the *rudos*, trying to goad a reaction; some of the most persistent, inventive and funniest hecklers are housewives. The wrestling arena is one of the only places in urban Mexico where you can vent steam against some huge muscular brute and not have to flee for your life.

The audience leaves the arena smiling; for a few hours they, or their stand-ins, were able to do battle with the forces of evil and, if not win, at least fight fairly and with all their ability and strength. As they walk out into the night and an uncertain future, they seem to say that in the never-ending war for a better life, this is the most that can be expected.

El Psicodélico unmasks Kaos in the Cuatro Caminos bullring

eccentric 12-sided **Siquieros Polyforum**, designed by the artist David Alfaro Siquieros and covered with wild murals. The interior contains exhibition spaces, a theater and a huge mural by Siquieros called 'The March of Humanity', which mixes sculpture and painting. A few blocks further down, Calle Holbein turns right (west) to the **National Soccer Stadium** and the **Plaza Mexico** bullfighting arena, supposedly the world's largest with seating for 64,000. The **Teatro Insurgentes** at the corner of Calle Mercaderes has a huge mosaic (1951–53) by Diego Rivera entitled 'The History of Theater in Mexico'. At the time of writing there were rumors the theater was to be torn down.

SAN ANGEL
After crossing Avda Miguel Angel de Quevedo, Insurgentes enters the San Angel neighborhood. This was originally an Aztec town named Chimalistac; during the Colonial era it became a popular weekend retreat for Mexico City's wealthy. In the early 20th century, when the rich began to move to Lomas de Chapultepec and other newly built enclaves, artists and intellectuals moved into their mansions. This 'intellectual tendency' was reinforced in the 1950s by the construction of UNAM's University City just to the south. San Angel is one of the last places in the city where you can walk on quiet, tree-lined cobblestone streets and get a sense of what life was like before the industrial era. The **Jardín de Bonilla**, just after Avda Miguel Angel de Quevedo, contains the **Alvaro Obregón Monument**, which marks the spot where, in 1928, this Mexican president was assassinated by a Cristero fanatic. The arm that Obregón lost in a 1915 battle used to float in a glass jar of formaldehyde on a shelf inside the monument; the arm was recently returned to his family and cremated, but the jar is still visible.

Avda La Paz climbs the hill on the other side of Insurgentes to the heart of San Angel. The **Convento del Carmen** to the left on Avda Revolución was founded in 1613 by the Carmelite order, and was one of the most luxurious of the monasteries around Mexico City. Many of these riches are preserved in the **Museo del Carmen** (10–5 daily), which houses colonial furniture, religious paintings and, in the basement, the mummified corpses of a number of monks—making it a popular tourist destination for Mexicans. Across Revolución and a block up the hill takes you to the **Plaza San Jacinto**, which on Saturdays hosts the **Bazar Sabado**, a huge crafts market that attracts bus-loads of tourists. The side streets here are lined with beautiful colonial mansions behind huge stone walls.

Returning to Avda Revolución, two blocks north from Avda La Paz stands the **Museo Carrillo Gil**, with an excellent permanent collection of Mexican and foreign paintings, including Rivera, Orozco and Picasso, as well as temporary exhibitions. Across the avenue, Calle Altavista heads five blocks west through a charming neighborhood to the **Antigua Hacienda de Goycoechea**, once a favorite resting spot for General Santa Ana, and now the **San Angel Inn,** one of the finest and most expensive restaurants in the city. Even if you do not eat here, it is worth a visit just to see the grounds.

COYOACÁN

Three kilometers (two miles) to the east of San Angel, on Avda Miguel Angel de Queve-do, lies Coyoacán, another suburb filled with attractive colonial buildings. Coyoacán was one of the earliest pre-Hispanic settlements on the shores of the Valley of Mexico's net-work of lakes, and Cortés made it his capital immediately after he captured Tenochtitlán. Like San Angel, it is famous for being home to many prominent artists and intellectuals. Coyoacán's main square is the **Plaza Hidalgo**, five blocks north of Miguel Angel de Quevedo on Calle Felipe Carrillo Puerto. The north side of the square is occupied by the **Casa de Cortés** (16th century), which now houses offices of the municipal government. This is said to be the spot where Cortés tortured Cuauhtemoc to force him to reveal the location of the Aztec treasure, and also where Cortés murdered his Spanish wife with his bare hands. Anti-Spanish murals by Diego Rivera decorate the interior. The **Iglesia de San Juan Bautista** across the plaza was begun in 1552, and heavily reconstructed in 1804. The glory of the original decor can be seen in the **Capilla del Sagrario**, to the left of the altar.

A half block to the east on Avda Hidalgo stands the **Museo Nacional de Culturas Populares**, which has exhibitions on such amusing subjects as old radio shows, circuses and professional wrestling. The **Capilla de la Concepcion** (18th century) on the pretty little **Plaza de la Conchita**, two blocks southeast of Plaza Hidalgo, contains ornate gilt retables. A short walk five blocks north of the plaza takes you to the fascinating **Frida Kahlo Museum** (Tues–Sun, 10–2, 3–6). This was the house and studio of Kahlo, the artist who is now a cult figure, and her lover Diego Rivera; it is preserved as they left it. The rooms are filled with their art collection, folk and archeological artefacts as well as interesting personal possessions like the bed Kahlo spent years in as an invalid and the painting she was working on when she died—a portrait of Stalin. A few blocks away at 45 Calle Viena stands the fortified home-in-exile of the Russian communist **Leon Trot-sky**, who was murdered here in 1940 by a Stalinist agent. The building is now a **museum** (Tues–Fri, 10.30–2, 3–5; Sat–Sun, 1–4) manned by Trotskyite volunteers from around the world, and you can see Trotsky's grave, the bullet holes in the walls from an earlier unsuccessful assassination attempt, and Trotsky's desk as he left it on the day of his death. The **Churubusco** neighborhood just to the east contains the huge Churubusco Film Studios, which unfortunately tourists are not allowed to visit. A few kilometers to the south, just west of Avda Division del Norte, stands the **Museo Anahuacalli** (Tues–Sun, 10–2, 3–6), which houses Diego Rivera's pre-Columbian art collection in a building built of black volcanic stone and designed with Indian motifs by the artist himself.

UNAM AND CUICUILCO

After passing through San Angel, Avda Insurgentes enters the **Ciudad Universitaria**, the main campus of the Universidad Nacional Autonimía de México, also known as UNAM.

Patriotic ceremony in the Zócalo

During the 1960s and 1970s, UNAM was a hotbed of political activism, but the current crop of students are definitely more career-oriented (although you do see hippies around the Humanities Building selling jewelry and left-wing books). On the right is the enormous **Mexico 68 Olympic Stadium**, built to resemble either a volcanic cone or a sombrero, and with a huge mosaic by Diego Rivera along the exterior. Across Insurgentes begins the vast expanse of the university campus. The ten-story **Library** is decorated with a cryptic mosaic by Juan O'Gorman, depicting Mexican and European knowledge, while the nearby **Rectory** has a relief-mosaic by David Alfaro Siquieros that shows students being egged on by workers. The campus also houses theaters, museums with temporary exhibitions and sculpture and botanical gardens, but it is best to take wheeled transport to see them, because the distances in the hot sun are great.

South of UNAM, immediately after Insurgentes crosses the Periférico, you reach the ruins of Cuicuilco on the left. Around AD 100, this Late-Formative site was buried under a huge lava flow; it was excavated during the 1930s. The main structure is a round tiered pyramid 23 meters (75 feet) tall and 118 meters (388 feet) wide—with an altar on top. The small **museum** contains many artefacts found on the site, including an incense burner modeled in the shape of the Fire God. The **Olympic Village** that housed the athletes in 1968 stands across Avda Insurgentes.

XOCHIMILCO

About 24 kilometers (15 miles) southeast of the Zócalo lie the floating gardens of Xo-chimilco ('Place Where Flowers Grow' in Nahuatl). In pre-Hispanic times, this town was the breadbasket of the Valley of Mexico; residents grew huge amounts of flowers and vegetables on *chinampas*, a type of reed and mud platform raised out of the shallow lake waters. When the Spanish arrived, they called it the 'American Venice'. The area of culti-vation is now greatly reduced because of the draining of the lakes and encroaching ur-banization. Nevertheless, Xochimilco is a hugely popular weekend excursion for Mexico City residents. Visitors should hire a flower-garlanded boat—you will be approached by many touts—and cruise the polluted waters of the canals for a couple of hours. As you drift along, you will be approached by water-born vendors selling flowers, food and music—whole *mariachi* bands take to the water as well. downtown Xochimilco has a **market** that draws many Indians on Saturdays, and the Franciscan **Templo de San Ber-nardo** (begun 1543) with a magnificent main altar.

Around Mexico City

Introduction

Pre-Hispanic civilizations thrived in the region comprising the Valley of Mexico, outside the Federal District, and the valleys beyond the ring of volcanic mountains. The Olmecs, Teotihuacános, Mayas, Toltecs, Tolteca-Chichimecas and Aztecs all built major cities here, and some of their monuments, like the pyramids in Teotihuacán, are wonders of the world. This area was also the center of colonial development and contains many of the most elaborate churches in Mexico. Today, this region is heavily urbanized, but you can still easily escape into the glories of the past.

The state of Mexico, popularly called **Edomex** (short for *Estado de México*), includes Teotihuacán, the most renowned and unforgettable archeological site in Mexico. This vast ruined city, which is bisected by the Avenue of the Dead, contains the enormous Pyramids of the Sun and Moon and numerous palaces decorated with newly discovered murals. In the heart of the traditional town of Tepotzotlán stands one of the most ornate baroque churches in Mexico. Edomex's capital, the industrial city of Toluca, attracts thousands of Indian craftsmen to its famous Friday market. At the eastern boundary of the state stand the massive volcanoes of Popocatépetl and Iztaccíhuatl, which are popular hiking and mountain climbing areas.

The mild climate of the state of Morelos has made it a popular vacation spot since Aztec times. Cuernavaca, the capital, is still the favorite weekend destination of Mexico City's wealthy and powerful. Among its sights are a pyramid, Cortés' palace, beautiful gardens, many artisans markets and a huge, old cathedral. In the countryside you can find fascinating but infrequently visited archeological sites like Tepoztlán and Xochicalco. The city of Taxco, just over the border in the state of Guerrero, is a colonial jewel. Its cobblestone streets, red tile roofed houses and fantastically ornate Santa Prisca church were originally built by silver barons. Today, Taxco is home to an industry devoted to the manufacture and sale of high-quality silver jewelry—a bargain-hunter's dream.

Surrounded by wealthier and more populous states, Hidalgo is something of an enigma. Nevertheless, the archeological site of Tula in the southwest of the state is worth visiting. Its huge stone warrior-columns, called 'Atlantes', provide a fascinating glimpse into the warlike Toltec civilization. Pachuca, the capital, is a mining city with an excellent complex of museums built in an old convent.

The state of Puebla was long the second most important region in Mexico after the capital. Now somewhat eclipsed by the industrial north, it is still home to some of the finest colonial architecture in Mexico. The center of Puebla, the capital, is filled with churches and mansions covered with the distinctive local tiles. The cathedral is a colonial masterpiece, and the Capilla del Rosario in the church of Santo Domingo is lined with remarkable gilt carvings covering every square inch of the interior. Puebla is also known for its culinary specialties, particularly the spicy *mole a la poblana* sauce and *camotes*, a delicious local candy made from sweet potatoes. Cholula, on the western outskirts of Puebla, was an important Indian sacred center and contains the partially excavated Great Pyramid, the most massive structure in the New World. Nearby are the scintillating churches of Tonanzintla and Acatepec. Tehuacán, at the southwest end of the state, is renowned for its mineral springs and spas.

Tlaxcala, the smallest state in Mexico, is home to the colorful pre-Hispanic murals of Cacaxtla and the confection-like baroque church of Ocotlán, just above the state capital.

Getting There

Almost all the sights in the state of Mexico lie within two hours of downtown Mexico City—even with traffic jams. To reach the great pyramids of Teotihuacán, take Mexico 85 (the Pachuca toll road) north and turn east at the Teotihuacán exit, from which it is another 25 kilometers (16 miles). Buses for the ruins leave frequently from the Indios Verdes metro station and also from the Terminal Norte bus station. The baroque monastery of Tepotzotlán stands a few kilometers west of the Mexico 57 route to Querétaro; the exit is 42 kilometers (26 miles) north of downtown Mexico City. Toluca, famous for its market, lies due west of the capital on Mexico 15, 67 kilometers (42 miles) from the Zócalo. Many buses and (slower) trains also run this route. Malinalco, with a pyramid carved of solid rock, is ten kilometers (six miles) east of Tenancingo on Mexico 55, between Toluca and Tasco. The pilgrimage site of Chalma lies a few kilometers further east. The great volcanoes of Popocatepetl and Iztaccihuatl stand east of Mexico City and may be reached from Amecameca.

The state of Morelos lies just over the mountains south of Mexico City. Cuernavaca is 53 kilometers (33 miles) south of the capital on Mexico 95, a scenic toll road. Dozens of buses run here daily from the Terminal del Sur. The site of Tepoztlán lies 26 kilometers (16 miles) east of Cuernavaca, while the ruins of Xochicalco stand a few kilometers east of the Mexico 95 exit, 25 kilometers (15.5 miles) south of the city. Mexico 95 continues south to the state of Guerrero, and the turn-off for the silver city of Tasco is just south of the border. The Olmec carvings of Chalcatzingo are found near the town of Jonacatepec off Mexico 160, 20 kilometers (12 miles) southeast of Cuautla.

(above) View from the Pyramid of the Moon down the Avenue of the Dead, Teotihuacán; (below) Pyramid of the Sun

The main sight in the state of Hidalgo, the Toltec city of Tula, stands just above the city of Tula de Allende 18 kilometers (11 miles) from Mexico 57—the Querétaro highway, 57 kilometers (35 miles) north of Mexico City. Pachuca, the state capital, lies 69 kilometers (42 miles) northeast of Mexico City on Mexico 85.

The state of Puebla extends east of the huge volcanoes on the Valley of Mexico's eastern edge. Mexico 150 heads over the pine-forest-covered ridge 112 kilometers (70 miles) to Puebla, the state capital. Puebla's airport has regular flights to Tijuana and Guadalajara. Buses run here every 15 minutes from Mexico City's Terminal del Oriente. Trains to Puebla from the capital are very slow and continue either to the Jalapa and Veracruz or southeast to Oaxaca. East of Puebla, Mexico 150 runs down to Veracruz via Orizaba and Cordoba. The ruins of Cholula lie about ten kilometers (six miles) east of Puebla; frequent mini-buses ply the route. The mineral springs of Tehuacán are 100 kilometers (60 miles) southeast of Puebla on Mexico 150. Tehuacán also lies on the Puebla-Oaxaca train line, and by car you can reach Oaxaca via either Mexico 125 or 131.

The tiny state of Tlaxcala begins just north of Puebla's outskirts. The state capital, Tlaxcala, lies 33 kilometers (20 miles) from the city of Puebla. The Mayan murals of Cacaxtla are southwest of Tlaxcala, halfway to San Martin Texmelucan in Puebla.

State of Mexico

The state of Mexico rings the Valley of Mexico outside Mexico City and also bulges far to the southwest, almost to the Rio Balsas. The Valley of Mexico has been occupied for many millennia. In the town of Santa Isabel Iztapan, just north of Mexico City, ditch diggers found the remains of two mammoths that had been butchered with stone and obsidian knives around 12,000–10,000 BC. Closer to our era, settlements in this region show the influence of the Olmec culture centered on the Gulf coast. Just after the birth of Christ, a plan for a city was laid out in the northeastern corner of the Valley of Mexico. No one knows where the builders came from, but the city became Teotihuacán, the most powerful urban center in Mesoamerica for seven centuries and the site of the great Pyramids of the Sun and Moon, two of the marvels of the world. At its zenith around AD 600, Teotihuacán contained 200,000 people, making it the sixth largest city in the world at the time. Teotihuacán probably sustained itself through trade; the city contained wards for Zapotecs, Mayas and other tribes, and artefacts made here have been found as far away as Guatemala. Around AD 700 unknown tribes invaded and burned the city. The Toltecs and later the Aztecs made pilgrimages to Teotihuacán, because they believed the gods resided in the huge pyramids. The Toltecs controlled the Valley of Mexico from Tula, while the Otomis to the west had capitals in Toluca and Malinalco. After the Toltec collapse, their descendants mingled with the Otomis and Chichimecs from the north to become a new Toltec-Chichimec culture centered around the valley's network of lakes. The major settlements included Chalco and Texcoco, which was ruled by a family of philosopher kings. By 1427 these tribes had been subjugated by a savage tribe of Chichimecs, who called themselves the Mexica and had recently moved to Tenochtitlán, an island in the middle of the lakes. They founded the Aztec empire, which was to rule central Mexico for almost a century. When Bernal Díaz del Castillo entered the valley with Cortés, the marvelous scene before him led him to write: 'With such wondrous sights to gaze on we did not know what to say, or if this was real that we saw before our eyes.'

After the Conquest in 1521, Cortés and his captains divided the Valley of Mexico into *encomiendas*, large estates (Cortés took the largest). Mexico City became the Spanish capital and development quickly extended throughout the valley. In the following centuries, Indian culture disappeared under the onslaught of Franciscan and Dominican missionaries, new forms of agriculture, early industries, mines and epidemics. In November 1810, any hope of a speedy finish to Mexico's battle for independence ended when Miguel Hidalgo halted his army in a pass between Toluca and Mexico City and decided to return north rather than attack the capital. Over the next decade Toluca was the site of many battles between Morelos's army and the royalists. In 1910, Zapata's peasant revolutionary army entered the state from the south and within two years controlled Chalco and Amecameca on Mexico City's outskirts. Throughout much of the Revolution, hunger, disease and looting were rampant in the region. Over the last 40 years Mexico City has expanded its boundaries and transformed what were once quiet towns into heavily polluted suburbs. Only the southwest of the state remains agricultural.

Teotihuacan

There are two principal entrances to the enormous and unique site of Teotihuacán. At the south entrance stands the **museum**, with good exhibitions, rest rooms and a restaurant, and the Temple of Quetzalcoatl is a short walk into the site. The north entrance, over a kilometer away, is the closest to the Pyramids of the Sun and the Moon. Admission is charged every time you enter the grounds, so it is expensive to visit one end of the city and then drive over to the next. To see everything inexpensively, you must be prepared to walk. Arrive early, as the sun is intense—hats are a must—and beware of afternoon thunderstorms during the summer months. Teotihuacán is bisected by the **Avenue of the Dead**, which begins at the Pyramid of the Moon, passes the Citadel three kilometers (two miles) to the south and, although this part hasn't been reconstructed, continues for a further three kilometers. The city plan is oriented a little east of due north; archeologists believe that this alignment had astronomical significance. If you enter the site at the south entrance, the first building that faces you across the Avenue of the Dead

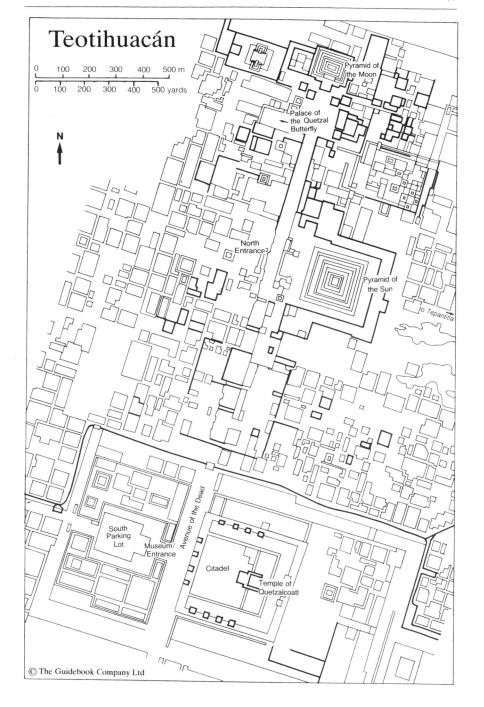

Teotihuacán

0 100 200 300 400 500 m

0 100 200 300 400 500 yards

N

Pyramid of the Moon

Palace of the Quetzal Butterfly

North Entrance

Pyramid of the Sun

to Tepantitla

Avenue of the Dead

South Parking Lot

Museum/ Entrance

Citadel

Temple of Quetzalcoatl

© The Guidebook Company Ltd

is the **Citadel**, so-called because this walled enclosure resembles a fortress. Thirteen temples stand along the Citadel's walls. Within this enclosure is the **Temple of Quetzalcoatl**, a low pyramid with six tiers. Each tier is decorated with alternating stone heads of the Feathered Serpent and the Fire Serpent, perhaps representing a mythic moment of creation. The pyramid was originally brightly painted and traces of a blue background may still be seen.

Returning to the Avenue of the Dead and heading north, on either side you will see remains of building complexes that were probably palaces. The ordinary citizens lived away from the avenue in densely packed complexes of apartments and courtyards. Archeologists believe that Teotihuacán developed through intensive trade rather than agriculture, and wards of the city were reserved for different tribes, including Mayas and Zapotecs. After a long walk you come to the **Pyramid of the Sun** looming on the right. Seventy meters (230 feet) tall, 225 meters (740 feet) to a side at the base, and containing 1,175,000 cubic meters of rubble fill, this pyramid is one of the wonders of the world. It was probably built around AD 100, a century or so before the Pyramid of the Moon. In the front is a plaza that was probably a ceremonial space. Archeologists believe that Teotihuacán's pyramids were not funerary monuments like the pyramids of Egypt. In 1971, they discovered a lava tube beneath the Pyramid of the Sun that had been artificially widened and ended in a chamber. This may have been the most important religious site in Teotihuacán: a kind of womb for the gods. At 2,300 meters (7,565 feet), the climb to the top of the Pyramid of the Sun literally takes your breath away, so take it slowly. The view is well worth it. Another site entrance lies behind the pyramid, and beyond it are the remains of **Tepantitla**, a residential quarter with what's left of a famous mural called the 'Paradise of Tlaloc'. The **Pyramid of the Moon** at the north end of the Avenue of the Dead is smaller and steeper and with a fine view down the avenue. All the major buildings in Teotihuacán were covered with plaster and painted, usually red—it must have been a splendid sight at sunset. On the west side of the plaza in front of the Pyramid of the Moon stands the **Palace of the Quetzal Butterfly**; the patio is surrounded with carvings of birds and butterflies and remnants of geometric murals. More murals are currently being restored in the palaces grouped at the north entrance to the site. There are sound and light shows at Teotihuacán at 7 pm (Spanish) and 8.15 pm (English), from October through June. The restaurants outside the site entrances are generally expensive; for cheaper food try the nearby town of San Juan Teotihuacán.

TEPOTZOTLÁN

The colonial town of Tepotzotlán lies two kilometers (1.25 miles) west of Mexico 57. In the heart of town stands one of the glories of the Mexican baroque, the **Church of San Francisco Javier**. The church was begun in 1664 and no expense was spared to make it

Apex of the churrigueresque,
the main altar of San Francisco Javier, Tepotzotlán

the most elaborate, both inside and out, in all Mexico. The churrigueresque façade, considered the country's finest, is a riot of intricate stonework; the interior contains five sumptuous floor-to-ceiling gilt retables covered with sculptures of saints and cherubim; and the **Camarín de la Virgen** is a seething mass of carving—vegetable and geometric motifs—from the ground up. Next door is the **Jesuit monastery**, which was founded in 1582 as a school for the study of Indian languages on land donated by an Indian convert. After the expulsion of the Jesuits in 1767, the monastery was converted into an ecclesiastical prison. Today, it is the **Museo del Virreynato**, containing collections of colonial secular and religious art. Inside are rooms devoted to religious treasures, an 18th-century pharmacy, armor, statuary, paintings and porcelain. The center of the monastery is a **cloister** planted with orange trees; the **chapel** next door is another baroque riot, although on a smaller scale. The monastery is surrounded by a lush garden filled with shade trees—it feels a long way from Mexico City. During the weeks before Christmas religious plays are held on the grounds and attract thousands to the town.The square around the church is lined with traditional restaurants, which are usually filled with urbanites on weekend afternoons.

TOLUCA

The state of Mexico's capital—the industrial city of Toluca (pop 600,000)—is known for its enormous **Friday market**. Thousands of Indian artisans from the surrounding villages and the state of Michoacán come to the market next to the central bus station to sell their crafts, including baskets, pottery and textiles. The preliminary prices are usually excessive, so bargain hard. The market is open the rest of the week as well, but the selection is smaller. More mundane articles, like plastic buckets, shoes, fruit, prepared food and so on are also available. Watch for pickpockets and don't get lost—the market is vast. At the **Casa de los Artesanías** on Paseo Tollocan 700, a few blocks east, you can buy reasonably priced local crafts in a less hectic setting. Toluca is not exactly a beauty spot, but there are other worthwhile sights, including the **Iglesia del Tercer Orden** (1585) near the Zócalo and the **Botanical Garden** with stained-glass greenhouses, one block east of the square.

MALINALCO AND CHALMA

The archeological site of Malinalco lies 11 kilometers (seven miles) east of Tenancingo, which is 48 kilometers (30 miles) south of Toluca. From the town's plaza you climb a steep path and come to a stone staircase at the top of which is the remarkable **Temple I**, which was cut in one piece from the side of the mountain. The entrance is through a stylized serpent's mouth, and inside you find stone carvings of eagles and a jaguar. This building was probably devoted to the worship of Quetzalcoatl and constructed on the orders of the Aztec emperors between 1501 and 1515. The remains of a pyramid and two more temples lie below Temple I. Back in town, the large **Augustinian convent** is worth visiting.

The tiny town of Chalma, east of Malinalco was a pilgrimage destination during pre-Hispanic times, when Indians worshipped images of their gods in a cave here. In 1539, two years after the arrival of Augustinian fathers, the image of **Santo Cristo de Chalma** miraculously appeared in the same cave. In 1550, the image was moved to a chapel and the church was begun in the 17th century. Chalma is one of the most popular pilgrimage spots in Mexico and attracts huge crowds on Sundays and religious holidays. In 1991, almost 50 of the faithful died in a panicked crowd that couldn't exit the church because there were too many entering. Chalma's streets are lined with stands selling religious memorabilia.

IZTACCÍHUATL AND POPCATÉPETL

On Mexico City's rare clear days (and early on some not-so-clear mornings) the twin volcanoes of Iztaccíhuatl ('The White Lady') and Popocatépetl ('Smoking Mountain') loom over the eastern skyline. 'Popo' at 5,465 meters (17,976 feet) is slightly higher than Iztaccíhuatl (5,230 meters, 17,203 feet) to the north. A road heading east from Amecameca winds up to **Paso de Cortés** in the saddle between the mountains. In 1519, Cortés' army marched through here on their way to Tenochtitlán. A road to the right leads up Popoc-atépetl to **Tlamacas**, a tiny settlement with a hostel for hikers and mountain climbers getting acclimatized to the altitude. The ascent of this volcano should only be attempted by experienced climbers with crampons and ice axes. The ascent of Iztaccíhuatl is slight-ly less difficult; the path begins at a parking lot 12 kilometers on a dirt road north of Paso de Cortés.

State of Morelos

The mild climates of the state of Morelos have always attracted more powerful cultures from less agreeable lands. Chalcatzingo lay on the western frontier of the Olmec expan-sion; a series of bas-reliefs on boulders here give glimpses of the Olmec religion. Xochi-calco, just southwest of Cuernavaca, became an important center after the fall of Teoti-huacán around AD 700. The city was probably inhabited by a tribe of Chontal-speaking Putun Maya, called the Olmeca-Xicallanca (no relation to the Olmecs), from the Gulf coast who worshipped the Feathered Serpent that surrounds the main temple here. In 1426, the kingdoms of Morelos were defeated by the Aztecs and huge piles of tribute were sent over the mountains to Tenochtitlán. The Aztec Emperor Motecuhzoma I built a luxuriant garden in Oaxtépec near Cuernavaca (then called Cuauhnahuac), which may have inspired the first European botanical gardens. In 1521, Cortés conquered the region,

(following pages) Popocatepetl volcano from the Puebla side

made it part of his *encomienda* and constructed the New World's first sugar refinery. He also built a palace in Cuernavaca, to which he retreated whenever the colonial politics became too much for him. Many other Spaniards also purchased sugar plantations in Morelos and imported African slaves to replace the Indians who died of disease and overwork. For centuries most of Morelos' land has been concentrated in the hands of a few, usually absentee landlords from Mexico City, and agrarian reform has been a burning issue here. Cuernavaca became the favorite vacation spot of first the *criollo* élite, then Emperor Maximilian, and now movie stars and politicians. The first *bandoleros*, peasant revolutionaries, sprang up in 1856 and were later crushed by Porfirio Díaz. *Bandolerismo* returned with a vengeance under the leadership of Emiliano Zapata. After his 'Liberating Army of the South' ousted Díaz' followers, he instituted his own brand of peasant communism and redistributed millions of acres of land to *campesinos*. The rich fled Cuernavaca for Mexico City. Zapata was assassinated on April 10, 1919 in a treacherous ambush ordered by President Carranza. At the end of the Revolution, Morelos' economy lay in ruins and reconstruction took decades.

CUERNAVACA

Morelos' capital, the ancient resort of Cuernavaca (pop 400,000), where Aztec emperors once disported, has grown rapidly over the last two decades; this has led to pollution and congestion. However, there are still enough trees, gardens and fine colonial buildings to make you forget urban woes. Cuernavaca remains the favorite weekend retreat of Mexico City's élite; politicians, businessmen, artists and movie stars relax in elaborate mansions hidden behind tall stone walls. The fanciest suburbs, where President Salinas de Gortari and Cantinflas have homes, are south of downtown. The city is famous for its mild climate. At 1,542 meters (5,072 feet), it is substantially lower than Mexico City; it is never too hot or too cold; and the sun comes out every day even during the rainy summer months. Cuernavaca is built on the southern slopes of the mountains that ring the Valley of Mexico, and the city's main street, **Avenida Morelos**, is the old Mexico City–Acapulco road (the new highway by-passes the town). The **Cathedral**, also called the Monastery and Temple of San Francisco, at Avdas Morelos and Hidalgo was begun in 1529 by Franciscans and is the fifth oldest church in Mexico. The exterior of this bulky, fort-like building is unadorned; the huge single-vaulted interior was renovated in 1961 with stark ecclesiastical decor and ugly stained glass. During the renovation, workmen discovered large oriental-style murals on the walls depicting a mass crucifixion. They were apparently painted during the 17th century by a Japanese convert inspired by the mass martyrization of 24 priests, including Mexico's first saint, in Japan. The Sunday masses (11 am) are accompanied by *mariachis* and are very popular. One of Cuernavaca's **artisans markets** stands just across Avda Hidalgo from the Cathedral. A few steps uphill on Avda

Morelos is the entrance to the **Jardín Borda** (small admission fee), once Emperor Maximilian and Empress Carlota's favorite promenade in Cuernavaca. The now-overgrown gardens were laid out in 1783 by Jose de la Borda, a silver magnate from Taxco, and contain paths among many trees, fountains and even a pool for small rowboats.

From the Cathedral, Avda Hidalgo heads east three blocks to the **Palacio de Cortés**. This crenelated fortress, constructed between 1522 and 1532, was Cortés' home and from it he controlled the vast holdings he owned as Marquis of the Valley of Oaxaca. A pyramid originally stood at this site, and you can still see some Aztec carved stones in front of the entrance. The palace is now the **Museo Regional Cuauhnahuac** (Tues–Sun, 10–5)—Cuauhnahuac is Cuernavaca's Indian name—and contains good exhibitions on Morelos' archeology on the first floor, with colonial to modern history on the second. The highlight is a series of murals on the second floor painted by Diego Rivera. Commissioned in the 1920s by the American ambassador, Dwight Morrow, they depict Mexican history from Cortés to Zapata in violently anti-Spanish and pro-Indian terms. The plaza just across from the palace entrance is usually filled with artisans making and selling crafts. The tree-filled **Plaza de Armas**, Cuernavaca's main square, is next door and is surrounded by pleasant, pricey outdoor cafés. A few blocks east of the train station (a long walk to the northeast, try a cab) is a small park containing the **Teopanzolco pyramid**, which is actually two pyramids, one superimposed on the other. The later of the two may have been under construction at the time of the Conquest. Cuernavaca's most famous hotel is the very expensive **Las Mañanitas** at Avda Morelos and Calle Linares; it is worth a visit to see the beautiful colonial building and the grounds filled with strolling peacocks and other exotic birds. The **Arena Isabel** for weekly professional wrestling and boxing matches is on Blvd Juárez, a block south of the Palacio de Cortés. Pullman de Morelos, with a terminal at Avda del Parque just west of the train station, is the main bus line for Mexico City. The Flecha Roja bus line, which runs the Acapulco–Mexico City route, has its terminal at Avda Morelos between Calles Arista and Victoria. The local university and many private schools offer popular Spanish language courses.

A road due east from the north end of Cuernavaca runs 26 kilometers (16 miles) to Tepoztlán, at the base of the wildly scenic Cerro de Tepozteco. The town—all winding cobblestone streets—is notable for its fort-like **Dominican church and convent** (begun 1565). The church is relatively elaborate, with a plateresque portal, but the monastery is one of the most austere and primitive in Mexico. A path from town leads up into a national park; after an hour-long hike more vertical than horizontal, you arrive at the **Tepoztlán ruins**. The main structure is a 20-meter (66-foot)-tall **pyramid** dated 1502, which is surrounded by lesser ruins. A huge statue of Tepoztecatl, a legendary warrior, was found on the site. The view is magnificent.

The ruins of **Xochicalco** are reached by turning right off Mexico 95, 25 kilometers

Exploding Souls

The solitary Mexican loves fiestas and public gatherings. Any occasion for getting together will serve, any pretext to stop the flow of time and commemorate men and events with festivals and ceremonies. We are a ritual people, and this characteristic enriches both our imaginations and our sensibilities, which are equally sharp and alert. The art of the fiesta has been debased almost everywhere else, but not in Mexico. There are few places in the world where it is possible to take part in a spectacle like our great religious fiestas with their violent primary colors, their bizarre costumes and dances, their fireworks and ceremonies, and their inexhaustible welter of surprises: the fruit, candy, toys and other objects sold on these days in the plazas and open-air markets.

Our calendar is crowded with fiestas. There are certain days when the whole country, from the most remote villages to the largest cities, prays, shouts, feasts, gets drunk and kills, in honor of the Virgin of Guadalupe or Benito Juárez. Each year on the fifteenth of September, at eleven o'clock at night, we celebrate the fiesta of the Grito in all the plazas of the Republic, and the excited crowds actually shout for a whole hour...the better, perhaps, to remain silent for the rest of the year. During the days before and after the twelfth of December, time comes to a full stop, and instead of pushing us toward a deceptive tomorrow that is always beyond our reach, offers us a complete and perfect today of dancing and revelry, of communion with the most ancient and secret Mexico. Time is no longer succession, and becomes what it originally was and is: the present, in which past and future are reconciled.

In all of these ceremonies—national or local, trade or family—the Mexican opens out. They all give him a chance to reveal himself and to converse with God, country, friends or relations. During these days the silent Mexican whistles, shouts, sings, shoots off fireworks, discharges his pistol into the air. He discharges his soul. And his shout, like the rockets we love so much, ascends to the heavens, explodes into green, red, blue, and white lights, and falls dizzily to earth with a trail of golden sparks. This is the night when friends who have not exchanged more than the prescribed courtesies for months get drunk together, trade confidences, weep over the same troubles, discover they are brothers, and sometimes, to prove it, kill each other. The night is full of songs and loud cries. The lover wakes up his sweetheart with an orchestra. There are jokes and conversations from balcony to balcony, sidewalk to sidewalk. Nobody talks quietly. Hats fly in the air. Laughter and curses ring like silver pesos. Guitars are brought out. Now and then, it is true, the happiness ends badly, in quarrels, insults, pistol shots, stabbings. But these too are part of the fiesta, for the Mexican does not seek amusement: he seeks to escape from himself, to leap over the wall of solitude that confines him during the rest of the year. All are possessed by violence and frenzy. Their souls explode like the colors and voices and emotions. Do they forget themselves and show their true faces? Nobody knows. The important thing is to go out, open a way, get drunk on noise, people, colors. Mexico is celebrating a fiesta. And this fiesta, shot through with lightning and delirium, is the brilliant reverse to our silence and apathy, our reticence and gloom.

Octavio Paz, *The Labryinth of Solitude*,
translated by Kemp, Milos and Belash

(15.5 miles) south of Cuernavaca, and taking the **ruinas** road a few kilometers west. The site is five kilometers (three miles) further, on the top of a hill. Founded around AD 700, Xochicalco was probably inhabited by the Olmeca-Xicallanca, a tribe of Putún Maya from the Gulf coast. They surrounded the hilltop with fortifications and built stone causeways to outlying settlements. The center of the town is the **Temple of the Feathered Serpent**, a tall platform surrounded by a deep relief of the serpent undulating around figures of seated, elaborately-dressed men. The remains of other temples, ball courts and dwellings, mostly unexcavated, can also be seen. The hill is perforated by caves and tunnels. One of the caves was probably used as an observatory, because it has a skyshaft through which the sun's rays reach the cave floor only on the summer solstice.

The rarely visited site of **Chalcatzingo** lies south of the Cuautla-Izucar de Matamoros road, near the town of Jonacatepec (almost at the Puebla border). The ruins are situated at the base of three 300-meter (986-foot)-tall rocks that rise dramatically out of the arid valley floor. The base of the rockfaces and of large boulders scattered nearby are carved with Olmec-style reliefs depicting rulers, warriors and deities. The actual settlement can be seen in platform mounds and terraces at the foot of the rocks.

TAXCO

Situated in the dry hills of northern Guerrero, the colonial silver mining city of Taxco (pop 120,000)—pronounced and spelled 'Tasco' by locals—has been attracting tourists for centuries. The authorities aim to keep it that way; development is restricted and all new construction, including the gas stations, must have whitewashed walls and red tile roofs. Although the silver mines are depleted (nearby fluorite and mercury mines are still producing), the city is now a center for silver jewelry manufacture and attracts buyers from around the world. The road from Mexico City passes the arches of an old **aqueduct** and then becomes Avenida John F Kennedy, along which you find the **tourism office** and the **bus stations**. Above this avenue, Taxco's winding streets all end up at the **Plaza Borda**, the main square named after the town's 18th-century benefactor, José de la Borda. According to local legend, Borda discovered the incredibly rich San Ignacio silver lode when his horse stumbled and broke open a rock to display pure silver ore.

As a way of giving thanks for this bounty, Borda built the **Iglesia de Santa Prisca** (1751–59), Taxco's great churrigueresque jewel, right on the plaza. No expense was spared, inside or out. The pink stone façade, which is best viewed at sunset, is an incredibly complicated intertwining mass of decoration and sculpture. It resembles nothing so much as a frozen baroque symphony. The central panel, Christ's Assumption, floats above the papal symbol of St Peter's keys and hat. The façade is only a warm-up for the interior, which contains nine gilt churrigueresque altars whose decoration, teeming with painted saints and cherubim, is even more complicated than the exterior. Under the arched painting of Santa Prisca, a Roman martyr, is the entrance to the **Chapel of the**

Indians, with three more gilt altars. The **Sacristy** contains masterpieces by Miguel Cabrera (1695–1768), a Zapotec Indian painter, depicting the life of the Virgin Mary. The church's jewel-encrusted monstrance (the receptacle for the Host in the mass), the most expensive religious object ever made in the New World, currently resides in Notre Dame in Paris. During Holy Week before Easter, the Society of Penitents, a local Catholic association, performs a 'solemn and interesting' procession: the arms of black-hooded *encruzados* are bound to 100-pound bundles of thorny branches; the *ánimas*, who represent souls in Purgatory, are chained together; and *los Cristos* carry crosses and pause now and then to flagellate themselves with leather straps lined with tacks. Borda went broke when San Ignacio dried up and, after a string of failures, found an even bigger silver lode in Zacatecas.

The **Museo Guillermo Spratling**, on Calle Veracruz behind the church, contains the archeological collection of William Spratling, the American architecture professor who came to Taxco in 1930 and opened the first silver workshop here. Spratling taught many local craftsmen and is responsible for the jewelry boom that continues today. Unfortunately, the museum is expensive, considering the exhibitions, and its collection of Olmec, Maya and west Mexican artefacts is haphazard and contains many fakes (some helpfully marked *reproducciones*). The Taxco history exhibition in the basement is being renovated. The **Casa Humboldt,** a block down Calle Juan Ruíz de Alarcon, was the house of the famed German explorer, Alexander von Humboldt, and is now being rebuilt. The **Casa Figueroa** half a block above the plaza, once the city museum, is also shut for repairs. Steps at the south end of the plaza lead down into the confusing, colorful **market,** which fills a ravine between Calles Veracruz and San Nicolás. Here you can find many jewelry wholesalers, retail crafts sellers and vendors of more mundane articles like fruits and clothing. For retail jewelry, try shops around the plaza and/or the Ballesteros store at 4 Calle Celos Muñoz (high-end merchandise). Stuart Cohen, a boutique owner from Alaska who buys silver in Taxco every year, gives this overview of the industry:

> Two kinds of jewelry are sold in Taxco: silver made from locally mined metal and alpaca, a nickel alloy usually inlaid with abalone and colored resins. The jewelry is produced by families of artisans who live in the hills around Taxco, and is then sold by merchants in town. Although new designs are often brought from outside, Taxco jewelry maintains its own particular style and feel. Silver's bullion value is now about five dollars an ounce. Taxco's silver jewelry wholesales by the gram at the equivalent of nine to 25 dollars an ounce, depending on the complexity of the work. In Europe and North America this same jewelry will retail for 36 to 120 dollars an ounce. Alpaca is even more profitable: an alpaca earring that costs 85 cents in Taxco can easily sell for eight to 12 dollars in the United States. It isn't hard to see why so many who come to Taxco have ecstatic visions of numbers with lots of zeroes behind them. Buyer beware—that could be an hallucination brought on by Taxco's winding streets and beautiful churches!

THE DAY OF THE DEAD

The Day of the Dead is a uniquely Mexican observance. The ceremonies reflect a mixture of Catholic and Pre-Columbian beliefs, and large quantities of charming yet macabre folk art are produced and exchanged during these rites. After the Conquest, Catholic teachings about death and the afterlife mingled with Aztec and Mixtec beliefs about the underworld, the dead returning to Earth on one day of the year and the ritual consumption of 'bread of the dead' associated with the god Huitzilipochtli. In traditional Mexican thought, life and death are not separate but different sides of the same coin, interacting in many ways. The dead provide continuity between the world of the living and the heavenly realm of God and the saints. If you are good on Earth, the dead can help you, and any success is due to their intervention. But if you are a sinner, their pleadings with the heavenly powers will be of no use. Between the evening of October 31 (the eve of All Saints' Day) and November 2 (the day after All Souls' Day), the dead return to commune with the living and are able to smell and taste their favorite foods and drinks.

A week or two before the Day of the Dead, many Mexicans begin to construct altars at home, at their workplace and in cemeteries. Depending on local custom and the amount of money available, these may be simple or elaborate constructions made from wood or wire frames. The frames are always decorated with yellow and orange marigold-like flowers, symbolic of the brief life of humans. The offerings on the altar include fruit, *pan de los muertos* ('bread of the dead'), pictures of holy figures, sugar or chocolate skulls called *calaveras*, paper cutouts with cheerfully morbid scenes, candles, photos of the dead, and food and drink. If the dead were children, toys will be placed on the altar. Some of the most elaborate altars are constructed by vendors in the huge market of La Merced in downtown Mexico City.

The Day of the Dead traditions differ in the various regions of Mexico, and neighboring towns may have completely different practices. The most elaborate celebrations are found in the traditional communities of the Central Highlands, particularly around Lake Pátzcuaro in Michoacán, in the mountains of Oaxaca, and in rural Morelos. In the Mexico City region, the town of Xochimilco, just to the south, also has well known observances. A month before the ceremony, the residents harvest and sell the crops from their *chinampas* (earthen platforms for growing, built in the shallow lake) in order to raise enough money to pay for the offerings. By the end of October, Xochimilco's market is filled with people from throughout the region, buying and selling flowers, fruit, candles, food and *calaveras*. The local version of *pan de los muertos* is a round, sweet bread with a knob of dough on the top. The night of October 31–November 1 is when the *angelitos*, the souls of dead children, return to Earth. Offerings of the children's favorite foods and toys as well as sugar skulls are placed on little altars in the homes while prayers are said. At 2 am the families repair to the cemetery to place flowers and light candles on the children's graves. The next day, the church bells peal with joy at the visit of the *angelitos*.

That same evening the bells begin to toll the death knell, because the souls of the *grandes*, the adults, are approaching. In the homes the women dismantle the little altars and invoke the spirits of their ancestors with prayers over the adult altar. Bread, fruit and candles are placed in the form of a cross on the altar and copal incense burners are lit. Food, usually chicken with *mole* and tortillas, and drink, including *pulque*, tequila and *mezcal*, are placed on the altar, so that the dead may enjoy smelling and tasting their favorite things. Between 10 pm and 2 am, a group of people who represent the souls who have no living relatives go from house to house, begging offerings through prayers and songs. Afterwards, the family once again goes to the cemetery and stays there for the rest of the night saying prayers, eating and drinking over the decorated and candle-lit tombs. On November 3rd, related households exchange the remaining offerings and then assemble to eat and drink yet again! For those who do not give offerings to their ancestors or seek to save a little money, the punishment is usually swift. The story goes that a women bought cheap little candles instead of the bigger traditional ones; when she returned home from the cemetery, she discovered that her house was on fire—the candle had burned down and set the altar aflame!

Today the Day of the Dead celebrations are slowly dying out under the onslaught of that American import—Halloween—which is being heavily promoted by TV and magazines. Nevertheless, Mexican culture is resilient; a synthesis of the two traditions may well occur.

Taxco's restaurants may be found around the plaza and along Calle San Nicolás. Restaurants Santa Fé and Tía Culla (on the second floor) on San Nicolás are recommended. The cheaper hotels are in the old part of town; the more luxurious resorts lie just off Avda Kennedy on the north and south sides of town.

State of Hidalgo

After the decline of Teotihuacán, a chief named Mixcoatl ('Cloud Serpent') led his tribe into the state of Hidalgo from the northwest. They were called the Toltecs, and Mixcoatl's son, the bearded and pale-skinned Topiltzín, founded their capital in Tula in southern Hidalgo around AD 950. The city was soon torn by a conflict between those who worshipped the peaceful Feathered Serpent, including Topiltzín, and those who followed the blood-thirsty god Tezcatlipoca ('Smoking Mirror'). Topiltzín was expelled from Tula around 987, and his subsequent wanderings south and east became the stuff of myth. According to one tale, he set sail in a raft from the Gulf coast vowing one day to return. (Motecuhzoma II remembered this story with fear when he heard of bearded white men landing on his shores.) With the warrior faction in power, the Toltecs extended their influence throughout central Mexico from Zacatecas to Oaxaca. The Aztecs later looked back on the Toltec era as a time of unparalleled prosperity.

In the mid-12th century, Tula collapsed due to internal strife, and the survivors streamed forth to conquer and settle lands as far away as Yucatán. Cortés entered Hidalgo in 1520, but he wasn't able to conquer the tribes there completely until 1530. The region was divided into *encomiendas*, and Spanish settlement surged when—from 1552 onwards—rich silver mines were discovered in Pachuca and Real del Monte. Pachuca's wealth made it an important prize for various armies; battles were fought here during the Insurgency, the US invasion, the Wars of Reform, the French invasion and the Revolution. Although Hidalgo is today surrounded by powerful neighbors, the trend towards increasing population and industrialization has largely by-passed the state.

TULA

The archeological site of Tula, once the capital of the warlike Toltec empire, sits on a hilltop east of Tula de Allende, a dusty town whose bustle is prompted by a nearby Pemex refinery. Unfortunately for visitors, many of Tula's great sculptures—the warrior-pillars—have been removed and replaced by copies. You can see them in the Anthropological Museum in Mexico City. The **museum** at the site entrance has an excellent exhibition on Tula's history and examples of Toltec pottery and stone work. A gift shop and a café are also on the premises. The city covered 14 square kilometers (5.4 square miles) at

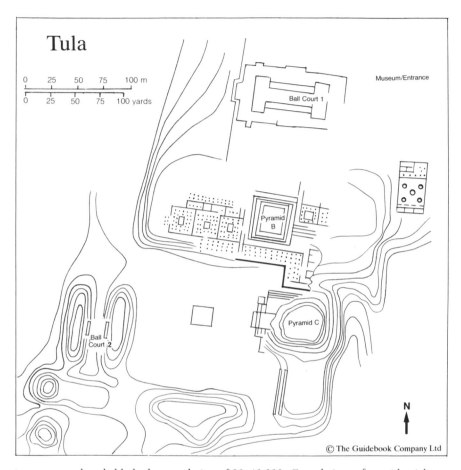

Tula

0   25   50   75   100 m

0   25   50   75   100 yards

Museum/Entrance

Ball Court 1

Pyramid B

Pyramid C

Ball Court 2

N

© The Guidebook Company Ltd

its apogee and probably had a population of 30–40,000. Foundations of a residential district can be seen immediately after passing through the entrance complex. The main ruins lie 600 meters (half a mile) down a walkway lined with exhortations like 'Walk, Observe and Enjoy!' on little signs (wear a hat too!).

The path takes you to **Ball Court No 1** on the right, whose design the Toltecs apparently copied from one at Xochicalco in Morelos. On the left stands the four-tiered **Pyramid B**, the most impressive structure on the site. A wall that runs along the pyramid's north side holds a 40-meter (131-foot) mural called the 'Serpent Wall', which depicts snakes eating human skeletons. Rows of square pillars abut the west side of the pyramid; these were probably meeting halls with muraled walls. More pillars range in front of the pyramid's staircase; these originally held reliefs of marching warriors and held up the roof of an entrance hall. Among the columns lie two *chac mools*, reclining stone figures with a dish in the mid-section that probably received human hearts. The sides of the pyramid are covered with reliefs symbolically depicting the main Toltec warrior orders: jaguars, coyotes, eagles eating hearts and monster-like faces that may be Quetzalcoatl. The platform on top of the pyramid held a temple with two rooms. The wooden roof of the first room was held up by four 'Atlantes', 4.6-meter (15-foot)-tall stone columns carved in the shape of Toltec warriors holding an *atlatl* (a stick for hurling arrows) in one hand and a copal incense pouch in the other. The warriors' chests are covered with stylized butterflies, the symbol of the Toltecs. Four square stone columns carved with warrior symbols held up the roof of the rear room, which was the site of the most important altar. The plaza south of Pyramid B has a small ceremonial platform in the center and the remains of **Pyramid C**. Only partially excavated, the latter was the largest structure in Tula. Another ball court lies west across the plaza.

Pachuca
Hidalgo's capital, the silver mining city of Pachuca (pop 320,000), lies in a valley between two arms of a mountain range. The highest point in town, at the top of the valley, is the still-active mine and ore-processing complex. Pachuca isn't a tourist-oriented city but nevertheless possesses some interesting sights. The **Plaza de la Independencia** is the main square; in its center stands an ornate 40-meter (131-foot)-tall **Clocktower** with the **tourism office** in the base. The **Church and Convent of San Francisco** (1590–98), five blocks south of the plaza, is now the **Centro Cultural de Hidalgo**. The white and gold interior of the church contains the mummified body of Santa Columba, who was martyred in Sens, France in AD 273. The other convent buildings have been converted to the **National Museum of Photography** (one of the best collections in Mexico), the **Archeology Museum**, the **Hidalgo Regional History Museum**, an art gallery, a cinema and a theater. The regional food specialties are *pastes*, meat pies originally brought here by English miners in the 19th century. The Hotel and Restaurant Noriega and the Restaurant Casino Español (2nd floor), both on Matamoros just off the Plaza de la Independencia, are recommended.

The scenic mining town of **Mineral del Monte** (also called Real de Monte) lies ten kilometers (six miles) into the hills to the east of Pachuca. The mine, still in operation, is just to the north of the entrance to town. Mineral del Monte's winding cobblestone streets are lined with whitewashed stone buildings. An overly realistic **sculpture of a heroic mineworker** stands in front of the market. The big church is **Nuestra Señora del Rosario**, which was begun in 1563 and renovated in the 18th century. Just up the hill stands the little **Capilla de Vera Cruz** (16th century), which contains interesting old wooden retables painted red. In 1766, Mineral del Monte was the site of the first strike

Toltec warriors, Tula

in Mexican history. Mineworkers disgusted by low pay and poor conditions rioted and killed the mayor. They were about to kill the mine owner when local authorities interceded and agreed to some of their demands. During the 19th century many of the mines were worked by prisoners.

State of Puebla

The state of Puebla is the site of one of the most important archeological finds in the New World. In caves of the Tehuacán Valley archeologists found tiny ears of domesticated corn dated around 3000 BC. These are the earliest yet discoveries of this crop, which became Mexico's 'staff of life' and without which the great developments of pre-Hispanic civilizations would have been impossible. Researchers theorize that corn was first domesticated between 7000 and 5000 BC, somewhere in the Puebla-Oaxaca region. The Puebla-area cultures were first influenced by the Olmecs and then by Teotihuacán and the Totonacs (in the region near El Tajín). The city of Cholula, which has an Olmec-style patio, possesses pure Teotihuacán-style murals on the exterior of the earliest pyramid. Around AD 900, the Olmeca-Xicallanca conquered Cholula and dedicated the Great Pyramid to the Feathered Serpent. By the time of the last reconstruction, this structure was the largest man-made object in the New World and rivalled the Pyramid of Cheops. In AD 1292, the Olmeca-Xicallanca were toppled by the Tolteca-Chichimeca and by the next century Cholula was an independent city-state. The Great Pyramid was abandoned in favor of a new temple to Quetzalcoatl.

In the 15th century, after decades of war, the Aztecs finally defeated the Cholulans and forced them to pay tribute to Tenochtitlán. By this time, Cholula was one of the most important religious centers in central Mexico—they had a temple for every day of the year—and was also known for high-quality ceramics that Motecuhzoma II dined off in the imperial palace. When Cortés advanced upon the Valley of Mexico in 1519, he stopped in Cholula, and his subsequent actions in the city remain controversial today. What is sure is that his troops massacred as many as 6,000 unarmed Cholulans in the main plaza. The question is: did he massacre them in self-defense, because they were planning to slaughter the Spaniards, or was this merely a way of broadcasting his power and ruthlessness to the Aztecs? Was he a mass-murderer or a simply a cunning general? The reality probably lies in between.

After the Conquest, the Spanish destroyed Cholula's 365 temples and declared they would replace every one of them with a Christian chapel (they only completed 40). In 1531, the city of Puebla was founded a few kilometers east, perhaps as a Catholic response to Cholula. Puebla, with its early ceramic and textile industries, quickly grew into Mexico's second most important city. Since many religious orders and a Jesuit college were based here, the city also became known as one of the most pious and conservative in Mexico, a reputation it retains today. The majority of the local Indians died in epidemics and their lands were taken over for large farms and cattle estates.

In 1811, Morelos entered the state with his insurgent army and fought the royalists successfully for five years until the tide of battle turned. The conservatives captured Puebla from the anti-clerical liberals in 1856, with much assistance from the pious citizenry. On May 5, 1862, Puebla was the scene of the most famous victory of the Mexican army. In a bloody, day-long battle, a troop of 2,000 Mexicans repelled 6,000 French soldiers weakened by Montezuma's Revenge. The hero of the day was a young general named Porfirio Díaz, who was catapulted to fame and eventually became Mexico's supreme dictator. The French returned a year later and bombarded and besieged Puebla. After two months of starvation and shell-shock, the Mexicans relinquished the city.

In 1910, a revolutionary activist named Aquiles Serdán was on the verge of calling for the armed overthrow of the dictator Díaz when a squad of soldiers circled his house in downtown Puebla and massacred him and his family, making them the first martyrs of the Mexican Revolution. The 1910–20 economic and political chaos led to severe starvation in Puebla and other cities. In 1920, President Carranza, on the run from Alvaro Obregón's army, was assassinated in the small town of Tlaxcalantongo by an Obregonista in his own bodyguard. Two of Puebla's post-Revolution governors, Manuel Avila

Camacho and Gustavo Díaz Ordáz (a dour conservative responsible for the 1968 Tlate-lolco student massacre), have gone on to become president.

PUEBLA

Puebla (pop 1,885,000) was Mexico's second largest city until this century when it was eclipsed by Guadalajara and Monterrey. Although Puebla is attempting an industrial comeback—there's a huge Volkswagen plant on the northern outskirts—the city's colonial core remains intact and covered with *azulejos*, the ornate local tiles. Puebla is built on a grid pattern and the main axes—Avdas 16 de Septiembre and 5 de Mayo (same street, different names) divide the town east-west; Avdas Reforma and Camacho do the same north-south—cross in the Zócalo. The huge, stern-looking **Cathedral** (begun 1539) occupies the south side of the **Zócalo,** a typical Mexican plaza with trees, benches and a fountain. One of the largest church structures in Mexico, the Cathedral possesses twin 69-meter (227-foot)-towers, the country's tallest, and a tile-covered dome. A little door in the north tower is open mornings from 11 to 12, and leads up to the bells and a sweeping view over Puebla. The vast interior is decorated with marble floors, onyx and gold leaf. The **tourism office** lies directly behind the Cathedral on Calle 5 Oriente. Next door stands the **Archbishop's Palace**, which houses the **Casa de Cultura** with temporary exhibitions on the first floor. The second floor is the **Biblioteca Palafoxiana**, a collection of rare books and manuscripts founded in 1647 and named after Puebla's most famous bishop, Juan de Palafox y Mendoza. The **Museo de Arte José Luis Bello y Gonzalez,** two blocks west of the Cathedral on Calle 3, is an amazing collection of decorative art amassed by a local businessman; it includes tiles, paintings made from feathers, ivory carvings, strange locks and ornate inlaid furniture.

A two-block walk north of the Zócalo on 5 de Mayo takes you to the **Templo de Santo Domingo,** a relatively plain church containing the most important shrine in Puebla. Just to the left of the main altar, the **Capilla del Rosario,** built by the Dominicans in 1534, takes your breath away. Above a dust guard of painted tiles that rises to shoulder level, it's covered all the way to the ceiling's point with gilt carvings of grape, vine and animal motifs; there are no architectural elements visible. Across the entry range the heads of a heavenly choir, and brightly painted—almost cartoonish—saints' sculptures extend from the walls. The centerpiece of the chapel is the altar containing the doll-like figure of the Virgin; it is one of the most venerated images in Mexico. The patron of seafarers, on holy days she wears a robe made of three kilos of pearls donated by sailors. The **Mercado Victoria,** one block north, was once Puebla's main market but is now mostly closed for renovations. Two blocks northeast, on Calle 3 Norte between Avdas 12 and 14, stands the **Santa Rosa Nunnery** (17th century), now the **Casa de Artesanías** (it has guided tours). Puebla's most famous culinary contribution to the world, *mole poblano* (a thick, dark sauce made from chocolate, chilli and ground spices), was invented by

(*facing page and above*) Aerial dance of the voladores in *Cuetzalán, Puebla;*
(*below*) The Totonac city of El Tajín, *a vision by Diego Rivera*

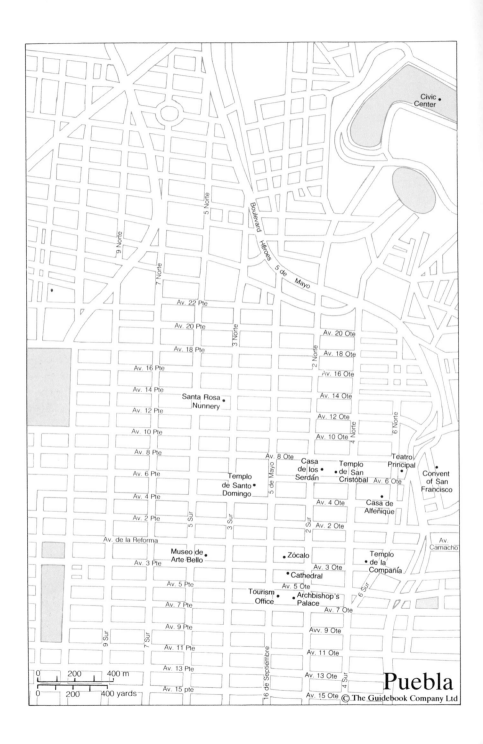

Civic Center

Boulevard Heroes 5 de Mayo

5 Norte

9 Norte

7 Norte

3 Norte

2 Norte

4 Norte

6 Norte

Av. 22 Pte

Av. 20 Pte

Av. 18 Pte

Av. 16 Pte

Av. 14 Pte

Santa Rosa Nunnery

Av. 12 Pte

Av. 10 Pte

Av. 8 Pte

Av. 6 Pte

Templo de Santo Domingo

Av. 4 Pte

Av. 2 Pte

5 Sur

3 Sur

Av. de la Reforma

Museo de Arte Bello

Av. 3 Pte

Av. 5 Pte

Av. 7 Pte

Av. 9 Pte

9 Sur

7 Sur

Av. 11 Pte

Av. 13 Pte

Av. 15 pte

Av. 20 Ote

Av. 18 Ote

Av. 16 Ote

Av. 14 Ote

Av. 12 Ote

Av. 10 Ote

Av. 8 Ote

5 de Mayo

2 Sur

Casa de los Serdán

Templo de San Cristóbal

Teatro Principal

Convent of San Francisco

Av. 6 Ote

Av. 4 Ote

Casa de Alfeñique

Av. 2 Ote

Zócalo

Av. 3 Ote

Cathedral

Av. 5 Ote

Templo de la Compañía

6 Sur

Av. Camacho

Tourism Office

Archbishop's Palace

Av. 7 Ote

Avv. 9 Ote

16 de Septiembre

Av. 11 Ote

Av. 13 Ote

4 Sur

Av. 15 Ote

0   200   400 m

0   200   400 yards

Puebla

© The Guidebook Company Ltd

nuns in the kitchen here. Another nunnery, **Santa Monica** at the corner of Avdas 18 and 5 de Mayo, contains hidden passages that were supposedly used to hide nuns during Mexico's long period of clerical prosecution. It is now the **Museo de Arte Religioso**.

One block east of the Capilla del Rosario, on Calle 2 North and Avda 6 East, the **Casa de los Serdán** was the home of a family of liberal activists opposed to the dictatorship of Porfírio Díaz. On November 20, 1910, Díaz' soldiers surrounded the house and, after a long gun battle, killed Aquiles Serdán and his family; they are considered the first martyrs of the Revolution. The house is now the **Museo de la Revolución**, and you can still see the bullet holes in the walls. The **Templo de San Cristóbal** next door contains onyx windows and a carved ceiling vault reminiscent of the Capilla del Rosario, but darker. This block of Avda 6 East is lined with shops devoted to the sale of *camotes*, delicious rolls of soft candy made from sweet potatoes and flavored with coconut, pineapple and other fruits. Avda 6 runs east two blocks into **Barrio del Artista** and the **Mercado Parian**. Once Puebla's artistic neighborhood, this area is now filled with stores selling low-quality souvenirs. The baroque **Teatro Principal** (1761), one of the oldest in Mexico, stands just north of the gift shops. Continuing east across the wide Blvd 5 de Mayo (not to be confused with the avenue), you come to the **Convent and Church of San Francisco** (begun 1535). The stark interior contains the body of Sebastian de Aparicio, a monk who built the first roads in Mexico and is now the patron of Mexican truck drivers. Paintings depicting his life decorate the walls. A room to one side is filled with amazing artworks made from votaries given in his memory. Icons of the monk for your dashboard are also sold.

Heading back to the Zócalo, you arrive at the **Casa de Alfeñique** at the corner of Calle 6 North and Avda 4 East, now the **Museo del Estado**. *Alfeñique* means 'spun sugar' and refers to the frothy white decorations on the building's façade. The interior contains exhibitions on pre-Hispanic and colonial history and local crafts. The **Templo de la Compañía** (1767) at Avda Camacho and Calle 4 South contains the tomb of La China Poblana, a legendary local figure. Supposedly a Mongol or Chinese princess, she arrived in Puebla, was adopted by a wealthy couple and became known for her Christian piety. Her oriental dress style became the fashion in the city and is still worn in traditional dances. A hill two kilometers (1.25 miles) north of the Zócalo, on Calle 2 North, is the site of the famous May 5, 1862 victory against the French. It is now the park-like **Civic Center**, which includes the **forts of Guadalupe and Loreto**, the **Anthropology and History Museum**, the **Natural History Museum** (under a pyramid) and the bullring. Mexico's only safari park, **Africam**, with 3,000 animals representing 250 species, lies 20 kilometers (12 miles) south of Puebla. Thrice-weekly professional wrestling matches are staged at the **Arena Puebla** on the corner of Calle 4 South and Avda 13 East. For local culinary specialties try the Fonda Santa Clara and Restaurant La Bola Roja. The new **bus station** is on the northern outskirts on Avda Carmen Serdán.

Quetzal dance, Puebla

CHOLULA

The archeological site of Cholula (pop 20,000) lies ten kilometers due west of Puebla on Avda Reforma. Many mini-buses run this route. In pre-Hispanic times this was one of the most important spiritual centers in central Mexico and contained around 400 shrines and 100,000 citizens. A small museum on the north side of the site contains a good diorama of the city as it looked at the Conquest. At first glance, the **Great Pyramid** looks like a large hill with a small church on top. However, if you enter the tunnel in the north side of the hill, you see that it is totally artificial. The narrow, somewhat claustrophobic tunnel passes through the four stages of the pyramid's construction; branching off from it are secret stairways used by the priests. Archeologists have excavated eight kilometers (five miles) of tunnels in the pyramid. The first pyramids were constructed from the sixth century on by groups associated with Teotihuacán; later, the Olmeca-Xicallanca captured Cholula, expanded the pyramid and dedicated it to the Feathered Serpent. By the time the Tolteca-Chichimeca conquered the area in the 13th century, the pyramid was the most massive in the world: 55 meters (180 feet) tall and 425 meters (1,400 feet) to a side. Various stairways lead up the hill to the small blue and white **Templo de**

Nuestra Señora de los Remedios (1597–1666) on top. On holy days, processions accompanied by bands, fireworks, flags and statues of saints wind up the hill to the church. At the base of the pyramid's south side, excavations partially expose the remains of the main staircase. Club Med has built a Villa Arqueológica hotel just south of the ruins.

Back in the town of Cholula, the **Church and Convent of San Francisco** (begun 1529) and the **Capilla Real**, with its dozens of little domes, are both worth visiting. The towns of **Acatepec** and **Tonantzintla** immediately south of Cholula contain the **Templo de San Francisco** (1788, reconstructed 1963) and the **Iglesia de Santa María Tonantzintla** (begun 1607), respectively. Both churches are covered inside and out with wildly ornate tiles and carved wood decoration crafted by local Indian artisans.

TEHUACÁN

The city of Tehuacán (pop 113,000) in the southeastern corner of the state of Puebla is famous for its mineral springs. (A bottle of soda water is popularly called a *tehuacán* throughout central Mexico.) Visitors enjoy relaxing in the bubbly waters of the many **spas and baths** on the outskirts of town. On or near the pleasant, tree-filled main plaza may be found the **Palacio del Gobierno**, with many murals, the **Franciscan Convent and Church** (1592–1697) and the tile-covered **Parroquia de la Concepcíon** (18th century).

State of Tlaxcala

The smallest state in Mexico, Tlaxcala, has always been densely settled. After the decline of Teotihuacán, a group of Olmeca-Xicallanca from the Gulf invaded central Mexico and built a hill-top city called Cacaxtla. In 1974, huge distinctly Mayan murals executed in intense colors were discovered here. Around AD 1100, the Olmeca-Xicallanca were expelled by a tribe of Tolteca-Chichimecas, later called the Tlaxcalans. Although they lived only 120 kilometers (75 miles) from the Aztec capital, the Tlaxcalans were fierce warriors and maintained their independence through constant battle. When Cortés' army entered the region with the Totonacs in 1519, Xicotencatl, the Tlaxcalan chief, saw that the balance of power in Mexico had suddenly shifted. After some initial hostilities, the Tlaxcalans decided to make peace and add their army to the Spanish force. The Tlaxcalans became the Spaniards' strongest allies and after the Conquest accompanied expeditions throughout Mexico. Tlaxcalan wards were built in Spanish settlements as far away as San Cristóbal in Chiapas and Santa Fé in distant New Mexico. However, the might of the Spanish bureaucracy soon whittled down their privileges, and they eventually suffered as much as the other tribes. Tlaxcala was one of the earliest sites of Christian evangelism; in 1530, the Franciscans began the construction of one of the first New

Blitzed

SEAT OF THE HISTORY OF THE CONQUEST
VISIT TLAXCALA!

read the Consul. (And how was it that, beside him, was standing a lemonade bottle half full of mescal, how had he obtained it so quickly, or Cervantes, repenting, thank God, of the stone, together with the tourist folder, to which was affixed a railway and bus timetable, brought it—or had he purchased it before, and if so, when?)

¡VISITE VD. TLAXCALA!

Sus Monumentos, Sitios Históricos y De Bellezas
Naturales. Lugar De Descanso, El Mejor Clima. El Aire Más Puro. El Cielo Más Azul.
¡TLAXCALA! SEDE DE LA HISTORIA DE LA CONQUISTA

'—this morning, when we were crossing the river there was this pulquería on the other side—'
'...La Sepultura?'
'—Indian sitting with his back against the wall—'

GEOGRAPHIC SITUATION

The State is located between 19° 06' 10" and 19° 44' 00" North latitude and between 0° 23' 38" and 1° 30' 34" Eastern longtitude from Mexico's meridian. Being its boundaries to the North-West and South with Puebla State, to the West with Mexico State and to the North-West with Hidalgo State. Its territorial extension is of 4,132 square kilometres. Its population is about 220,000 inhabitants, giving a density of 53 inhabitants to the square kilometre. It is situated in a valley surrounded by mountains, among them are those called Matlalcueyatl and Ixtaccihuatl.

'—Surely you remember, Yvonne, there was this pulquería—'
'—What a glorious morning it was!—'

CLIMATE

Intertropical and proper of highlands, regular and healthy. The malarial sickness is unknown.

'—well, Geoff said he was a Spaniard for one thing—'

'—but what difference—'

'So that the man beside the road may be an Indian, of course,' the Consul suddenly called from his stone retreat, though it was strange, nobody seemed to have heard him. 'And why an Indian? So that the incident may have some social significance to him, so that it should appear a kind of latter-day repercussion of the Conquest, if you please, so that that may in turn seem a repercussion of—'

'—crossing the river, a windmill—'

'Cervantes!'

'A stone...You want a stone, señor?'

HYDROGRAPHY

Zahuapan River—Streaming from Atoyac river and bordering the City of Tlaxcala, it supplies a great quantity of power to several factories; among the lagoons, the Acuitlapilco is the most notable and is lying two kilometres South from Tlaxcala City...Plenty of web-footed fowl is found in the first lagoon.

'—Geoff said the pub he came out of was a fascist joint. The El Amor de los Amores. What I gathered was he used to be the owner of it, though I think he's come down in the world and he just works there now...Have another bottle of beer?'

'Why not? Let's do.'

'What if this man by the roadside had been a fascist and your Spaniard a communist?'—In his stone retreat the Consul took a sip of mescal.— 'Never mind, I think your thief is a fascist, though of some ignominious sort, probably a spy on other spies or—'

'The way I feel, Hugh, I thought he must be just some poor man riding from market who'd taken too much pulque, and fell off his horse, and was being taken care of, but then we arrived, and he was robbed...Though do you know, I didn't notice a thing...I'm ashamed of myself.'

'Move his hat down though, so he can get some air.'

'—outside La Sepultura.'

Malcolm Lowry, Under the Volcano

World monasteries here. Although Tlaxcala adjoins the industrial boomtown of Puebla, the state has so far avoided the modern ills of overpopulation and pollution.

TLAXCALA

The state capital, Tlaxcala, is a traditional town with a population of 25,000. On the north side of the **Zócalo** stands the **Palacio del Gobierno** (16th century), with a façade of patterned bricks and ornate windows. The interior is decorated with a series of vivid **murals** (begun 1965) by Desiderio Hernandez Xochitiotzin, depicting Tlaxcala's turbulent history. Another park just southeast of the Zócalo is the entry to the complex of the **Convento de San Francisco** (begun 1525), one of the first four monasteries in Mexico. At this spot in 1520 the Spaniards baptized four Tlaxcalan chiefs. The exterior of the convent and church is austere and fort-like; next to the church is the **Open Chapel**, where mass was said when the huge crowds of Indian converts couldn't fit into the church. The church interior is lavish, with an Arab-style wooden ceiling considered the finest in Mexico, colorful tile floors and an 18th-century altar. The **Capilla del Tercer Orden** contains the original 16th-century pulpit and baptismal font. The neighboring monastery is now the **Museo Regional de Tlaxcala**, with archeological and historical collections, built around a cloister.

On a hilltop a kilometer east of the city stands the **Santuario de Nuestra Señora de Ocotlán** (1670), one of the most lavish churrigueresque churches in Mexico. You may reach it by local bus or walk up Calle Zitlalpopoca, three blocks north of the Zócalo. The church is covered with hexagonal bricks, and the carved white stone façade between the twin towers is a confection of elaborate decorations and religious sculptures. Inside, the **Camarín** behind the altar is an octagonal room lined with carvings by Francisco Miguel, an 18th-century Indian artist. Paintings on the walls depict the miracle that led to the church's construction: in 1536, a local Indian saw a tree on fire and doused the flames; inside the trunk he saw a pine statue of the Virgin, so he proceeded to build a shrine on the hillside for the image's safekeeping. That pine statue is now revered in the church's main altar.

CACAXTLA

The ruins of Cacaxtla, on a hilltop southwest of Tlaxcala, are the remains of the capital of the Olmeca-Xicallanca, a tribe of Putun Maya who flourished in central Mexico in the eighth and ninth centuries. In 1974, looters discovered a brightly colored mural on the site, and subsequent excavations unearthed another one nearby. They are the best preserved ancient murals found so far in Mexico. The murals were painted on the walls of Cacaxtla's palaces and are now protected from the elements by an enormous steel shed. The murals are sometimes only open in the morning, so it is best to visit then. A small

Maya warrior in eagle costume, Cacaxtla

museum stands at the site entrance. The **Palace of the Paintings** mural is divided into two: the north mural depicts a warrior-knight with jaguar feet standing on a jaguar; the south mural shows another warrior, this time with eagle feet and standing on a Feathered Serpent. In his arms he carries a stylized conch shell. The frame around him is decorated with turtles, snakes and snails. The **Building B** mural shows a great battle between jaguar and eagle knights, with grisly details like a man holding his entrails. Archeologists believe this scene represents a real battle that was possibly witnessed by the artist. The murals stand on the north side of the **Plaza Norte**; more palaces extend to the south.

The Colonial States

Introduction

Mexico's rich colonial legacy is centered in the fertile region north of Mexico City known as the Bajío. This is a broad valley that spans the central plateau from Querétaro in the east almost to Lake Chapala in the west, and from León in the north to Morelia in the south. The states of this region were the wealthiest of Spanish Mexico, encompassing prosperous estates, cities filled with ornate Baroque buildings and some of the richest silver mines in the world. This heritage can be seen in well-preserved pink stone cathedrals, palaces, convents, forts and aqueducts. In the states of Michoacán, Guanajuato, Querétaro and Jalisco there is also a vibrant culture of popular arts; Indian artisans in hundreds of little towns produce crafts objects, like the guitars of Paracho, Michoacán, which are famous around the world.

The city of Querétaro, less than two hours from Mexico City by highway, was a center of the anti-Spanish Insurgency in 1810 and retains its colonial charm. The air is clear, the pace is slower and the bells of the city's many churches resound throughout the day. The gilt interiors of the Santa Clara and Santa Rosa de Viterbo churches are masterpieces of the baroque at its most ornate. Querétaro also resonates with memories of the Emperor Maximilian, who was captured in a convent here in 1867 and executed on a hill outside the town. The state of Querétaro is a center of artisan work, and the crafts markets of Tequisquiapan and San Juan del Río are particularly worth a visit.

The state of Guanajuato was the birthplace of the Insurgency in the early 19th century. The state capital, also called Guanajuato, is dramatically situated in a narrow valley that compresses the many colonial buildings into a colorful hodgepodge of narrow streets and alleys. The fort-like Alhóndiga de Granaditas (the public granary) was the site of a savage rebel massacre in 1810 and is today an excellent museum. The city is the home to the famous Cervantino Festival, which brings the finest international artistic talent here for two weeks in November. The La Valenciana church situated on a hill above the city is considered the most beautiful church in Mexico. The state of Guanajuato also contains many other colonial towns, the most famous of which is San Miguel de Allende. It was the birthplace of the rebel Ignacio Allende, whose house is now a fine museum. This beautifully sited town is filled with colonial churches and plazas and contains famous art and language schools, a crafts market and a large community of American retirees.

The city of Aguascalientes has an attractive colonial heart at the Plaza de Armas but more business-oriented outskirts. The famous Mexican printmaker, Posada, was born here and an excellent display of his work may be seen at his museum. Every spring, Aguascalientes is home to the nationally famous San Marcos agricultural and artistic fair.

San Luis Potosí is filled with plazas surrounded by colonial churches, mansions, convents and government buildings. The Templo del Carmen contains the stunning gilt Virgin's chapel, a testament to the city's wealth under the Spanish kings. The Regional Museum is in an old convent; both the museum and the spun-sugar decor of its Aranzazu Chapel are worth a visit. San Luis also has a rich cultural life and now attracts people escaping from the pollution of Mexico City.

The state of Zacatecas is largely barren and covered with thorny scrub. Nevertheless, the state capital, also called Zacatecas, may have been the finest jewel in the colonial crown. The city is situated in a saddle between two hills, which are connected by a cable car that takes one up to clean, cool air and a huge vista. In the colonial heart of Zacatecas is the red stone Cathedral, with one of the finest and most ornate façades in all Mexico. The two Coronel museums contain the best collection of masks in the country as well as exhibits of artworks from around the world. The convent in nearby Guadalupe is a treasure of colonial religious art and an important pilgrimage site.

Jalisco is the home of Mexican cultural traditions like *mariachis, charrerías* (Mexican-style rodeos), tequila and the *jarabe tapatío,* also known as the Mexican Hat Dance. Guadalajara, the state capital, is Mexico's second largest city; it is modern and industrialized, yet still preserves a distinctive charm. The city's main sights are conveniently located near or along the Plaza Tapatío downtown and include the Cathedral, the Regional Museum and stunning murals by José Clemente Orozco. Jaliscan crafts are available in the San Juan market here or in the Tlaquepaque artisan's neighborhood. Excursions outside of Guadalajara include the town of Tequila's distilleries and the resort towns along Lake Chapala's northern shore.

Michoacán was the heart of the Tarascán Indian empire and retains much of its Indian flavor, particularly in the many small towns that specialize in crafts production. Morelia, the state capital, is filled with pink stone churches, colleges, mansions and theaters. The city's many museums contain excellent exhibitions on Tarascán culture, colonial life and on José María Morelos, the rebel leader who is the city's namesake. The Casa de Artesanías here is probably the largest crafts store in Mexico and sells the finest examples of artisan-work from throughout the state. Lake Pátzcuaro nearby is beautifully located amid forest-covered hills and was the center of the Tarascan kingdom. The red tile-roofed town of Pátzcuaro is a monument to the benevolent policies of Bishop Vasco de Quiroga, who built the enormous Basilica here and encouraged the Tarascans to sustain themselves through making crafts. Their products—the lacquerware is particularly excellent—may be seen in the local markets and boutiques. The town of Tzintzuntzán has the best preserved remnants of Tarascan pyramids, and the island of Janitzio is also a pleasant

COLONIAL ARCHITECTURE

For most of the colonial era Mexican architecture followed strict Spanish and European models. The magnificent exception is the 18th century, when Mexican building exploded into the ultra-baroque and distinctly Mexican style known as the churrigueresque, perhaps the most ornate in world architectural history.

The first building constructed by the Spanish in Mexico was a fortress at San Juan de Ulúa, next to Veracruz. Forts and fort-like motifs dominated Spanish buildings for the first decades of the colony. Cortés' mansion in Cuernavaca has thick walls topped with crenelations, a flat roof, his coat of arms over the entrance and an interior courtyard sur-

rounded by rooms. Many of these early buildings, like the Monte de Piedad in Mexico City, were first built on the foundations and with the stones of Indian temples. The typical church was built following the plan of Andalusian basilicas: a long nave flanked by two colonnades and aisles on the either side. Monasteries built around two-story cloisters were later attached. The church interiors often were decorated with *mudéjar*, or moorish-style, ornaments, including inlaid wood ceilings, carved tiles and octagonal columns. Open-air chapels were also built next to many early churches to accommodate the huge crowds of Indian converts; the one in the Franciscan monastery at Cholula resembles the great mosque in Córdoba, in southern Spain.

As the colony stabilized after 1550, more sophisticated architectural styles began to travel across the Atlantic; the Renaissance had arrived. The most common floor plan was now cross-shaped. Wooden church ceilings were replaced with barrel vaults, and these began to acquire Gothic ribs, as in Guadalajara Cathedral. The apse was filled with a retable, which is a complex of carved wooden panels covered with gilt ornaments, sculptures and paintings that provides a dramatic backdrop for the altar. The exteriors were relatively austere; the design of the façades, usually with columns and sculptures, followed the strict classical principles of harmony. Many of the great cathedrals, including those in Mexico City, Puebla, Morelia and Mérida, were begun during this era. Some church and residential entrances were designed in the more exuberant plateresque style, so named because it resembled the silversmith's art. The hallmarks of this style are flat-topped arches surrounded by purely ornamental carvings, often including the coats-of-arms and sculptures of the owners; this style may be seen on the Franciscan monastery in Xochimilco, and in the entrance to the Casa de Montejo in Mérida.

In the late 18th century, the old classical rules—form follows function and reverence for proportion—began to dissolve under an ever-growing zest for ornament, one of the hallmarks of the baroque era. The baroque soon became the dominant style, because the central religious and civic authorities no longer had absolute control over architectural design. Most new churches were funded by wealthy mine- and estate-owners, who had more daring tastes than the central powers. The Capilla del Rosario in Puebla is considered the masterpiece of the pure baroque. The gold and white carving is so fine and so all-encompassing that it is easy to see why the faithful think of it as a depiction of the fabric of

continues

(above) Churrigueresque: ornate tower of Santa Prisca, Taxco;
(below) baroque: pink stone façade of Santo Domingo, Zacatecas

Heaven. Nevertheless, this splendid ornamentation never departed from the basic architectonic structure to become an end in itself. Other fine examples of the baroque are the churches of Santo Domingo in Oaxaca, and of Acatepec and Tonantzintla, near Cholula in the state of Puebla.

Thus far Mexican architecture had followed the lead of Europe, but around 1730 architects developed the unique ultra-baroque style known as the churrigueresque. This was erroneously named after a Spanish architect, José de Churriguera, whose work was not in the least churrigueresque, but the name stuck—perhaps because it is onomatopoeically appropriate. The churrigueresque ignored the old classical rules and its architects did not even work from complete plans; they designed as they built. Instead of narrowing as they ascended, churches now expanded upward into a profusion of ornamentation. Classical columns were forgotten; the main supporting member was the *estipite*, a rectangular pillar covered with geometric, vegetal and sculptural ornamentation. Stone was not worked to look like stone but carved to resemble wood, ivory or fabric. The joy and intensity of the churrigueresque reflected the piety of the Mexican people during the 18th century, and the faithful flocked to worship at these churches.

The three churrigueresque masterpieces are churches in Tepotzotlán, Taxco and Tlaxcala, all within a day-trip of Mexico City. The church of the Jesuit seminary in Tepotzotlán contains 11 gilt retables that are so deep and complex you appear to be on the sea floor looking up at a huge wall of coral reef. Taxco's smaller church of Santa Prisca has a baroque façade and a breathtaking interior that houses more gilt retables, which are identical

(above) Colonial Madonna and Child in the Museum of the Virreynato, Tepotzotlán; (below) detail of the façade of Chihuahua Cathedral

except for the paintings and sculpture. The church at Ocotlán, on a hillside above Tlaxcala, has an ornate whitewashed façade and twin towers, which break the classical rules by widening as they ascend. The finest example of the churrigueresque in Mexico City is the *estipite*-covered façade of the Sagrario Metropolitano on the Zócalo. The church at La Valenciana, just outside of Guanajuato, is a churrigueresque gem, and the interiors of the churches of Santa Rosa and Santa Clara in Querétaro are also particularly fine.

In 1785, the Academy of San Carlos for the study of art and architecture was founded by royal decree in Mexico City. The academicians were heavily influenced by the 'Rationalist' movement in Europe and quickly decided that the churrigueresque was imbalanced, arbitrary, confusing, top-heavy and, worse still, 'deformed'. They also discovered that many of the churrigueresque architects had not been professionally trained. New rules were published: only architects approved by the academy would be given major projects, and only architects who built in the new neo-classical style would be approved. The neo-classical was a return to the old principles of proportion and functionalism, with an even greater severity than the pre-baroque era. The result was buildings like the College of Mines in Mexico City, which is very symmetrical and orderly (very French) but also cold and rather obvious. The academy planned to strip the ornament off the churrigueresque churches and rebuild them more tastefully; luckily, the Wars of Independence intervened, and by the time stability returned decades later, tastes had changed and the churrigueresque was preserved.

(above) Alabaster: St Sebastian imported from China, Tepotzotlán; (below) folk baroque: interior of Santa Maria Tonantzintla, Puebla

excursion. Uruapan, an attractive small city, is a good base for exploring the crafts towns of Western Michoacán and the Paricutín volcano.

Getting There

The main roads to Querétaro are Mexico 57, the highway from Mexico City that continues north to San Luis Potosí, and Mexico 45 from León and Guanajuato. Querétaro is on the Constitucionalista train line from Mexico City, which continues north to Guanajuato or San Luis Potosí, and also on the Ciudad Juárez–Mexico City line. Daily service to Guadalajara is also available. The nearest major airports are Mexico City or León, Guanajuato.

The city of Guanajuato is 22 kilometers (14 miles) north of Mexico 45, which runs between Querétaro and León. Mexico 45 also connects Celaya, Salamanca and Irapuato. Guanajuato may also be reached via Mexico 110 from Dolores Hidalgo, and over 87 narrow and potholed kilometers (54 miles) from San Miguel de Allende. The latter town is on Mexico 111, about 40 kilometers (25 miles) north of Querétaro. Guanajuato and San Miguel de Allende are on different branches of the Constitucionalista rail line, which meet in Querétaro and head to Mexico City. The División del Norte train between Ciudad Juárez and Mexico City stops at León and Irapuato. The new international airport in León is served by flights from Hermosillo, Los Angeles, Mazatlán, Mexico City and Tijuana.

The main roads to Aguascalientes are Mexico 45 from Zacatecas and León, Mexico 80 from San Luis Potosí, and Mexico 54 and 70 from Guadalajara. The train lines originating in Ciudad Juárez and Zacatecas to Mexico City pass through here daily, and there is also a slow train service to San Luis Potosí. Aguascalientes' airport is served by direct flights from Mazatlán, Mexico City and Tijuana.

San Luis Potosí may be reached by car or bus via Mexico 80 from Aguascalientes, Mexico 70 from Tampico, Mexico 49 from Zacatecas and Mexico 57 from Saltillo and Querétaro. San Luis Potosí is on the Regiomontano line between Monterrey and Mexico City; it is also the origin for the Constitucionalista train that runs through the Bajío to Mexico City. Direct flights from Mexico City and Monterrey fly to San Luis Potosí.

Zacatecas is reached from Durango on Mexico 45, Saltillo on Mexico 54, San Luis Potosí on Mexico 49, Aguascalientes on Mexico 45 and Guadalajara on Mexico 54. Zacatecas is the terminal for the Zacatecan line that runs to Mexico City via Aguascalientes; other trains run the División del Norte route, changing at Pescador for Durango. There are direct flights to Zacatecas' international airport from Los Angeles, Tijuana and Mexico City.

Guadalajara is a major transportation hub. It may be reached from Mexico City on Mexico 15 via Toluca and Morelia, or on Mexico 45 and 90 via Querétaro. Mexico 15 continues to the Pacific after Tepic and becomes the Coast Highway. The resort of Manzanillo may be reached via Colima on Mexico 54 south; Mexico 54 north connects with Zacatecas and Aguascalientes. The Tapatío luxury train that runs daily between Mexico City and Guadalajara is one of Mexico's most popular train rides. Another luxury train, the Colimense, heads to Manzanillo on the coast via Colima. There are also two trains, the Pacífico and the Sinaloense, which serve cities along the coast up to Mexicali. A local train to Irapuato connects with the División del Norte line to Ciudad Juárez. Direct flights from Acapulco, Cancún, Chicago, Chihuahua, Cincinnati, Ciudad Juárez, Ciudad Obregón, Culiacán, Dallas, Detroit, Hermosillo, Houston, Ixtapa–Zihuatenejo, La Paz, Los Angeles, Los Cabos, Manzanillo, Mazatlán, Mexicali, Mexico City, Monterrey, Oaxaca, Philadelphia, Puerto Vallarta, San Diego, San Francisco, San José, Tijuana and Torreón land at Guadalajara's international airport. For Puerto Vallarta, see the Pacific chapter, p 165.

The main towns of the mountainous state of Michoacán may be reached by Mexico 15 from Mexico City, Mexico 35 from Guadalajara or Mexico 43 from Salamanca in Guanajuato. Morelia, Pátzcuaro and Uruapan are connected by Mexico 14. A scenic road travels from Uruapan down to the coast near Lázaro Cárdenas, from which it is two hours to Ixtapa-Zihuatenejo in Guerrero. The Purepecha train line winds through Michoacán's beautiful hills from Uruapan to Mexico City via Pátzcuaro and Morelia. There are small airports in Uruapan and Morelia, with flights from Lázaro Cárdenas on the coast and Mexico City.

State of Querétaro

Before the arrival of the Spaniards, Querétaro was on the border between the great Mesoamerican civilizations to the south and the barbarian Chichimecs. The principal inhabitants were the Otomi tribes, who had a fairly developed culture influenced by the Toltecs and the Aztecs. As the Tarascán empire based in Michoacán ascended, they began to expand into Querétaro. In 1446, the Aztecs defeated the Tarascans here, pushed them back to Michoacán and established military posts to protect against Chichimec raids. In 1531, a local Otomi chief named Conín was converted to Christianity and agreed to help the Spaniards colonize Querétaro. Rebaptized Hernando de Tápia, he led an expedition of converted Indians and Spaniards across the state, founding communities and convincing the Indians to give up their pagan beliefs. On July 25, 1531, the local chiefs agreed to convert, but only after a symbolic battle without weapons. According to legend, the battle ended when a cloud came across the sun and a cross and the image of the apostle Santiago appeared in the sky.

The city of Querétaro was founded at that site. The state was originally just a way-station on the road between Zacatecas and Mexico City. As the silver mines to the north prospered so did Querétaro's mining supply, agricultural, cattle and industrial enterprises; within decades it was the third richest city in Mexico, after the capital and Puebla. At the end of the 17th century, the Franciscans built in Querétaro the Colegio Apostólico de Propaganda Fidé de la Santísima Cruz de los Milagros, from which famous missionaries like Junípero Serra evangelized among the Indians of Northern Mexico. In the early 19th century, Querétaro became a center of the rebellion against the Spanish. The principal conspirators—Hidalgo, Allende, the Aldama brothers among others—met at the house of Querétaro's *corregidor* (the mayor) and planned to begin the rebellion on October 4, 1810. The conspiracy was discovered on September 11 but the *corregidor's* wife, Doña Josefa Ortíz de Domínguez, was able to warn Hidalgo and he started the revolt before the Spanish could arrest them. In February 1848, at the end of the US invasion of Mexico, the peace treaty was ratified in Querétaro's Templo de la Congregación. Two decades later another invasion, this time by the French, ended in Querétaro. After the Emperor Maximilian was forced from the capital in 1867, he retreated to Querétaro, where his army was besieged for three months until he was captured by the liberal forces under Mariano Escobedo. He was sentenced to death in the Teatro de la República, and on June 19 was executed by a firing squad on the Cerro de las Campanas just outside town. As the Mexican Revolution drew to a close, Venustiano Carranza named Querétaro his provisional capital, and on February 5, 1917 the Mexican Constitution—still in use today—was signed in the Teatro de la República. In the same theater in 1929, President Plutarco Calles inaugurated the Partido Nacional Revoluciónario, a precursor to today's ruling Partido Revoluciónario Institucional (PRI).

QUERÉTARO

The city of Querétaro (pop 300,000), situated in a broad valley of the same name, is clean, unhurried and filled with churches, squares and low colonial buildings. Between the lanes of the Mexico City highway south of town stands a huge **statue of Conín**, the Otomi Indian chief who converted to Christianity and convinced the local Indians to surrender peacefully to the Spanish. Querétaro's two main streets are **Avenidas Benito Juárez** and **Corregidora**, which run parallel north from the **Alameda**. The latter tree-filled park is surrounded by modern hotels, the **central bus station** at the south end and the main shopping district to the west. The center of town is the **Plaza Principal** between Juárez and Corregidora. The **Templo de San Francisco** on the east side was erected by Franciscans between 1540 and 1550. The interior, which is covered with *trompe l'oeil* decorations, contains the image of Santa Maria del Pueblito, the patroness of Querétaro. Next door stands the Franciscan convent (begun 1540), now the **Regional Museum**,

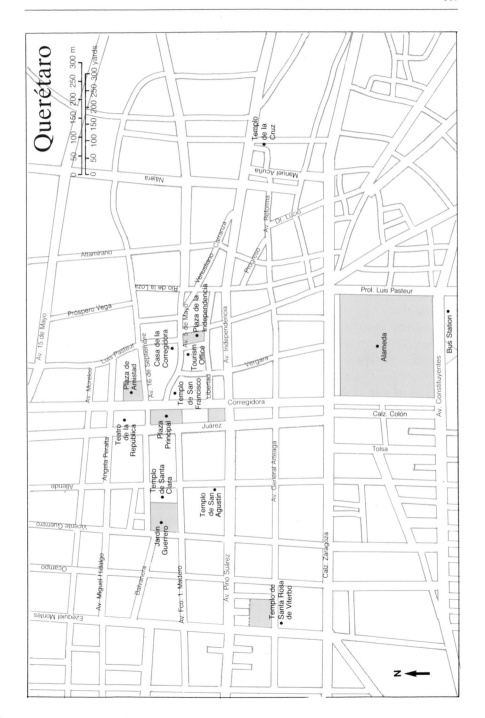

Querétaro

which encloses two beautiful patios. The museum contains the table on which the 1848 peace treaty with the United States was signed, exhibits on the Insurgency and the execution of Maximilian and a large collection of religious art. The streets behind the museum have become an attractive pedestrian area lined with colonial buildings.

Two blocks east on Avda 5 de Mayo takes one to the **Plaza de la Independencia**. At the north end is the **Casa de la Corregidora** (1770), now the Palacio del Gobierno, from which Doña Josefa Ortíz de Domínguez warned Miguel Hidalgo that their conspiracy against the Spanish had been discovered. The **tourist office** sits on the west side next to the Casa Ecala, an 18th-century mansion. The plaza also contains boutiques, restaurants and the more elegant hotels. The antique shop at 8 Avda Luis Pasteur displays many mementoes of 19th-century Querétaro. In the small **Plaza de Amistad**, a block north of the Plaza Principal, stands a **monument to La Corregidora** that looks very much like the Statue of Liberty. Outdoor cafés and restaurants popular with students ring the square. The **Teatro de la República** (1845–52) at the corner of Juárez and Angela Peralta was the site of the Emperor Maximilian's trial and sentencing; it is also where the Mexican Constitution of 1917 was drafted and signed. The plush interior with four tiers of boxes is worth a visit.

The **Jardín Guerrero**, two blocks west of the Plaza Principal, contains the **Neptune Fountain** (1797) designed by the famous colonial architect, Eduardo Tresguerras. It stands before the **Templo de Santa Clara**, which was founded in 1633 as a nunnery and later became La Corregidora's prison after her arrest. While the exterior is comparatively austere (in the style of Querétaro baroque), the interior is a fecund outpouring of the churrigueresque (see p 114). The walls are lined with intricately carved gilt wood retables that surround sculptures and religious paintings. The upper and lower choruses are also models of profusion. The 1804 **Cathedral** at the corner of Ocampo and Madero has a colonnaded red stone façade and a Gothic interior. The **Templo de San Agustín** (1731–45), one block south of Santa Clara, is topped by a tile dome surrounded by stone sculptures of angels playing musical instruments. The convent next door (often closed) contains a superb cloister surrounded by elaborately carved columns. Continuing south on Avda Allende one comes to the **Casa de los Perros** ('House of the Dogs'), an 18th-century mansion with six gargoyles in the form of dogs jutting from the façade. The **Templo de Santa Rosa de Viterbo** (completed 1752), four blocks west of Avda Juárez on Avda General Arteaga, is one of the masterpieces of Querétaro baroque. The two flying buttresses on the exterior hold carved reliefs of grotesque faces grimacing at passers-by. Supposedly, the architect, Mariano de las Casas, added these to thumb his nose at those who doubted his ability. Like the Santa Clara church, the interior contains ornate gilt retables worked around devotional paintings. The back of the church contains a series of paintings of the Twelve Apostles and, behind a finely worked iron grill, the chorus where the nuns sat during services.

Six blocks east of Avda Corregidora, on Independencia, stands the **Templo de la Santa Cruz** (founded 1683), on the site of Querétaro's conquest on July 25, 1531. The church and convent were founded as the Colegio de Propaganda Fidé (College for the Propagation of the Faith), the first such institution in North America, which sent famous missionaries like Fray Junípero Serra across northern Mexico. After Maximilian retreated from Mexico City in 1867, he made the convent his headquarters. Juárez' forces captured him here on May 15, 1867 and imprisoned him in a monastic cell off the cloister. You can still see the breach in the wall through which the liberal troops entered the convent. The **aqueduct** (1726–35) nearby is nine kilometers (six miles) long (almost half underground) and carried water to the city over 74 arches. There's a good view from a **vista** on top of the hill here, and La Corregidora is buried in the neighboring **cemetery**. The **Cerro de las Campanas**, a hill northwest of the center (a long walk), was the location of Maximilian's execution on June 19, 1867. His family built a small chapel in his memory here that exhibits mementoes of his life and last hours. The hill is also the site of a looming **statue of Benito Juárez**, who ratified the execution. Querétaro is most crowded during the **Festival of December**, when thousands flock to the city for dances, parades, cultural events and the ritual burning of the Tree of Friendship to symbolize the new year.

The towns of Tequisquiapan and San Juan del Río, just off the highway to Mexico City, are also worth a visit. **Tequisquiapan**, which is known for its crafts, has a large and pleasant **Plaza Cívica**. The **Mercado Municipal** and **Mercado de Artesanías**, one block east, sell a wide variety of locally produced crafts (basketry, hats, etc) and candies. **San Juan del Río** contains a pedestrian-only center along Avda Juárez Poniente lined with inexpensive restaurants. The 18th-century churches of **La Parroquia** and **del Sagrado Corazón**, two blocks east, were built for the segregated Spanish and the Indian populations respectively. The **Templo de Santo Domingo** (1690–1734), at the north end of the pedestrian area, has a rich baroque façade and a less interesting interior. The convent next door now holds the city hall. On Avda Juárez heading to Querétaro are the **Templo y Hospital de San Juan de Dios** (17th century) and the fine 1710 **San Juan del Río Bridge**, which spans the San Juan River over five arches. San Juan del Río is known for its gem-polishing industry, particularly local opals.

A long (six hours) and extremely winding road leads from Querétaro into the northeast corner of the state. Here, in a rugged, empty corner of the Sierra Madre Oriental known as the Sierra Gorda, stand five richly ornate 18th-century Franciscan missions at **Tancoyol, Conca, Jalpán de Serra, Tilaco** and **Landa de Matamoros**. There are resort hotels in Jalpán and Conca.

State of Guanajuato

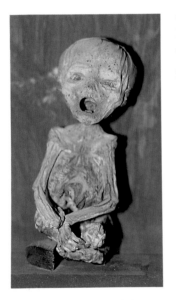

The earliest developed society in Guanajuato was the Chupicuaro Culture that lasted from 500 BC to AD 200. The Chupicuaro buried their dead with elaborate offerings of pottery, figurines and dogs (perhaps to guide the dead to the underworld). After AD 1400, Tarascans from Michoacán conquered the territory and made it part of their empire. The first Spaniard to explore Guanajuato was the conquistador, Cristóbal de Olíd, who in 1522 passed through on his way to the Pacific. Later, Spanish expeditions and Augustinian friars entered the state and founded settlements in Acámbaro and Apaseo. They were accompanied by Otomi Indians, early converts to Christianity, who helped populate new Spanish towns like Celaya and Salamanca. In 1553, the great silver and gold mines of Guanajuato were discovered and this discovery led to the rapid creation of Spanish *presidios, haciendas,* ranches and roads in the state. The Chichimecs attacked the colonizers but were gradually pushed back. In 1589, the Colegio de la Purísima was founded by the Jesuits and soon Guanajuato became a center of the missionary effort. In the early 19th century, Guanajuato, San Miguel and Dolores were centers of the anti-Spanish conspiracy led by Miguel Hidalgo, Ignaçio Allende, the Aldama brothers and Mariano Abasolo.

Early on September 16, 1810, Hidalgo, a radical priest, gave the *Grito de Dolores*—the 'shout' for the beginning of the rebellion—in the little town of Dolores. His little band of Indian and *mestizo* followers marched south, picking up recruits along the way, and captured and pillaged San Miguel that same night. In less than two weeks, Hidalgo had a ragged but enthusiastic army of 25,000 behind him and was at the gates to Guanajuato. He demanded the surrender of the Spanish administration and of the wealthy citizenry barricaded in the fortified Alhóndiga de Granaditas (the public granary). The Spanish refused and, after hours of bloody assaults, a rebel named Pipila set fire to the gates and the insurgents poured in behind him. Hundreds of Spaniards were massacred and the town was sacked, extinguishing any hope of a peaceful settlement and causing wealthy Mexicans to side with the colonial administration. Hidalgo, Allende and other rebel leaders were finally captured and executed in Coahuila; for the next ten years, their

'World's smallest mummy', Guanajuato

severed heads were displayed on poles over the Alhóndiga. In 1858, Benito Juárez, then head of the Supreme Court, went to Guanajuato and declared himself President, a right granted him by the Constitution. This act led to the outbreak of the liberal-conservative war of the late 1850s. Perhaps the bloodiest battle in Mexican history occurred outside Celaya in April 1915, when in wave after wave of suicidal cavalry charges, Villa's troops threw themselves against the barbed wire and entrenched soldiers of Obregón's position, only to be finally defeated.

León was a center of the Cristero rebellion in 1926 and 1927, and in 1937, the Unión Nacional Sinarquista, a militant, rightist Catholic party, was founded there. Today, the state is one of the manufacturing centers of Mexico; Irapuato and Salamanca have heavy industries and León is the shoe-making capital of the world.

GUANAJUATO

The city of Guanajuato (pop 150,000) is situated in a narrow valley in the foothills of the Sierra de Guanajuato. Maps of the city resemble a plate of spaghetti, because there are no right angles, streets turn into alleys or dead ends, and the city is so compressed that they need a network of underground streets to ease the congestion. The main street is **Avenida Juárez** and most of the sights are either here or along the parallel **Calle Pocitos**. Juárez turns into the main road to the León-Querétaro highway and passes the new **central bus station** about seven kilometers (four miles) out of town. The massive **Alhóndiga de Granaditas** (1798–1809) was built as the public grain warehouse and then fortified to double as a citadel. On September 28, 1810, Miguel Hidalgo's insurgent army stormed the Alhóndiga and slaughtered the Spanish soldiers and wealthy citizens who had taken refuge inside. The building is now an excellent museum (Tues–Sat, 10–1.30 and 4–7; Sun, 10–2.30) with exhibits on the Chupicuaro Indian culture, the Insurgency, local crafts and so on. One gallery is devoted to the art of Hermenegildo Bustos (1832–

Two citizens of 19th century Guanajuato in a remarkable state of preservation

Nothing Moved

The Austrian Government had a memorial chapel set up on the site where Maximilian and his two aides were shot. It is a drab little brown-stone building, more like a guard-house, standing on top of a bare, dun hill among rubble and sparse agaves. It was built in 1901—some thirty years after the event—and now belongs to the Mexican nation, and is administered by the Instituto Nacional de Antropología e Historia, which provides a custodian, but not his shelter, who on the approach of visitors rises from under a stone to sell for the price of threepence a ticket of admission and a picture postcard of the graceless memorial. The same institution runs the collection of Maximilian miscellany, exhibited in a room at the Federal Palace of Querétaro. We wandered about the array of photographs, medals, captured banners; peered at scraps of handwriting under glass. The inkstand used by the court martial...The stools Generals Mejija and Miramón, the two aides that died, sat on during the trial...Somebody's top boots...Swords...

The custodian was following us around. 'Accomodate yourselves. Your Excellencies are missing the coffin.

'Please to approach again. It is the coffin of Don Masimiliano. Do not think that because it is empty, it is not the true coffin. La Mamacita sent another when Don Masimiliano was taken across the sea, but this is the true coffin of Don Masimiliano. General Juárez came to look at Don Masimiliano in this coffin.

'Your Excellencies have not noted the bloodstain. Please to look inside. Is it not shaped like a hand? Your Excellencies have not noted well. Favour to use this glass. To make it larger.'

A braided coat...The facsimile of the death sentence...A daguerreotype of the Princess Salm-Salm on horse-back...

'And he could have got away,' said E. 'It was usual. When the Princess Salm-Salm came back from San Luis Potosí she was so frantic that she

> *managed to persuade him. She, and the Belgian and Austrian ministers, arranged it all. They bribed everybody. It cost a fortune. A Juarista general would have had to flee with them. When all was ready, they put a cloak around him, and then they realised they would have to do something about his fair beard. No one else had a beard like that. That must have brought it home to him: he refused to move. Perhaps, it seemed all so shabby. They argued with him. Meanwhile, the guard had changed. The new men were not bribed. It was too late.'*
>
> *'And this is the syringe Don Masimiliano was embalmed with. Please to look again: it is the embalming syringe of Don Masimiliano. 'Do your Excellencies understand? The embalming syringe. The syringe for embalming Don Masimiliano after he was dead.*
>
> *'Please, Excellency, does the other Excellency not understand? It is of much interest. It is the embalming syringe. Favour to explain.'*
>
> Sybille Bedford, *A Visit to Don Ottavio*

1907), a local painter whose painstakingly accurate portraits of the cross-eyed men and mustachioed women of Guanajuato's pious citizenry bring to mind Albrecht Dürer. Allegorical murals about local history by José Chávez Morado decorate the stairways. The **Museo Diego Rivera** (Tues–Sat, 10–1 and 4–7; Sun, 10–2.30) at Pocitos 47 was the birthplace of the world famous Mexican muralist. Rivera, an arch-radical in art, politics and lifestyle, sprang from this typically Catholic and conservative Guanajuato household. The upper floors contain exhibitions of lesser works from all phases of Rivera's career, including adolescent sketches, his cubist phase and roughs for his murals.

Returning down the hill from the Alhóndiga to Juárez, one comes to the cast iron arches of the **Mercado Hidalgo** (1910). The interior, which resembles a blimp hangar, contains food stalls on the ground floor and handicrafts stands along the second floor walkway. The **Jardín Morelos** on Juárez, just east of the market, leads to the **Templo de San Roque**. Every spring, the university theater stages plays by Cervantes in the plaza in front of the church. At the Plazuela de Los Angeles, Juárez makes a sharp turn to the left, and the Callejón de Patrocinio heads to the right and leads to the **Callejón del Beso** ('Alley of the Kiss'). The houses along this alley are so narrow that people can kiss from

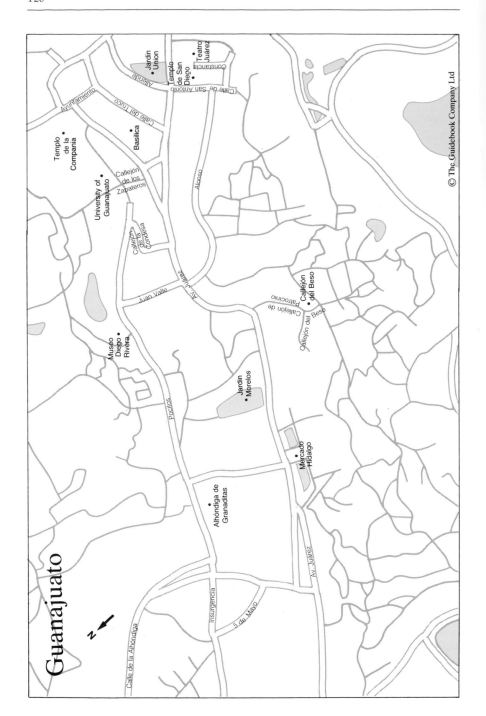

Guanajuato

Jardín Union
Teatro Juárez
Constancia
Templo de San Diego
Calle de San Antonio
Alhóndiga
Calle del Truco
Templo de la Compañía
Basílica
Callejón de los Zapateros
University of Guanajuato
Callejón de la Condesa
Av. Juárez
Alonso
Callejón del Beso
Callejón de Patrocinio
Callejón del Beso
Juan Valle
Museo Diego Rivera
Pocitos
Jardín Morelos
Mercado Hidalgo
Alhóndiga de Granaditas
Av. Juárez
Insurgencia
5 de Mayo
Calle de la Alhóndiga
N

opposite balconies and, of course, do. Up the Callejón del Condesa, passing the **Palacio Legislativo**, and on to Pocitos, one comes to the **University of Guanajuato**. The grand staircase in front climbs about halfway up this medieval style seven story building. The **Templo de la Compañía** (1747), just east, was built by the Jesuits as a seminary and contains a collection of paintings by Miguel Cabrera, a renowned religious artist. Juárez continues to the triangular **Plaza de la Paz**, which is adorned by the **Casa de los Condes de Rul y Valenciana**, an 18th-century silver baron's mansion designed by Eduardo Tresguerras, the famous baroque architect. The east end of the plaza is dominated by the **Basilica** (1671–96). The interior of this imposing building contains dozens of crystal chandeliers; one, known as 'The Spider', may be the largest in Mexico. The bells, which toll hourly, are particularly fine. The **Jardín Unión**, one block east, is a triangular oasis enclosing trees, benches and a bandstand, and is lined with restaurants (the one in the Posada Santa Fe is recommended). From the park there is a view of the heroic **statue of Pipila**, the mineworker who in 1810 breached the door of the Alhóndiga, up on the hill. Side by side at the south end of the park stand the **Templo de San Diego** (1784), with an ornate neo-classical façade, and the colonnaded **Teatro Juárez** (1903). The latter is the main theater for the world-famous Cervantino Festival and has a profusely decorated, horseshoe-shaped interior.

South of Juárez lies a warren of narrow alleys winding through residential neighborhoods filled with more modest colonial buildings—but it's well worth a walk. The Calle de la Alhóndiga, which begins at the base of the granary (take the bus here), passes by the luxury hotels and heads five kilometers (three miles) up into the hills, to **La Valenciana**. This community was built at the entrance of what was once the most productive silver mine in the world. The **Templo de San Cayetano** (1765–1788) in the town here is one of the most beautiful baroque churches in Mexico. The gorgeous churrigeresque red stone façade is intricately carved with vegetal motifs, cherubs and the Holy Trinity in the center. The stone interior contains three ornate gilt wood altars with important statues of saints, a carved wood and ivory pulpit and beautiful reliefs around the door. From the steps there's a view of the valley and the mine-head nearby. A ten-minute walk on an abandoned road takes one to the **La Valenciana Mine**, where there's a small chapel and a statue of Cervantes in the garden nearby. A wall keeps you from falling into the 525-meter (1,726-foot)-deep mineshaft. Craftspeople sell jewelry, clothes and leather goods. The **Panoramic Highway** that connects with Calle Alhóndiga circles the valley above the city and provides a vista at the Pipila statue.

From the bus stop opposite the Mercado Hidalgo, the 'Panteón' or 'Momias' bus leads up to the municipal cemetery and Guanajuato's most popular and notorious tourist attraction. The **Museo de las Momias** (3,000 pesos admission, more for cameras; daily 9–6) contains the mummified bodies of 114 Guanajuato citizens who died from accidents, gunshots, stabbings and illnesses and who were exhumed from the cemetery between 1865 and 1975. Because of the dry air and the mineral content of the soil, they are all in a remarkable state of preservation. The bathrooms are at the end of the museum. Child guides will recite the story of the mummies in a nasal sing-song (Spanish only); beware, if they're interrupted they have to start again at the beginning. The local candy specialties are called *alfeñiques*, also known as *charamuscos*—taffy pulled in the shape of corpses smoking cigarettes and holding bottles of tequila! Every year Guanajuato stages the **Festival Cervantino**, a two-week festival of the arts held in October. The festival used to attract top world artists—Baryshnikov, Pavarotti, Sting—but recent budgetary restrictions have made the line-ups slightly more modest. Nevertheless, it is a unique display of international drama, pop and classical music, dance, painting and sculpture. Tourists wishing to visit at this time should book well in advance. In the mountains east of town there's a huge **statue of Christ**, perhaps the tallest in the world, on top of the Cerro de Cubilete, a popular destination for pilgrims. Geographers have declared that this spot also marks the geographical center of Mexico.

SAN MIGUEL DE ALLENDE

The popular tourist destination of San Miguel de Allende (pop 50,000) is built on a hillside looking northwest across a wide valley to the Sierra de Guanajuato. Narrow cobblestone streets follow the contours of the hill and make heavy traffic unviable, so the town retains its pre-industrial charm. San Miguel has been named a national monument and all construction has to be approved by a panel of preservationists. The **Jardín Principal**, the town's center, is where locals meet and read newspapers. The **Parroquia de San Miguel** at the south side of the plaza has fantastic Gothic spires that tower over the 17th-century church. The red stone spires were built by an Indian master mason, Zeferino Gutiérrez, in 1880. Behind the main altar is the **Camarín del Virgen** ('Dressing Room of the Virgin'), a chapel designed by the famous colonial architect Tresguerras. Before he became leader of a revolutionary army, the insurgent priest, Miguel Hidalgo, performed masses in this church. Next door stands the **Iglesia de San Rafael**, a much more homely church containing crude frescoes of grapevines and flowers. The **Allende House** on the other side of the Parroquia was the home of Domingo Allende and the birthplace of his brother, the revolutionary leader Ignacio Allende. In 1809, it was a meeting place for the insurgent conspirators. The house is now the **Museum of History and Archeology**, which includes exhibits on local archeology, the Virreynato period and on the birth of the anti-Spanish movement in the officer corps of the local militias.

The west, north and east sides of the Jardín are occupied the **Casa del Mayorazgo de la Canal**, the **Casa del Mariscal Don Francisco Lanzagorta** (now a hotel) and the **Casa de los Condes de Loja** respectively, all fine colonial mansions. The **Iglesia de San Francisco** (begun 1779), just northeast of the Jardín, has a fine baroque façade. One block

San Miguel De Allende

© The Guidebook Company Ltd

further north stands the **Oratorio de San Felipe Neri** (finished 1712), whose churrigueresque façade shows Indian influences in its abundant vegetal motifs. The interior contains a series of paintings depicting the saint's life. Next door is the **Santa Casa de Loreto** (1735), a copy of a church in Loreto, Italy. Behind and around these churches are the stands of the lively **Mercado Ignacio Ramírez**, which sells mainly fruits and vegetables. The neighboring **Artisans' Market** sells crafts from throughout Mexico, mainly to bus tour groups—consequently the prices are high. Down the hill at the corner of Calles Canal and Macías stands the **Iglesia y Convento de la Concepción** (begun 1734) with a dome by Zeferino Gutiérrez. The convent is now the **Cultural Center**, known locally as Bellas Artes, which offers renowned art, music and dance classes. Some of the most famous Mexican artists, including David Siquieros, have taught here, and the walls are decorated with many murals by Siquieros and others. Language and art classes are also given at the **Instituto Allende**, housed in the 1735 mansion of the Conde de la Canal on Calle San Antonio at the south end of San Miguel. San Miguel's residents frequently celebrate religious festivals, particularly during Easter Week, on September 29 (St Michael's Day) and leading up to Christmas. During San Miguel's fair in September there's a bull run through the center of town. Although San Miguel looks low-key and tasteful, prices here are quite high, reflecting the influence of abundant dollars.

Dolores Hidalgo, forty kilometers (25 miles) north of San Miguel, was the birthplace of the independence movement led by Miguel Hidalgo. Every September 16, Mexicans around the world celebrate his 1810 *Grito de Dolores* ('Shout of Dolores') that announced the beginning of the armed struggle. On the main square, facing a **statue of Hidalgo**, stands the **Parroquia** (1712), the church from which Hidalgo gave his 'shout'. The **Palacio Municipal**, also on the square, is the birthplace of the insurgent, Mariano Abasolo. The **Museo Casa de Hidalgo** at the corner of Calles Hidalgo and Morelos reverentially displays items owned by the 'Father of the Country'.

Atotonilco, halfway between Dolores and San Miguel, is worth a stop to visit the **Santuario de Jesús Nazareno** (begun 1740). The frescoed interior was decorated by native artists, who gave the church a unique exuberance. When Hidalgo's army began its march south, they took possession of a banner of the Virgin of Guadalupe from this church and made it the symbol of their battle against the Spaniards.

CELAYA AND LEÓN

Celaya was the home of Eduardo Tresguerras, the neo-classical architect who built many of the greatest churches of the Bajío region. Two of his masterworks may be seen here. The domed **Templo del Carmen** was originally built in 1597, but later burned, and was rebuilt by Tresguerras in 1807. His fine **bridge** (1803–09) spans the Laja River. Celaya is famous in Mexico for a candy spread called *cajeta*, made from sweetened and condensed goat's milk. It's not to everybody's taste, but those that like it can't get enough.

León (pop 1,000,000) is not only a shoe-making mecca, it also has Guanajuato's largest airport. Shoe fanatics must visit the **Plaza del Zapato**, with over 60 shops near the central bus station. The **Templo Expiatorio** at Calles Juan Valle and Madero is a huge Gothic cathedral that has been under construction since 1921. León's hub is two plazas linked by pedestrian-only streets and lined with many shoe stores, cafés and medium-priced hotels. Nearby is the enormous, austere **Cathedral** (1746–65), the **Palacio Municipal** and the **Casa de las Monas** (1870), with caryatids in the form of Indian women holding up interior columns.

State of Aguascalientes

Not much is known about pre-Conquest Aguascalientes. The area was occupied by Zacatecos and Chichimecs, and the city of Aguascalientes sits on a network of tunnels apparently used by an unknown tribe. After Beltrán de Guzmán's 1530 expedition to Zacatecas passed through Aguascalientes and killed many Indians, the native tribes withdrew to the mountains. The main road to the Zacatecas mines led through Aguascalientes, and all travelers had to contend with bands of marauding Indians. Finally, a series of *presidios* was built, one of which became the city of Aguascalientes (founded 1575). Because of disease and Indian raids, the latter was soon abandoned; it was resettled in 1596 and became part of the state of Zacatecas. Soon the first Franciscan missionaries arrived. During the 18th century silver was discovered, and since some of the mines were owned by Jesuits, they used the profits to finance their missions. Gradually, Aguascalientes became an agricultural and industrial center, achieving statehood in 1835. In October 1914, a convention was held there to decide who would become the next president of Mexico. All the main revolutionary factions attended, fully armed, and the proceedings soon deteriorated into a violent squabble. On one side were the peasant revolutionary armies of Villa and Zapata, on the other were the bourgeois revolutionaries who supported Carranza and Obregón. When they finally decided on a candidate—Eulalio Gutiérrez—Carranza rejected him and ordered his delegates to withdraw. This action led to five more years of bloody civil war all across Mexico. Nevertheless, some of the egalitarian measures first proposed at the Convention of Aguascalientes, such as land redistribution, became law in the following decades.

AGUASCALIENTES

The city of Aguascalientes (pop 422,000) lies in a rich agricultural plain. In the middle of the **Plaza de Armas**, the central square, stands a 21-meter (63-foot) **column** topped by a statue of an eagle and a serpent, which commemorates the founding of the city on October 22, 1575. The **Cathedral** (1704–38) opposite is under restoration, but you can see the four statues of bishops on the façade and the gilt interior of the dome. The **Palacio del Gobierno** (tourist office) next door was built in 1665 as the residence of a wealthy local family. The gracious arcaded patios are lined with murals by Oswaldo Barra Cunningham, a Chilean ex-student of Diego Rivera, who began to paint them in 1960 and continues to do so. The murals' subject matter is local culture, and noteworthy is the one representing the San Marcos Fair (a nationally famous agricultural fair celebrated in April) on the second floor. The 17th-century **Municipal Palace** to the left is less interesting. The **Teatro Morelos** (1884), an ornate Porfiriato building that is now a national monument, was the site of the epochal 1914–15 Convention of Aguascalientes, at which the main factions of the Mexican Revolution couldn't agree and so led the country into five more years of bloody battle. About seven blocks south of the main square, the **Templo del Encino** contains retables illustrating the Stations of the Cross as well as the venerated image of a black Christ. The **Museo Posada** next door contains exhibitions on José Guadalupe Posada (1852–1913), Mexico's most famous printmaker. The collection exhibits hundreds of his blunt images of executions, murders, accidents, monsters, miracles and scandals, as well as his famous *calaveras* ('skeletons'). These heavily influenced many 20th-century artists, including Diego Rivera, who considered Posada's art the most

Overview of Guanajuato from the statue of Pipila

purely Mexican he had experienced. Nearby is a luxurious, empty private amusement park built for the employees of a local furniture factory.

The **Museo de Aguascalientes** at 505, Calle Zaragoza contains works by local artists in a Greek-style Porfiriato building. The **Templo de San Antonio** across the street is a small but extremely ornate late 19th-century church designed by a local architect. The nearest hot springs, which the city is named after, are at the **Balneario Ojo Caliente** (public pools, tennis courts) on Calzada Revolución, heading toward San Luis Potosí. Aguascalientes is an important clothing manufacturing center; local products, particularly sweaters and lace, may be bought at **Plaza Vestir** on Blvd José María Chávez. The city is extremely crowded during the April San Marcos Fair, 'The Fair of All Fairs', when thousands come to see the exhibits, cockfights, bull-fights and literary events—so book ahead. The area is known for its San Marcos brand wine and for the quality of its fighting *toros*.

State of San Luis Potosí

San Luis Potosí was divided between the Huastecs, who occupied the southeastern corner of the state, and the Chichimecs who roamed the rest. The Huastecs, who spoke a Mayan language, apparently flourished between AD 800 and 1200, but not enough systematic investigation has been done to know much about them. According to the Aztecs, they were the inventors of pulque, the alcoholic beverage made from maguey juice, and the Aztecs considered them notorious drunkards and lechers. Their descendants still occupy the same territory today. Cortés and Nuño Beltrán de Guzmán passed through San Luis Potosí as they jockeyed for control of north and central Mexico. The belligerence of the Indians and the far more attractive silver discoveries in Zacatecas kept San Luis Potosí free of settlers for decades. The period between 1550 and 1590 was the era of the Chichimec War, and the only Spaniards who dared enter were Augustinian and Franciscan missionaries accompanied by soldiers. In 1583, Fray Diego de la Magdalena founded a small mission for local Indians at the site of San Luis Potosí. With the discovery of the San Pedro mines in 1592, settlers finally began arriving in the territory. The silver-rich areas in the hills lacked water, so the miners settled in the San Luis Valley and officially founded the city on November 3, 1592. Within three decades it was the third most important city in Mexico after the capital and Puebla.

In 1623, the Jesuits established a famous college there and evangelized in the state until their expulsion from Mexico in 1767. As they left the city was rocked by earthquakes, which were interpreted as a sign from God. In 1800, a mountain of gold and silver was found in Catorce, now the ghost town of Real de Catorce, and for a century it was the third most productive mine in Mexico.

In 1910, the anti-Díaz campaigner, Francisco Madero, was arrested for daring to challenge the dictator and thrown into San Luis Potosí's jail. He later escaped from the city to the United States, from where he issued his *Plan of San Luis Potosí*, a call for Mexicans to take up arms against Díaz. During the subsequent Revolution the city fell into the hands of *federales*, constitutionalists and Villa's troops at one time or another. The end of the Revolution was not the end of political turmoil in San Luis Potosí: after President Cárdenas' expropriation of foreign oil companies in 1938, San Luis Potosí's political strong man, General Saturnino Cedillo (perhaps under the influence of oil company agents), declared that the state didn't recognize Cárdenas' authority. Cárdenas rushed the federal army to the state and quickly squashed the rebellion, killing Cedillo. In 1960, Salvador Nava was cheated of his victory in the gubernatorial elections and his followers staged a noisy protest in the main square. Security forces from Mexico City quelled the demonstration with bloody force. In 1991, the past repeated itself: Nava ran again for governor, was cheated once more and staged a protest march to Mexico City. This time President Salinas de Gortari, who is acutely conscious of foreign opinion, nullified the results, sent his own party's candidate off in disgrace and scheduled new elections.

San Luis Potosí

Lying in the center of a rich mining, agricultural and industrial region, San Luis Potosí (pop 800,000) is the state capital. The city is crowded and polluted but nevertheless has more than enough attractions to make a visit worthwhile. Downtown San Luis Potosí is designed on a grid of narrow streets and squares that are lined with ornate colonial and Porfiriato buildings and churches. The center of town is the **Jardín Hidalgo**, also called the Plaza de Armas, a pleasant square with many benches shaded by trees. The east side of the Jardín is dominated by the baroque **Cathedral** (begun in 1670). The two bell-towers possess three tiers of columns intricately carved with vines. The blue and gold interior incorporates neo-classical and neo-byzantine elements. Next door is the **Palacio Municipal** (1838) built as a residence for the bishop. The **tourism office** is on Calle Othon, opposite the side of the Cathedral.

The **Palacio del Gobierno** (1789–1816), across the Jardín Hidalgo, was the residence of many 19th-century Mexican presidents, including Juárez, who signed Maximilian's death warrant here. The Palacio has a small museum to Juárez on the second floor. On the corner of Avdas Aldama and Madero is the **Caja Real** ('Royal Treasury'), a baroque building that held the locally-mined silver destined for the King of Spain. A ramped staircase off the courtyard was built so that the *burros* could carry the silver up to the safes. The statue of the Virgin over the entry was given to the city by King Charles III of Spain. A block north is the **Plaza de Fundadores**, a large square with the main **University Building** and the **Capilla de Loreto** (1700), considered the finest Jesuit-built church in Mexico. The popular **La Parroquia** restaurant is on the south side of the plaza. Three blocks south of Avda Aldama is the **Plaza de San Francisco**, a quiet tree-lined square. The **Museo de Artesanías** on the square has a large gift shop selling Mexican crafts and temporary exhibitions. The **Templo de San Francisco** (begun 1686) next door possesses a fine pink limestone façade, important religious paintings and a blue and white-tiled dome. This church is the centerpiece of a Franciscan convent complex begun in 1591. Around the corner on Avda Galeana, the **Museo Regional Potosino** (free: Tues–Sun, 10–1 and 3–6; Sat, 10–12; Sun, 10–1) occupies the old convent. The first floor is devoted to a large, haphazard collection of Mesoamerican artefacts that looks unchanged since the museum opened in 1952. On the second floor is the **Capilla de Aránzazu** (1609), a small but ornate and brightly painted chapel. The **Templo de Carmen** (1749–64) on the **Plaza del Carmen**, three blocks east of the Cathedral, is San Luis Potosí's most beautiful baroque church. The façade is one huge and elaborate carving, and the interior is filled with gold leaf-covered stone work. A unique relief of dozens of brightly painted cherubim peeking out of billowing white clouds surrounds the entrance to the chapel. The **Virgin's Chapel** within is covered floor to ceiling with gold leaf and has an enormous gold scallop over the altar. At the south end of the plaza, the **Teatro de la Paz** (1894), a colonnaded neo-classical Porfiriato monument, was completely and unattractively remodelled inside in 1949. The 19th-century mansion facing the theater is now the **National Mask Museum** (free: Tues–Fri, 10–2 and 4–8; Sat–Sun, 10–2). The collection contains hundreds of ceremonial masks worn by indigenous groups throughout Mexico, as well as some pre-Columbian masks (although the Coronel Museum in Zacatecas is better). Behind the Templo del Carmen is the **Alameda**, a large tree-filled park that unfortunately is surrounded by avenues congested with buses spewing diesel fumes. At the north end there are a number of inexpensive **cafeterias** and the **train station.** Two amusing murals in the station show the perils of travel before the railway arrived—thievery and stubborn *burros*—and of steamship travel: a group of superior *gringos* looking down their noses at Mexican dockworkers. Avda Universidad at the south end of the Alameda leads to the **bullring** and the **central bus station** (right at the huge Juárez monument). **Avda Venustiano Carranza,** west of the city center, is the main shopping street.

State of Zacatecas

Archeologists believe that the state of Zacatecas was on the border between the Chichimecs and the more advanced civilizations to the south. A tribe known as the Zacatecos occupied well-developed urban areas at La Florida, Alta Vista and La Quemada. The latter was constructed within a hilltop fortress, perhaps as a front line against Chichimec invasion. Alta Vista was the center of a mining region, whose products were sent to Teotihuacán to be used as ceremonial objects. The western border of the state was occupied by a less advanced tribe called the Caxcanes. In 1530, the first Spaniards entered Zacatecas under the orders of Beltrán de Guzmán. Miguel de Ibarra's expedition reached Zacatecas in 1541 and encountered fierce opposition from the Caxcanes. This battle became so intense that it threatened Guadalajara, and the army was called in finally to defeat the Indians. In 1548, huge deposits of silver and gold were found near the town of Nuestra Señora de los Remedios de Zacatecas, today's state capital, and a horde of prospectors and adventurers descended on the state. Within a few years this region was producing a third of all Mexican silver. As the metal flowed out in wagon trains, settlers, tax collectors, priests, building materials and luxury items flowed in.

By 1700, Zacatecas was the home of churches, palaces, mansions, luxurious convents and ambitious public monuments. The city also became the center for the evangelization of the north. In 1707, the Franciscans founded the Colegio Apostólico de Propaganda Fidé in Guadalupe, ten kilometers (six miles) out of town. This was one of the three most important missionary training institutions in Mexico and its influence changed the face of the north. During the fight for independence from Spain, Zacatecans gave important early help to the cause, and Miguel Hidalgo's army captured the city in 1810 shortly after his victory in Guanajuato. The troubles of the 19th century led to a drop in Zacatecan silver production, but this picked up again under Díaz' pro-business dictatorship. In June 1914, Venustiano Carranza, Villa's commanding officer, ordered him to attack Zacatecas, which was occupied by President Huerta's federal troops. Villa refused, Carranza fired him and Villa attacked the city to spite his former boss. After two days of fighting,

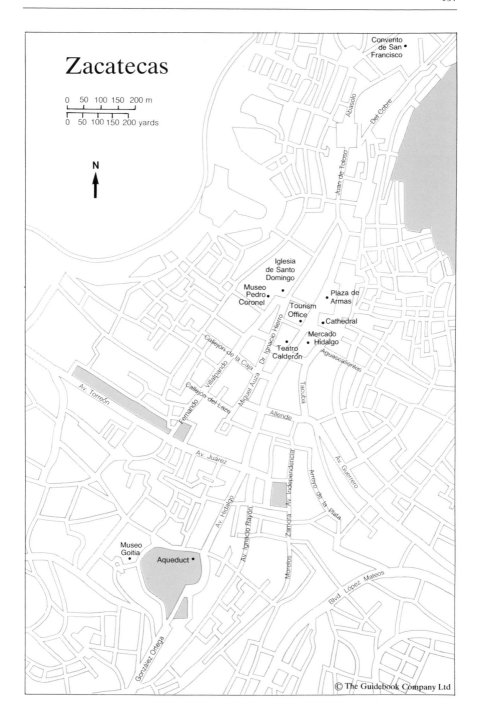

Zacatecas

0   50 100 150 200 m

0   50 100 150 200 yards

N

Convento
de San •
Francisco

Abasolo

Del Cobre

Juan de Tolosa

Iglesia
de Santo
Domingo

Museo
Pedro •
Coronel

Plaza de
• Armas

Tourism
Office
•

• Cathedral

Mercado
• Hidalgo

Aguascalientes

Teatro
Calderón

Dr. Ignacio Hierro

Callejón de la Caja

Villalpando

Miguel Auza

Callejón del Lazo

Fernando

Av. Torreón

Tacuba

Allende

Av. Juárez

Av. Hidalgo

Av. Ignacio Rayón

Zamora

Av. Independencia

Arroyo de la Plata

Av. Guerrero

Morelos

Museo
Goitia
•

Aqueduct •

Blvd López Mateos

González Ortega

© The Guidebook Company Ltd

the *federales* retreated. Villa had won a major victory but had also opened a dangerous crack in the coalition against Huerta. In the late 1920s, Zacatecas was one of the centers of the Cristero rebellion against the anti-Catholic policies of President Calles. Silver is no longer as plentiful or as valuable—although the mines are still worked—but the city retains the charms of a showplace of the colonial era.

ZACATECAS

The pink limestone city of Zacatecas (pop 150,000) is nestled in a ravine between two hills that rise out of a barren plain occupied by only a few widely scattered ranches. At 2,495 meters (8,207 feet) the air is thin and the city gets cold at night—so avoid over-exertion and bring a sweater. The mine owners spared no expense in the construction of the splendid **Cathedral**, which was begun in 1612 and completed in the mid-18th century. The façade is a riot of vine and flower motifs winding around statues of Christ, the 12 Apostles, various bishops, angels and cherubs. It's best seen at sunset. The interior, with fine stone arches, is more austere, partly due to repeated plunderings during the 19th century. The **Plaza de Armas** on the north side of the Cathedral is also bordered by a silver baron's mansion (1727), which is now the **Palacio del Gobierno** and contains a mural of Zacatecas' history. The **tourism offices** are opposite, across the square. The **Mercado Hidalgo**, housed in an elegant 1889 Greek temple-like building just south of the Cathedral, was the city market for decades until it was damaged in a fire. Now it is an upscale mall with restaurants, cafés and shops selling crafts, leather goods and Zacatecan wine (recommended). The **Teatro Calderón** across the street is a fine 1891 building with an elegant interior. A short street uphill from the Cathedral leads to the small **Iglesia de Santo Domingo** (1746–1769). Although the exterior is plain, the interior is filled with churrigesque carved wood retables covered with gold leaf. The ex-monastery next door is now the **Museo Pedro Coronel** (Fri–Wed, 10–2 and 4–7), one of two excellent and surprising museums donated to the city by the Coronel brothers, local engineers. The first floor contains the historical library and collections of Pre-Columbian art, while on the second floor are exhibitions of Oriental and African art, Piranesi and Hogarth prints, classical sculpture and modern prints.

North from the Plaza de Armas, Calle Juan de Toloso passes the **Founders' Fountain** and comes to the **Templo y Convento de San Francisco**. The oldest building in Zacatecas (1567), the complex lay in ruins from 1857 until it was recently reconstructed to become the **Museo Rafael Coronel** (Thur–Tues, 10–2 and 4–7). The highpoint of the museum is the best collection of Mexican masks in the country. Dozens of each mask type—animals, satans, skeletons, conquistadors—are exhibited together, making the display visually stunning as well as anthropologically interesting. Other collections include pre-Hispanic clay figurines and marionettes from Zacatecas and Tlaxcala. The **Teleférico**, about six steep blocks uphill on the Callejón García Rojas from the Plaza de Armas, is the cable car that crosses above the city to the Cerro de la Bufa park. The cars run every six minutes (crowded on weekends). On the **Cerro de la Bufa** there is the small **Capilla de los Remédios** with a venerated image of the Virgin de Patrocínio, the **Museo Toma de Zacatecas** (Tues–Sun, 10–4.30) commemorating Pancho Villa's victory over the Federal Army in Zacatecas on June 23, 1914, and an excellent view of the city and the country east and west.

Avenida Hidalgo, south of the Cathedral, runs into a park containing the remains of the city's **aqueduct**, which was rendered inoperable by Villa's forces after his victory. Nearby is the **Museo Francisco Goitia**, named after the visionary 20th-century Zacatecas painter known for his bleak images. It contains a collection of Goitia's works as well as those by other modern Zacatecan artists. The hills around Zacatecas are filled with still operating mines. The **La Eden Mine**, just above the **Alameda Park**, offers guided tours of the mining operation (no longer producing) by miniature railway. The local candy is *queso de tuna*, a hard jelly made from the fruit of the prickly pear cactus. Zacatecas is a town of coffee aficionados; in the Acropolis Café in the Mercado Hidalgo, patrons make art on their saucers from Turkish coffee grounds. The best images—Jesus, Che Guevara, Venus de Milo—hang on the walls. Good restaur ts may be found in the basement of the market along Calle Tacuba.

The town of **Guadalupe**, now a suburb of Zacatecas eight kilometers (five miles) down the highway east, contains the **Convent of Guadalupe**, founded in 1707 by the Franciscans as the College for the Propagation of the Faith. From here missionaries spread the word throughout northern Mexico and the American Southwest. The church is a masterpiece of Mexican baroque, with an interior covered with paintings by the top colonial artists, and is a popular pilgrimage site. The gilt **Capilla de Nápoles** nearby has one of the richest interiors of any church in Mexico. The convent's museums are open Tuesday–Sunday, 10–5.

The Zacatecan ruins of **La Quemada**, also called Chicomostoc, are about 40 kilometers (25 miles) south of Zacatecas, on Mexico 54 to Guadalajara.

State of Jalisco

In 1962, a mammoth skeleton was discovered just west of Lake Chapala in the state of Jalisco. The mammoth may have been killed by prehistoric hunters, of whom there is ample evidence around the state. After 300 BC, Jalisco was occupied by the tribes of the Tomb Culture, who also thrived in neighboring Nayarit and Colima. These peoples were

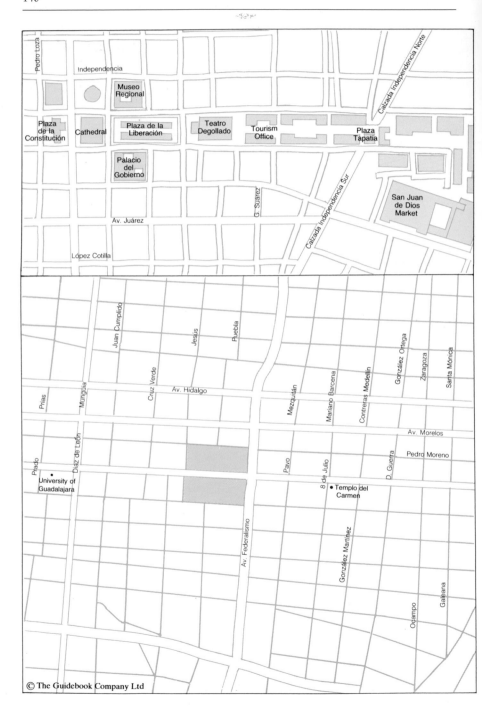

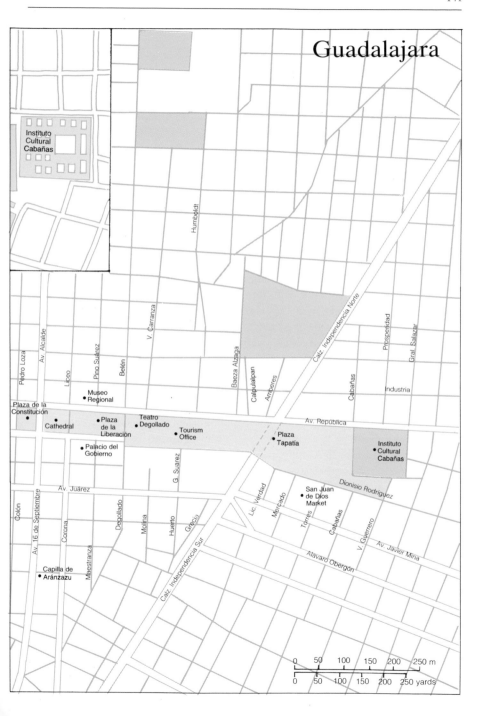

Guadalajara

remarkable for their shaft-tombs filled with lively pottery figures depicting dancers, musicians, shamans, warriors, couples, houses, animals, and so on. These may have represented the world of the dead. In the Post-Classic era (AD 800–1521), Jalisco saw great demographic and cultural development, including gold and silver working, textile manufacturing and intensive agriculture. During the 1520s various conquistador relatives of Cortés tried to set up little kingdoms in Jalisco but failed. In 1530, after his rape of Michoacán, the brutal Nuño Beltrán de Guzmán arrived in the territory determined to succeed. He conquered the Pacific Coast up to Sonora and founded the Province of Nueva Galicia with himself as governor. His capital was Guadalajara, originally called Villa del Espíritu Santo, which moved three times before arriving at its present site in the Valley of Atemajaco. In 1536, Guzmán was recalled to Spain to account for his actions and was never allowed to return to Mexico. Nueva Galicia grew rapidly with the discovery of rich mines and the establishment of huge plantations and cattle ranches; Guadalajara, as its capital, boomed. There were battles with the Indians into the 19th century, but the vigorous evangelization initiated by the Franciscans tempered their ardor.

In 1810, Guadalajara was one of the four Mexican cities with a printing press. When Miguel Hidalgo with his insurgent army entered the city in November of that year, one of his first actions was to set the press rolling with decrees abolishing slavery, the alcohol tax, the expropriation of peasant lands and Indian tribute. In early 1811, royalist troops caught up with the insurgent troops and routed them at the Calderón Bridge near Guadalajara. Hidalgo and the remnants of his army fled north, hoping to find money and supplies, but they were captured two months later. Guadalajara weathered the battles between liberals and conservatives and the French occupation, becoming by 1900 the second largest city in Mexico. During the Revolution many residents starved because of the blockades imposed on food and water by the warring parties. In 1926 and 1927, Jalisco was the center for the Cristero rebellion against the anti-clerical laws of President Calles. Bands of Cristero guerrillas torched schools, blew up police stations and dynamited the Mexico–Guadalajara train. In retaliation the army executed priests and sacked churches, turning them into stables. The heart of the rebellion was the Los Altos district of northeastern Jalisco, a region of deep conservatism and intense machismo.

GUADALAJARA
Guadalajara (pop 3.4 million) is at once a modern, industrial metropolis and a cradle of traditional Mexican culture—tequila, *charros*, *mariachis*, cockfights, and so on. Residents call themselves *tapatios*, from the Nahuatl word *tlapatiotl*, which means 'price of merchandise'—a testament to the locals' business skills. The main sights are conveniently located in the center of the city on a 12-block-long strip of colonial buildings and pedestrian malls between the Cathedral and the Cabañas Cultural Institute. The **Cathedral** (begun 1561) has a wide stone façade topped with twin towers that were rebuilt after

Water carriers, early 1900s, Guadalajara

their destruction in the 1818 earthquake. The white and gold, rib-vaulted interior contains the hands of Santa Inocenta, a Roman martyr, and tombs of many bishops in the Capilla del Santísimo. Murillo's famous *Immaculate Conception* painting hangs in the sacristy, which is often locked. The Cathedral faces the **Plaza de la Constitución**, the north side of which is occupied by the **Palacio Municipal** (1952). Next door is a park containing the **Rotunda of Illustrious Men**, a tribute to renowned Jaliscans. The **Museo Regional de Guadalajara** occupies an old seminary building (begun 1701) that was later a barracks and prison, and then a school. The excellent exhibitions include a mammoth skeleton excavated near Zacoalco in 1962, lively offering figurines from the Tomb Culture of western Mexico, the ethnography of the Huichol and Cora Indians, and a large collection of colonial religious art.

Across the **Plaza de la Liberación** (statue of Miguel Hidalgo) stands the **Palacio del Gobierno** (18th century), which contains two ferocious murals by José Clemente Orozco, Jalisco's most famous muralist. The first, above the main staircase, depicts an enor-

Treasures from Guadalajara Regional Museum (clockwise from top left) ceramic couple from Nayarit Tomb Culture burial; Michoacán flute; incense burner, Tomb Culture; belted Maya ballplayer; (center) ritual dance figurines from Tomb Culture burial

mous Hidalgo brandishing a burning brand above a violent battle that includes carica-
tures of Hitler, Stalin and Mussolini. The second is painted above the hall of the state
congress (ask the guard to turn on the lights) and depicts a slightly more pacific Hidalgo.
The **Teatro Degollada** (1856–66), at the opposite end of the plaza from the Cathedral, is
a colonnaded neo-classical edifice with a relief of Apollo and the Muses on the façade.
The luxurious gold and velvet interior (open 10–2) contains five tiers of boxes and a
mural of the Olympian gods on the ceiling. The Ballet Folklórico performs here every
Sunday. The **Templo Santa Maria de Gracia** (1661), at the corner of Avdas Carranza and
Hidalgo, has an austere stone interior and an ornate altar. At the back of the Teatro Degollada is a bronze relief commemorating the founding of the city on February 15,
1542. It looks over the **Plaza de los Fundadores**, supposedly on the exact site of the
fourth and final establishment of Guadalajara. This plaza marks the beginning of the
Plaza Tapatía (inaugurated 1982), five blocks of pleasant pedestrian malls and fountains
lined with cafés and a few shops. The **tourist office** is here at the corner of Avdas Morelos and Suarez. Midpoint in the plaza, steps lead down to the massive **San Juan de Dios
market**, where hundreds of vendors on multiple levels sell inexpensive crafts, *huaraches*
(leather sandals), fruits, vegetables, candy, hats, leather jackets and prepared foods.
There are often musical groups perfoming in the market's patio.

Just south of the market on Independencia is the **Plazuela de los Mariachis**, which—
like Mexico City's Plaza Garibaldi—is where bands of musicians congregate to look for
work and serenade visitors in the dozens of restaurants here (most active at night). At
the end of the Plaza Tapatía sits the massive **Instituo Cultural Cabañas** (1805–10).
Originally built as an orphanage around a plan containing 23 patios, it later became a
barracks and a prison before being converted into an arts center and school in 1979. José
Clemente Orozco painted the interior of the institute's central chapel between 1935 and
1939, and it is now considered his greatest work. The centerpiece is the 'Man of Fire', a
huge hovering figure of flame surrounded by figures representing Earth, Air and Water.
Other panels depict pre-Hispanic cannibalism, missionaries, conquistadors and a Cortés
constructed out of steel beams and bolts. The **Templo y Convento de San Francisco**
(begun 1542) on Avda 16 de Septiembre, five blocks south of the Cathedral, was once a
huge Franciscan monastic complex; now only the church and the **Capilla de Aránzazu**
(1749–52) across the street are still standing. The church has a plateresque façade and an
interior that was stripped bare and set on fire by an anti-clerical mob in 1936. The churrigueresque Capilla de Aranzazu contains three ornately carved gilt altars, a beautifully
frescoed ceiling and an elaborate depiction of the Franciscan order's genealogical tree.
The **Biblioteca Iberoamericana** at Avdas Colón and Moreno near the Cathedral is
housed in the ex-Iglesia de Santo Tomás (begun 1591), originally a Jesuit seminary and
now part of the University of Guadalajara. The ceiling is decorated with a red-tinged,

neo-primitive mural (1926) by David Alfaro Siquieros and Amado de la Cueva, depicting the history of Mexico's working class, which was apparently never finished. The **Templo del Carmen**, west of downtown at Avdas Juárez and 8 de Julio (1687–90, rebuilt 1820–30), is a small church extravagantly covered in gilt from floor to ceiling and also containing fine religious paintings and a carved gold pulpit. On weekends, local hippies sell crafts and jewelry at the side of the ex-convent, now an art gallery, across the street.

Avenida Juárez heading west is lined with restaurants, upscale shops and old mansions. The **University of Guadalajara** building at Avdas Juárez and Enrique Díaz de León contains two more murals by José Clemente Orozco, depicting the failure of the commu-

Side streets of Guadalajara

nist revolution and poverty and starvation. Juárez continues out to the **Arches Monument**, a triumphal arch built in 1942 to commemorate the 400th anniversary of the city. There's a **tourist office** in the base and a viewing platform on top. On the outskirts of Guadalajara there are a number of modern malls with hundreds of shops, including **Plaza del Sol**, south on Avda Lopez Mateos, and **Plaza Mexico**, west on Avda Mexico. The **Tlaquepaque** neighborhood, four kilometers (2.5 miles) southeast of downtown, was until recently an autonomous village that specialized in blown-glass crafts. Today, it's part of the big city and the central plaza has been converted into a pedestrian mall, lined with craft stores and factories selling colored glassware, pottery and textiles. The famous Mexican artist, **Sergio Bustamante** (known for his surreal ceramic objects), has a gallery in a colonial house on Calle Independencia. Next door is the **Regional Ceramics Museum**. Another ex-village, **Zapopán**, on Guadalajara's northwestern outskirts, contains a famous **Basilica** with a much-venerated image, the Virgin of Zapopán (enormous

Guadalajara Cathedral from the Plaza de la Liberación

fiesta on October 12). The sprawling new **central bus station** is 14 kilometers (nine miles) southeast of downtown (taxis expensive, but there are many local buses). *Charrerías*, Mexico's colorful variants on the rodeo, are celebrated Sundays at noon at one of Guadalajara's many *charro* arenas, including De Jalisco (tel 19-32-32) at Avdas Dr Michel and Las Palmas and La Generala (tel 33-06-16) at 201 Hidalgo.

Guadalajarans' favorite weekend destination is **Lake Chapala**, 53 kilometers (33 miles) due south. This vast, shallow and weedy lake is 86 kilometers (53 miles) by 25 kilometers (16 miles) at its widest. D H Lawrence wrote his Mexico novel, *The Plumed Serpent*, in the town of **Chapala**, which is also the thinly disguised setting for the book. Lawrence's house is at 307 Zaragoza. Local villagers traditionally make their living from fishing, but pollution has drastically reduced the catches. Chapala and the towns of **Ajijic** and **Jocotepec** to the west contain many American retirees, resorts, country clubs, boats for hire and vendors of local crafts.

The small town of **Tequila**, 60 kilometers (37 miles) west of Guadalajara on the Nayarit road, is the home of the Cuervo and Sauza distilleries, both of which may be toured. The town, originally home of the Tequila Indians, lies in the middle of fields of blue maguey, from which tequila is manufactured. Tequila distilleries have been operating here since the early 18th century. The volcano of Tequila (3,000 meters, or 9,868 feet) looms nearby.

For a description of **Puerto Vallarta**, see The Pacific States, p 165.

State of Michoacán

Michoacán, which means 'Place of the Masters of Fish' in Nahuatl, was originally inhabited by tribes of the Chupicuaro culture from Guanajuato. In the 12th century, a group that called themselves the Purépecha, now known as the Tarascans, arrived in the region of Lake Pátzcuaro and became 'Masters of the Fish'. They established capitals at Pátzcuaro, Ihuatzio and Tzintzuntzan, all around the lake, and developed advanced political, economic and religious systems. At Tzintzuntzan, the last Tarascan capital, one can still see their *yacates*, rectangular stepped platforms attached to circular stepped pyramids. Their kings, called Kasonsis, were buried with elaborate rites reminiscent of Ancient Egypt, during which their servants were sacrificed and interred with them. In the 15th century, the Aztecs attacked Michoacán and were repeatedly defeated, thereby increasing Tarascan prestige and power. In 1520, Cuitlahuac, the penultimate Aztec emperor, appealed to the Tarascans for help in defeating the Spanish, but the Tarascan Kasonsi Zuangua declined.

After Cortés' victory, he sent emissaries to Tzintzuntzan to initiate peaceful relations (his forces were too weak for another war). Later, Zuanga's successor, Tangaxoan II, recognized the Spaniards' power and traveled to Cortés' palace in Coyoacán in order to give the conquistador vassalage. In 1528, Cortés was directed to return to Spain and power fell into the hands of Nuño Beltrán de Guzmán, who ordered Tangaxoan to Mexico City and executed him. Beltrán de Guzmán then led a bloody expedition into Michoacán in which he burned villages and murdered or enslaved thousands of Indians. In 1538, Vasco de Quiroga, a humanist judge and later bishop of Michoacán, moved to the territory to try and heal some of the wounds opened by Beltrán de Guzmán. In Pátzcuaro he founded one of the first hospitals in Mexico, and he formed utopian communities in which Indians were taught crafts and self-government. He is still affectionately called 'Tato Vasco' and worshipped as a saint in Michoacán. Nevertheless, many Indians died of famine and disease. Morelia, founded in 1541 as Valladolid, contained many religious colleges that turned into centers of intellectual ferment.

By 1800, Michoacán was a center of mining, sugar cane plantations, textile and furniture manufacture, and educated *criollos* could turn their attention to more important things, like independence from Spain. A brilliant local priest, Miguel Hidalgo, became rector of the Colegio de San Nicolás in Valladolid before moving to Dolores, Guanajuato, in order to start the rebellion. When Hidalgo's army approached the city in November 1810, the residents joyfully welcomed him. After Hidalgo's execution, an old student of his named José María Morelos took up his banner and started a revolutionary army that marched victoriously all the way to Oaxaca; however, in 1815 he was captured and executed. A third Michoacán native, Agustin Iturbide, became the commander of a royalist army, changed sides and then named himself Emperor of Mexico after the ouster of the Spaniards; he was exiled in disgrace in 1823. Valladolid was renamed Morelia in 1828 (not Iturbide).

Of all those heroes remembered in Michoacán, the name of Lázaro Cárdenas, Michoacán's governor between 1928 and 1932, is most revered today. He restructured the state's politics and economy, personally opened hundreds of rural schools, redistributed the lands of the huge estates and encouraged direct contact with the people, particularly Indians and peasants. Cárdenas went on to become the most popular president in Mexican history. His son, Cuauhtemoc Cárdenas, was also Michoacán's governor and is now seeking to become president as the leader of a left-wing opposition party.

MORELIA

The red stone colonial city of Morelia (pop 449,000) is situated in the valley of the same name on the edge of the Michoacán highlands. The **Plaza de Armas** is the center of the city and most of the sights are within easy walking distance. The plaza is filled with trees and benches and surrounded on three sides by **Los Portales**, a series of arcades containing restaurants, outdoor cafés and hotels. The **Cathedral** (1640–1706) is a massive pink

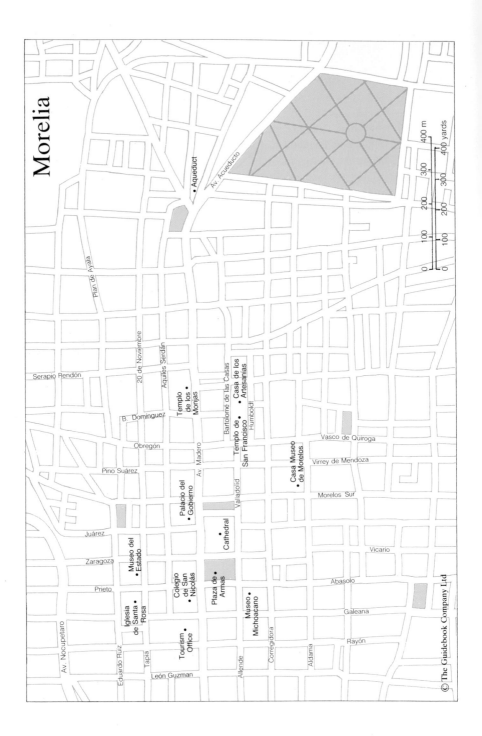

Morelia

Aqueduct •

Av. Acueducto

400 m
400 yards

Plan de Ayala

Serapio Rendón

20 de Noviembre

Aquiles Serdán

Templo
de los •
Monjas

B. Domínguez

Bartolomé de las Casas

Casa de los •
Artesanías

Humboldt

Obregón

Av. Madero

Templo de •
San Francisco

Vasco de Quiroga

Pino Suárez

Casa Museo •
de Morelos

Virrey de Mendoza

Palacio del
• Gobierno

Valladolid

Morelos Sur

Juárez

Cathedral •

Vicario

Zaragoza

Museo del
• Estado

Colegio
de San
Nicolás

Plaza de •
Armas

Abasolo

Prieto

Av. Nocupetaro

Iglesia
de Santa •
Rosa

Museo •
Michoacano

Galeana

Eduardo Ruiz

Tapia

Tourism •
Office

Allende

Corregidora

Aldama

Rayón

León Guzman

edifice with two large towers and a relief of the Ascension above the doors. The interior contains a large silver altarpiece and a venerated image of Christ made from corn to the left. The sacristy has a good collection of religious paintings. The **Palacio del Gobierno** across Avda Madero (the main street) was originally built as a seminary with a fine patio. The **Museo Michoacana**, in an 18th-century mansion at the southwest corner of the Plaza de Armas, exhibits a good collection of local archeological remains. The **Colegio de San Nicolás**, just west on Madero, was founded in 1540 (it may be the oldest institute of higher education in the New World) by Vasco de Quiroga and moved to Morelia around 1600. Miguel Hidalgo, José Maíia Morelos and other insurgents studied here, and Hidalgo was the Colegio's rector before he moved to Dolores in Guanajuato. Although it's still used a school, visitors may see a statue of Hidalgo in the courtyard and a mural along the second-floor walkway. The **Palacio Clavijero** (1660) across the street was built by Jesuits as a seminary, later became a prison and now contains government departments, including the **tourism office**. The **Biblioteca** in the seminary's old church has shelves covered with rare books and murals on the walls.

Just north on the Avda Nigromante stands the **Mercado de Dulces**, which specializes in Michoacán's many local candy delicacies, including chocolate from Uruapan, *ate* (fruit jam) and *chongos* (an incredibly sweet chewy curd) from Zamora. The **Iglesia de Santa Rosa** (16th century) across Avda Tapia from the **Plaza de las Rosas** is an ex-convent church, now a music conservatory, with three stunning gilt altars and walls covered with floral frescoes. The **Museo del Estado** at the corner of Avdas Tapia and Guillermo Prieto contains archeological and historical exhibitions and a particularly good display on Michoacán's ethnography (dances, food, crafts, etc) on the second floor. The enormous **Ex-Convento del Carmen** on Avda Morelos Norte is now the Casa de la Cultura, with art classes, exhibitions and performances. The **Templo de San Francisco** on Avda Vallodolid, three blocks east of the Cathedral, is a large church with a fine gold and white interior that fronts on a cobble-stoned plaza often filled with vendors. The **Casa de las Artesanías** in the old convent next door is probably the largest crafts store in Mexico. Selling only products of Michoacán, the store exhibits artisan work by type—pottery, woodwork, textiles, lacquerware, metalwork—on the first floor; on the second floor, each of the state's principal crafts-producing towns has a room in which they sell their merchandise. There is also a café on the first floor.

The **Casa Museo de Morelos** at Avdas Morelos Sur and Aldama was the anti-Spanish insurgent's home in the early 19th century and exhibits uniforms and other items from his life. Six blocks east of the Cathedral on Avda Madero stand the **Templo de los Monjas** (17th century), containing *trompe l'oeil* decor and a vivid painting of the Flagellation, and the neighboring **Palacio Federal**, another ex-convent. Madero continues east to the **Aqueduct** (1785–89), originally 26 kilometers (16 miles) long, now with only 253 arches remaining. To the south of the aqueduct is the tree-filled **Cuauhtemoc Park**; to the north is the **Ex-Convento de San Diego**, now the law school, with a heroic **Equestrian Statue of Morelos** (1910–13) in the plaza. The **central bus station** occupies the corner of Avdas Eduardo Ruiz and Rayón, six blocks northwest of the Cathedral.

PÁTZCUARO

The large, beautiful **Lake Pátzcuaro**, located in the Michoacán highlands 45 kilometers (28 miles) west of Morelia, is surrounded by traditional villages and also contains settlements on islands in the middle of the lake. The most important of these is Pátzcuaro (pop 65,000), about two kilometers (1.25 miles) south of the lake. The **Basilica de la Virgen de la Salud** (begun 1554) was planned by Vasco de Quiroga as the seat of his bishopric. This enormous, single-vaulted edifice was never finished—and was partially destroyed by two 19th-century earthquakes—but retains a rough charm. The altar holds the venerated image of the Virgen de la Salud, which according to legend was molded from corn-stalk paste and found floating in a canoe on the lake. The Basilica also contains the remains of Don Vasco, who is locally considered a saint. Behind the building are the foundations of the pre-Hispanic Tarascán capital that stood here. Crafts are sold in the square in front of the church. The **Museo de Artes Populares**, just south of the Basilica, exhibits excellent examples of crafts from throughout Michoacán. The building was constructed by de Quiroga to be the first home of the Colegio de San Nicolás, now in Morelia. The **Templo de la Compañía** (1540) next door was the cathedral until the Basilica was fit for use in 1565. The simple interior conserves wood floors and a single-vaulted wood beam ceiling. Just past the **Templo del Sagrario**, another early church, stands the **Casa de los Once Patios**, which was built as a hospital by Don Vasco. Now it is filled with craft boutiques selling scarves, lacquer, furniture, basketry, masks and so on.

Pátzcuaro is centered on two squares just downhill from the Basilica. The **Plaza Vasco de Quiroga**, the larger of two, is usually filled with vendors making furniture and selling them and other crafts to the tourist trade. The **Palacio Municipal**, on the west side of the plaza, contains the **tourist office**. The plaza's other sides are lined with hotels, restaurants and the **Casa del Gigante** (1663), a Spanish count's mansion on the east side, which contains a statue of a giant guarding the main stairway. The good hat store on the north side also sells traditional rubberized ponchos. The **Plaza Gertrudis Bocanegra** is where the locals prefer to walk. The **Biblioteca Pública** on the north end occupies an old church and contains a large and complicated mural (1942) by Juan O'Gorman, depicting the conquest and subjugation of the Indians. The vans that stop on Avda Obregón heading downhill take passengers to the railway station and the ferry landing. The **market** begins east of the plaza and covers several square blocks with stands selling fruits, vegetables, whitefish and crayfish from the lake, candies, crafts, etc. The **Santuario de Guada-**

lupe (19th century) west of the market is rather plain, except for the fishing nets strung from the rafters. The **central bus station** is southwest of town on the ring road.

From the **Embarcadero**, or ferry dock, launches leave regularly for Janítzio, an island in Lake Pátzcuaro. The road up to the dock is lined with gift shops and restaurants specializing in lake whitefish. **Janítzio** (half-hour boatride) is a peaked island populated by fishermen. It once was the capital of the Tarascan kingdom. Paths lined with modest souvenir shops (wooden boats, 'Memory of Janitzio' mugs and dresses) and restaurants run by the fishermen's wives climb the hill up to a heroic 40-meter (132-foot)-tall **Monument to Morelos** with his fist upraised. The interior of this rather ugly statue is lined with a mural by Ramón Alva de la Canal depicting Morelos's life, which spirals up the walls to his head. Local fishermen skim over Lake Pátzcuaro in little canoes powered by square-tipped oars and cast distinctive butterfly-shaped nets for the whitefish. To reach the other islands of the lake—Tecuén, Yunuén, and Pacanda—a private launch must be hired.

The smaller towns surrounding Lake Pátzcuaro are also worth a visit. **Ihuatzio** and **Tzintzuntzan** along the eastern shore are both the location of Tarascán ruins. Tzintzuntzan was the Tarascán capital on the arrival of the Spaniards, and its archeological site, **Las Yacates**, contains the largest and best preserved complex of *yacates,* which are connected circular and rectangular stepped pyramids. The centerpiece of the town, one kilometer (0.6 miles) away, is the **Convento de Santa Ana** (16th century), where Vasco de Quiroga founded his first church in Michoacán. The interior contains the venerated image of the **Señor del Rescate**. The other towns, including **Quiroga**, **Chupicuaro**, **Erongaricuaro** and **Jaracuaro**, are all traditional Indian communities inhabited by fishermen and artisans.

Uruapan

Set on the slopes of the sierra, Uruapan (pop 250,000), which may mean in Tarascán 'Place of Eternal Spring', is a good base for exploration of the Michoacán highlands. The city's center is a three-block-long square called the **Plaza Morelos**, which is lined with crowded arcades. The **16th century chapel** built on the plaza by Fray Juan de San Miguel stands on the site of the Tarascáns' Temple of the Sun; it is now the state artisanry shop. The **Santo Sepulcro** next door was built by Fray Juan as a hospital for Indians stricken with pestilence; it is now the **Museo Huatepero**, exhibiting crafts from the surrounding villages (ceramics, shawls, furniture, straw figures and masks). The streets behind these buildings are filled with the stalls of the **market**, and there is a precinct of cheap food stands (local specialties) behind the undistinguished **Cathedral** also on the plaza. The **Parque Nacional Eduardo Ruiz** at the west end of town is filled with streams, waterfalls and forest. The central bus station is northeast of downtown on Calzada Benito Juárez.

(above) *Tarascan Indian paddles across Lake Pátzcuaro;*
(below) *Lake Pátzcuaro, with the island town of Janitzio to the left*

The hills around Uruapan are covered with avocado orchards.

Paracho, 38 kilometers (24 miles) north of Uruapan, is famous for its wooden musical instruments—violins, cellos, and particularly guitars. Locals believe that it was Vasco de Quiroga himself who originally taught them guitar-making. A side road halfway between Paracho and Uruapan leads to **Angahuan**, the jumping-off point for the 50-year-old **Paricutín volcano**. From here you can rent a horse or hike to the peak of volcano, 14 kilometers (nine miles) south. In 1942, a peasant noticed that his field was beginning to tremble and swell upward. The bulge grew into a hill and on February 20, 1943 blew its top, spewing lava over the nearby towns of San Juan and Paricutín. San Juan's church spires can still be seen above the lava flow, three kilometers (1.9 miles) from Angahuan. Plants and trees have recently begun to grow on the lava.

The Pacific

Introduction

The slopes of the western Sierra Madre swoop down to the Pacific Ocean between the state of Sinaloa and the Isthmus of Tehuantepec far to the south, providing a dramatic setting for many of Mexico's most famous resorts. These same mountains were home to the Tomb Culture that produced lively, painted terracotta figurines in the centuries before Christ. Some of the least Westernized indigenous groups in Mexico—the Cora and Huichol—still occupy the most remote regions of the sierra.

Sinaloa is mostly hot, flat agricultural land. Mazatlán has an exciting history going back centuries and is now a seasoned resort. Eating buckets of fresh shrimp and deep-sea fishing for sailfish are popular recreations.

The up-and-coming resort of San Blas on Nayarit's coast was the port for the Spanish Pacific fleet, and now attracts visitors for wildlife adventures. The island town of Mexcaltitán nearby is a miniature Venice in the middle of a tropical lagoon. Nayarit's capital, Tepic, with good museums and a relaxed atmosphere, is a pleasant place to stop after too much sightseeing.

Puerto Vallarta, in the state of Guadalajara, has one of the most beautiful settings of any resort; it nestles against a range of steep palm-tree-covered hills that are green year-round. Although the resort is currently undergoing a construction boom, it is still low-key enough for a relaxed vacation.

Colima contains the resort of Manzanillo, which is famous for the Moorish fantasy hotel, Las Hadas, and miles of white beaches. The state capital, Colima, is a colonial city with good food and friendly surroundings.

The mountainous state of Guerrero contains two popular resorts, Ixtapa-Zihuatenejo and Acapulco. The former is schizophrenic: Ixtapa is an ultra-modern, American-style resort area; Zihuatenejo is a small Mexican fishing village that is preferred by more budget-minded travelers. Acapulco, the grandfather of Mexican resorts, is built on the steep hills that ring a beautiful natural harbor. Day or night the view is striking. This was the home port for the famous *Nao de China*, the boat that carried spices and other luxury items from the Orient to the New World during the colonial era. Acapulco contains a fascinating mix of foreign visitors staying in space-age hotels, rich and middle-class Mexicans from the capital and poorer Acapulqueños, many of whom are descendants of African slaves.

Getting There

Mexico 15, the Pacific highway, cuts through the state of Sinaloa and connects the cities of Los Mochis, Culiacán and Mazatlán. The Pacífico train line plies the same route, linking Mexicali with Guadalajara. Inland Mexico is reached via the Chihuahua-Pacífico train that departs daily from Los Mochis and also via Mexico 40, the scenic highway that runs from Mazatlán to Durango and eventually reaches the Gulf. An express passengers-only ferry travels daily between Topolobampo and La Paz on Baja California. A slower vehicle ferry runs daily from Mazatlán to La Paz. Airports in Los Mochis and Culiacán receive flights from Chihuahua, Ciudad Obregón, Durango, Guadalajara, Hermosillo, La Paz, Mazatlán, Mexicali, Mexico City, Monterrey, Tijuana and Torreón. Mazatlán's international airport is served by direct flights from the above-mentioned Mexican cities as well as Aguascalientes, Denver, León, Los Angeles, Los Cabos, Phoenix, Portland, Puerto Vallarta, San Diego, San Francisco, Seattle and Tucson.

Mexico 15, the Pacific highway, turns inland at Tepic, Nayarit's capital, and heads to Guadalajara. The coast road becomes Mexico 200 and runs to Puerto Vallarta and points south. Tepic is also on the Pacífico train line that runs between Guadalajara and Mexicali. Tepic's airport has daily flights from Mexico City and Tijuana.

Puerto Vallarta lies on Mexico 200, the windy two-lane road that runs along the Pacific south of Tepic to Manzanillo. It is far easier to reach the resort by air. Puerto Vallarta's international airport receives flights from Guadalajara, Houston, Ixtapa, La Paz, Los Angeles, Los Cabos, Mazatlán, Mexico City, Miami, Monterrey, San Francisco, San Diego, San José, Seattle and Tijuana.

Mexico 200 runs along the coast of the tiny state of Colima, passing Manzanillo along the way. Just before Armería, 200 connects with Mexico 110, a highway that leads to the city of Colima and continues to Guadalajara. The latter stretch, with the Colima volcano looming in the west, is particularly scenic. The Colimense train line connects the beaches of Manzanillo and the city of Colima with Guadalajara and includes luxury service. Manzanillo's airport has services from Guadalajara, Los Angeles and Mexico City, and flights from Mexico City and Tijuana land at Colima.

Mexico 200 continues south along the empty beaches of Michoacán's coast and reaches the state of Guerrero at the Río Balsas. It passes Ixtapa-Zihuatenejo, then Acapulco, and proceeds south and east through Oaxaca and Chiapas all the way to the Guatemalan border. The section between Acapulco and Pinotepa Nacional in Oaxaca has a reputation for bandits. Mexico 134, a scenic road from Toluca, hits Mexico 200 just above Ixtapa. Acapulco is 417 kilometers (259 miles) from Mexico City on Mexico 95, which also passes through Cuernavaca and Chilpancingo. It can be extremely crowded on holidays. Taxco is a short detour off 95 between Iguala and the Morelos border. There is no train service in the state of Guerrero. Ixtapa has an international airport with flights from Guadalajara, Houston, Los Angeles, Mexico City and San Francisco. Acapulco's international airport is served by flights from Chicago, Dallas, Fort Myers, Guadalajara, Houston, Los Angeles, Mexico City, New York, Omaha, Puerto Escondido, San José (Costa Rica), Tampico, Tijuana and Tulsa.

State of Sinaloa

The state of Sinaloa was the home of the Culture of Aztatlán until about AD 900. Centered in Culiacán and Guasave, the Aztatlán peoples built ceremonial centers with raised platforms, pyramids and ball courts. Their dead were buried with offerings of ceramic figures placed in large funerary urns. At the time of the Conquest, Sinaloa was occupied by eight less-developed tribes, including the Mayos, the Guasaves and the Chichimecs in the sierra. Nuño Beltrán de Guzmán invaded the region in 1530 and founded his capital in Culiacán. Large-scale Spanish settlement began at the end of the 16th century, with the discovery of mines in the sierra. During the 19th century, Sinaloa's principal port, Mazatlán, was the site of many battles. In 1847, the United States blockaded and then captured the town; Juárez' liberals defeated the conservatives here in 1859; the French bombarded and captured Mazatlán in 1864; and in 1914, the revolutionary army defeated Huerta's forces here after a long siege. During World War II, the Japanese cut the supply of opium and its derivatives, like morphine, from the Orient, and Sinaloa leaped into the breach. Large fields of opium poppies were planted for both legal and illegal use. Since then the culture of drug smuggling has thrived, particularly in Culiacán. Today, Sinaloa is also an important producer of many legal crops, like sugar cane.

Los Mochis

Los Mochis (pop 200,000) is a glorified crossroads town and agricultural center that sprang up at the intersection of the Chihuahua–Pacífico railway and the Pacific highway. Buses for Mochis' hotels (Hotel Santa Anita downtown is recommended) meet passengers at the arrival of the train every evening. (For a description of the Chihuahua–Pacífico route, see 'Chihuahua', p 188.) Downtown Los Mochis is built on a grid pattern, with restaurants and the market within walking distance. During the summer, the heat is oppressive and locals head to the nearby port of **Topolobampo** (24 kilometers, or 15 miles) on the Sea of Cortés. This is mainly a fish processing town and also has the dock for the **express passenger-only ferry to La Paz** (four hours, daily departures). Excursion boats are available for hire.

Port of Mazatlán, Sinaloa

CULIACÁN

Culiacán (pop 700,000), the state capital, is rarely visited by tourists and acquired a notorious reputation because of shootouts between bands of police competing over the drug trade. President Salinas de Gortari's clean-up campaign has apparently cleansed the force of the most corrupt officers. The vast majority of Culiacán's citizens have always plied more peaceable occupations. Downtown Culiacán is clean, modern and lively, perhaps due to the nearby **University of Sinaloa**. The main square, the **Centro Cívico Constitucion**, lies at the foot of the large white **Cathedral** (18th century). The **Malecón**, the waterside drive, runs along the banks of the Río Culiacán. Culiacán also contains a shrine to **Jesús Malverde**, a smuggler hanged in 1909, who is now considered a saint by local *bandidos*. There's a good vista over the city from the **Capilla de la Guadalupana**, in the hills above town.

MAZATLÁN

The Pacific resort and fishing port of Mazatlán (pop 450,000), just south of the Tropic of Cancer, is divided into two zones: downtown on a rocky peninsula jutting out into the Pacific; and the resort areas along the beaches to the north. Although the Spanish settled here in 1540, nothing remains of colonial Mazatlán (which means 'Leg of Deer' in Nahuatl). It was an important fishing town and nothing else for centuries, until Californian sportfishermen discovered the offshore attractions in the 1920s. The cramped, Mexican downtown, also known as the Puerto Viejo, is centered on the **Plaza Principal**, with the **Basilica of the Immaculate Conception** (1856–99) on one side. Just to the north is the large **municipal market**, containing inexpensive local crafts and food stalls. The cheap hotels are centered in this district. Top Mexican entertainers perform in the large **Teatro Angela Peralta** (two blocks south of the cathedral), named after the famous diva, 'The Mexican Nightingale', who died here of cholera. The **Cerro de Nevería** ('Ice Cream Hill'), which looms over the town, has a great view of the **Dos Hermanos** rocks offshore and the beautiful sunsets. There are vistas from the **statue of the Mazatlecán woman** and the **Pergola** lookout. The tip of the peninsula is a rock called El Crestón; on the western side is a **lighthouse**, which locals say is the highest in the world. The **sportfishing fleet** docks along the pier at the south side of El Creston. Offshore you can catch marlin, sailfish, shark, red snapper, tuna, dorado and bonito. The terminal for the ferry to La Paz is also located here. The **Avenida del Mar**, heading north from downtown along the beach, is the main drag of the resort section. The first three kilometers (1.9 miles) run past the older hotels and the less attractive beaches. The small **aquarium** (big sign) is one block inland, across the street from the **Carnival grounds**.

At Punta Camarón, Avda del Mar turns a bit inland and becomes the **Calz Camaron-Sabalo**, the heart of the **Zona Dorado**, the luxury hotel zone. The **bullring** is one kilometer (0.62 miles) inland on Calz Rafael Buena; bullfight season is December–April. The Zona Dorado is extremely built-up and Americanized, with gift shops, fast food restaurants, laundromats, condos, and money exchanges lining Calz Camarón-Sabalo. The **arts and crafts center** and the enormous **Sea Shell City** gift shop are on Avda Loiza, just west of the main strip. The hotel zone ends at the Camino Real hotel at Punta Sabalo. The most popular way of seeing Mazatlán is in *pulmonías* ('pneumonias'), a local type of open-air taxi. Downtown you also may take *arañas* ('spiders'), horse-drawn two wheel buggies. Shrimp, *bargo* (grilled red snapper) and *pescado sarandeado* (fish in *papillote*) are the local culinary specialties. The most popular drink is Pacifico beer, brewed here in Mazatlán. The **tourist office** (9 am–4 pm) is in the Los Sabalos Hotel on Avda Loiza.

The small town of **Concordia** on Mex 40, 46 kilometers (29 miles) inland, is a pleasant excursion from Mazatlán. Founded in 1563 amid the jungles of the Sierra Madre Occidental foothills, this town of small whitewashed buildings grouped around a plaza contains the baroque **Iglesia de San Sebastián** (18th century). Mex 40 continues up through the sierra's wild and mountainous terrain, past some of the most stunning views in Mexico, to the city of Durango. **Rosario**, 88 kilometers (55 miles) south of Mazatlán on Mex 15, is worth visiting for the **Iglesia de la Misión de Nuestra Señora del Rosario** (18th century), with a splendid gold altar in the interior.

State of Nayarit

Nayarit was one of the centers of the Tomb Culture, also found in Jalisco and Colima. Probably flourishing in the last few centuries BC, these peoples buried their dead at the bottom of long shafts in ceremonies accompanied by elaborate offerings of painted terracotta figurines, many depicting male-female pairs (perhaps ancestors). Others portrayed whole towns, including houses, temples and the citizenry. The first Spaniard arrived in Nayarit in 1524, but it was Nuño Beltrán de Guzmán who conquered the region in 1529. He founded Compostela, the first capital of the province of Nueva Galicia, on the site of Tepic, an Indian town. Later, Compostela was moved south, and Tepic returned to its original name and eventually became the capital. Nayarit's sierra was the stronghold of the Cora and Huichol tribes, who resisted the Spanish military and evangelists until well into the 18th century. They remain amongst the least assimilated of the Indian groups. In 1767, Charles III of Spain chose the small Nayarit harbor of San Blas to be the port for his Pacific fleet. He wanted to strengthen his hold on the Californias and counter the Russians, who were colonizing Alaska. During the mid-19th century, Nayarit was ruled by Lozada, 'The Tiger of Alicia', who began his career as a smuggler and later became a general on the side of the conservatives and then the French imperialists. In the 1860s, he decided to make the poverty-stricken Indians of the sierra his cause and led an Indian army on Guadalajara in a renewal of the War of the Castes. The Mexican army wounded, captured and quickly executed 'El Tigre'.

TEPIC

Visitors usually stop briefly in Tepic (pop 200,000), Nayarit's capital, on their way somewhere else. Nevertheless, this small city in the foothills of the sierra has enough sights to make a short stay worthwhile. **Avda Mexico** is the main street and connects the **Plaza Principal**, surrounded by arcades and the gothic **Cathedral** (1891), and the **Plaza de los Constituyentes**. The **Museo de Nayarit**, on the corner of Avda Mexico and Calle Zapata, contains exhibits on Huichol crafts, including fine examples of their psychedelic yarn paintings, archeological artefacts, colonial paintings and a giant stuffed crocodile. There is one **tourism office** at the corner of Avda Mexico and Allende, and another at the restored **Convento de la Cruz de Zacate** (16th century), on top of a hill about one kilometer further out on Avda Mexico. The convent contains a miraculously long-lasting cross made of grass (Cruz de Zacate), which is still green after several centuries.

The **Palacio del Gobierno** on the Plaza de los.Constituyentes has murals depicting Nayarit's history. The famous Mexican poet, **Amado Nervo**, was born in the house at 284 Calle Zacatecas, which is now a museum of his life. Most of the hotels are around the Plaza Principal; many restaurants are located on Avda Mexico. Restaurant Lupita, at the

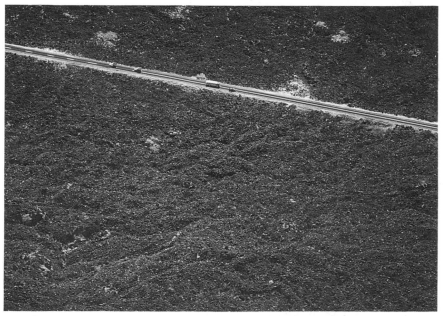

*(facing page) Sugar cane fields, Nayarit; (above) ruins of the
San Blas Counting House; (below) a highway, Nayarit*

corner of Calles Allende and Morelos, serves cheap typical dishes popular with locals. Shops selling Huichol and Cora crafts are on Avda Mexico; Indians in traditional costume also sell their work on the streets.

SAN BLAS

The small town of San Blas (pop 5,000), 70 kilometers (43 miles) WNW of Tepic, was a bustling port of 30,000 and the main Pacific base for the Spanish navy in the late 18th century. It is today a small resort and the colonial edifices lie in ruins. San Blas is built on a spit of land between the Pacific and a series of mangrove and jungle-lined estuaries filled with wildlife. The climate is almost always hot and is unpleasant during sand fly season. The road into town passes the **Cerro de la Contaduria** on the right, which was the original site of San Blas. Here you may clamber around the ruins of the fortified **Counting House** (1770), the **Templo de Nuestra Señora del Rosario** (begun 1769) and many houses. Downtown is centered on the **Plaza Principal**, around which are clustered the bus station, the market and the tourism office. The ruins of the 19th-century **Customs House** lie three blocks east of the plaza on Juárez. The municipal dock is just beyond. From here boats leave for the **Islas Marías**, Mexico's principal penal colony for hardened felons. Another landing, at the bridge next to the Cerro de la Contaduria, serves excursion boats heading up the estuary to the **La Tovara springs**. The dense green vegetation along the way is filled with tropical birds and the waters hold turtles, fish and occasional caymans. La Tovara is a freshwater spring and a popular swimming hole. The nearest beach to San Blas is the **Playa Borrego**, just south of town; other beaches may be reached along the road to Santa Cruz that cuts south along the Bahía Matanchen after La Tovara.

MEXCALTITÁN

The remarkable Venice-like town of Mexcaltitán (pop 2,000) lies on an island in the middle of a lagoon west of the town of Santiago Ixcuintla, and is only accessible by passenger ferry. Two sets of parallel streets running east–west and north–south cross the island; the rectangle they form in the center is the main square. The streets are lined with strangely tall benches, whose use only becomes apparent during the rainy season. Then the lagoon floods the town and the benches become docks and sidewalks for the inhabitants. Mexcaltitán's residents make their living from netting the freshwater shrimps that fill the lagoon. The local culinary specialty is *textihuille*, shrimp with *mole* sauce. None of the whitewashed buildings is more than a century old, but archeologists believe the island has been inhabited since pre-Hispanic times. In fact, Mexcaltitán is currently the front-runner for being the site of Aztlán, the mythic island home of the Aztecs. Today Mexican presidents make annual pilgrimages to celebrate the town as the 'Navel of Mexicanness'. Mexcaltitán, which until the 1950s lived in utter obscurity, is now a pawn in the elaborate game of self-legitimization played by Mexican politicians.

State of Jalisco

(see also Colonial States, p 139)

PUERTO VALLARTA

The Pacific resort of Puerto Vallarta (pop 100,000), part of Jalisco state, is set against the steep green hills that arc around the enormous Banderas Bay, one of the largest on the coast. The first settlement on this site was the Sánchez family farm, founded in 1851. Development proceeded at a snail's pace, because the area was only accessible by boat. The airport and the Tepic road did not open until 1968. The bay first reached the attention of the outside world in the 1950s, when John Huston filmed *The Night of the Iguana* at Mismaloya, at the south end. Liz Taylor and Richard Burton, the stars, had just begun their romance and scandal-hungry reporters flocked to the set. Puerto Vallarta became a favorite hideaway for the Hollywood jet-set, and the regular tourists followed when the first big hotels opened in the mid-1960s.

Puerto Vallarta is divided into three areas: downtown, the crowded north beach hotel zone, and the more exclusive hotel and condo zone south of downtown. Zoning ordinances have kept downtown buildings relatively low, with whitewashed walls and red tile roofs (prices are still high though). The **Río Cualé** bisects downtown, and most of the sights are within four blocks of the bridges. The tower of the **Parroquia de Nuestra Señora de Guadalupe** (1930–66) is topped with a brick rendering of the Spanish crown. The **Palacio Municipal** on the **Plaza de Armas**, a block downhill from the church, contains the **tourism office**. The **Aquiles Serdán Theater**, which presents top Mexican entertainers, stands between the plaza and the sea. The streets around the plaza are lined with gift shops, restaurants and the cheaper hotels. Three blocks south of the plaza, a bridge spans the Río Cualé. A stairway leads down to **Cuale Island** in the middle of the river, where you find more gift shops and the small **archeological museum**. The south side of downtown contains more restaurants and cheap hotels, as well as the **bus offices** for the various lines spread out on Calles Pino Suárez and Ignacio Vallarta. The **Playa de los Muertos**, a few blocks further south, is the most popular beach for locals. The beachfront Paseo Díaz Ordáz, which heads north from the Plaza de Armas becomes **Avda Mexico**, the main street for the northern hotel zone. It's lined with big luxury hotels, malls and condominiums and eventually passes the **airport**, becoming Mex 200.

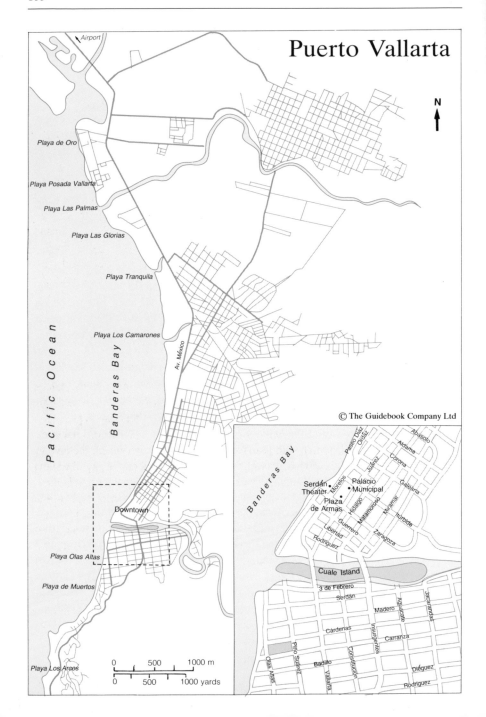

Puerto Vallarta

N

Airport

Playa de Oro

Playa Posada Vallarta

Playa Las Palmas

Playa Las Glorias

Playa Tranquila

Playa Los Camarones

Pacific Ocean

Banderas Bay

Av. México

© The Guidebook Company Ltd

Downtown

Playa Olas Altas

Playa de Muertos

Playa Los Arcos

0   500   1000 m

0   500   1000 yards

Banderas Bay

Serdán Theater

Palacio Municipal

Plaza de Armas

Paseo Díaz Ordaz

Juárez

Morelos

Hidalgo

Matamoros

Guerrero

Libertad

Rodríguez

Abasolo

Aldama

Corona

Galeana

Miramar

Iturbide

Zaragoza

Cuale Island

3 de Febrero

Serdán

Madero

Cárdenas

Aguacate

Insurgentes

Constitución

Carranza

Jacarandas

Olas Altas

Pino Suárez

Badillo

Vallarta

Diéguez

Rodríguez

The better beaches, **Playa los Camarones**, **Playa Tranquila**, **Playa las Gloria** and **Playa de Oro**, begin two kilometers (1.25 miles) north of downtown. The southern coast of Banderas Bay is also lined with beaches; they are smaller and harder to reach, but they may be cleaner and less crowded. South of downtown, Mex 200 winds along the rocks above the blue water and passes more exclusive hotels and condo complexes. Some of these are perched on hills so steep that residents need elevators to reach them. The big rocks offshore are called **Los Arcos**, after the natural archways carved in them by the waves. They are a popular destination for snorkelers. **Mismaloya**, ten kilometers (six miles) south, is a beach at the mouth of a jungle stream. Until recently it was a small fishing village, but a large condo edifice has just been erected here. A dirt road beside the stream leads up into the jungle to a restaurant. These trees may look familiar to moviegoers, because the Schwarzenegger movie, *Predator*, was filmed here. Mex 200 turns inland and heads up a narrow valley lined with waterfalls and then enters a hotter, drier and less interesting landscape. The two small resorts of **Melaque** and **Barra de Navidad** are 209 kilometers (130 miles) south of Puerto Vallarta, almost at the border of the state of Colima.

State of Colima

Some of the liveliest burial offerings of the Tomb Culture have been found in the state of Colima. The most famous are the 'little dogs' that perhaps represent the dogs who led the dead into the underworld. Figurines of warriors brandishing clubs that may depict shamans in ritual dances have also been found. In 1522, Cortés sent Cristóbal de Olid into the west to find a large island rich with pearls and inhabited only by women: the mythic Amazonas. He found Colima instead, and the first Spanish settlement, the city of Colima, was established in 1523. Cortés founded Manzanillo, originally named Santiago de Buena Esperanza, as a shipbuilding port for his expeditions to Central America. Colima and Manzanillo were the only Spanish towns in the region for centuries, since settlers were attracted by richer mines and farmlands elsewhere. They were also deterred by the state's frequent earthquakes and the threat of the Colima volcano, which last erupted in 1913 (and sent out warning tremors in early 1991).

MANZANILLO
The resort of Manzanillo (pop 70,000) is also an important industrial port and the end of a train line from Guadalajara. The resort areas are spread along the wide beaches of Manzanillo and Santiago Bays, and a peninsula at the east end of the Manzanillo Bay holds the port installations and the old downtown. The resort development began in the

late 1970s with the completion of Mex 200, the coastal road. Downtown Manzanillo is cramped, smelly and dirty; you can easily imagine why the town had a reputation among sailors as an unhealthy hellhole during the 19th century. The center of town is the **Jardín Alvaro Obregón**, along the portside **Malecón**, with a view of the Mexican Navy and commercial piers. Most of the cheap hotels are found here. The main church, the **Iglesia de Nuestra Señora de Guadalupe**, stands one block southwest. The dirty municipal beach, **Playa San Pedrito**, is about half a kilometre east of downtown.

The resort zone is right across a channel from this beach, but to reach it you have to take a circuitous road around the lagoon. The first half of the resort zone arcs along a long spit of land, with the **Brisas**, **Azul** and **Salagua** beaches heading west. The main road, which is actually Mex 200, is lined with big and small hotels, condos, supermarkets, car rentals, restaurants and a few malls. This portion of Manzanillo Bay ends at the rocky Santiago Peninsula, which is topped by the enormous white moorish fantasy **Las Hadas** resort. Built by a Bolivian tin baron for his jet-set friends, Las Hadas was the other featured attraction of the movie, *10*, starring Bo Derek and Dudley Moore. West of this peninsula, less crowded beaches curve along **Santiago Bay**. The resort ends at **Juluapán Peninsula**, from which a rock in the shape of an elephant juts. The **Elephant Rock Beach** just below is accessible only by boat. Sailfishing is very popular in Manzanillo, and all other water sports are available. West of Manzanillo, Mex 200 heads through many kilometers of coconut groves on the way to Puerto Vallarta. To the east of town, the road heads along a 26-kilometer-long (16-mile) sandbar between the Pacific and the Cuyutlán Lagoon, before turning inland.

COLIMA

The state capital, Colima (pop 150,000), is situated in a broad agricultural valley in the foothills of the Sierra Madre Occidental. Most tourists whiz past on their way from Guadalajara to the coast, but Colima has enough sights to make a short stay rewarding. The **Plaza Principal**, with a bandstand in the middle and surrounded by colonnades, is the center of town. The east side is dominated by the neo-classical **Cathedral**, originally erected in the 1530s and renovated in 1894. The **Palacio del Gobierno** next door is decorated with historical murals by Jorge Chávez Carrillo. At the southwest corner of the square, the **Museo del Estado de Colima** contains a room filled with Tomb Culture figurines, including pot-bellied dogs, pregnant women, couples and gymnasts. The **Hotel Ceballos** occupies the north end of the square and is worth visiting to see the renovated interior (the guest rooms are disappointing). A store on the ground floor, the **Casa Ceballos**, changes money and sells lingerie, postcards, figurine reproductions, hats and old coins. The main shopping street, **Avenida Madero**, heads east from the plaza to the **Jardín Núñez**. Behind the auto parts store on the east side of the park is a private **antique** car museum, open at the store owner's whim. The **Museo de las Culturas de Occidente**, with a large Tomb Culture display, stands at the corner of Avda Carranza and Calz Pedro Galvan in the northeastern corner of the city. Colima crafts and ethnography are on display at the **Museo de la Máscara, la Danza y el Arte Popular del Occidente**, at the corner of Calles Gallardo and 27 de Septiembre, seven blocks north of the main plaza. For the best local cuisine, try Restaurante Naranjos on Calle Barreda, just north of Avda Madero. Colima's candy specialty is *cocada*, made from coconut, sugar and milk and sold throughout the city. You may see local men wearing a unique type of hat with leather reinforcements across the crown, called *golimotes*. In the old days these were bigger, had more leather and doubled as shields.

The highway from Guadalajara passes east of the looming **Colima Volcano** (3,820 meters, or 12,566 feet), which last erupted in 1941 and is definitely still active. Behind it in the state of Jalisco stands the dormant, snow-capped **Nevado de Colima** (4,240 meters, or 13,947 feet). Hikers can reach the summits from trails that begin in the towns of Atenquique and Fresnito in Jalisco.

State of Guerrero

Before the arrival of the Spanish, Guerrero's fate was to be surrounded by larger and more powerful Indian cultures. The Olmec Culture, based on the Veracruz coast, contributed remarkable cave paintings (900–700 BC) found near Oxtotitlán and Juxtlahuaca, in the eastern Guerrero sierra. At one time or another Guerrero's tribes were conquered by and had to pay tribute to Teotihuacán and the Toltecs from the Valley of Mexico, the Mixtecs from Oaxaca, the Tarascans from Michoacán and, finally, the Aztecs. Many Guerreran ceremonial objects have been found in Tenochtitlán (Mexico City).

In 1523, an expedition sent by Cortés reached the mouth of the Río Balsas, and the deep natural harbor of Acapulco was discovered shortly thereafter. After silver was found at Taxco and other sites, Spanish settlers poured into the region. Acapulco became the sole legal port for the *Nao de China*, the galleon that plied the Pacific between Mexico and the Orient. A road was built to carry the silks, spices and other luxuries up to Mexico City, and African slaves were imported to work in the harbor. Guerrero became a showplace of the Virreynato, and many distinguished visitors, including a Japanese delegation in 1614 and Alexander von Humboldt in the early 19th century, visited Acapulco and the silver mines.

In 1809, Miguel Hidalgo delegated José María Morelos to take the battle for independence into the south. With the help of Vicente Guerrero, after whom the state is

(top, bottom and above right) Michoacán's unspoiled Pacific coast

(below left) downtown Puerta Vallarta; (below right)
diving from the rocks at La Quebrada, Acapulco

named, he formed a ragged army that had great early success, capturing Taxco in 1811 and Acapulco, briefly, in 1813. That same year, insurgent delegates from throughout Mexico convened a congress in Chilpancingo to determine the country's future shape; they signed the *Act of Independence* in early 1814. The tide of battle turned in 1815, when Morelos was captured and executed, leaving Guerrero to continue the fight. Guerrero went on to become a liberal president of Mexico in 1829–30, until he was overthrown and executed by his conservative vice president. After independence in 1821, Acapulco lost its lock on trade to the Orient and began a slow decline that lasted until the beginnings of tourism in the 1920s. In this century, poverty, corruption and unequal distribution of power have led to frequent peasant rebellions in Guerrero, and many governors have resigned or been ousted before serving full terms.

IXTAPA–ZIHUATENEJO
The fraternal twin towns of Ixtapa and Zihuatenejo on the Guerrero coast, 239 kilometers (149 miles) west of Acapulco, offer contrasting experiences for visitors. Zihuatenejo is a small fishing village that has gradually attracted more and more tourists, yet still retains its original charm. On the other side of a craggy hill, Ixtapa is a carefully planned Cancún-style resort with big, modern hotels along a beach and almost no Mexican identity. The cobblestone streets of Zihuatenejo are built around the small bay of the same name, and almost all the attractions are spread along the beachfront **Paseo Costera**. Here you will find the **tourism office**, the small **El Patio archeological museum** and the **Plaza de Armas**. A block inland from the plaza stands the **artisans' market**. The beach here, **Playa Zihuatenejo**, is dirty; the Paseo Costera heading east along the bay ends at the much more attractive **La Ropa** beach. The **Playa Las Gatas** over some rocks at the south end of the bay, has good snorkeling. The cheap hotels are downtown, while the more upscale ones are found east along the Paseo Costera. The new **central bus station** is northeast of town near Mex 200.

Two roads lead from Zihuatenejo to Ixtapa five kilometers (three miles) west, the Camino Viejo and Mex 200—with frequent buses and relatively inexpensive taxis serving the route. **Paseo Ixtapa** is the resort zone's main avenue and passes the **18-hole golf course** at the entrance to Ixtapa. A line of huge hotels and condo complexes is built along the Playa del Palmar; just inland is a zone of malls, restaurants and discos that Fonatur, the Mexican tourist development agency, carefully restrains from overdevelopment. Big Pacific breakers crash directly onto the beach, and the undertow makes it too dangerous for swimming. The Paseo de las Garzas passes a line of condominiums and runs over a causeway to a rocky island just west of the hotel zone and ends at the Club Med and **Playa Linda**. There are secluded beaches along this road, and you have a great sunset view from the **lookout** at Punta Ixtapa. Excursion boats take snorkelers to the rocks offshore.

ACAPULCO

A steep range of coastal hills circles Acapulco Bay and provides a dramatic setting for the city of Acapulco (pop near 1,000,000), the oldest of Mexico's Pacific resorts. The city surrounds the bay and has also spread inland into the valley beyond the hills. Unfortunately, earthquakes, battles and rampant development have destroyed most of Acapulco's colonial monuments. Nevertheless, there are enough sights to fill a day of dedicated tourism. The real emphasis in Acapulco is on pleasure and relaxation; the city contains some of Mexico's most luxurious hotels, finest restaurants and flashiest discos. Acapulco's climate rarely changes: it's hot year round (rest at midday), and it rains—pours for a few hours every afternoon—in summer and early autumn.

The waterside **Avenida Costera Miguel Alemán**, called the 'Costera' for short, is Acapulco's main boulevard, and an enjoyable day (and night) can be spent just people-watching here. Taxis are plentiful and inexpensive; buses are rarer and dirt-cheap. The mid-point of this avenue is the **Ignacio Altamirano Park**, more popularly called Papagayo Park, which is more or less the dividing line between the old and new resort areas. Papagayo contains a small amusement park, open air restaurants and a popular public beach. Although Acapulco Bay is lined with beaches, swimming is not recommended because the waters are dirty—there's lots of floating garbage—and shark-infested. That doesn't faze the parasailers and jet skiers. Tourists on the beaches are continually pestered by vendors. The **Estrella de Oro bus station** is just northeast of Papagayo at the corner of Avdas Insurgentes and Cuauhtemoc. East of Papagayo, Miguel Alemán passes through the **main hotel strip**, with malls, restaurants and discos filling the spaces between the ultramodern multi-story edifices. Just beyond the **Acapulco Golf Club** on the left is the **Acapulco International Center**, which contains a small **archeological museum**, a **theater** and the state **tourism offices**. The **CiCi Acapulco children's park**, with water rides and dolphin shows, is two blocks further down Miguel Aleman on the right. Passing the enormous **Artesanías Finas de Acapulco**, a large crafts store, on the left, the avenue becomes the Scenic Highway and winds up into the hills. After a stunning view of the harbor from the **Las Brisas hotel**, one of the most expensive in Mexico, the highway heads east to the **airport**. More luxury hotels, including the enormous Acapulco Princess, lie in this direction.

Returning to Papagayo Park, Miguel Alemán heads west to old Acapulco. On the left is the regional **SECTUR (Secretaría de Turismo) office**. The street to the right, just past the supermarket, leads to the **Arena Coliseo** for boxing and professional wrestling. The vast **municipal market** is two blocks inland, at the corner of Avdas Mendoza and Cuauhtemoc. Miguel Alemán bulges around a small hill, on top of which sits the **San Diego Fort**, Acapulco's bulwark against foreign invaders and home-grown revolutionaries. The fort, which was reconstructed in 1783 after the 1776 earthquake, was repeatedly

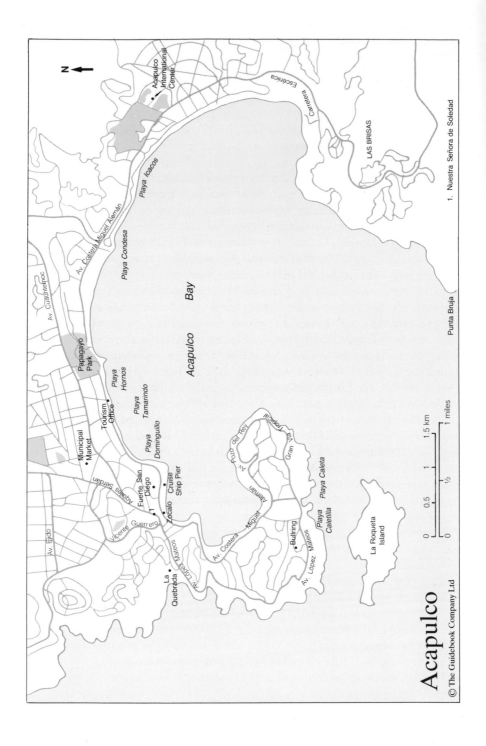

Acapulco

© The Guidebook Company Ltd

1. Nuestra Señora de Soledad

attacked by both sides during the 1810–20 Insurgency, by the French in 1863, and during the 1910–20 Revolution. Today it is the **Acapulco Historical Museum** (hours variable; most recently Tues–Sat, 10.30–4.30) and contains air-conditioned exhibits on Acapulco history and the *Nao de China*'s trade with the Orient. The fort is surrounded by a maze of tiny houses that gives visitors an idea of Acapulqueños' life away from the resort zone.

The **cruise ship docking pier** occupies the waterfront opposite the fort. Miguel Alemán next runs into the un-touristy **Zócalo**, the heart of downtown Acapulco. This slightly grubby tree-filled square is surrounded by cafés, cheaper hotels, gift shops, Woolworths and Sanborn's. At the north end of the Zócalo, the modern **Nuestra Señora de Soledad church** has a large white dome capping a blue and gold mosaic interior. Avenida López Mateos at the back of the church leads up the hill to **La Quebrada**, the jumping-off point for the famous divers of Acapulco. Since 1934, these divers have been jumping off the rocks from 35 meters (115 feet) high, and occasionally from points higher, into the dangerous surf below, bringing Acapulco more media coverage than any marketing campaign could possibly accomplish. There are performances at 1, 7.15, 8.15, 9.15 and 10.30 pm; the performances are especially dramatic at sunset onwards, when the divers hold torches. You can either watch the divers from the viewing platforms (admission fee collected by the divers' union) or from the patios of the Hotel El Mirador, which also charges admission unless you arrive early. La Quebrada is at the base of the **Peninsula de las Playas**, which forms the western arm of Acapulco Bay. A scenic road circumnavigates the peninsula, which is covered with mansions and condos, and eventually runs back into Avda Costera Miguel Alemán. The **bullring** stands at the south side of the peninsula; under the waters offshore off **Caleta** and **Caletilla beaches** stands the **Underwater Shrine of the Virgin of Guadalupe**, a popular dive spot. The **La Roqueta island**, with a beach and snorkeling, lies just beyond and is only accessible by boat.

Note: For the silver city of Taxco, see Morelos in 'Around Mexico City', p 90.

The North

Introduction

The North is the region of Mexico least visited by tourists. For that reason the area's stunning, largely barren scenery and bustling colonial cities are more attractive to some visitors. Others prefer the string of wild border towns that run along the US–Mexican frontier from the Gulf of Mexico to the Pacific. Lovers of empty and untouched desert can realize all their passions here.

The desert state of Sonora has the region's finest beaches, particularly around Guaymas, a modern capital in Hermosillo, and a string of little towns with 17th-century mission churches in the sierra. Mexico's turbulent history weighs heavily in Chihuahua: the capital is filled with beautiful colonial and 19th-century buildings and has excellent museums commemorating the Wars of Reform and the Revolution. The Wild West still lives here in the garb of the cowboys from the surrounding cattle ranches. The Copper Canyon train ride from Chihuahua to the Pacific passes through some of the wildest country in Mexico and is a must for any visitor to the area. Coahuila is largely farmland and empty desert, but the capital of Saltillo contains many small jewels of colonial architecture, like its Cathedral. Monterrey, the capital of Nuevo León, is Northern Mexico's powerhouse: a crowded, polluted, business-minded city with one of the highest per capita incomes in Mexico. Nevertheless, it has enough museums, colonial buildings, luxury hotels and gourmet restaurants to make a visit worthwhile. Tamaulipas is known for its rowdy border towns, empty beaches and the dirty yet thriving port of Tampico. Durango contains a fine colonial capital and rugged mountain scenery, which has been used as a backdrop for many Hollywood Westerns.

Getting There

Airplanes are the most efficient way to travel across the huge empty spaces between the sites of tourist interest in Northern Mexico. Nevertheless, the landscape is striking enough to justify a longer trip by car or bus. Mexicali, Nogales, Ciudad Juárez, Ojinaga, Piedras Negras, Nuevo Laredo, Reynosa and Matamoros are all terminals for the slow but scenic trains to Mexico City.

Sonora has five border crossings with the State of Arizona: San Luis Río Colorado, Sonoyta, Nogales, Naco and Agua Prieta. Mexico 2 runs along the border from San Luis Río Colorado, bends south to meet Mexico 15, returns to the border at Agua Prieta and heads east toward Ciudad Juárez. Mexico 15, which begins at Nogales and passes through Hermosillo and Guaymas, is the main Pacific coast highway, turning inland at Tepíc and ending in Mexico City. The Pacífico train lines from Mexicali and Nogales meet at Benjamín Hill and head south through Hermosillo and Guaymas to Guadalajara. Direct flights connect Hermosillo, the state capital, with Mexico City, Guadalajara, Chihuahua, Ciudad Obregón, Los Mochis, Tijuana and Tucson. There are flights to Guaymas from La Paz and Tucson. Guaymas also has a thrice-weekly car ferry that runs to Santa Rosalía in Baja California Sur.

Chihuahua is reached via car from New Mexico at Rodrigo M Quevedo, and from Texas at Ciudad Juárez, El Porvenir and Ojinaga. Mexico 45 begins at Ciudad Juárez, connects with Mexico 16 from Ojinaga at Chihuahua and heads south to Mexico City. The Division del Norte train service begins at Ciudad Juárez and passes through Chihuahua on its way south. Chihuahua is also the terminal (separate train station) for the Chihuahua–Pacífico railway, one of the most spectacular trips in Mexico, which runs down to Los Mochis on the coast. This train is the only way to go directly from Chihuahua to the Pacific by land, since the mountains are so rugged that no paved roads have been built. By air, Chihuahua may be reached from Ciudad Juárez, Hermosillo, Mexico City, Monterrey and Torreón. Direct flights from Chihuahua, Mexico City and Mazatlán also land at Ciudad Juárez.

Coahuila has border crossings with Texas at Acuna and Piedras Negras. Mexico 57 originates at Piedras Negras and heads south through Saltillo on its way to Mexico City. Mexico 40 connects Saltillo with Monterrey and Reynosa to the east, and to Mazatlán via Torreón and Durango to the west. Piedras Negras is the terminal for the Coahuilense train that runs to Saltillo and connects there with the Regiomontano service to Mexico City. The nearest large airport to Saltillo is Monterrey's, about two hours away.

A new border crossing was recently inaugurated at Columbia (close to President Salinas de Gortari's family home), giving Nuevo León its first direct connection with Texas. It's still quicker to get to Monterrey from Texas via Nuevo Laredo or the Reynosa area in Tamaulipas. Mexico 85, which begins at Nuevo Laredo, bisects the state north-south and connects Monterrey with Mexico City. Mexico 40, the main east–west route, runs from Reynosa to Mazatlán through Monterrey. The Regiomontano train originates at Nuevo Laredo and stops at Monterrey on its way south to Mexico City via San Luis Potosí. Monterrey has a major international airport, which is reached by direct flights from Cancún, Chicago, Chihuahua, Dallas, Guadalajara, Houston, Los Angeles, Mazatlán, Mexico City, San Luis Potosí and Tijuana.

Tamaulipas has major border crossings into Texas at Nuevo Laredo, Reynosa and Matamoros and four smaller ones along Mexico 2. The latter road parallels the border from Nuevo Laredo to Matamoros. Mexico 40 heads west from Reynosa through Monterrey all the way to the Pacific. Mexico 180 begins in Matamoros and runs along

Malgré Tout

Félix Maldonaldo hailed a one-peso cab and relaxed, the first client in this collective taxi. In front of the Cathedral, a man dressed in overalls was skimming a long aluminum tube above the paving stones. He was crowned by headphones connected to the tube and to a receiving apparatus strung across his chest and secured by suspenders. He was muttering something. The cab driver laughed and said, Now you've seen the Cathedral nut, he's been searching for Moctezuma's treasure for years.

The taxi stopped at every corner to pick up passengers. First, two nuns got in on the corner of Motolinía. He knew they were nuns by the hair severely drawn back into a bun, the absence of makeup, the black dresses, the rosaries and scapulars. Since they were forbidden to go out into the street wearing their habits, they'd found a new uniform. They chose to get in front with the driver. He treated them like old friends, as if he saw them every day. 'Hel-lo, Sisters, how's it going today?' The nuns giggled and blushed, covering their mouths with their hands, and one of them tried to catch Félix's eye in the rear-view mirror.

When the taxi stopped at Gante, Félix drew back his legs to make room for a girl dressed in white, a nurse. She carried cellophane-wrapped syringes, vials, and ampules. She asked Félix to slide over. He said no, he would be getting out soon. Where? At the Cuauhtémoc traffic circle across from the Hilton. Well, she was getting out before that, in front of the Hotel Reforma. Come on, she was in a hurry, she had to give an injection to a tourist, a gringo tourist dying of typhoid. Moctezuma's revenge, Félix said. What? Don't be a creep, move over. Félix said certainly not, a gentleman always gives his place to a lady. He got out of the taxi so the nurse could get in. She looked at him suspiciously while behind the peso cab a long line of taxis were tooting their horns.

'Step on it, they're about to climb up my ass,' the driver said.

'So who said chivalry's dead?' The nurse smiled and offered an Adams chiclet to Félix, who took it, not to offend her. And he made no *effort to press against the girl. He respected the empty space between them. It wasn't empty long. In front of the Palacio de Bellas Artes, a dark, fat woman stopped the taxi. To prove to the nurse that he was gallant with ugly as well as pretty women, Félix attempted to get out, but the fat woman was in too much of a hurry. She was carrying a brimming basket, which she lifted into the taxi. She sprawled face-down across Félix's legs, her head plowing silently into the nurse's lap. The nuns giggled. The fat woman propped her basket on Félix's knees and, groaning, struggled to seat herself. Dozens of peeping yellow chicks erupted from the basket, swarming around Félix's feet and climbing his shoulders. Félix was afraid he was going to crush them.*

The fat woman settled into her seat, clutching the empty basket. When she saw that the chicks had gotten out, she flung the basket aside, striking the nuns, grabbed Félix by the neck, and flailing about, tried to collect the chicks. Félix's face was plastered with feathers like adolescent down.

Ahead, a student with a pile of books under his arm was flagging down the taxi. The driver slowed to pick him up. Félix protested, sneezing through a myriad of feathers, and the nurse seconded him. There wasn't room. Four could ride in the back. 'In the front too,' one of the nuns giggled. And when the fat woman shrieked, 'God help us, the chicks have escaped,' one of the nuns giggled, 'Did she say God help us, we're about to be raped?' The driver said he had to make his living any way he could and anyone who didn't like it could get out and get a taxi all to himself, two and a half pesos before the meter ever started ticking.

The student approached the halted taxi, running lightly in his tennis shoes in spite of his load of books. He ran with both arms crossed over his chest. Maldonaldo, hissing in protest, noted this curious detail. A girl with a head of tight curls emerged from behind a statue whose pedestal bore the inscription 'Malgré tout'—in spite of every-thing. She grabbed the student's hand and the two piled into the rear of the taxi. They said excuse me, but inevitably stepped on several chicks. The fat woman shrieked again, struck at the student with her basket, and the girl asked whether this was a taxi or a mobile food-stamp market. Félix dreamily gazed at the receding statue, a marble

continues

woman in an abject posture, naked, poised for the outrage of sodomy, 'Malgré tout'.

Books spilled to the floor, killing more chicks, as the student perched on the nurse's knees. She didn't seem to mind. Félix took his eyes from the statue to glare with scorn and anger at the nurse through the crook of the fat woman's arm, and pulled the student's girlfriend towards him, forcing her onto her knees. The girl slapped him and called to the student: 'The pig's trying to feel me up, Emiliano.' The student took advantage of the diversion to turn to the nurse, wink, and stroke the back of her knees. 'Are we going to have to get out,' he said to Félix, 'and settle things? You're asking for it, not me.'

The student spoke in a nasal voice, his girl urging him on: 'Let him have it, Emiliano'; and Emiliano: 'Keep your hands off my baby.' Through the open window, a lottery vendor thrust under Félix's nose a handful of black and purple sheets still smelling of fresh ink. 'Here's your dream come true, señor. Ending in seven. So you can marry this nice lady.' 'What lady?' Félix retorted with assumed innocence. 'You're looking for trouble and you're going to get it,' growled the student. The nuns giggled and asked to get out. The girlfriend noticed that the student was eyeing the nurse with interest and said, 'Let's get up in front, Emiliano.'

As the nuns were climbing out, the student got out of the left side of the taxi to avoid stumbling over Félix, and the driver said, 'Don't go out on that side, you stupid jerk, I'm the one who'll get the fine.' The girlfriend with her head like a woolly black sheep pinched Félix's knee on the way. Only Félix noticed in the midst of the confusion that the giggling nuns had stopped beside one of the many statues of heroes along the Paseo de la Reforma. One of them raised her skirts and whirled her leg as if dancing the can-can. The taxi shot away, leaving the student and his girl scuffling in the middle of the street. Then he remembered his books, shouted, 'The books', and ran after the taxi, but couldn't catch up.

Carlos Fuentes, *The Hydra Head*, translated by M S Peden

the Gulf coast via Tampico all the way to Cancún. The Tamaulipeco train line travels from Matamoros to Reynosa and Monterrey, where it connects with the Regiomontano line to Mexico City. Tamaulipas' largest airports are at Matamoros, Nuevo Laredo and Tampico, all with direct flights from Mexico City.

The city of Durango is reached by Mexico 45 from Ciudad Juárez to the north and Zacatecas to the south. Mexico 40 passes through the city on its way to Mazatlán from Reynosa via Torreón. The section between Durango and Mazatlán traverses stunning mountain scenery, which approaches but does not quite equal that along the Chihuahua-Pacífico railway. Trains run from Durango to Zacatecas with a change at Pescador. Durango's international airport is served by flights from Mazatlán and Mexico City.

State of Sonora

Before the arrival of the Spaniards, the vast arid reaches of northern Mexico were occupied by a loose association of tribes known as the Desert Culture. These nomadic, warlike hunter-gatherers, called the Chichimec by the Aztecs, fiercely resisted attempts at subjugation by the 'civilized' south. The northwest was inhabited by tribes that were affiliated not with Mexico but with the kiva-building cultures of the southwestern United States. The apex of these groups in Mexico was Paquimé, a highly-developed city near Casas Grandes in northern Chihuahua, which for two centuries was the crucial trade link between Aztecs and the southwest.

The first Europeans to travel across northern Mexico were Alvar Núñez Cabeza de Vaca, two companions and an African slave, who were the only survivors of a 1528 shipwreck on the Texas coast. Cabeza de Vaca's party wandered across the southwest and northern Mexico for eight years, dependent on the Indians for food, water and clothing, before arriving at Culiacán on the Pacific Coast in 1536. The authorities eagerly questioned them about the existence of Cibola, a fabled country with seven cities of gold; Cabeza de Vaca confirmed that they had heard of cities to the north of their route. Cabeza de Vaca later conquered Paraguay and died in a Madrid jail. His tales lived on to fuel another Spanish rush for mythic gold and led to the colonization of the southern half of North America.

No state in Mexico had a longer and bloodier history of European-Indian confrontation than Sonora. It was the home of the Pima, Opoto, Papago and Yaqui tribes, who came under the influence of the Paquimé culture. In 1531 and 1533, Spanish expeditions reached Sonora but were repelled by the indigenous tribes, particularly the Yaquis, who didn't stop fighting the Spanish and their descendants until 1910. After Cabeza de Vaca emerged from the desert in 1536, the viceroy sent Francisco Vázquez de Coronado to find the mythic cities of gold. He marched through Sonora all the way to Great Bend, Kansas, but only returned with tales of 'shaggy cows'—buffaloes. No Spanish settlements took hold until 1563, when Francisco de Ibarra entered Sonora from Durango and constructed a line of *presidios* (small forts) in the sierra. In the 17th century, the Jesuits led by Father Francisco Eusebio Kino began missionizing Mexico's northwest and had to face fierce Indian resistance. The colonizing of Sonora finally picked up momentum in the 1700s, after gold and silver mines were found in the mountains. In the unsettled period after Mexico's independence, settlers faced almost continual raids by Yaquis, Papagos and Apaches forced out of the north by American ranchers. William Walker, the American adventurer, tried to form an independent Republic of Sonora in 1853, but was defeated by Mexican soldiers and forced to flee to San Diego. During Porfírio Díaz' reign, foreign copper companies purchased the major mines in Sonora, and the rebellious Yaquis were rounded up and sent as slave labor to the henequen plantations of distant Yucatán, where many of them died. They returned after Díaz was defeated in 1911 and fought in the revolutionary army of Alvaro Obregón, beginning their integration into Mexican life. Hermosillo, Sonora's capital, was originally an Indian village named Pitic; in the 18th century it became a Jesuit mission and then a *presidio*. Named after a general

San Carlos, Sonora

in the War of Independence, Hermosillo is the center of a rich farming district. Guaymas, which was discovered by Francisco de Ulloa in 1539, became the port for Sonora's mines during the 19th century. The US Navy bombarded it in 1846, William Walker looted the town in 1853, and the French occupied it between 1865 and 1866. Tourism is increasingly important for Guaymas, but the port and a large copper smelter are the main industries.

THE BORDER

Northern Sonora is a landscape of forbidding barrenness. Between **San Luis Río Colorado** (tourist motels and nightlife) and **Sonoyta** (motel), Mexico 2 passes through pancake-flat desert and a moonscape of black rock hills dotted with cacti. The border here is a waist-high fence; in the evening young Mexicans carrying jugs of water jump it and take their chances with the US Border Patrol and the desert heat. The road turns south through **Caborca**, which has a mission church built by the renowned Jesuit, Eusebio Kino. In 1857, a group of American mercenaries led by H A Crabb attacked the town; after six days of fighting they were captured and executed. The latter event is celebrated every year on April 6. Mexico 2 then reaches Mexico 15, the Pacific Coast highway from Nogales. On the Arizona border, **Nogales** is a major freight crossing, founded in 1882 with the arrival of the railway. The main street is Avenida Obregón, which begins at the border and is lined with tourist-oriented bars, restaurants and hotels. Further east on Mexico 2 is the smaller border town of **Agua Prieta**, across from Douglas, Arizona. Built by the railway on the line that shipped copper ore from Sonoran mines to US refineries, it contains the usual border town amusements on a small scale. Mexico 2 continues east through the desert to the state of Chihuahua.

HERMOSILLO

Mexico 15 heads south through scrub covered desert to Hermosillo, the state capital. In the center of an agricultural district, Hermosillo is a clean, wealthy, city (pop 700,000) whose expansion has been fueled by a new Ford Motors plant. In summer it is extremely hot. The outer suburbs have strip shopping malls, fast food and gaudy Chinese restaurants, giving the town an American feel. Hermosillo is dominated by the **Cerro de la Campana**, a pointed hill with a vista on top. The old center of town is the tree-lined **Plaza de Zaragoza**. On one side is the white-washed **Cathedral of the Ascension** (1779), with a large dome on a rather small base. The **Palacio del Gobierno** nearby has a startling neo-Futurist mural on the ground level and a realistic but apocalyptic view of Sonoran history on the second floor. The new center of town is the **Boulevard Eusebio Kino**, which heads northeast from the Plaza de Zaragoza, passes the entrance to the train station and becomes the road to Nogales. This avenue is lined with upscale hotels, restaurants and shops. Other points of interest are the **University of Sonora**, one of the best in northern Mexico, and the **Museum of Sonora**, which is housed in a large mausoleum-like building and contains a locally famous **mummy**. The nearest beach to Hermosillo is **Bahía Kino**, 107 kilometers (66 miles) to the west.

GUAYMAS
On the coast 143 kilometers (89 miles) south of Hermosillo, the port city of Guaymas nestles against a rocky peninsula along the north side of Guaymas Bay. It is home to one of Mexico's largest fishing fleets (and accompanying fish-packing plants) as well as a smoke-belching copper refinery and a large power plant. The **Church of San Fernando**, built by Jesuits in 1751, is the main attraction downtown. The **Palacio Municipal** near the bus station is built in the shape of a castle and has a reputation among locals as being a den of thieves. Most tourists in the area stay in **Bahía de San Carlos**, 22 kilometers (14 miles) north of Guaymas. American-style hotels, a Club Med and campgrounds are built on the beaches around this bay lined with barren rock hills. *Catch-22* was filmed here, as film buffs will soon recognize.

State of Chihuahua

Chihuahua, the largest state in Mexico, was inhabited in the south by Desert Culture tribes and in the north by the Paquimé culture, part of the Mogollan tradition of the American Southwest. Paquimé, now called Casas Grandes, was the most highly developed city in Northern Mexico. Its ceremonial plazas, temples and ball courts strongly resemble those found in the Valley of Mexico. Archeologists have found storage rooms filled with turquoise and pens that they think held parrots and macaws from the south. Paquimé's development began around AD 1060, when envoys from Central Mexico visited the city and fashioned it into a center for trading ceremonial commodities between north and south. For unknown reasons Paquimé began to decline around AD 1261, and after a disastrous fire in 1340, the city was abandoned. Cabeza de Vaca passed through Ciudad Juárez in 1533 or 1534, but it wasn't until 1563 and Francisco de Ibarra's exploration of Nuevo Vizcaya (Durango and Chihuahua) that Spanish settlement began. Rich mines were discovered in the sierra but the Spanish had to battle continuous Indian raids to profit from them. The Jesuits and the Franciscans divided the territory for evangelization, the former taking the sierra and the latter taking the plains, where many were killed by Apaches.

During the 18th century, *presidios* were built to protect the mines and the huge cattle estates from the Indians. In 1811, after their capture near Monclova, Coahuila, the insurgent revolutionaries, Miguel Hidalgo, Ignacio Allende and Juan Aldama, were taken to

Chihuahua, tried and executed by firing squad on the site of the present Palacio del Gobierno. Over the next century Chihuahua was the scene of many foreign invasions and locally bred revolutionary battles. The only time of peace came under the Porfiriato, when the poor were worked to death on the flourishing cattle estates and mines. The US army invaded in 1847, Juárez and his government were chased around the state by French forces from 1864 to 1866, and numerous important battles were fought here during the 1910–20 Revolution, when Pancho Villa made Chihuahua the stronghold of his army. In 1916, Villa raided Columbus, New Mexico and President Wilson sent a punitive expedition under General Pershing to punish the Mexicans. They wandered around the Chihuahuan desert for weeks, unable to find Villa, and finally withdrew. Today, the state is peaceful, although the Wild West tradition endures.

Ciudad Juárez
Ciudad Juárez, across the Río Bravo (known as the Río Grande in the US) from El Paso, Texas, is the second largest border city (pop over 1,000,000) after Tijuana. It is hot in the summer, cold in winter, crowded and dusty. On the outskirts are many American and Japanese-owned *maquiladora* (assembly) plants. The border area was the site of a recent US-Mexican land dispute over a sudden oxbow that formed in the Río Bravo and caused Mexico to lose a few acres of land. After years of negotiations, the US recently returned it to Mexicans, who have constructed a patriotic park on the site. Travelers enter Juárez from El Paso via the Santa Fé Street or Stanton Street bridges. Immigration is at the latter, if you're traveling further into Mexico. The downtown is centered on the **Plaza Principal**, with the **Cathedral**, which is built on the site of the original mission, on one side and the **Palacio Municipal** on the other. Ciudad Juárez' new **Museum** is intended as an introduction to Mexico for tourists. The city's entertainment possibilities are manifold: gift shops, restaurants, cantinas, the famous horse racing track, a *jai alai frontón* (pelota court) and an enormous red light district. Visitors looking for the more dangerous types of fun should know that Ciudad Juárez has the highest murder rate in Mexico. The cheaper hotels are downtown, while the upscale ones are in the new shopping malls and along the Paseo Triunfo de la República, south of town.

Casas Grandes
The Paquimé ruins are most easily reached from Ciudad Juárez on Mexico 2 west, and then turning south on Mexico 23 at the town of Janos. From Chihuahua it's a four- to five-hour journey via Mexico 45 north, and then turning east just before El Sueco. **Nuevo Casas Grandes**, the nearest large town (hotels), was founded in the early 1900s by a breakaway Mormon sect that wanted to continue practising polygamy. The **Paquimé ruins** are next to the town of **Casas Grandes**, seven kilometers (four miles) to

(*above*) *Cusarare Falls in the Barranca de Cobre, Chihuahua;*
(*below left*) *Tarahumara cave dwelling;* (*below right*) *Tarahumara elder*

*Tarahumara Easter Fiesta: (above left and right) The Pharisees;
(below) Pharisees soldiers on the Way of the Cross*

the west. On the site may be seen adobe communal houses once five storeys high, platform temple mounds, pyramids, plazas, a Mesoamerican-style ball court and a complicated system of stone-lined channels that brought water to every building. The sun can be intense; wear a hat.

CHIHUAHUA

Set squarely in the middle of the state, the city of Chihuahua (pop 800,000) abuts the foothills of the Sierra Madre Occidental to the west and the high central desert to the east. Chihuahua is built along the banks of the small Río Chuvíscar, and most of the sights are within walking distance. Travelers wishing to take the scenic train through the Copper Canyon to the Pacific should buy tickets immediately on arrival. The crowded **bus station** near the river is always a colorful scene. Here sober-looking Mennonite families in overalls and blue dresses and bonnets mingle with barefoot, round-faced Tarahumara Indian women in bright, gypsy-like skirts with many petticoats. The **Plaza de Armas**, the main square, is a few blocks walk uphill through the red light district. At night the power lines and window sills around the square are covered with thousands of swallows; they have inspired 'Las Golondrinas', a nostalgic song about Chihuahua.

The twin towers of the baroque **Cathedral** (built 1724–1826), one of the finest churches in northern Mexico, soar above an ornate façade. The other sides of the Plaza de Armas are occupied by mansions built by landowners and industrialists under Porfírio Díaz and now turned into banks. Behind the Cathedral the streets are lined with cowboy wear and boots stores. Most of the customers are authentic cowboys from the surrounding cattle ranches. East of the plaza, **Calle Libertad** is a pedestrian walkway lined with shoe stores and ice cream parlors. The **Museo Casa de Juárez** (Mon–Fri, 9–4.30) on Calle Juárez is a colonial house in which President Juárez lived during the French intervention in the 1860s. The **Palacio Federal** on Avenida Carranza has a small museum in the basement, which displays the cell where the revolutionary priest, Miguel Hidalgo, was held prior to his execution. The actual site of his death on July 30, 1811 is marked by a shrine next door in the **Palacio del Gobierno**, a big Porfiriato edifice. The **Regional Museum** at 401, 4th St is an ornate Victorian-style mansion decorated with Greco-Roman, Art Nouveau and Louis XV flourishes. Built by a wealthy engineer in 1907, it was quarters for Pancho Villa and Venustiano Carranza at different times during the Revolution. The museum has rotating exhibitions and a small display of Paquimé pots on the second floor. Among the notable decorations are the Little Red Riding Hood-inspired children's room and the Art Nouveau toilet paper holder in the parent's bathroom.

Quinta Luz, a rambling house in a nearby residential neighborhood, was the home of Pancho Villa and Luz Corral, his official wife (he fathered children by at least 26 other women), and is now an excellent museum devoted to Villa and the Revolution. Prominently displayed is the bullet-riddled 1922 Dodge in which Villa was assassinated on July

20, 1923 in Hidalgo de Parral. The first floor is devoted to his bedroom, study and dining room, all originally furnished; on the second floor are exhibits of weapons, saddles, photos and other artefacts of the Revolution. The **Centro Cultural Chihuahua**, in a Porfiriato palace at Calle Aldama and Avda Ocampo, has a good exhibition of the Paquimé Culture from Casas Grandes on the second floor. The **main train station** for the Ciudad Juárez–Mexico City line is north of downtown, at the corner of Avda Tecnológico and Avda División del Norte. The **Chihuahua–Pacífico train station** is south, behind the prison at 20th Street and Calle Mendez. Travelers hoping to see a chihuahua (the breed of dog) in Chihuahua are almost always disappointed.

COPPER CANYON TRAIN

The 673-kilometer (417-mile) train ride between Chihuahua and Los Mochis on the Pacific Coast is the most spectacular rail journey in Mexico. It is also the quickest way to go by land from Chihuahua to the coast. Originally conceived in the 19th century, the Chihuahua–Pacífico railway, which passes through some of the roughest country in Mexico, was completed in 1961. The heart of the trip is called the Barranca del Cobre (the 'Copper Canyon', after a copper mine), but is more properly known as the Sierra del Tarahumara, after the local Indian tribe. In this sierra a network of five major canyons (each of which is deeper than the Grand Canyon at some point) drains into the Río Fuerte. Due to this terrain, the Tarahumara, who call themselves the Raramuri, may be the least assimilated Indian tribe in Mexico; they still live a deeply traditional life. A running Tarahumara is the logo of the railway. Four trains, two first-class (buy tickets in advance) and two second, ply the route daily in each direction. First class leaves Los Mochis and Chihuahua at 7 am, and second class departs an hour later. Vendors sell water and other provisions at embarkation. First class, which provides air-conditioning, comfortable reserved seats and a dining car, takes 13 to 14 hours, while second class takes at least 17 hours and is, said a local, 'very dirty'. To enjoy it, he added, 'bring lots to eat, lots to drink and a guitar, and don't mind that you're barely moving along'. The best seats are on the left heading to Los Mochis, and on the right in the other direction.

The railway crosses 39 bridges and goes through 86 tunnels. After leaving Chihuahua, the train winds through a rich agricultural zone in the center of which is the city of **Cuauhtemoc**. This community was founded in 1921 by Mennonites, a Protestant sect from Northern Germany who immigrated here to escape oppression. They were given a huge land grant by President Alvaro Obregón and have made the valley the most productive in Mexico. Four hours out, the train enters pine-forested canyons and valleys. Logging is the major legitimate industry in the sierra (marijuana cultivation and drug smuggling are the main illegitimate ones). At 2,430 meters (8,000 feet), **San Juanita**, a lumber town smelling of resin, is the coldest town in Mexico. **Creel** (pop 5,000), named after a Chihuahua governor, is the largest town in the sierra and has a gift store in the Tarahu-

MEXICAN MURALS

It is inevitable that Mexico should be covered with murals. Its block and cement walls are covered with huge expanses of plaster: the natural canvas for the muralist.

Muralism's antecedents in Mexico are ancient. Mesoamerican temples and pyramids were covered with plaster and painted in bright colors. Remarkably preserved murals depicting battles and the glorification of rulers may still be seen at the site of Cacaxtla in the State of Tlaxcala. After the fall of Tenochtitlán, the conquistadors destroyed all the murals they could find, considering them pagan idolatry. Nevertheless, the mural tradition lived on, because Spanish evangelists, in desperate need of Catholic images as instructional aids for the masses of new converts, enlisted Indian artists to cover the walls of the newly built fortified convents. During the 17th- and 18th-century ascendancy of the baroque and churrigueresque style, muralism fell out of favor because artists preferred to cover the walls with architectural ornament and sculpture rather than paint. By Independence, mural painting techniques had essentially been forgotten.

Muralism's revival began at the end of Mexico's century-long spasm of often violent self-discovery, which commenced after Independence in 1821. The muralists' artistic inspiration was the work of the newspaper lithographer, José Guadalupe Posada (1852–1913), whose prints of accidents, murders, hangings and fiestas were the only art that reflected the real Mexico of the streets. The artistic élite of the time painted in the manner of European schools like the Impressionists, and their work had almost no Mexican characteristics. The spark for the revival of mural painting was lit by a radical painter and teacher known as Dr Atl, who had admired the great church murals of Europe and knew of the Mesoamerican tradition. He encouraged his students at the Academy of San Carlos, including José Clemente Orozco, to develop a new, monumental, public and popular art that communicated through the medium of murals. Their plans were interrupted by the Revolution, which had a crucial effect on young artists' training.

continues

Insurgent firebrand Miguel Hidalgo depicted in an
Orozco mural in the Palacio del Gobierno, Guadalajara

The Revolution destroyed Mexico's rigid social and economic hierarchies. All the ethnic groups were stirred around as if in a great pot and, for the first time, they were forced to confront each other face to face. Peasant revolutionaries from Morelos rode into Mexico City wearing broad *sombreros* and ate in downtown restaurants with bandoliers strapped to their chests. For the first time, the young art students became aware of the richness and complexity of their culture. Their experiences during the Revolution, either working for Dr Atl's consitutionalist newspaper or actually fighting in the army, also politicized the artists. After the fighting stopped, they wanted to continue the Revolution through other means, and many of them became Marxists.

In 1922, José Vasconcelos, the militant Secretary of Education, commissioned a group of young artists to decorate the walls of the National Preparatory School in Mexico City. The first task of this group, which included Diego Rivera, José Clemente Orozco and David Alfaro Siquieros—the three greatest Mexican muralists—was actually to figure out how to paint murals, because the techniques had been lost. Their earliest efforts were not always successful and some have all but disappeared. However, within a few months, the muralists began to show progress both in technique and subject matter.

The National Preparatory School murals fulfilled two out of three of Dr Atl's requirements for the new art: they were monumental and they were public. Here were bold, larger-than-life figures placed on a huge expanse of wall for the greatest dramatic effect. The subject matter was often simplistically didactic: the horrors of war, the corruption of the Europeanized upper classes, the evil of Cortés and the conquistadors and the essential virtue of the poor, oppressed Indian peasants and factory workers. The Aztec civilization was looked back on as a Utopian idyll.

The public reaction to these first murals was uniformly negative; people did not mind the agitprop content so much as the crude style—they thought it ugly. All three of the great muralists were forced to spend significant periods abroad until the outcry over their works died down. They returned when the administration changed and new political protectors emerged to give them commissions. Nevertheless, the influence of time and international attention gradually began to change public perceptions. Mexicans realized that the muralists had taken

continues

(*above*) Child Hero of Chapultepec, *mural in Chapultepec Castle, Mexico City;*
(*below*) 19th-century tequila manufacture, *mural at the Sauza distillery, Jalisco*

great steps in building a national identity based not on foreign models but on Mexico's glorious past and rich culture. Today, Mexican muralism is viewed as a true reflection of the soul of 20th-century Mexico and, along with Mesoamerican art and churrigueresque architecture, is considered one of the great artistic achievements of the Mexican people.

Orozco The dark, expressionistic paintings of José Clemente Orozco (1883–1949) are the least political and most emotion-filled of the 'Big Three' Mexican muralists. Born in the State of Jalisco, he moved to Mexico City as a child and, while walking to and from school, used to gaze into the window of Posada's printing office and watch the master at work. In the early 1930s, in order to escape the constant public protests against his work, he traveled to the US, where he painted murals at Pomono College in California and Dartmouth College in New Hampshire. When he returned, he was commissioned to decorate various public buildings in Guadalajara and, over the next few years, created his masterworks there. Orozco based his subjects on the same themes as the other muralists—Mexico's Indian heritage, the conquistadors, the fight for independence—but his treatments were open to many more interpretations. For example, his looming green and gray portrait of Cortés with legs made from steel girders in Guadalajara's Hospital Cabañas is seen by some as a portrait of a monster, but by others as a depiction of naked (not necessarily evil) power. This intensely personal vision, combined with a superlative command of technique, has led many critics to call Orozco the most complete artist of all the muralists.

Rivera Diego Rivera (1885–1957) was the most flamboyant character in 20th-century Mexican culture. He was born in the conservative Catholic city of Guanajuato and showed artistic promise early. After his family moved to Mexico City, he enrolled at the Academy of San Carlos; he became a star pupil and won a grant to study abroad. Rivera lived in Europe from 1907 to 1921, befriended the great intellectuals and artists of the time, including Apollinaire, Cocteau and Picasso, and was soon adept in the latest artistic styles, particularly Cubism. However, when he returned to Mexico, he favored a style that was purely Mexican in both form and content. Rivera's greatest murals, like those in the Secretariat of Education and the National Palace in Mexico City, illustrate his boundless energy and imagination. During his life he covered literally hundreds of thousands of meters of wall with works that depict the richness of traditional Mexico and the corruption of international capitalism. Wherever he traveled, scandal followed him, either because of the radical themes in his paintings—he used to paint with a revolver at his waist for protection—or because of his tempestuous personal life. His great love was the painter, Frida Kahlo, but that did not prevent him from having many other affairs. Politically, Rivera was a diehard leftist for most of his career, but his inability to toe the party line got him ejected from the Communist Party. He also flirted briefly with fascism, and when the big public commissions dried up at the end of his life, he became a portraitist and the darling of Mexican society. As the scandals and politics recede into history, Rivera's great respect for the fecundity and beauty of Mexican culture shines forth undimmed.

Siquieros David Alfaro Siquieros (1896–1974) was a man of action. His brushes were often laid down for years at a time while he pursued his often violent career as a political activist. Born in Chihuahua, he moved to Mexico City, enrolled at the Academy of San Carlos and soon became embroiled in a strike for which he was sent to jail at the age of 13—the first of many occasions. During the Revolution, he enlisted in the consitutionalist army and worked his way up the ranks, becoming a lieutenant while still a teenager. Siquieros organized his fellow muralists at the National Preparatory School into a trade union and soon was a national leader of left-wing unions. As an artist, he was fascinated by the latest technology. On his return from a trip to the US, he brought with him spray guns, resins and industrial paints, using them to create bright, three-dimensional murals with violent, didactic images. A devoted Stalinist, Siquieros fought in the Spanish Civil War. On his return, he participated in the 1940 machine-gun attack on the Mexico City home of León Trotsky, which left one person dead but Trotsky unharmed (he was successfully assassinated a few months later). It seemed that the only time Siquieros had to paint was when he was in jail. His activism continued to the end of his life; at the age of 64, he was imprisoned for four years for attempting to overthrow President López Mateos. Siquieros' greatest work, his Polyforum next to the Hotel Mexico in Mexico City, was the culmination of his fascination with new materials and techniques (aluminum, resins and three-dimensional murals) and of his commitment to revolutionary politics. The title of the Polyforum is 'The March of Humanity from Earth to the Cosmos: Misery and Science.'

mara Mission, a bank and a few hotels. At the **Hotel Parador de la Montaña** you can organize excursions on horse or by foot into the canyons. From Creel an occasionally paved road winds through the sierra to numerous small Tarahumara villages. For hours the train runs along a ridge offering only tantalizing glimpses of the network of canyons below. Finally, at **Divisadero del Barranca** the ground drops away into the main canyon. The train stops for 20 minutes; from the lookout you can see the jungled canyon floor at least 1,000 meters (3,300 feet) below. Indian vendors sell crafts, mostly basketry, and food to the passengers. The **Cabañas Divisadero Barrancas** hotel is perched on the cliff next to the lookout. Four kilometers (2.5 miles) further on there is a stop at the castle-like **Posada Barrancas Hotel**. After a smelly maintenance stop at San Rafael, the train comes to **Cuiteco**, a small town with a 1684 mission in the middle of apple orchard country.

Then the train begins its precipitous drop to sea level, and the air becomes warmer and the vegetation tropical. **Bahuichivo** is the pickup point for the **Hotel Misión** in Cerocahui, a scenic village on the rim of the enormous Urique Canyon. The train enters the steep and narrow canyon of the Río Septentrion; the next three hours are the most stunning of the trip. Huge rock walls soar above the canyon bottom and far above you may see the tracery of waterfalls cascading hundreds of feet. (The sharp-eyed may also see the occasional wreckage of freight trains in the river below.) The train passes a sign commemorating the inauguration of the railway (you can't see it until you are past it), enters the longest tunnel (935 meters, or 3,074 feet) of the trip and then loops down to the town of **Temoris**, founded in 1677 by missionaries. Towering cones of rock loom above the town like battlements. For the next two hours along the canyon there's no sign of human habitation except railworkers' huts. The canyon floor is covered with jungle in which parrots may be glimpsed. The train rolls out into a wider valley and cuts through some foothills that mark the beginning of the state of Sinaloa. After a long haul across a depressing scrub-covered plain as the sun sets, the first-class train reaches Los Mochis about 8.30 pm (one-hour time change). Forty-eight kilometers (30 miles) before Los Mochis is the station at **San Blas**, where the Chihuahua–Pacífico line meets the Pacific Coast line between Mexicali and Tepic. Buses for the major hotels meet passengers at the Los Mochis station.

HIDALGO DEL PARRAL

On the road to Durango in the southern part of Chihuahua is the historical town of **Hidalgo de Parral**. Founded in 1629 as a mining town, it was capital of the province of Nueva Vizcaya (comprising Durango and Chihuahua) from 1640 to 1731. Many of Chihuahua's Indians were enslaved to work the mines. It was briefly Juárez' capital in 1865. On July 20, 1923, Pancho Villa and five of his bodyguards drove through Hidalgo de Parral and were slain in an ambush that was implicitly approved by Mexico City. The

Wine festival, Coahuila

Museo de Pancho Villa in the public library has a large collection of photos and other mementoes of his life. The **Templo de San Nicolás**, founded in 1629, was the site of a mass hanging of rebel Indian leaders in 1676. The **Templo de Nuestra Señora del Rayo** ('Church of Our Lady of Lightning'), finished in 1728, was partially financed—according to legend—by a Tarahumara Indian, who appeared every week with a ball of gold in his hands and then disappeared into the hills.

State of Coahuila

The high plateau of Coahuila was occupied by little-known Desert Culture tribes before the arrival of the Spanish. Missionaries were the first explorers of the territory but Indian resistance slowed the process of colonization. Saltillo was founded in 1575 and became the economic center for the state's cattle ranches. Saltillo's annual fair, still active today, was the most important trade fair for northern Mexico and attracted goods from Europe and Asia as well as other parts of Mexico. During the early 19th century, Saltillo became the capital of the merged territories of Coahuila and Texas, which led to political friction between American settlers and Spanish authorities. After the US invasion in 1846, in which Saltillo was occupied, and the Treaty of 1848, Texas was separated for good from Coahuila.

In 1909, a Coahuila politician, Francisco I Madero, published a book called *The Presidential Succession of 1910*, which heralded the imminent collapse of Díaz' dictatorship. The shock waves from this book led to an armed rebellion and Díaz' defeat and exile. Madero went on to become president. After he was assassinated by Victoriano Huerta, Coahuila's governor, Venustiano Carranza, proclaimed the beginning of an armed struggle to overthrow Huerta. In 1914, the cotton and industrial town of Torreón was the site of Pancho Villa's greatest victory at the head of Carranza's forces. For five days Villa's men attacked Huerta's strongly entrenched troops and finally, through sheer bravery and savage fighting, forced them to withdraw. Later, Villa and Carranza became mortal enemies, and Villa relied on the people of Coahuila, particularly Torreón, to provide the money and supplies to furnish his army. During the presidency of Lázaro Cárdenas, the cotton fields around Torreón were the site of the most ambitious of Cárdenas's land redistribution programs; over 8 million acres of prime farmland along with new schools and hospitals were given to the peasants.

Coahuila is one of the least populous states in Mexico. **Ciudad Acuña** and **Piedras Negras**, the state's two border towns, are opposite Del Río and Eagle Pass, Texas, respectively, and offer numerous cantinas, restaurants, motels and gift shops. **Monclova**, 250 kilometers (154 miles) south, possesses the enormous Altos Hornos iron- and steel-making complex, one of the largest in Mexico. In 1811, Miguel Hidalgo and the other leaders of the Insurgency against the Spanish were captured nearby.

In the south of Coahuila and one to two hours west of Monterrey, **Saltillo** (pop 650,000) is a popular weekend destination for *regiomontanos* (Monterrey residents) seeking to escape pollution and traffic jams. The air is clear and the city has a relaxed pace, even though it is the state capital. The **Cathedral**, constructed between 1746 and 1800, is a masterpiece of the churrigueresque style. The façade is ornately carved and above it rise twin towers with fluted columns. Across the street is the red stone **Palacio del Gobierno** (1808), with copious murals by Tarazona, a Spanish painter. **Avenida Allende**, which turns into **Boulevard Venustiano Carranza**, is Saltillo's main street and leads to the **Alameda**, a large park shaded by many trees. Saltillo's most famous craft items are *serapes*, which are for sale at the **Mercado Juárez**, two blocks south of the Cathedral. The 9 bus leaves from the side of the market to the **Central Bus Station** (good roast goat restaurant across the street), northwest of town. The mid-range hotels are downtown, while the expensive ones are on the Paseo de la Reforma, heading east toward the **fairgrounds** (the fair is in August). **El Tapanco** at 225, Allende Sur, near the Cathedral, has the best local cuisine.

Torreón, in the southwest corner of Coahuila, is an overgrown farm town, which also has the largest copper refinery in Mexico. It is in the middle of the La Laguna agricultural district on the banks of the Río Nazas, opposite the twin cities of Gómez Palacio and Ciudad Lerdo in the state of Durango. On a hill above the cities stands a **15-meter (50-foot) concrete Christ** embracing the scene with outstretched arms. Torreón's broad streets are laid out on a widely spaced grid, giving it the feel of a city in the American Midwest. There are no particular tourist sights in Torreón, although the tree-lined **Alameda** is a nice place to stroll on hot days. The most charming hotel in town is the **Río Nazas**, a highrise whose decor hasn't changed since the 1950s. Sam Peckinpah's *The Wild Bunch* was filmed around Torreón and in Parras, halfway to Saltillo.

State of Nuevo León

Not much is known about the Desert Culture tribes of Nuevo León, despite the many cave paintings and petroglyphs they left in the mountains. Two years after Cabeza de Vaca passed along the northern border of the state, Spanish adventurers founded a town at the site of Monterrey but deserted it shortly thereafter. In 1579, Luis de Carvajal, usually called 'luckless' by historians, received permission to found the New Kingdom of León in northern Mexico. Carvajal was a Portugese Jew who converted to Christianity, and he settled one hundred Jewish families in Monterrey. Unfortunately, he made enemies of the neighboring Spanish governors, who denounced him to the Inquisition. Carvajal died in jail, Monterrey was abandoned and many of the Jews died at the stake in Mexico City's Zócalo. The final, lasting founding of Monterrey came in 1596 at the hands of Diego de Montemayor, who named the city after the viceroy, the Count of Monterrey. The city became the economic center for Nuevo León's mines and vast cattle and sheep ranches.

Like many northern Mexico cities, Monterrey was captured by the Americans during their 1846 invasion, and two decades later it became the provisional capital of Juárez' government while he was being chased by the French. More than any other city in Mexico, Monterrey boomed under Porfirio Díaz and became the industrial capital. Mexico's largest steel mill opened here in 1890, and the next year José Schneider opened the Cerveceria Cuauhtemoc, soon the largest brewery. During this period the first family corporate dynasties were founded; some of these, like the Garza Sadas, continue to wield immense power and wealth.

The state of Nuevo León contains the bustling industrial and corporate center of Monterrey—the most Americanized city in Mexico—and little else. In the north there's a new multi-lane border crossing at **Columbia**, about 50 kilometers (31 miles) west of Nuevo Laredo. **Monterrey** (pop 3,000,000), Mexico's third largest city, is built in a valley

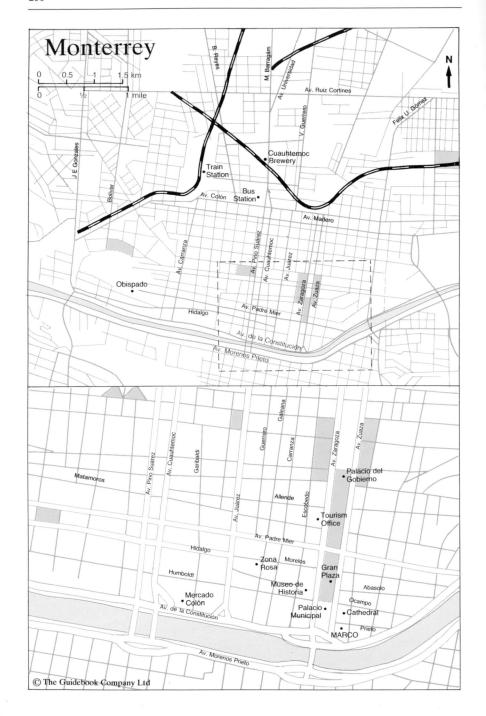

Monterrey

0   0.5   1   1.5 km
0   ½   1 mile

N

B. Reyes
M. Barragám
Av. Universidad
Av. Ruiz Cortines
V. Guerrero
Felix U. Gómez
J. E. Gonzales
Bolívar

Cuauhtemoc Brewery

Train Station

Bus Station

Av. Colón

Av. Madero

Obispado

Av. Carranza
Av. Pino Suárez
Av. Cuauhtemoc
Av. Juárez
Av. Zaragoza
Av. Zuaza

Av. Padre Mier

Hidalgo

Av. de la Constitución

Av. Morenos Prieto

Galeana
Guerrero
Carranza
Av. Zaragoza
Av. Zuaza

Matamoros

Av. Pino Suárez
Av. Cuauhtemoc
Garibaldi

Palacio del Gobierno

Av. Juárez

Allende

Escobedo

Tourism Office

Av. Padre Mier

Hidalgo

Humboldt

Zona Rosa   Morelos

Gran Plaza

Abasolo

Mercado Colón

Museo de Historia

Ocampo

Av. de la Constitución

Palacio Municipal

Cathedral

Prieto

MARCO

Av. Morenos Prieto

© The Guidebook Company Ltd

between three craggy hills at the edge of the Sierra Madre Oriental. The **Cerro de la Silla**, which looms to the east, is the symbol of the city. The oldest part of the city is built along the **Río de Santa Catarina**, which is channeled to avoid floods. Monterrey's heart is the **Gran Plaza**, an ambitious, multi-level civic complex with many monuments and fountains, mixing the colonial with the ultra-modern. At the south end of the plaza stands the **Cathedral**, now dwarfed by modern buildings. This pink stone building was begun in 1635, heavily damaged during the US invasion of 1846–47, and only finished in 1899. Next door is the new **Museo de Arte Contemporáneo de Monterrey** (MARCO). This dramatic building (open Tues–Sun, 11–5), designed by Ricardo Legorreta, is a testament to Monterrey's desire to be considered a 'world-class city'. The spacious interior has rotating exhibitions of Latin American and world art 'on the cutting edge'. The south end of the plaza is dominated by the new **Palacio Municipal**. The **Faro de Comercio** ('Lighthouse of Commerce'), across from the Cathedral, is a tall orange stucco obelisk from which a laser beam shines forth every evening. The **Museo de Historia**, in a colonial building just west of the obelisk, has good exhibitions on local history from pre-Hispanic times through the Revolution. Further north, the plaza is lined by mirrored glass and concrete governmental buildings, including courts, the **Palacio Legislativo** (tourism office next door) and the **Teatro de la Ciudad**. A staircase in the middle of the plaza leads to an underground mall and parking garage. The plaza ends at the 1895 **Palacio del Gobierno**.

The streets west of the plaza comprise the **Zona Rosa**, the downtown shopping area with many pedestrian walkways, restaurants and expensive hotels. Pancho Villa once rode into the elegant lobby of the **Gran Hotel Ancira** on his horse. The **Mercado Colón** on Avda Constitución, near the river, is a good place to shop for food and inexpensive crafts. The two main downtown avenues, Pino Suárez and Cuauhtemoc, run north from the river, pass the triumphal **Arco de la Independencia**, and merge near the enormous **Central Bus Station**. The **train station** is two blocks west. The huge brick **Cuauhtemoc Brewery**, founded in 1891, has daily tours of the factory, a **beer garden** where you can enjoy free bottles of Carta Blanca, and a small museum. Also on the grounds is the **Mexican Baseball Hall of Fame**, with pictures of American as well as Mexican stars who played here. The **bullring**, **Niños Heroes Park** and the **University** are all on Avda Alfonso Reyes heading north. The **Obispado**, constructed between 1785 and 1790 on a small hill west of downtown (too far to walk), was the home of Monterrey's bishops, a fort during the American invasion, and heavily damaged by cannons in the Revolution. It now contains a museum of local history and a good collection of religious art. Monterrey's wealthy live and shop in the luxurious **Colonia del Valle** and **Garza García** neighborhoods, southwest of the city. The hills around Monterrey have caves, hot springs, waterfalls and resorts for those wanting to escape the city's heat and pollution.

State of Tamaulipas

The southern part of the coastal state of Tamaulipas was occupied by the Huastecs, a tribe distantly related, linguistically at least, to the Mayas further south. Various expeditions of conquistadors, Juan de Grijalva and Cortés among them, competed in trying to subdue the Huastecs, but all withdrew after much bloodshed. Although the first mission was planted in 1544, it wasn't until the mid-18th century that the Spanish had more than a precarious hold on the state. In 1749, Don José de Escandón was granted permission to settle the northern and interior portions of Tamaulipas. Spanish cattle ranchers fought Huastecs, Apaches and Comanches from the north well into the 19th century. In 1829, Spanish troops, in one last desperate attempt to retake their colony, landed at Tampico and managed to repulse Santa Ana's troops. Santa Ana besieged the town and, after being weakened by the tropical heat and yellow fever, the Spaniards finally surrendered. The American fleet of General Winfield Scott landed at Matamoros and Tampico in 1847, before heading south to capture Mexico City. After Texas became part of the United States in 1848, 500 Mexicans from the town of Laredo moved across the river to Mexico and founded Nuevo Laredo. Under Porfírio Díaz, Tampico became a major industrial port, rivalling Veracruz. At the end of the century an American oil man named Edward Doheny struck oil near Tampico, and by 1914 the city was the center of the richest oil-producing area in the world. Boom times lasted until 1921, when salt water began appearing in the wells.

Tamaulipas' three border towns—Nuevo Laredo, Reynosa and Matamoros— all lie on the Río Bravo opposite Laredo, Hidalgo and Brownsville, Texas respectively. The area is a center of winter vegetable production on rich irrigated agricultural lands. The three cities contain nightlife and gift shops aimed at the 'walk-in' tourist trade from Texas. **Nuevo Laredo** is the largest (pop 400,000), with most of the tourist businesses on **Avda Guerrero** and a popular horse racing track south of town. The **Cadillac Bar**, Nuevo Laredo's most famous cantina, has spawned a chain of restaurants across the United States. **Reynosa** (pop 350,000) is better known as a center of oil and gas refineries. **Matamoros** (pop 350,000) has become notorious because of the 'narcosatanic' drug gang that operated nearby, and because of a recent prison rebellion that exposed widespread corruption in the local police force. Nevertheless, prudent visitors should have no problems. **Avenida Obregón** at the foot of the International Bridge is the main street. Near the **Plaza Hidalgo** is a market for tourist handicrafts. Good deserted beaches may be found east of Mexico 180 heading south. **Tampico** (pop 638,000), at the mouth of the Río Panuco on the border with the state of Veracruz, is a major oil refinery center and the second largest port in Mexico. It contains many hotels and lots of port atmosphere.

State of Durango

Before the Conquest, the Tepehuans, the Acaxees and the Chichimecs occupied the territory of Durango. Archeologists theorize that, because of their traditions of human sacrifice, the ball game and constant warfare, the Acaxees were related to the Mexica, who went on to conquer the Valley of Mexico. In 1552, Gínes Vázquez del Mercado and 100 adventurers marched into Durango looking for the fabled cities of gold. He found only a mountain of iron ore and an army of warlike Indians, who mortally wounded him. At the foot of that mountain, now called the Cerro de Mercado, the Spaniards founded the city of Durango in 1563. The areas of Durango and Chihuahua were administered as the province of Nueva Vizcaya until 1786. In the early 17th century, all three Indian tribes rebelled, killing many Jesuit missionaries, and were crushed with much bloodshed. The Indians revolted again during the period of national chaos after Mexico's independence, causing the Durango government to proclaim a bounty of 200 pesos for one live Indian and 250 pesos for one dead. Durango was the scene of battles between the constitutionalists and conservatives in 1858, the French and Juárez' forces in 1864 and 1866, and Pancho Villa's army and federal troops in 1914.

This large northwestern state is divided between farm country in the north and east, and the largely impassable Sierra Madre Occidental to the south. The city of **Durango** (pop 400,000), the capital, lies at the foot of the **Cerro de los Remedios**, a long ridge with a scenic chapel on top. The center of town is the **Plaza de Armas**, on the north side of which is the sprawling **Cathedral**. Begun in 1695, the building's recently renovated interior is punctuated by imposing stone arches. The **Palacio del Gobierno** (tourist office) was a 17th-century mansion constructed for a local militia leader. The **Museo Regional** occupies the ground floor of the Avocado Building near the main square. The surrounding blocks are the old residential neighborhood filled with elegant houses. One of these was the birthplace of Dolores Del Río, the famous Mexican actress, on August 3, 1908. Scorpions encased in blocks of plastic are Durango's main gift item. The city's outskirts are filled with belching factories.

However, the countryside along Mexico 45 north of town is extremely scenic and was used as the setting for many Hollywood Westerns. The towns of **Villa del Oeste** and **Chupadero**, about ten kilometers (six miles) north, are actually old stage sets for some John Wayne movies, including *Big Jake* and *Chisum*. **Mexico 40** from Durango to Mazatlán passes through some stunning mountain terrain, which almost rivals the Copper Canyon Railway for scenery.

Baja California

Introduction

In less than three decades the 1,300-kilometer (800-mile)-long peninsula of Baja California has become the prime destination for outdoor recreation enthusiasts. It's particularly popular with Californians, who own many condos and vacation homes here. The entire west coast is lined with beaches and excellent surfing waters. The peninsula's many islands and harbors delight boaters. Both the Pacific and the Sea of Cortés are filled with one of the richest and most varied stocks of game fish in the world. Ensenada, Loreto, La Paz and Cabo San Lucas have the main sportfishing fleets. Inland, there's opportunity for hiking in the national parks that run along Baja's sierra. Baja contains a number of unique plant species, including the enormous cordon cactus, the ocotillo with thorny whip-like branches, the cirio (a tree with a tapering trunk up to 20 meters (62 feet) tall and pencil-like branches), and the elephant tree with thick branches and papery bark. Baja's most famous natural attraction is the whale nursery in Scammon's Lagoon, just south of the 28th Parallel. Every winter, the lagoon is filled with California grey whales that frolic and give birth in the crystal clear waters. There are also large sea-lion and dolphin populations around Loreto and Cabo San Lucas.

The historical attractions on Baja are fewer: a string of mission churches that run the length of the peninsula. The first and most famous still stands in Loreto. There are good historical museums in Tijuana, Loreto and La Paz. For border town action, Tijuana and Mexicali are the places to visit, although Ensenada has some of the same atmosphere. The main resort areas are near Loreto and La Paz, and in Cabo San Lucas and San José del Cabo at the tip of the peninsula.

Getting There

More people cross at Tijuana than at any other point along the 3,225-kilometer (2,000-mile)-long US–Mexico border. The San Ysidro–Tijuana border crossing can be reached by car on US 5 and 895, by bus and by the inexpensive (US$1.50) red trolley that begins in downtown San Diego, 24 kilometers (15 miles) to the north, and makes frequent stops along the way. From the crossing it's an easy walk into downtown Tijuana. If you're planning on traveling further into Mexico, fill out a tourist card in the office on the Mexican side of the crossing. US citizens on day trips need only a driver's license or

Whip-like cirio tree, unique to Baja

other valid ID to pass through US Customs on the way back. There is another auto crossing at Otay, eight kilometers (five miles) east on California 117, also known as Otay Mesa Rd. The rest of Baja may be reached via Mexico 1, either a toll highway to Ensenada, or the old two-lane road. The only land connection to lower Mexico is Mexico 2, which runs due east via Tecate and Mexicali, both of which have border crossings. One section of this road just east of La Rumorosa is notoriously dangerous because of its hairpin turns and lack of guard rails. Mexicali also has the nearest railway station, the terminus for the line from Guadalajara and Mexico City. The fast train to the capital is supposed to take 44 hours, the slow train 57.

Tijuana's international airport is just to the west of the Otay crossing. From here you can catch flights to Puerto Vallarta, La Paz, Hermosillo, Guadalajara, Monterrey, Aguascalientes and Mexico City on Aeromexico; Mexicana flies to Monterrey, Guadalajara, Zacatecas, Mexico City and Cancún; and Aero California has flights to Aguascalientes, Colima, Culiacán, Guadalajara, La Paz, Los Mochis, Mazatlán and Mexico City.

Most buses south into Baja and for lower Mexico use the huge new Central de Autobuses, east of downtown at the beginning of the airport road. This is one of the highest volume bus stations in Mexico, so be prepared for long lines, especially on holidays. (Mexicans and Central Americans arriving here, particularly young men traveling light, are met at the door by *polleros*, professional illegal alien smugglers, offering their services in crossing the border.) The main lines are Tres Estrellas de Oro, Transportes del Norte de Sonora and Transportes del Pacífico for points in Mexico; Baja is served by ABC and Tres Estrellas de Oro.

All of Baja below Tijuana is connected by Mexico 1, which winds the 1,300-kilometer (800-mile) length of the peninsula. The middle peninsula is particularly barren, and drivers should bring good spare tires and extra oil and water. There are regular gas stations every 100 kilometers (62 miles) or so and the road is patrolled by the Green Angels. By car, it takes two long days to reach Los Cabos; it's at least 20 hours by long distance bus. At the time of writing there was a car ferry from Santa Rosalia to Guaymas in Sonora three times a week.

The next major airport is at Loreto, from which there are daily flights to La Paz and Los Angeles on Aeromexico and Aero California. La Paz' international airport is served by flights to Los Angeles, Guaymas, Culiacán, Puerto Vallarta and Mexico City on Aeromexico, and to Culiacán, Loreto, Los Mochis, Mazatlán and Tijuana on Aero California. Two ferries leave daily from La Paz to Topolobampo and Mazatlán on the Mexican mainland. The passengers-only Baja Express leaves from the Malecón and takes four hours to Topolobampo (tickets at the pier). The slower Sematur ferry carries vehicles and takes 10–20 hours to reach Mazatlán. Line up very early for tickets at the Sematur office at Calles Cinco de Mayo and Guillermo Prieto in La Paz. Cabo San Lucas and San José del

Cabo are served by the Los Cabos international airport, a few kilometers north of the latter town. Mexicana has flights to Denver, Los Angeles, San Francisco, Guadalajara, Mazatlán, Puerto Vallarta and Mexico City; Aeromexico flies to Culiacán, Guaymas, Los Angeles, Puerto Vallarta, Tijuana and Mexico City; Aero California serves Los Angeles, Phoenix and San Diego; and Alaska Airlines to San Diego and points north. The ferry from Cabo San Lucas to Puerto Vallarta is no longer running.

History

The first evidence of human habitation in Baja comes from shell middens found in Pichilingue, near La Paz. Cave and cliff paintings of hunting scenes and animal motifs have been found in central (near San Ignacio) and southern Baja. Before the Spanish arrived there were eight tribes of hunter-gatherers who eked out an existence from the peninsula's rocky ground and from the rich waters of the Sea of Cortés. The lack of rainfall and freshwater springs effectively barred the existence of any communities of more than a few hundred people and of any advanced culture.

The first European contact with Baja came in 1533, when a Spanish expedition financed by Cortés and led by his navigator, Fortun Ximénez, landed at Los Cabos and near La Paz. At the latter site they had a violent battle with the local Indians, in which Ximénez was killed. A bloody 200-year saga of European-native conflict began. Cortés himself landed at Pichilingue on May 3, 1535, and founded a settlement there named Puerto de Santa Cruz. This town was soon abandoned due to the lack of food and water, as were all subsequent attempts at settlement of the peninsula until well into the next century. In 1539, Francisco de Ulloa penetrated to the northernmost point of the Sea of Cortés, and then circumnavigated Baja and became the first to explore the coast along Southern California. Another Spanish explorer, Sebastián Vizaino, landed at Puerto de Santa Cruz in 1596 and renamed it La Paz, because he was met by Indians bearing gifts of fish, meat and fruit. During the first two centuries of Spanish rule, the only successful attempt at exploitation of Baja was the black pearl fishery off the southeast coast. By the mid-17th century this too was depleted.

In 1697, the Jesuits convinced the royal authorities that their zeal, faith and organizational expertise could succeed where the Spanish warrior-entrepreneurs had failed. The Virrey granted them almost complete political, economic and religious power over Baja. For the next 150 years, first the Jesuits, next the Franciscans, and lastly the Dominicans ruled Baja. Their legacy can be seen in the dozens of small mission churches that dot the peninsula from Tijuana to Los Cabos.

The missionaries started their campaign in Loreto, about two-thirds of the way down the peninsula, where there was a reliable freshwater spring and no reminders of the failures in La Paz. On October 25, 1697, Padre Juan María de Salvatierra began building the Nuestra Señora de Loreto church. Over the next 75 years the Jesuits built 18 churches in southern Baja. They also began converting the Indians and taught them farming and crafts to encourage them to adopt a more sedentary and Christian life. Of far greater influence on the Indians were the Old World diseases the fathers unknowingly brought with them; the indigenous population was decimated. The native tribes did not always react kindly to the priest's activities: there were frequent Indian raids on the mission settlements. The bloodiest was in 1734, when Indians around San José del Cabo began an uprising that killed many Spaniards and could only be put down by colonial troops from the mainland. In 1767, the Jesuits, whose power vexed the Spanish monarch Charles III, were expelled from Mexico. In Baja the vacuum was filled first by the Franciscans, who missionized the mid-peninsula region, and then by the Dominicans, who built churches in northern Baja. Their power was gradually weakened until 1834, when the Mexican government ousted them from the peninsula.

Mission of San Ignacio, Baja California Sur

The colonial government had been encouraging the secular presence in Baja since the 1760s. Farmers and fishermen were settled there, and mines opened at Santa Ana and at El Triunfo near La Paz. Cabo San Lucas was the haunt of pirates and scavengers who tried to lure ships onto the rocks, and an English pirate named Cromwell made La Paz his base. In 1828, the capital was moved from Loreto to La Paz, where most of the population was concentrated, after a hurricane nearly destroyed the mission town.

During the 19th century, both Baja and Upper California began to attract mercenary adventurers and foreign governments, because they realized that Mexico's hold on the region was tenuous. In 1822, an adventurer named Thomas Cochrane with two Chilean ships full of soldiers took San José del Cabo, but the lack of food and water forced him to withdraw. The Americans invaded Baja at the same time as they attacked mainland Mexico in 1846. The US Navy blockaded Baja's main ports, and an invasion force marched around between San José del Cabo and La Paz, meeting only weak resistance. During the treaty negotiations in 1848, the Mexicans agreed to accept the loss of Upper California, New Mexico, Texas and Louisiana (in return for US$15 million) but refused to cede Baja as well. The last invasion of Baja came in 1853, at the hands of William Walker, the notorious American mercenary. He tried to form an independent Republic of Sonora from the states of Sonora and Baja California. His troops captured La Paz and San José del Cabo but were defeated in Sinaloa. Later, Mexican troops forced him to flee to the United States.

Baja remained isolated from the waves of violence that swept across Mexico in the second half of the 19th century and the first decades of the 20th. The peninsula remained in the hands of Juárez' republicans during the short, disastrous reign of Maximilian and Carlota. By this time, most of the Indians had been killed by disease and poverty. The peninsula was carved up into huge cattle estates founded when the mission lands were secularized. During the 1910–20 Revolution, Baja's Liberal Party, led by Ricardo Flores Magón, controlled the governments of the southern towns for a few months. Their radical universalist platform confused many locals, and they were replaced by more conservative governments.

In 1889, the land of a ranch and frontier post named Punta Tía Juana, just south of the US border, was subdivided into lots and the building of a town began. It had been an outpost of the mission in San Diego until the property was confiscated in 1834. Tijuana, as it was known, had 733 inhabitants by 1910, and in the next decade a bullring and a horse track were built. Tijuana soon became a staging point for Mexican workers trying to enter the US illegally. After Prohibition was enacted, tourists flooded the town looking for booze, sex and gambling. During the Depression, Mexicans escaping the hard times north of the border settled here, causing another population jump. Tijuana continued to rely on the illicit economy until 1965, when the first *maquiladora* (assembly plant for US and other foreign manufacturers) opened here. Today the *maquiladoras* rival tourism and illegal emigrants as the pillars of Tijuana's economy. Unfortunately, some of these plants have dangerous work conditions and spew untreated waste into the rivers and atmosphere. With a population of at least a million, Tijuana sprawls for miles south of the border and attracts immigrants both rich and poor from all over Mexico who want to settle here.

Ensenada was a frequent stop-off for the galleons plying the Manila–Acapulco route during the Colonial era, but the lack of water prohibited permanent settlement. During the 19th century, it became a cattle ranch and then a booming port serving the nearby goldmines, which were discovered in 1870. Until 1915 it was both the largest city and the capital of Baja Norte. The spill-over from Prohibition led to another boom, and the Los Angeles glitterati flocked to the luxurious new casino. Although the wild times still continue, in a muted way, Ensenada is now home to one of Mexico's largest fishing fleets.

The rest of Baja remained isolated from the world well into the 1950s. La Paz was accessible by air, but the other towns were only connected by a single-lane dirt-and-rock track that took a month in a jeep to traverse in its entirety. Then Baja was discovered by American sportsmen and nature-lovers. Fishermen discovered black marlin and roosterfish off Los Cabos, surfers realized that the Pacific coast had great waves all the way down to the tip, and naturalists began to investigate the grey whale breeding grounds and the peninsula's unique flora. The Mexican government completed Highway 1, a two-lane blacktop, in the 1960s, and the modern era came to Baja. Its most visible manifestation is the Baja 1000, a dangerous off-road vehicle race that winds through the hills and deserts of Baja Norte. Today many Mexicans complain that the peninsula, with all its resorts and California cars on Highway 1, has finally been annexed by the United States. Nevertheless, the vast majority of Baja remains untouched.

Baja Norte

Tijuana

After leaving the Mexican Customs area, the visitor can either take a taxi or follow the pedestrian walkway to downtown. The walkway passes through a large mall filled with gift stores, bars and restaurants catering to American tourists. From the footbridge across the Tijuana River, there is a view of the Operation Desert Storm surplus-steel tank road, which runs for ten kilometers (six miles) along the border as a wall against illegal aliens. Every evening, in an absurd ritual, hundreds of youths gather just to the west of the bridge and climb across the wall in large groups. The odds are that in such numbers the

Cantina troubadour

US Border Patrol can't capture them all. (The other main illegal crossing is just east of the Otay border post.) Vendors sell sweaters to people from the south not used to Tijuana's evening chill. It's not safe to get closer to the wall, especially at night.

The walkway divides here. Straight ahead is an area of more malls and the **Mexitlán** amusement park, a new multi-media exhibition of the wonders of Mexico in miniature, with restaurants and gift shops (adult admission US$10). Nearby is the **Centro Cultural Tijuana** arts complex, with an Omnimax theater, concert hall and a museum with a good introduction to Mexican history and culture and temporary exhibits. The walkway to the right, at the end of the bridge, leads between more gift shops to Avda Revolución and the heart of downtown. The **red light district**, possibly the largest in Mexico, begins at Calle

1 and Avda Revolución, and heads down the hill to the river. Prostitutes stand outside cheap hotels and read Mexican comic books, fights spill out of bars onto the street, and the police are a long time coming. In the other direction on Avda Revolución are the bright lights of the main shopping district, which runs until Calle 11. At street level, shops sell discount perfumes and drugs, Mexican liquor, jewelry, leather, whips and switchblades. On the side streets you can be married or divorced and get cheap auto bodywork, painting and upholstery. The second floors have been taken over by restaurants and discos, and the hooting of gringo revelers resounds late into the night. The **Jai Alai Frontón**, on Revolución between 7 and 8, is a brightly painted reminder of more elegant days and has a sculpture of a *jai alai* player on top of a globe at the entrance. Tijuana has two **bullrings**, one near downtown on Boulevard Agua Caliente and the other—the 'Bullring by the Sea'—is seven kilometers (four miles) west on the beach, immediately south of the border fence. The beach is attractive but the water is extremely polluted. The fancy **Hippodrome** (horse racing track) is on Boulevard Gustavo Díaz Ordaz, near the more expensive hotels and restaurants.

Tecate, a border town 49 kilometers (30 miles) east of Tijuana, is the center of a wine-growing region and gives its name to the popular Mexican beer brewed here.

MEXICALI

The road east of Tijuana climbs over a high plateau to 1,000 meters (3,300 feet) in altitude, then drops sharply just after La Rumorosa, where the gullies between the hairpin turns are filled with literally hundreds of cars, trucks and buses that have fallen over the edge. The road then flattens out across a dry lake bed before it reaches Mexicali (pop over 500,000), the hottest city in Mexico. Summertime temperatures in this booming border town frequently reach the mid 40'sC (around 110F); during the winter there are frosts. The dusty and congested downtown begins where California 111 reaches the border at Calexico, on the American side. Avenidas Colón and Madero, which run parallel to the border, are the main streets, with many hotels, restaurants, bars and gift shops. There is a tiny **Regional Museum** at Avda Obregón and Calle L, at the east end of town. The rest of Mexicali is a hodgepodge of rich neighborhoods and slums packed as close to the border as possible. At the south end of town is a new **Centro Cívico y Comercial** complex (fancy shops) near the **bullring**. A huge statue of Mexican President Lázaro Cárdenas, looking strangely like Chairman Mao, stands at the nearby intersection. To the east of Mexicali is an area of rich, irrigated farmland.

ENSENADA

As a four-lane toll road and a two-lane freeway, Mexico 1 runs along the coast south of Tijuana before turning inland just after Ensenada (where the toll road ends). The coast here is lined with trailer parks, condos and hotels mostly catering to Californians. The first town is **Rosarito** (many new condo complexes), which is dwarfed by the enormous thermo-electric plant right on the beach. During the holidays US students and surfers flock to the beach campgrounds along this stretch. Just before Ensenada the road runs along the top of two towering cliffs, Punta Salsipuedes and Punta San Miguel, with excellent views. Thirty-nine kilometers (24 miles) north on Mexico 3 to Tecate is the town of **Guadalupe**, founded by Russian immigrants, with a Russian-style church.

Ensenada (pop 250,000) is situated at the mouth of a valley on the north side of the Bahía Todos Santos. The largest tuna fleet in Mexico anchors in the port, and there are fish-processing factories just north of town. Boulevard Lázaro Cárdenas, which runs parallel to the harbor, and Calle López Mateos just inland are the main tourist streets, with most of the hotels. The old Spanish colonial-style casino, now the **Centro Social, Cívico y Cultural de Ensenada**, is at the south end of Lázaro Cárdenas. It attracted gamblers from Prohibition until 1938, when gambling was outlawed in Mexico, and the boxer Jack Dempsey was hired to attract the high rollers. Now a banquet hall, you can still roam around the elegant interior. The **Plaza Cívica** on Lázaro Cárdenas is a small park with colossal heads of the Mexican patriots, Juárez, Hidalgo and Carranza, and a monument to martyrs of US aggression in Veracruz and Mexico City. The **sportfishing fleet dock** is right on the harbor with party boats and charters. Next door is the **fish market**, whose main attraction is the stalls selling fish and shrimp tacos, ceviche and oysters to crowds of hungry tourists.

Further inland, on Avda Ruíz just off Avda López Mateos, is **Hussong's**, a cantina founded in 1892 and Ensenada's most famous tourist attraction. Day or night, it's full of enthusiasts downing oceans of tequila and beer. Ensenada is littered with gift shops selling 'authentic', 'original' and 'official' Hussong's merchandise. There are many other bars in this area, as well dozens of pool halls frequented by locals. The **Bodegas de Santo Tomás Winery** at Avda Macheros and Calle 7 produces some of Mexico's finest wine, from grapes grown south of Ensenada, and has daily tours. Sixteen kilometers (ten miles) south of town there's a turn-off to **Cabo Punta Banda**, at the south end of Todos Santos Bay. Here the surf pushes water as much as 16 meters (52 feet) into the air, through a blowhole known as **La Bufadora** (parking and gift shops).

Lower Baja Norte

From Ensenada, Mexico 3 heads east 219 kilometers (136 miles) across the peninsula (through pine forests in the sierra) to **San Felipe**, a small fishing port that doubles in size from October through June with vacationers, retirees and fishermen. From here Mexico 5 runs north to Mexicali.

South of Ensenada, Mexico 1 runs along the Pacific coast through small towns like

Santo Tomás, which were founded as mission settlements. Dirt tracks to the west lead to many campgrounds and surfing and fishing spots. Below Colnett a road leads into the sierra and the **Parque Nacional Sierra de San Pedro Mártir**, with pine forests, a stupendous view and the 3,100-meter (10,200-foot) bulk of Pico del Diablo looming nearby. Eight kilometers (five miles) east of Colonia Guerrero there are the ruins of the **Mission of Santo Domingo**, built by monks in 1775. At **San Quintín** there are a number of motels and views of a range of small volcanic cones along a cape west of town and a volcanic island offshore. After **El Rosario** (mission ruins), the road cuts to the center of the peninsula through a unique landscape of deserts populated by strange cacti and elephant trees. There are more mission ruins in **San Fernando** and **Santa Inés**. Ninety-two kilometers (58 miles) below the latter town a turn-off leads to **Bahía de los Angeles**, a popular fishing and boating resort set in a dramatic bay surrounded by barren hills (motels and trailer parks). The Angel de la Guarda island, Baja's largest, is offshore and is a popular excursion spot. Dolphins and whales are frequent visitors. Mexico 1 continues back on the Pacific coast down to the 28th Parallel, which is the border between Baja California Norte and Baja California Sur.

Baja Sur

GUERRERO NEGRO

Immediately south of the 28th Parallel, Guerrero Negro (cheap hotels) is the nearest town to the Ojo de Liebre lagoon, also known as **Scammon's Lagoon**, which serves as a winter (December–April) birthing ground for the California Grey Whale, until recently an endangered species. The whales migrate yearly from the Bering Sea. The lagoon is an inlet off the Bahía Sebastián Vizcaino (the Spanish discoverer of the bay in 1596) and was named after an American whaling captain who explored the area in 1857. Several dirt roads from town lead to the best whale watching points. The lagoon, now a national park, is also filled with other marine life, including sharks, octopuses, lobsters, oysters and a wide variety of fish. South of town is one of the largest salt evaporation fields in the world.

Mexico 1 now heads east across the barren Vizcaino Desert. **San Ignacio**, 123 kilometers (76 miles) from Guerrero Negro, is like an oasis in a small valley filled with palm trees. There's a stone mission church (1728) and pre-Columbian cave paintings on the cliff walls near town. The road continues to the Sea of Cortés coast, with the enormous cone of the Las Vírgenes volcano on the left. **Santa Rosalía**, the port and smelter for nearby copper mines, is a bustling little city. The cast-iron **Templo de Santa Rosalia** near the main square was ordered by French mining company engineers from Gustave

*(above) Pelicans, Los Cabos; (below) Los Frailes, the rocks that divide
the Pacific from the Sea of Cortez at Cabo San Lucas*

Eiffel, the designer of the tower in Paris, and was delivered in pieces by freighter in 1905. A ferry to Guaymas leaves three times a week. **Mulege**, 63 kilometers (39 miles) down the coast, is a garden-like town; each house is surrounded by fruit and palm trees. The mission church was constructed on a huge rock near town. Cave paintings are nearby, and excellent beaches are three kilometers (1.8 miles) away. At the south end of the Bahía Concepción, halfway between Mulege and Loreto, is the **Playa Santísima**, a beautiful half-moon of sand with camping and some semi-permanent vacation homes.

LORETO

'The Historical Capital of the Californias', Loreto has recently been given a new **Malecón** (seaside drive), an ambitious street plan and an international airport. According to the government tourist development agency, Fonatur, this palm tree-filled town will soon be a major tourist destination. Loreto has yet to grow into its new clothes: inland most of the streets are unpaved, and the pace is still somnolent. In the center of town is the Baja's oldest structure, the **Parroquia de Nuestra Señora de Loreto** stone church, one block inland from the water. Begun in 1697 by the Jesuits, the inscription over the door reads: 'Head and Mother of the Mission of Lower and Upper California'. The interior is a long, simple vault with a gilt gold altar at the end, containing a gold and silver image of the Virgin and Child. Next door is the **Museum of the Missions** (Mon–Fri, 9–12.30 and 1–4), with good displays on church and Baja history. On the same plaza is the whitewashed city hall/police station building. A bust of Padre Juan María de Salvatierra, founder of the mission, decorates the plaza. Most of the hotels and restaurants are spread along the Malecón. The fishing dock is at the north end of town. Fonatur is also developing **Nopolo**, eight kilometers (five miles) down the road.

LA PAZ

Between Loreto and La Paz, Mexico 1 runs mostly through flat desert and irrigated farmland. La Paz, the largest city (pop 160,000) and the capital of Baja Sur since 1829, is situated on the south shore of the Bahía La Paz on the Sea of Cortés. Although it does have tourist attractions, it is also a free port and the economic center of the southern peninsula. The old center of town is the **Plaza Constitución**. On one side is the **Palacio del Gobierno**, which contains a museum that recounts Baja history through paintings by local artists. Opposite is the **Cathedral**, built in 1861 on the foundations of the original mission. The new center is where the **Malecón**, also called Paseo Alvaro Obregón, meets Calle 16 de Septiembre. The latter is the main shopping street, with department stores, boutiques selling cheap gifts from Taiwan and Chinese restaurants. There's a **tourism kiosk** in the Parque de Amistad on the Malecón, next to the ferry terminals. Fishing charters, glass bottom boat rides and day cruises to Los Cabos and offshore islands are all available on the waterfront. At the east end of the Malecón is the terminal for buses to the Pichilingue beaches and Los Cabos. The **Museo de Antropología** at Calles Cinco de Mayo and Altamirano (15-minute walk from Malecón), is the best museum in Baja. It has excellent displays on Baja history and culture and also features good traveling exhibits. On the road to **Pichilingue**, site of Cortés' first settlement 18 kilometers (11 miles) northeast, are many beaches popular with La Paz residents.

Los Cabos

Mexico 1 divides 30 kilometers (19 miles) south of La Paz and forms a loop that circumnavigates the tip of Baja California. The road east to San José del Cabo passes through some semi-deserted silver mining towns, **El Triunfo** and **San Antonio** (nice mission), before crossing the Tropic of Cancer just after the picturesque town of **Santiago**. It reaches the southern coast at **San José del Cabo** (pop 10,000), a rapidly developing resort that attracts many American retirees as residents, as well as tourists. The palm tree-lined downtown centered on **Parque Mijares** has many shops and restaurants. The **Templo de San José** was built in 1940 on the original mission church foundations, and has a mosaic depicting the 1734 Indian rebellion over the door. The Boulevard Antonio Mijares leads down to the water. On the beach are the large Fonatur-developed hotel and condo complexes, which include golf courses and RV parks. They could easily have been transported bodily from Southern California.

Heading west along the water, the road passes some discrete (Hotel Cabo San Lucas) and outlandish (Melia Cabo Real) luxury hotels. **Cabo San Lucas**, 33 kilometers (20 miles) from San José, is nestled against a spur of giant rocks at the southernmost tip of Baja California. The rocks, called **Los Frailes** ('The Friars'), arch out into the choppy blue water and divide the Sea of Cortés from the Pacific. Although it's a paradise for surfers, the undertow and crashing waves make the area, especially the Pacific side, too dangerous for swimming, except in a few secluded coves. SEDUE (Secretariat of Urban Development and Ecology) has built dirt access roads to all the beaches around Cabo San Lucas—a rare democratic gesture. The town is built around the harbor east of the rocks. This is home port to one of the most famous sport billfishing fleets in the world. Offshore are rich waters for blue and striped marlin, sailfish, wahoo, tuna, dorado and blue sharks. November through January is the high season, and light tackle fishing is the local specialty. The harborside area is being built into a condo/mall complex, while the Mexican neighborhoods, many still unpaved, are on the hill further inland. **Calle Hidalgo** is the town's 'downtown', and most restaurants may be found here or on the Malecón (Calle Lázaro Cárdenas). The Hotel Hacienda, on the east side of the harbor, claims to have the only really safe beach in town.

After Cabo San Lucas the road curves north to La Paz, along miles of empty beaches with crashing surf. A pleasant stop is **Todos Santos**, a tree-lined town on a hill above the Pacific, just south of the Tropic of Cancer.

The South

Introduction

South Mexico encompasses the country as it narrows down to the Isthmus of Tehuantepec and beyond to the Guatemala border. This region contains the remains of the great Olmec, Zapotec, Totonac and Maya civilizations. Their descendants still occupy the same territory, and many live in traditional villages little changed by modern culture.

Although northernmost Veracruz is not far from the US border, the state is included in this section because its culture, both modern and ancient, is 'southern'. The slightly dilapidated colonial port city of Veracruz possesses a heroic past and a fascinating Mexican-Caribbean *jarocho* culture. El Tajín's Totonac ruins are one of the greatest and least visited ancient cities in Mexico. The state capital, Jalapa, contains an excellent new archeology museum featuring Olmec, Totonac and Maya relics.

Oaxaca is one of Mexico's most popular tourist destinations. The capital, Oaxaca, is a colonial city filled with red and green stone churches and offering excellent regional cuisine, hundreds of crafts shops and a charming Zócalo. Just to the west stands the ancient Zapotec capital of Monte Albán, spectacularly situated on a hilltop overlooking the Valley of Oaxaca. The valley east of Oaxaca contains traditional craft-making towns, colonial churches and many Zapotec and Mixtec ruins, including Mitla with its ornate mosaic walls. Beach lovers can find surfing in Puerto Escondido, an ultra-laid back atmosphere in Puerto Angel and luxury resorts in Huatulco.

Chiapas has the most durable Indian culture in Mexico. The dramatic Cañon del Sumidero to the east of the modern state capital of Tuxta Gutiérrez is outdone only by the Barranca del Cobre in Chihuahua. San Cristóbal de las Casas is the cultural capital of the Chiapas Highlands; its clear atmosphere, red tile roofs, many churches and rich artisan tradition make it a magnet for tourists from around the world. This city is surrounded by Maya villages where Indians wear traditional dress and practice a mix of Christian and ancient religions. The highlands slope down to the endangered Lacandón rain forest, one of the last in Mexico, and the Maya cities of Bonampak and Yaxchilán. Palenque, considered the most beautiful ancient city in Mexico, is situated on the edge of the jungle in northern Chiapas.

The steamy coastal state of Tabasco has been taken over by the oil industry. The modern state capital of Villahermosa has two good museums of Olmec and Maya archeology.

Triqui Indian woman, Oaxaca

Getting There

The main road to the state of Veracruz from Mexico City is the toll highway via Puebla, which ends east of Córdoba and becomes Mexico 150 to the city of Veracruz. Mexico 180, the Gulf coast highway, traverses the state from Tampico in the north all the way to Coatzacoalcos and Tabasco. The sites of El Tajín and Zempoala, the city of Veracruz and the volcanic region of the Tuxtlas are all on or near this road. At Acayucán Mexico 180 meets Mexico 185, the road that crosses the Isthmus of Tehuantepec, where Mexico is narrowest, and ends at the Pacific. Jalapa, the state capital, lies in the mountains northwest of Veracruz on Mexico 140, which continues into Puebla and hits the Mexico City toll road. Veracruz is served by two train lines from Mexico City, both of which pass through Puebla, Córdoba and Orizaba. The first, the Jarocho, ends in Veracruz after a ten-hour trip. The second is the Mexico City–Mérida train, which passes through Coatzacoalcos and Palenque, Chiapas on its way to the Yucatán Peninsula. Due to the oil industry, Veracruz has a bounteous supply of airports. The following are the major airports and the cities from which there are direct flights: Veracruz—Ciudad del Carmen, Matamoros, Mérida, Mexico City, Minatitlán, Monterrey, Poza Rica, Reynosa, Tampico and Villahermosa; Tampico—Brownsville, Ciudad del Carmen, Matamoros, Mexico City, Minatitlán, Monterrey, Poza Rica, Veracruz and Villahermosa; Poza Rica—Mexico City, Minatitlán, Reynosa, Tampico and Veracruz; Minatitlán—Mérida, Mexico City, Monterrey, Poza Rica, Reynosa, Tampico and Veracruz; Jalapa—Mexico City.

There are two scenic roads to Oaxaca from Puebla. The first runs south via Izúcar de Matamoros and passes by some interesting, but rarely visited, monasteries and small archeological sites in northwestern Oaxaca. The second and faster heads west to the mineral spring town of Tehuacán before turning south to Oaxaca and descending over dry, largely uninhabited mountains. The road from the city of Oaxaca to Puerto Angel on the coast has to cross the steep Sierra Madre del Sur. This narrow, windy and spectacularly scenic road is not for the faint-hearted: it is frequently fog-bound, rock falls are common and the road is filled with big timber trucks. Another road heads southeast of Oaxaca to Tehuantepec, near Salina Cruz on the coast. It passes through largely empty countryside that has a reputation for bandits. Mexico 200, the Pacific 'highway', runs along the coast from Guerrero to Chiapas via Puerto Escondido, Puerto Angel, Tehuantepec and Juchitán de Zaragoza. Just north of Juchitán, the highway hits Mexico 185, which crosses the Isthmus of Tehuantepec to the state of Veracruz. The town at the crossroads here is called La Ventosa, 'The Windy Place', because the breezes get so strong that they blow vehicles off the road. The Oaxaqueño train that runs from Mexico City to Oaxaca via Puebla and Tehuacán is scheduled to take 12.5 hours. The city of

Oaxaca's airport is served by flights from Acapulco, Cancún, Guadalajara, Huatulco, Mérida, Mexico City, Puerto Escondido, Tijuana, Tuxtla Gutiérrez and Villahermosa. The resorts of Puerto Escondido and Huatulco both have airline terminals made out of giant thatched beach huts. The former's airport can be reached directly from Huatulco, Mexico City and Oaxaca; the latter's from Acapulco, Los Angeles, Mexico City and Oaxaca.

Chiapas, Mexico's southernmost state, may be reached from Mexico 190, which branches off from Mexico 200 just inside Oaxaca, or via Mexico 195, due south from Villahermosa in Tabasco. Mexico 190 passes through the state capital, Tuxtla Gutiérrez, and then heads up to San Cristóbal de las Casas. Mexico 195 hits this road halfway between these two cities. Mexico 190 continues east to the Guatemalan border at Ciudad Cuauhtémoc via Comitán de Domínguez. Just east of San Cristóbal, Mexico 199 branches north and descends from the highlands to the ruins of Palenque and Mexico 186, the inland route between Villahermosa and Campeche. Mexico 200 runs east from Oaxaca along the coast via Tonalá and ends at Tapachula. Just east of Tapachula are two border crossings into Guatemala, Ciudad Hidalgo and Talisman (the latter is closer and higher volume). Chiapas' main airports are at Tuxtla Gutiérrez (direct flights from Cancún, Mérida, Mexico City, Oaxaca, Tapachula and Villahermosa), which is the nearest to San Cristóbal, and Tapachula (direct flights from Guadalajara, Mexico City, Monterrey and Tuxtla Gutiérrez). From Palenque's small airport you can charter light planes to fly you to the sites of Bonampak and Yaxchilán along the Usumacinta River on the Guatemalan border. You may also reach Bonampak via a rough road that heads here from Palenque; then you have to take a 3–4 hour hike through the jungle to reach the ruins. The last portion of the land trip to Yaxchilán must be taken by boat on the Usumacinta.

The state of Tabasco lies on Mexico 180, the Gulf coast highway. At Villahermosa, the state capital, you can either continue along the coast to Campeche (tolls, and a ferry at Ciudad del Carmen) or head inland on Mexico 186, which meets 180 at Champotón in Campeche. Mexico 195 runs due south of Villahermosa to the Chiapas Highlands. The Mexico City–Mérida train line passes through southern Tabasco; the nearest station to Villahermosa is Teapa, 53 kilometers (34 miles) south. Villahermosa's airport is served by flights from Cancún, Chetumal, Ciudad del Carmen, Mérida, Mexico City, Minatitlán, Monterrey, Oaxaca, Tampico, Tuxtla Gutiérrez and Veracruz.

State of Veracruz

The Gulf coast lowlands of Veracruz and western Tabasco saw the birth of Mesoamerica's first civilization—the Olmecs. Between 1200 and 900 BC, an elaborate religious and administrative center was built on top of a mesa at San Lorenzo Tenochtitlán. The

Tlacotalpán, the most typical Veracruzan town, celebrates the Fiesta of the Virgin of Candelaria

Olmecs sculpted the mesa with thousands of tons of fill, perhaps into the shape of a giant bird, and constructed an intricate drainage system. Most impressively, they dragged huge basalt blocks from the volcanic region of the Tuxtlas 80 kilometers (50 miles) away and carved them into colossal heads and other monuments weighing many tons. San Lorenzo was violently destroyed around 900 BC, and the centers of Olmec culture became La Venta in Tabasco and Tres Zapotes, just west of the Tuxtlas. After the Olmec decline, a new culture, the Totonacs (who may or not be related to the present day people of the same name), sprung forth in northern Veracruz. Their capital was El Tajín, which reached its zenith between AD 600 and 900. The Totonacs were infatuated with the pre-Columbian ball game; there at least eleven ball courts on the site, and many ritual objects associated with the game have been found. Death and the ball game were closely linked in Totonac life: the losers were sacrificed. El Tajín was destroyed by fire, perhaps by the Chichimecs. The contemporaneous Remojadas culture in central Veracruz is known for their clay tomb offerings, including the 'smiling children' figurines that may represent the effects of hallucinogens. During the pre-Conquest era, Veracruz was divided between the Putún Maya (known to the Aztecs as the Olmeca-Xicallanca) in the south, the Totonac's descendants in city-states like Zempoala in the center, and in the north by the Huastecs, a Maya-speaking tribe.

In 1518, Juan de Grijalva's expedition landed on San Juan de Ulúa island off present-day Veracruz city. The Spaniards returned under Cortés and founded the Villa Rica de

Vera Cruz, their first settlement on the New World mainland, at the same spot on April 22, 1519. After organizing the first *ayuntamiento* (municipal government), Cortés marched north to Zempoala to meet with the Totonacs. With the help of La Malinche, his Indian translator and mistress, he cemented an alliance with the Totonacs and together they marched inland toward the Aztec capital. The Spaniards found Veracruz' hot, swampy location disease-ridden and filled with mosquitoes; they moved the city three times before returning it to its original site in 1599. After the Conquest, Veracruz became the sole Mexican port for the fleet that sailed between Cádiz in Spain and the New World. In 1587, the city of Jalapa was founded in the mountains to the west, so that traders could have a more pleasant spot to do business. The fleet arrived every two to five years, and Veracruz and later Jalapa were the site of a trade fair that lasted two or three months. Tons of Mexican silver flowed into the Spanish king's ships, while the luxury goods of the Old World headed to the wealthy of Mexico City. During the 16th and 17th centuries, masses of Veracruz' Indians died of epidemics and overwork on Spanish sugar plantations and estates. African slaves, thought to be tougher and harder working, were imported to take their place.

From 1569 to 1609, the slopes of the Orizaba volcano were the site of an independent state of escaped slaves and criminals ruled by a fugitive slave named Yanga. When

A toro balks at a fiesta bullring, Tlacotalpán

the outlaws got too ambitious and threatened nearby towns, Spanish soldiers captured Yanga and ended his republic. The riches of the Gulf made Veracruz a frequent target for pirates. In 1683, a pirate named Lorencillo locked the inhabitants in the cathedral, sacked the town and held the richest citizens for ransom. By the time the army managed to repel him, 400 Veracruzans were dead. After independence, the anti-pirate fortress of San Juan de Ulúa became the last piece of land given up by the Spaniards; their garrison held on to the fort until 1825. Mexico was torn by political turbulence during the decades that followed, and the property of many foreign nationals was destroyed, including that of a French pastry cook whose confections were eaten by Mexican soldiers. In what became known as the War of the Cakes, the French government demanded reparations, and, when these were not forthcoming, blockaded, bombarded and invaded the port of Veracruz. General Santa Ana's troops beat them back, and the Mexicans agreed to pay a reduced sum. Veracruz was next invaded by the United States under General Winfield Scott, who bombarded the port in 1846 and captured it the following year. The French invaded again in 1862, paving the way for the arrival of the hapless Emperor Maximilian and Empress Carlota. Carlota broke into tears at their rude reception and at the squalor of the port.

In 1914, American sailors invaded again in a hopeless effort to bring order to the chaos of Revolutionary Mexico. Four young Mexican naval cadets who died in the fighting are now national martyrs. The Americans withdrew so that Venustiano Carranza, who was menaced by the approach of Villa's army, could move his capital from Mexico City to Veracruz. Over the last few decades, the discovery of large oilfields has spurred an economic boom in southern Veracruz. Meanwhile, the port of Veracruz, once Mexico's most active, has stagnated because corruption and high docking costs make Tampico and Houston, Texas less expensive for shipping.

VERACRUZ

The port city of Veracruz (pop 476,000) is much faded by sun, salt, humidity and time. Ever since airlines replaced ocean liners and cargo ships started preferring cheaper ports like Houston, Veracruz has lost its luster as one of the foremost cities of Mexico. Nevertheless, the city's heroic history and unique *jarocho* (Veracruzan) Mexican-Caribbean culture make a visit worthwhile. Veracruz' heat and humidity slows the daytime pace; at night the town comes out to stroll along the Malecón and to dance in the main square. The **Plaza de la Constitución** is Veracruz' heart. Many evenings, particularly on weekends, a big band plays Veracruzan dance tunes, like the *bamba*, while dozens of elegant couples—the men wearing wide-brimmed hats—whirl around the plaza. You can also find traditional *marimba* (wooden xylophone) bands playing in the many restaurants that surround the plaza. The east side is bounded by the portaled **Palacio Municipal**, in the ground floor of which you find the **tourism office**. The white **Cathedral** (1721) across the street is revered by locals and has a pleasant, cool interior. The vast **La Parroquia restaurant** opposite the Cathedral entrance is a Veracruz institution. The white tile interior is filled day and night with local citizenry chatting, idling and drinking gallons of coffee (observe the huge, ornate urns) while ceiling fans flutter overhead. Clinking your glass is the signal for the white-jacketed waiter to bring hot milk for your coffee. The food is also recommended. Medium-priced hotels surround the plaza. **Avenida de la Independencia**, which runs along the plaza's west side, is the main shopping street. A walk one block northeast brings you to the long rectangle of the **Plaza de la República**. Vendors navigate the plaza selling pineapple juice from pineapple-shaped containers strapped to their backs. The east side of the plaza is occupied by various public edifices: the **Customs House**, **Port Services** and the **Post Office**. The first and last are ornate buildings from the reign of Porfirio Díaz, who embarked on a massive public works program to upgrade the port in the late 19th century. Opposite the modern Port Services building stands the **Benito Juárez lighthouse** (1872), now the **Museo de la Reforma**, which contains a pantheon of statues of Juárez and other politicians of the 1850–70 era. The **railway station** (1873) stands on the north side of the plaza.

A ramp just to the left of the station leads to the **Castillo de San Juan de Ulúa** (Tues–Sun, 9–5). It is too far to walk; take the 'Castillo' buses from the plaza or a car; the fort is the second to last right before the Pemex terminal at the end of the road. Once an island, San Juan de Ulúa is now a long pier lined with industrial terminals that curves around the seaward side of the port. In 1519, Cortés set out from this site on his expedition to conquer the Aztec empire. The fort is actually one big fort surrounded by three smaller ones. Battlements, a lighthouse, cave-like rooms with stalactites and a view of the port make the fort great for clambering around. A small museum gives a history of the site. The earliest buildings were begun in the mid-16th century and construction and expansion continued until the 1850s. Under Porfirio Díaz it was a notorious political prison; many died of disease and maltreatment, and during high tide the cells flooded. You are not allowed into the fort's battery, in which the Mexican Navy still stores working weapons.

Returning to the Plaza de Republica, Avda Lavandero Y Coss heads south and is lined with stalls selling cheerfully tacky souvenirs, like novelty T-shirts and 'Memory of Veracruz' bottle openers. In two blocks it hits the **Malecón**, the main port-side avenue and promenade, and the souvenir stands continue around the corner to the left. Across the street stands the **Mercado de Artesanías**, which sells more of the same in a more expensive setting. The Malecón runs east past the new La Parroquia restaurant (same idea, but the atmosphere isn't the same), the Hotel Emporio (expensive, recommended) and the yellow **Museo y Faro Venustiano Carranza**. The latter building was President Carranza's

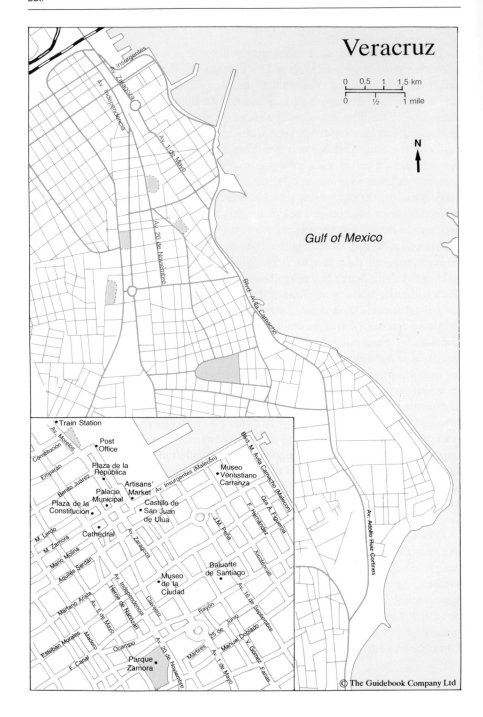

Veracruz

headquarters in 1915, when he made Veracruz his capital during the Revolution. Today, it is the headquarters of the 3rd Naval Zone and contains a free museum (Tues–Sun, 9–1 and 4–6) of Carranza's career that includes many photos, his bedroom and a shrine to the Mexican Constitution. Out front stands a heroic sculpture of Carranza that could have been placed in any city in the ex-Soviet Union and labeled Friedrich Engels. The modern **Bank of Pemex** edifice at the end of the Malecón is fronted by a statue of a thick-bodied female nude being netted by two thick-bodied fishermen and a monument to the naval cadets who were killed in the 1914 American invasion. Tourist launches leave from the dock here for tours of the harbor and to the offshore **Island of Sacrifices** (so-called because the conquistadors found the remains of sacrificed humans here), a popular picnic and swimming spot. The Malecón continues for miles south along the polluted waterfront; sights include the yacht club, Mexican Navy ships, the aquarium (dirty and depressing) and youths selling big bags of cooked shrimp and limes to passing cars.

Returning downtown, the **Museo de la Ciudad** (Tues–Fri, 10–2 and 4–8; Sat–Sun, 9–4, free) at Avdas Zaragoza between Morales and Canal, four blocks south of the main plaza, contains exhibitions on the state from the Conquest and World War II, including the African slave trade to the Gulf coast and both US invasions. The second floor is devoted to displays of *jarocho* culture—food, dance and music. A short walk east on Avda Canal will take you to the **Instituto Veracruzano de Cultura**, a former church hospital that has been converted into galleries, dance spaces, a theater and a crafts shop. Continuing east, you come to the **Baluarte de Santiago** (1635), the last remnant of the fortifications that protected Veracruz from invasion. This small fort, which you enter via a drawbridge, contains a collection of gold money and jewelry, supposedly from a sunken Spanish galleon. These were discovered by an octopus fisherman in the late 1970s and partially melted down by a local jeweler before the authorities heard about the find and confiscated the lot. Avda Independencia heads six blocks south from the Plaza de la Constitución and runs into the **Parque Zamora**, just west of which is the large **municipal market**. The **central bus station** is ten blocks south of this park on Avda Salvador Díaz Mirón. The big shopping centers and expensive beachfront hotels lie along Blvd Ruíz Cortines, about four kilometers (2.5 miles) south of downtown.

Veracruz' cuisine is a happy mixture of Mexican and Caribbean; specialties include *huachinango a la Veracruzana* (red snapper with green olives, chillies, tomatoes and capers), *arroz con plátano* (rice with fried plantains, usually served with beans) and *seviche* (spicy pickled raw fish). Mangoes and pineapples are delicious here. Unfortunately, downtown Veracruz has a shortage of good seafood restaurants; most locals head to the beachfront town of **Boca del Río** 13 kilometers (eight miles) south and savor *jarocho* specialties at restaurants like Pardino's. Veracruz' principal festivals are the debauched Carnival—Mexico's most famous—and **El Viejo** ('The Old Man') on New Year's Eve. The town's rich musical tradition has given birth to talents like the chanteuse, La Toña Negra, and Agustín Lara, Mexico's most famous songwriter.

ZEMPOALA

The ruins of the Totonac city of Zempoala lie 40 kilometers (25 miles) north of Veracruz, just west of the coast highway. Unfortunately, the temples have been over-restored and consequently the site looks somewhat sterile. In 1519, a Totonac chieftain called by the Spanish the 'Fat Cacique' invited the conquistadors to Zempoala. A Spanish scout was so dazzled by the whitewashed walls that he informed Cortés that the Totonacs built their homes of silver. When Cortés arrived, he reached an agreement with the 'Fat Cacique'; the Spaniards would protect the Totonacs from the Aztecs, who were demanding a heavy burden of tribute, and the Totonacs would provide Cortés' expedition with warriors and porters. This treaty proved crucial in the conquistadors' eventual victory over Tenochtitlán. In 1520, Cortés was forced to make a speedy return visit to Zempoala from Tenochtitlán to counter a punitive expedition from Cuba led by Pánfilo Narváez. Late one stormy night Cortés' troops attacked Narváez' men, who were sleeping on top of Zempoala's pyramids, killed five and put out Narváez' eye.

Zempoala is situated on the coastal plain among sugar cane fields and palm trees. Just before you reach the center of the small town of Zempoala, turn right to the site entrance. A small **museum** containing an interesting ceramic skeleton stands just left of the entrance. Directly opposite stands the **Templo Mayor**, an 11-meter (36-foot)-tall platform pyramid. It abuts another temple known as **Las Chimeneas**, due to the hollow columns in front of it. Cortés and his men were probably quartered here. Across the plaza from this temple stand the **Great Pyramid** (a wide rectangular platform) and the circular **Temple of the Wind God**. Two smaller temples lie in the sugar cane fields behind Las Chimeneas. Another stands in the village across the main road.

EL TAJÍN

The ruins of El Tajín, the most important site yet found on the Gulf coast, are packed into a valley in the first foothills of the Sierra Madre Oriental. Papantla, the nearest town, is eight kilometers (five miles) east over potholed roads. El Tajín was inhabited by the Totonacs, whose relationship with the present-day peoples of the same name is under debate. Excavations of the site are currently under way, and many of the temples are being restored. One of the great attractions of El Tajín are the **Voladores** ('Fliers') who perform a unique and dangerous ritual on a 20-meter (66-foot)-pole next to the parking lot. Five men in traditional costumes climb the pole; one sits on top and plays a flute and drum, while the others wrap four ropes around the top and tie the ends to their waists. At the musician's signal, the four fling themselves into space and slowly whirl to the

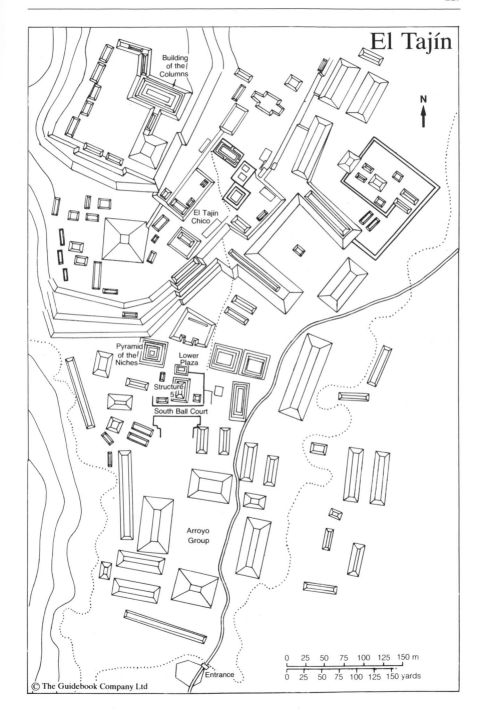

El Tajín

Building of the Columns

N

El Tajín Chico

Pyramid of the Niches

Lower Plaza

Structure 5

South Ball Court

Arroyo Group

| 0 | 25 | 50 | 75 | 100 | 125 | 150 m |

| 0 | 25 | 50 | 75 | 100 | 125 | 150 yards |

Entrance

© The Guidebook Company Ltd

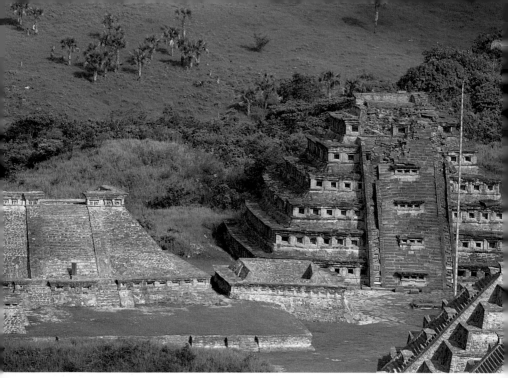

The Pyramid of the Niches, El Tajín

ground as the ropes play out. At the last minute they perform a neat flip and land on their feet. Representations of this dance have been found on pre-Columbian Totonac reliefs, but the original meaning has been lost. The *Voladores* usually perform around mid-day and whenever a large enough crowd is present. The small **museum** on one side of the parking lot was under renovation at the time of writing.

The main path winds between temples more densely packed than any other site yet found. The first grouping, the **Lower Plaza**, contains the pyramid known as **Structure 5**, on the steps of which stands a stone monument representing the Death God. The **South Ball Court** just below this pyramid is lined with reliefs, one of which shows ballplayers sacrificing one of their own, perhaps a member of the losing team, while the Death God oversees (the Death God is ubiquitous on the site). Other reliefs depict warriors and gods drinking pulque. The **Pyramid of the Niches** on the opposite side of Structure 5 is El Tajín's most famous building. This 18-meter (60-foot)-tall, six-tier structure is perforated with 365 niches, which obviously represent the days of the year. Inside, archeologists have found another pyramid, smaller but otherwise identical. The path continues up a flight of steps to the **El Tajín Chico** section of the site. The buildings here are mostly unrestored, but you can see that many were built with stone mosaic patterns on the exterior (possibly influenced by the Puuc Maya of Yucatán). The **Building of the Columns**, which abuts the hillside, contained columns carved with warriors, sacrifices and date glyphs. Many more structures are visible along the ridge to the north and in the neighboring valleys around the site.

The traditional town of **Papantla** is the most popular base for visiting El Tajín. The main square contains a pole for *Voladores* and a grotesque concrete relief depicting Totonac history (there is another at the sports center south of town). Local crafts, particularly textiles, may be found in the market. The Hotel El Tajín is recommended. Other visitors stay in **Poza Rica**, due west of El Tajín on a terrible 'paved' road. This city is dominated by a huge refinery with hissing pipes and constantly burning oil flares, but it has a better selection of hotels. The coast south of El Tajín is lined with small beach hotels and trailer parks under the palm trees. **Lagunas Verdes**, south of Nautla, is Mexico's only nuclear power plant.

JALAPA

Jalapa (also spelled 'Xalapa'), Veracruz' capital (pop 250,000), is situated in a cool and usually cloud-covered zone halfway up the mountains from the coast. The hills around are covered with coffee plantations. At the center of town stands the **Cathedral** (1773), which was completely renovated in the Gothic style during the 19th century. The floor slopes noticeably from the altar down to the main entrance. Across Avda Juan de la Luz Enríquez are the **Palacio Municipal** and the **Palacio del Gobierno**. The latter fronts on the small **Juárez Park**, Jalapa's central square. Behind the Palacio Municipal on Calle Zaragoza are two good restaurants: Café La Parroquia, which attracts an intellectual crowd, and Casona del Beatrice for Mexican cuisine. Jalapa's real attraction lies north of downtown on Avda Xalapa, the Mexico City road.

The **Museo de Antropología** is one of Mexico's finest museums (in organization and labelling it is superior to the anthropology museum in Mexico City). The building, which opened in 1986, is stunning—a series of marble-lined exhibition halls that cascade gently down a slope. The displays focus only on the cultures of Veracruz, from the earliest to present-day indigenous groups. The first rooms are devoted to the Olmecs and include colossal heads from San Lorenzo. Then follow exhibitions on Central Veracruz (frescoes from El Higuera and El Zapotal ceramic funerary sculptures), El Tajín, Zempoala, osteology (the study of bones) and current ethnography. Around 3,000 artefacts are on display, and the museum apparently keeps many times that number in storage.

ORIZABA AND CÓRDOBA

Orizaba (pop 140,000), on the southern slopes of the volcano of the same name (at 5,747 meters, or 18,904 feet, Mexico's highest point), is one of the wettest spots in the country. The town is built around several natural springs; the Río Blanco flowing off the volcano cuts through town, which has a rainfall so famous for its constancy that it is named the *chipi-chipi* (drizzle). The springs have attracted many industries, including the Moctezuma brewery, but downtown still has some colonial charms, including many churches with baroque façades. The cast-iron **Palacio Municipal** at one corner of the **Parque del Castillo**, the main square, was originally the Belgian pavilion for the late 19th-century Paris International Exhibition. The town of **Fortín de las Flores**, 14 kilometers (nine miles) east down the mountain, is devoted to the production of flowers. The Hotel Fortín de las Flores here was formerly the Hacienda de las Animas, the retreat of Emperor Maximilian and Empress Carlota. **Córdoba** (pop 110,000) further down the slopes is the center of the flower-, fruit-, coffee- and sugar cane-growing region. The extremely pleasant **Zócalo** is surrounded by portals. The Hotel Ceballos (an old mansion) on the northeastern corner was the site of the signing of the 1821 Treaty of Córdoba by Agustín de Iturbide and the Virrey, which brought an end to the War of Independence. The **Parroquia** at the opposite end of the Zócalo is worth a visit. **Yanga**, the next town toward Veracruz, was named after the escaped slave leader who led a rebellion in the region around 1600. The original inhabitants were African slaves.

THE TUXTLAS

The Tuxtlas are a region of volcanic hills that rise on the Gulf coast about 125 kilometers (78 miles) south of Veracruz. Mistakenly called the 'Switzerland of Mexico' by Alexander von Humboldt, they are a series of hills, lakes and volcanic cones covered with lush vegetation that culminate in the volcanoes of San Martin (1,650 meters, or 5,427 feet) and Santa Marta (1,700 meters, or 5,592 feet). Crops like tobacco and the blackest, richest beans in Mexico thrive in the volcanic soil. The region is also known for the many local witches, who convene an annual meeting on top of the San Martín volcano. **Catemaco** is a resort town on the edge of Lake Catemaco, which fills an old volcano cone 11 kilometers (seven miles) wide and eight meters (24 feet) deep. The **Malecón** is lined with restaurants specializing in snails and **Mojarra de Catemaco**, a perch-like fish you can watch being netted while you eat. Launches are available along the waterfront to take you on tours of the lake, including a shrine, some small archeological sites and the spring for Coyamé brand mineral water, which is bottled in town. Inland the streets are muddy and broken. The **Santuario** contains a venerated image of Nuestra Señora del Carmen. Pilgrims carrying bouquets of green herbs brush the altar's window and then their faces and bodies with the leaves.

The town of **San Andrés Tuxtla**, 12 kilometers (seven miles) west, is the Tuxtla's commercial center. There are no real tourist sights downtown, but the **Parque Lerdo** is congenial in the evenings when the entire town seems to be either perambulating or sitting in the surrounding cafés. The Hotel del Parque is highly recommended (try the restaurant's *frijoles*—refried beans). The cave-like Restaurant Guadalajara del Noche on Avda Juárez serves local specialties. San Andrés is also the center of the local cigar industry: Te-Amo, Santa Clara and San Andrés all have factories here, and you may visit the last two on the west end of town. The **Laguna Encantada** ('Enchanted Lagoon') on an unmarked road north of town is so called because the water level rises when the weather is dry and falls when it rains.

From Siluapán, on the road toward Catemaco, another road heads eight kilometers (five miles) south to the **Cascades of Eyipantla**. At the parking area children working in teams take charge of you. One guards your car, while the other guides you down to the falls and recites their history and vital statistics in a nasal sing-song. You descend 244 broken and slippery concrete steps to the base of the falls, which are 45 meters (148 feet) high and 40 meters (131 feet) wide. The constant mist waters a lush plant life on the walls. Many Mexican movies and soap operas were filmed here. The red tile-roofed town of **Santiago Tuxtla**, 14 kilometers (nine miles) west of San Andrés, is smaller and more traditional. The **Plaza Principal** contains a 40-ton **Olmec colossal head**, the largest ever found, which in 1970 was towed four kilometers (2.5 miles) from its original site by Pemex engineers. It is also distinctive because the face has closed eyes, perhaps representing a dead chief. The **Museo Tuxteco** on the plaza is rather expensive considering the small collection. The highlights are a small colossal head and frog, snail and rabbit head sculptures, all Olmec. The Hotel Castellanos across the plaza stands out in this setting: it is a modern, circular highrise. The Olmec site of **Tres Zapotes** lies on the plain west of Santiago.

The city of **Coatzacoalcos**, on the coast south of the Tuxtlas, is a major oil port. It was founded in 1522 as the Villa de Espíritu Santo by Gonzalo de Sandoval and then abandoned for almost three centuries. Since oil was discovered nearby in the 1960s, Coatzacoalcos has become a boomtown with a lively commercial downtown, expensive hotels and a long stretch of dirty beach. Its inland sister city, **Minatitlán**, has the honor of possessing the first oil refinery built in Mexico and the beginning of an oil pipeline that runs to Salina Cruz on the Pacific. A thick haze hangs overhead.

State of Oaxaca

The first settlements with a clear social hierarchy began to appear in the Valley of Oaxaca between 1150 and 850 BC. Around 500 BC, a hilltop at the junction of the valley's three arms was levelled off, and construction began on the Zapotec city of Monte Albán, one of the most long-lived of the major pre-Columbian cities. The exterior of one of the first temples was lined with a series of bas-reliefs called the **Danzantes** ('Dancers'), which may actually represent dead and mutilated captive chiefs. These reliefs also contain hieroglyphic texts that represent the earliest known dates marked in the 52-year calendar system. Archeologists believe that the Zapotecs invented this system, which was used by all the great Mesoamerican cultures to the end of the Classic era (AD 900). The Zapotec state also included cities like Yagul, Zaachila and Teotitlán. Before its abandonment around AD 700, Monte Albán had a population of 25,000 and covered 6.5 square kilometers (2.5 square miles). In the centuries that followed the Zapotec collapse, the Mixtec tribes of northwestern Oaxaca began to develop and reach beyond their mountainous homeland. The Mixtec history is chronicled in eight codices (folding paper books) that tell of the linking of the Mixtecs with the remains of the Zapotec nobility through intermarriage and the gradual Mixtec takeover of Zapotec cities.

In the 15th century, the Aztecs made repeated attempts to conquer Oaxaca but were themselves overthrown before they could accomplish this. Cortés was tantalized by tales of Oaxaca's wealth and sent an expedition led by Luis Marín to the south; the Zapotecs and Mixtecs successfully repelled him. While Cortés was away in Spain being dubbed Marquis of the Valley of Oaxaca, his rivals conquered the state and founded the Villa de Antequera de Oaxyacán in the valley east of Monte Albán. The Dominicans arrived and built monasteries there and in the northwestern mountains. Until Acapulco opened in 1578, the little harbor of Huatulco was the principal Mexican port for trade to Peru and Central America. The Spanish divided Oaxaca into huge *encomiendas*, and the majority of Indians died from disease and overwork in mines, sugar plantations and estates. A 1570 Indian rebellion was violently crushed.

Nevertheless, in 1800 Oaxaca was still predominately Indian, and 20 languages and many more dialects were spoken here. In 1810, dozens of conspirators were shot before they could take arms against the royalist government. José María Morelos' army captured Oaxaca in 1812, but the royalists returned the favor in 1815. In 1848, a liberal lawyer of Zapotec Indian descent named Benito Juárez became governor; his term was marked by economic progress, political order, public works and school construction. One of his allies was a young local officer named Porfirio Díaz (who later turned against him). Juárez went on to become president, and his stern, Lincolnesque figure dominated Mexican politics for two decades. Oaxaca was isolated from the main movements of the Revolution. Today, Oaxaca is occasionally torn by violence erupting from land tenure disputes, whose foundations were laid by the 16th-century Spanish administration.

Oaxaca

The state capital, Oaxaca (pop 150,000 plus), has been a popular tourist destination at least since D H Lawrence stayed here in the early part of the century. The city is situated in the Valley of Oaxaca just east of the famous Zapotec site of Monte Albán. Oaxaca combines a wealth of beautiful red and green stone colonial buildings with a central location for visiting the pre-Columbian ruins, monasteries and Indian villages of the surrounding valleys. The tree-filled **Zócalo** brings together tourists and locals alike to

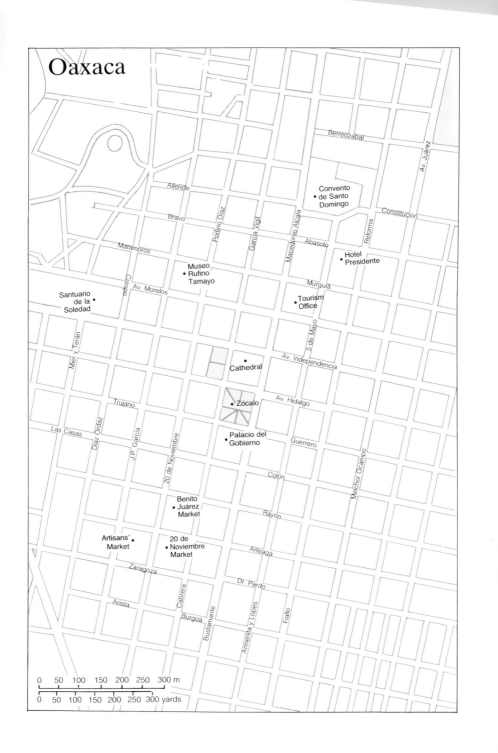

Oaxaca

Berreozabal

Av. Juárez

Allende

Convento
de Santo
Domingo

Constitución

Bravo

Porfirio Díaz

García Vigil

Macedonio Alcalá

Abasolo

Reforma

Matamoros

Hotel
Presidente

Crespo

Av. Morelos

Museo
Rufino
Tamayo

Murguía

Santuario
de la
Soledad

Tourism
Office

Mier y Terán

5 de Mayo

Av. Independencia

Cathedral

Trujano

Zócalo

Av. Hidalgo

Las Casas

Díaz Ordaz

J.P. García

20 de Noviembre

Palacio del
Gobierno

Guerrero

Melchor Ocampo

Colón

Benito
Juárez
Market

Rayón

Artisans'
Market

20 de
Noviembre
Market

Arteaga

Zaragoza

Cabrera

Dr. Pardo

Arista

Burgoa

Bustamante

Armenta y López

Fiallo

0   50   100   150   200   250   300 m

0   50   100   150   200   250   300 yards

Imagination

It was by now quite dark and the high point of the devotions had been reached. Slowly a procession began to form up behind the Cristo, once more recumbent in its crystal bier. The litany had stopped and the priest was nowhere to be seen.

They carried the life-size wooden figure lying in the glass case out of the main doors of the church and into the churchyard. Everyone in the congregation joined the procession. Sixteen men staggered beneath the weight of the bier. One of them was the young husband who had been sitting opposite me in the cloister. He had fought his way at the last moment to the altar rails to secure his honour. Immediately behind the Cristo other men, who had been pushed aside in the struggle, pressed forward, eager for signs of failing strength among those who had succeeded. Behind them, sixteen women staggered in the same way under another litter supporting the rocking but upright statue of Christ's mother. Behind them trailed the rest of the penitents. The procession was lit by a few candles. Beyond the churchyard wall was the noise and brilliance of the fair. Against this explosive background the dark figures of the worshippers seemed all the more intent on their unlit purpose. What they were doing had to be done in the dark space between fun-fair and church. There was a terrible determination in the scattered chorus of voices that sustained a mournful hymn against the thunder of commerce. Real grief was evident. It was as though a real mother was following the dead body of her real son. If the sixteen men had been carrying one of their own family, they could not have mourned him with more passion. This was what the Indians understood by belief. They did not merely believe in Christ. They went further. They invented him. From the shadows at their feet occasional voices still called out, traders rattling rattles, offering food, crying their wares to those who processed by. And yet there was no feeling of irreverence. The Indian imagination could as easily manage the discord of commerce and religion as it could bridge the space between grief

> *their world. They had taken the characters of Christ and Mary out of the Gospel*
> *story and recast them in an entirely Indian tragedy. To an outsider the words*
> *of the drama seemed familiar, the figures in the cast were authentic. Nothing*
> *had been omitted, but inaccessible meaning had been added. The grief of this*
> *pueblo del Señor was far too genuine and far too private. Cristo had been*
> *kidnapped, overwhelmed, diminished.*
>
> Patrick Marnham, *So Far From God*

listen to police band concerts on the bandstand, dine in the surrounding cafés and res-taurants, or simply watch the scene. Many medium-priced hotels are also on or near this plaza. The red stone **Cathedral** on the north end of the Zócalo was built between 1702 and 1738 on the site of an earlier church. The interior contains large stone columns, green painted vaults and gold chandeliers. In the **Capilla del Señor del Rayo** to the left of the altar hangs a venerated and rather grisly crucifix. The **Palacio del Gobierno** across the Zócalo contains a fine courtyard and a grand staircase decorated with a mural of Oaxacan history, including the Zapotecs, Monte Albán and a huge, looming head of Benito Juárez. Five blocks north of the Zócalo on Calle Macedonio Alcalá stands the **Convento y Templo de Santo Domingo** (1570–1608 building, 1650–1700 interior) with one of the most ornate church interiors in Mexico. The exterior is forbidding, because the structure was fortified for protection during unrest. During the 19th-century wars for independence and later for reform, the church was used as a barracks and then as a pris-on, ruining many of the decorations (since restored). The ceiling just inside the entrance is carved with a family tree tracing the Dominican order from Abraham to the Virgin Mary and to various monks and bishops via a branching grapevine. The main temple contains gold and white walls, a gilt altarpiece and, above the choir, a dome decorated with vividly painted—almost cartoonish—busts of Catholic saints rising to the peak. The 18th-century **Capilla del Rosario** is decorated with more gilt carvings and sculptures of church fathers. Evenings are a good time to visit because the ceilings are illuminated.

A pedestrian street just west of the church is filled during the day with Indian women weaving brightly colored textiles on waist looms. The convent (17th century) next door is now the **Museo del Estado** (Tues–Sat, 10–6; Sun, 9–5), which contains large and good historical, archeological and ethnographic collections in a beautiful two-story building constructed around two cloisters. Highlights include the Mixtec treasure of Tomb Seven from Monte Albán, one of the most elaborate tomb offerings ever found—pearls, jade and gold jewelry, engraved jaguar and eagle bones, and a skull decorated with tiny pieces of turquoise mosaic. The ethnographic collection has displays on Oaxacan costumes, musical instruments and social and religious beliefs. The **Casa de Juárez**, one block west on Calle García Vigil between Carranza and Quetzalcoatl, was Benito Juárez' home and workplace when he was apprenticed to a local printer as a teenager. The ARIPO crafts store is one block north at 809 García Vigil. Returning down the hill, the **Museo Rufino Tamayo** at the corner of Avda Morelos and Calle P Díaz contains the archeological collection of the famous muralist, an Oaxacan native son. Pieces include Tomb Culture figurines from the Pacific Coast, Monte Albán funerary urns, Remojadas 'laughing children', a fresco from Teotihuacán and a Classic Maya stela from Campeche, all well labeled in Spanish. The **Templo de San Felipe Neri** across the street is under renovation.

The **Santuario de la Soledad**, two blocks west on Avda Morelos, has a yellow and green stone baroque façade and contains the 17th-century statue of the Virgen de la Soledad, the most revered icon in Oaxaca. The **tourism office** is at the corner of Avda Morelos and Cinco de Mayo. The city's most luxurious hotel, the **Hotel Presidente**, a block north on Cinco de Mayo, is built within the walls of the Convento de la Compañía (17th century), which lay in ruins for many years. It is worth a visit if just to see the swimming pool lying in the middle of the old cloister. Vendors sell carved wooden ani-

A Zapotec potter and (right) his inspiration, Tehuantepec

mals and other crafts in the little square just north of the hotel. The old **Benito Juárez market**, one block south of the Zócalo, collects vendors selling clothes, crafts, leather and food under a tin roof. Indian women sell herbs and vegetables in the corners. One block further south is the **20th of November market**, which is devoted to prepared food. You enter via a long smoky hall, where vendors sell meats and sausages cooked on charcoal braziers; the main room is filled with food stalls with bright blue and green benches, patronized by Indian families spooning down spicy soups and other dishes. The street at the south end of this market is lined with chocolate grinders, whose

aroma permeates the atmosphere. Across the street at the corner of Avda Zaragoza and 20 de Noviembre is the **artisans market**, where you can buy clothing, serapes, rugs and ceramics. The **new market** is west of town on the Periférico next to the **second-class bus station** and the road to Monte Albán. The **railway station** is a few blocks north at the corner of the Periférico and Calz Madero. The **first-class bus station** is situated about 12 blocks due north of Avda Morelos, on Calz Niños Heroes.

Oaxaca's culinary specialties usually include the local variety of *mole* sauce, which is milder and slightly sweeter (it is sometimes made with bananas) than in Puebla. It is particularly tasty in a *tamale*, usually chicken and *mole* encased in cornmeal and steamed in a banana leaf. For a variety of local tastes, try the *tablitas* platter, which includes spicy local sausage, *quesadillas*, two types of local cheese, roast pork, beef, chicken tacos and a *mole tamale*. Oaxaca's typical chilli *salsa* is dark red and gives a warm burn, not a three-alarm fire like the Yucatecán *habanero* chilli sauce. Mezcal, a firewater made from the maguey plant, is the favorite local drink; make sure the bottle says '100% maguey'—others are just flavored alcohol.

Monte Albán

The Zapotec capital of Monte Albán stands on a terraced hilltop just east of Oaxaca. The ruins road begins at the second-class bus station and winds up the hill past instant slums clutching the slope. (At this rate of expansion, they will reach the ruins in a year or two.) Archeologists have divided Monte Albán's history into four phases: Monte Albán I (500–200 BC), Monte Albán II (200 BC–AD 250), Monte Albán III (AD 250–700), and Monte Albán IV (AD 700–800). Monte Albán V (800–1521) refers to the period in the Valley of Oaxaca after the city's abandonment.

You can easily see the reason for the city's location: the hilltop commands the three main arms of the Valley of Oaxaca. At the entrance is a small **museum/cafeteria/gift shop/book store complex**. A statue of the famous Mexican archeologist, Alfonso Caso, stands nearby, usually with a cigarette in his mouth (as in life). In the museum are many of the best preserved *Danzantes* ('Dancers') and *Nadadores* ('Swimmers') reliefs from the Monte Albán I era. Caso discovered the great Mixtec burial offering in **Tomb Seven**, now partially restored, just north of the parking lot. Most people head left from the museum and enter the site via the Gran Plaza. This tour will avoid the crowds and head straight for the entrance to **Tomb 104**, the most elaborate yet found. Steps lead down to the tomb door, over which sits an urn depicting the Rain God. Built during the Monte Albán III phase, the tomb is a shrunken copy of a Zapotec temple. The stone door slab is covered with hieroglyphs and the tomb walls are painted with polychrome frescoes portraying a procession of deities. The less well-preserved **Tombs 103 and 172** are nearby. Turning left, you face the semi-restored **North Platform**, the largest single structure on the site, which may have been an administrative center. There is a sunken patio in the center of the platform and remains of columns that probably held up the roof of a temple; tombs and a drainage system have been found in the interior.

The **Gran Plaza**, Monte Albán's main ceremonial space, begins at the foot of the North Platform's grand staircase. **Building IV**, a well-preserved rectangular platform at the northeast corner of the plaza, is pierced by a tunnel. The next building is one of Monte Albán's earliest; its sides are lined with the famous *Danzantes* and *Nadadores* reliefs. Glyphs on the stones represent dates and names, probably of the subjects. After years of debate, archeologists seem to have agreed that these figures—naked, contorted and with stylized blood streaming from their genitals—represent dead and mutilated royal captives. **Building M** just beyond is a replica of Building IV. The **South Platform** at the southern end of the plaza is only partially excavated; from here you have a spectacular view of the valley. Directly opposite this platform's staircase stands the unique, arrowhead-shaped **Building J**, which points southeast at a 45-degree angle to all the other temples; researchers have discovered that it is aligned with the star Capella, raising the possibility that it was an observatory. A tunnel lined with *Danzantes* reliefs (probably from some other building) cuts through the interior, and the outer walls are faced with reliefs that represent cities subjugated by the Zapotecs. Three more connected structures occupy the center of the plaza, **Buildings G, H and I**, all built on top of a rock outcropping. More temples line the east side of the plaza; the small **Pyramid** in the center contains a tunnel. A **ball court** sits at the plaza's northeast corner; small and relatively unadorned, it was probably built during one of Monte Albán's earlier phases. The terraced slopes below the hilltop were covered with residential zones and are largely unexcavated.

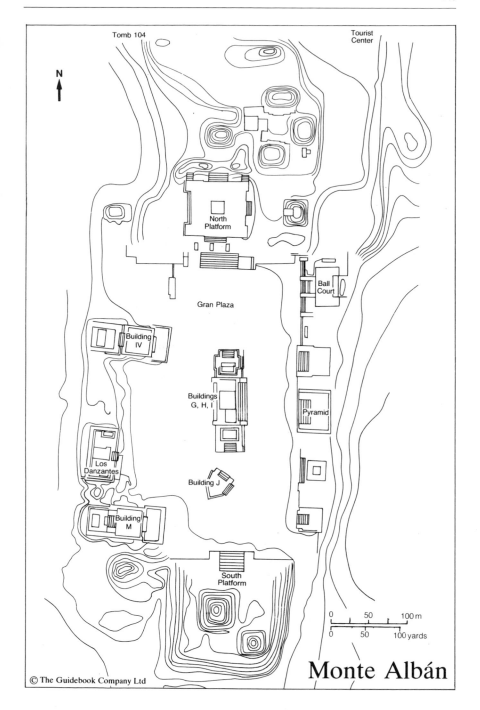

Monte Albán

THE MITLA ROAD

The 45 kilometers (28 miles) of Mexico 190 between Oaxaca and the ruins of Mitla are packed with enough sights for a very full day's excursion. In the town of Santa María, 12 kilometers east (seven miles), stands the **tree of El Tule**, said to be Mexico's largest and oldest—at least 2,000 years old. This cypress is 40 meters (132 feet) tall; 28 men with arms extended and fingers touching are needed to encompass the tree's girth; ten people can stand in the cavity inside the trunk. The town of **Tlacochahuaya** at kilometer 18 (mile 11) contains the 16th-century Dominican **Templo de San Jerónimo**. These friars eschewed extravagance, particularly in the form of gold, so the now-dilapidated interior is decorated with crude but charming frescoes and wood carvings. Paintings by the Zapotec Indian artist, Juan de Arrúe, surround the altar. **Dainzu**, six kilometers (seven miles) further east, was a Zapotec town of about 1,000 inhabitants on a hillside one kilometer (0.62 miles) south of the highway. The restored temple, **Building A**, which abuts the hillside, is surrounded by reliefs depicting ballplayers. Facing the east staircase are a ball court and a tomb with a stylized jaguar or bat (or monstrous combination of both) carved over the lintel.

The town of **Teotitlán del Valle**, up the hill north of the highway, is famous for its blankets, rugs and serapes. Nearly every house has a loom, and the inhabitants hang samples of their craft over the door to let you know what is for sale. Also try the **artisans market** in the town center. Just beyond the Teotitlán turnoff lies the mostly unexcavated site of **Lambityeco**. Just to the left of the largest temple, known as **Mound 195**, is a patio with stone friezes depicting six men and a women of Zapotec royalty. The building complex of **Mound 190** is decorated with two ferocious reconstructed stucco heads of the Rain God. These structures were built between AD 650 and 700, relatively late in the Zapotec era.

Tlacolula is a bustling market town 33 kilometers east of Oaxaca. The **Santuario del Señor de Tlacolula**, visible from the highway, is notable for its **Capilla del Rosario**. Like the chapel of the same name in Oaxaca, this one has elaborately carved white and gold decor. The sculptures are decidedly more gory; they depict saints frozen in the instant of their martyrdom, with daggers in their chest, holding their head in their hands, their cranium split by an axe or simply in their various positions of crucifixion.

At kilometer 35 (21 miles) from Oaxaca, a road leads two kilometers (1.2 miles) to the site of **Yagul** on a stone mesa covered with cacti and bushes. There's a great view to the north and south. A fortress occupied the hilltop on the right of the parking lot, and you can still see remains of the walls. A path heads to the left up to the **Palace of Six Patios**, a maze-like network of rooms that were probably used both as residences and for administration. To the south are the remains of a larger patio and a ball court. The latter abuts a temple mound forming a side of another patio that was lined with tombs. The largest of these is **Tomb 30**, with sculptures on either side of the entrance. A stone frog sculpture also sits in the patio.

The ruins of **Mitla**, in the town of the same name, are considered by some the most aesthetically pleasing of any Zapotec site. Mitla, which means 'Place of the Dead' in Nahuatl, was the Zapotec capital after the abandonment of Monte Albán. According to the Spaniards, it was the seat of the Zapotec king and high priest, and their greatest chiefs and warriors were buried in an immense and ghastly chamber beneath the temples. It is rumored that Spanish priests found the chamber but were so horrified they resealed it and hid the entrance again. Mitla's most important structures are complexes of three adjoining patios, surrounded by rooms for administrative functions or used as royal residences. These complexes are faced with distinctive yellow stone mosaics in 14 different intricate running patterns—a style unique to Mitla. The road loops around the ruins, and the site entrance is just below the artisans market. The northernmost building complex, to the right, is the **Church Group**, so-called because a Catholic church (16th century) was built on the foundations and with the stones of the southernmost patio. The interior contains an interesting painting of a man in armor falling off his horse in battle and many flower decorations around the altar. The next group downhill, the **Group of the Columns**, is the largest, best preserved and most impressive. It was probably the residence of the Zapotec king. The north side of the nearest patio is the **Hall of the Columns**, with six stone columns. From this hall you go back to the **Patio of the Mosaics**, which contains the finest Mitla mosaics. The southern patio of this complex contains two cruciform tombs beneath the staircase. Two other complexes outside the site fence may also be visited: the **Adobe Group** to the west, with a Catholic shrine on top of the pyramid, and the **Arroyo Group** to the south.

Many other mounds and other Zapotec ruins are visible in town and in the surrounding countryside. Mitla town is filled with shops selling mezcal and crafts. A visit to the **Frissel Museum/Posada La Sorpresa**, just west of the main plaza, is recommended. The museum (donation suggested) contains many fine Zapotec funerary urns and other artefacts. It occupies the same building as the Posada La Sorpresa, which has four rooms for overnight stays and a good, inexpensive restaurant.

THE OAXACA COAST

In 1965, **Puerto Escondido** was a fishing village with 400 inhabitants; today it has an international airport. In the intervening years the beaches and waves were discovered by the surfing set, and nature lovers found the wonders of the marine life, like turtle nesting grounds and manta rays cavorting in the waters offshore. Despite these changes, Puerto Escondido remains surprisingly small and relaxed. From Acapulco and the airport to the west, the first beach is **Playa Bacocho**, at the foot of a neighborhood of vacation homes and discos. There are smaller beaches at **Carrizalilla** and **Puerto Angelito**. Mexico 200, the coast road, cuts through downtown and divides the tourist zone from the Mexican business district. The heart of the latter is Mexico 131, the Oaxaca road, which turns left from Mexico 200; the cheaper hotels and the bus station are within the first three blocks. A right turn here takes you downhill to **Avda Pérez Gasga**, a pedestrian-only street that runs along Escondido Bay for five blocks lined with tourist hotels and seafood restaurants. The beach here is the home of the small fishing fleet. Pérez Gasga then returns to Mexico 200, which continues east along the long straight stretch of **Playa Zicatela**. The surf here is too dangerous for swimming but perfect for surfing; tournaments are held here during the winter season.

After a hair-raising ride over the Sierra Madre del Sur, Mexico 175, the most direct route from Oaxaca to the coast, hits Mexico 200, 71 kilometers (44 miles) east of Puerto Escondido. The town of **Pochutla** just before the crossroads is a lively, dirty town of 15,000 with two passable hotels and a bus station. After passing the coast road, Mexico 175 continues nine kilometers (six miles) down through dry hills to the tiny beach resort/fishing village of **Puerto Angel**, where the '60s counterculture still lives. Two rocky hills enclose the little town harbor; a hotel and lighthouse stand on top of the western hill. The fishing fleet pulls up on the town beach; most swimmers use the **Playa del Panteón**, named after the nearby cemetery on the harbor's west side. Downtown Puerto Angel consists of a few hotels and guest houses, open-air seafood restaurants, the navy base, a small supermarket, the post office and a number of snack counters. The bumpy harbor road climbs west over the hill and heads to the renowned hippie haven of **El Zipólite**. The beachfront is lined with one shack-like hammock hotel after another. Inland pigs root through the garbage strewn over the ground. About two-thirds of the way down the beach, the hotels thin out and it becomes more pleasant. A path leads over the rocky point at the end to another, emptier beach. The huge surf here makes swimming too dangerous; nude sunbathing is the favorite tourist activity. More beaches may be reached east of Puerto Angel by heading 200 meters up the Pochutla road and turning right at the Corona sign marked **Playa Estacahuite**.

About 45 kilometers (28 miles) east of Pochutla, Mexico 200 reaches the antithesis of Puerto Angel, the new luxury resort of **Huatulco**. According to rumor, President López Portillo and his mistress, the Minister of Tourism, were floating offshore of Huatulco's nine beautiful little bays in a private yacht when they hit on the idea of building an expensive resort here. Until that fateful day in 1982, the little village of Santa Cruz Huatulco had lived in obscurity for hundreds of years. Its only claim to fame was the remains of the cross planted here by the conquistadors in the early 16th century. The villagers have been moved to the town of Santa María, 15 kilometers (nine miles) east on Mexico 200, near the airport. However, there is still friction with the locals, because the holy cross is a major pilgrimage icon, and the faithful refuse to move out of the way of progress. Huatulco is linked by a new four-lane road that winds between the bays and connects the newly rebuilt town on the west end with the east bay hotels. The **Zócalo** is now surrounded by gift shops, and water taxis leave from the new dock and head to the hotels or various beaches. To the east of town there's a large golf course and another smaller mall and restaurant area near the Sheraton. Many hotels and condo complexes are under construction, and Huatulco's roads are filled with construction equipment grinding back and forth and kicking up clouds of dust.

After a monotonous ride through empty hills, one reaches the city of **Salina Cruz** on the southern end of the Isthmus of Tehuantepec, Mexico narrowest point. This industrial city and oil port is the terminal for the trans-Isthmus railway and the pipeline from Minatitlán. Downtown, ugly new development has obliterated all but a few older buildings, and the beach is cut off from town by the rail yards. The red-tile-roofed town of **Tehuantepec**, 17 kilometers (11 miles) north on the banks of the river of the same name, is infinitely more interesting. The original Indians here were the Huaves, who are thought to come from Central or South America. The traditional society of the Isthmus is matriarchal, and the women wear embroidered gold and red blouses, floor-length red, pink or blue skirts and ribbons braided into their hair. They run all the market stalls and are driven through the streets on the platforms of Tehuantepec's motor-tricycles like portly goddesses surveying their domain. Many of the men now work in Salina Cruz' oil refinery, and these new wages have tilted the balance of power in their favor. The town is famous for its frequent and colorful festivals, in which each neighborhood celebrates its patron saints with special dances (Jan 15–22, June 20–30 and August 17). **Juchitán de Zaragoza**, 40 kilometers (25 miles) northeast, may be Tehuantepec's future: charmless and industrialized. However, the market—still ruled by women—remains a stronghold of tradition and is worth a visit to see the live iguanas, armadillos and local crafts for sale.

State of Chiapas

Among the earliest signs of man in Chiapas are projectiles and stone implements, dated 5000 BC, found in a cave near Ocozocautla. Early Chiapans probably spoke a form of the Maya language; their settlements included Chiapa de Corzo and Izapa on the Guatemala border, where Olmec influences starting in 1000 BC have been found. Southeastern Chiapas and the neighboring area of Guatemala saw the rise of the culture of Izapa around 600 BC. Throughout this area archeologists have traced the evolution of Olmec gods and religious forms to the Maya civilization, concluding that Izapa was the crucial link between the two cultures. Beginning around AD 150, the rapid expansion of Maya culture in the Peten jungle of northwestern Guatemala led to the founding of Maya centers along the Usumacinta River (the border between Guatemala and Mexico). Important city-states here included Yaxchilán, Piedras Negras, Bonampak and Palenque, 50 kilometers (31 miles) to the west. In the fifth century, this region was conquered by and paid tribute to Teotihuacan.

After Teotihuacan began to collapse in the next century, the Maya city-states leaped into a period of incredible growth and cultural richness. Ornate polychrome vases, stelas with finely carved reliefs, steep pyramids containing elaborate tombs and, most importantly, a highly developed written language all give evidence of one of the greatest Mesoamerican cultures. Thanks to recent breakthroughs, we can now translate the hieroglyphs and read the history of the Maya kings. The site of Palenque, which lies in the hills at the western boundary of the Usumacinta floodplain, reached its apogee after AD 600. In 615, Lord Pacal took the throne at the age of 12 and ruled for 68 years. He built the Temple of the Inscriptions, and when he died he was buried deep inside, in one of the most elaborate tombs ever found. His son Chan-Bahlum then took power, and the Temples of the Sun, the Cross and the Foliated Cross were lined with reliefs celebrating that event. Construction stopped and Palenque was mysteriously abandoned around AD 800.

In 1946, a group of Lacandon Mayas showed a photographer a stupendous series of murals inside a temple in the ruins of Bonampak. Dated AD 790, they glorify Bonampak's rulers and the accession of a baby to the throne through scenes of battle, torture of captives and ritual dances; the city was abandoned before the murals could be completed. From 900 onwards, the center of Maya life in Chiapas moved to the highlands. Here more modest city-states, like the Tzeltales in Yaxbite and the Tzotziles in Zinacantán, maintained the traditions of the Classic Maya. When the Spanish arrived, the Mayas were so torn by ritual warfare between the nine tribes that they could not defend themselves effectively.

The first Spaniard to enter Chiapas was Gonzalo de Sandoval in 1522. In 1524, Luis Marín, still smarting from his defeat in Oaxaca, led his troops to the highlands and defeated the Tzotziles in a fierce battle at Zinacantán. The Spanish did not have the resources to sustain their victory and soon withdrew. In 1527, they attacked the highlands again under Diego de Mazariego. At the battle of Tepetchia, the Indians threw themselves into the Canon del Sumidero rather than surrender. Mazariego founded the Spanish settlements known today as San Cristóbal de las Casas (it has had ten name changes since 1528) and Chiapa de Corzo. The Spanish treatment of the Chiapan Indians was notoriously bad. Between 1524 and 1549, thousands were sold as slaves to Veracruz and Nicaragua, and many more died of epidemics and overwork on the *encomiendas*.

The Indians eventually found a protector in San Cristóbal's bishop, Bartolomé de las Casas, whose passionate petitions to the royal administration led to better treatment of the Indians. Nevertheless, there were violent rebellions by the Tzeltales in 1712 and in 1868, when the Chamulas killed their curate and teacher and fought several bloody battles with the Mexican army. From 1744 until 1821, Chiapas was under the administrative control of the province of Guatemala. Today, poverty is endemic, particularly in the highlands, and sporadic violence continues due to tension between Indian peasants, landlords, the Catholic church and Protestant evangelists—religion, land and politics are inseparable in the area. Chiapas' natural marvels, like the Lacandon rain forest, are threatened by loggers and oil exploration.

Tuxtla Gutiérrez

Chiapas' capital, Tuxtla Gutiérrez (pop 150,000), is a hot, modern and commercial city visited by tourists mostly as an overnight stop before entering the highlands, which begin just to the east. If you have been in the highlands for a while, Tuxtla Gutiérrez' lively pace and bright lights may be a welcome change. Chiapas' principal airport—the nearest to San Cristóbal—is 30 kilometers (19 miles) northeast of the capital. **Avenida Central** running east-west divides the city into north and south and bisects the **Plaza Principal**. This broad plaza is lined with the modern state and municipal government buildings. The **Catedral de San Marcos** on the south half of the plaza is a white barrel-vaulted structure notable for its belltower. As the chimes ring the hour, a little door opens in the tower's side and a parade of saints circles around a track and re-enters the tower through another door.

Avenida Central is lined with the better hotels and restaurants. The **municipal market**, four blocks south of the plaza, is decorated with amusing cartoonish murals of Chiapan culture that were painted by a Japanese artist, Prof Shinobu Tobita. Tuxtla Gutiérrez' main tourist sights are in the **civic center**, five blocks north on Calle 5 Oriente. The **Museo Regional** is divided into halls for pre-Columbian archeology, post-Conquest history and temporary exhibitions. The artefacts are interesting but they are confusingly displayed and poorly labeled. The **Botanical Gardens** nearby are a pleasant place to walk in the mid-day heat. Just northeast of this complex is the entrance to the excellent park-like **zoo**, also called ZOO-MAT (Tues–Sun, 8.30–5.30), which is filled with animals indigenous to Chiapas, including jaguars, snakes, macaws and butterflies. The **State Artisans Store** on Avda Central West, across the street from the Hotel Bonampak sells a high quality selection of crafts from around the state. The Cristóbal Colón and Transportes Tuxtla bus stations are at 268, 2A Avda Norte Poniente and 712, 2A Avda Sur Oriente respectively. Reasonably priced collective taxis to San Cristóbal leave from the corner of 3A Avda Sur and 7A Calle Oriente.

CHIAPA DE CORZO AND CAÑÓN DEL SUMIDERO

The picturesque colonial town of Chiapa de Corzo on the Río Grijalva, 15 kilometers (nine miles) east of Tuxtla Gutiérrez, is the embarkation point for the spectacular Cañón del Sumidero. This site has been an important settlement at least since 1500 BC. A stone found here bears the earliest Long Count date that has been deciphered: December 8, 36 BC. The Spanish town was founded in 1528 as Chiapa de los Indios by Diego de Mazariegos, who built it as a settlement for those Indians who had not thrown themselves into the canyon on their defeat. The **fountain** (1562) in the middle of the plaza is capped with an elaborate cupola supposedly in the shape of Queen Isabella's crown. The small **Museum of Lacquer** (free) on the plaza contains a collection of lacquer crafts from Mexico and Central America as well as a gift shop. The **church** (1554–72) at the bottom of the plaza was part of a Dominican convent. **Temple ruins** may be seen on the road heading up to San Cristóbal. Collective taxis back to Tuxtla Gutiérrez depart from the north side of the plaza.

There are two landings for the launches down the spectacular **Cañón del Sumidero**: one below the bridge, three kilometers (two miles) west of Chiapa de Corzo; the other, south of the plaza in town. The cost of the 12-seat launches is usually divided between as many passengers as show up. On slow days it may take half an hour for a boat to fill up. The two-hour boat ride takes you down the Río Grijalva between sheer cliffs that soar as much as 1,000 meters (3,290 feet) above you. The other sights include caves, the 'Christmas Tree' waterfall and many birds, including pelicans, herons, egrets and cormorants. The boatman gives you ample time for photography. The launch turns around at a huge hydroelectric dam, beside which stands a monumental Soviet-style sculpture of the dam's engineer and his heroic workers. The launches are equipped with canvas roofs in case it rains and, occasionally, with life jackets.

SAN CRISTÓBAL DE LAS CASAS

Situated in a high valley (2,100 meters, or 6,907 feet) in the middle of Chiapas' Central Mesa, **San Cristóbal de las Casas** (pop 90,000) is the commercial and cultural center of the highlands. The valley is surrounded by some of the most traditional and poverty-stricken Indian villages in Mexico. The region's many charms have made San Cristóbal a major stopping point of the **Ruta Maya**, the tourist route that extends north to Yucatán and east to Guatemala. The city also has a small but rapidly growing expatriate community, which may soon become a substantial influence here like it has in San Miguel de Allende. San Cristóbal is a small city of red tile roofs and church towers set against pine forest-covered hills. The air is clear and cool, and downtown is relatively peaceful because the streets are generally too narrow for much traffic. The **Zócalo** is the center of town, and it is dominated by the imposing, colonnaded **Palacio Municipal**, which was rebuilt after it was burned during an 1863 political rebellion. The **tourism office** in the first

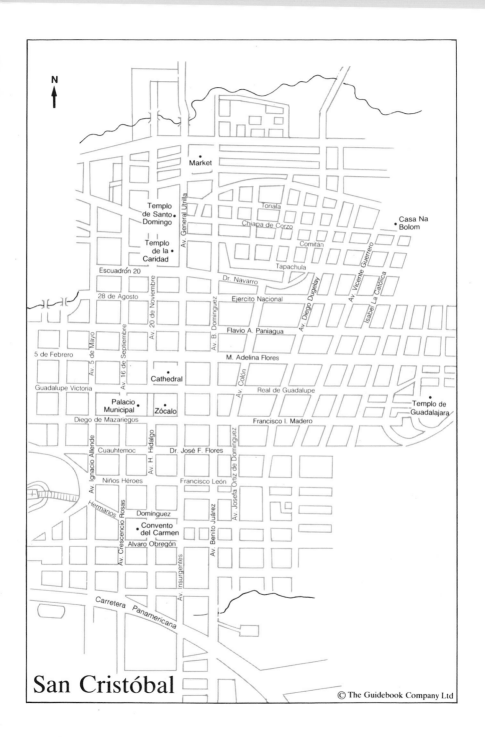

Market

Templo de Santo Domingo

Tonala

Chiapa de Corzo

Casa Na Bolom

Templo de la Caridad

Comitán

Av. General Utrilla

Escuadrón 20

Tapachula

Dr. Navarro

28 de Agosto

Ejercito Nacional

Av. 20 de Noviembre

Av. B. Dominguez

Av. Diego Dugelay

Av. Vicente Guerrero

Isabel La Católica

Flavio A. Paniagua

Av. 5 de Mayo

M. Adelina Flores

5 de Febrero

Av. 16 de Septiembre

Cathedral

Colón

Guadalupe Victoria

Av. Colón

Real de Guadalupe

Palacio Municipal

Zócalo

Templo de Guadalajara

Diego de Mazariegos

Francisco I. Madero

Cuauhtemoc

Av. Ignacio Allende

Av. Hidalgo

Dr. José F. Flores

Av. H.

Av. Josefa Ortiz de Dominguez

Niños Héroes

Francisco León

Hermanos

Av. Crescencio Rosas

Dominguez

Av. Benito Juárez

Convento del Carmen

Alvaro Obregón

Av. Insurgentes

Carretera Panamericana

San Cristóbal

© The Guidebook Company Ltd

floor has a message board for rides and hotel and restaurant descriptions. The side of the **Cathedral** (begun 1528, remodeled in the 18th century) runs along the northern side of the Zócalo. The interior contains massive Corinthian columns and carved gilt altars. From 1544 to 45, this was the seat of San Cristóbal's most famous bishop, Bartolomé de las Casas, the protector of the Indians. The other two sides of the Zócalo are occupied by hotels and banks. The streets around the center are lined with low-key shopping plazas set in old patios with boutiques, gift shops, cafés, restaurants and bookstores.

Avenida General Utrillo heads four blocks north from the square to the **Templo de la Caridad** (1712). This church's patroness, the Virgin of Charity, became the symbol of the Spanish forces when they squashed an Indian rebellion that took the image of the Virgin of the Rosary as its protector. Except for a gilt baroque altarpiece, the interior is rather plain. The **Templo y Convento de Santo Domingo** (begun 1547) next door contains San Cristóbal's most beautiful church, which was built during the 18th century. The church is covered with an ornate baroque façade carved with a jungle of vegetal motifs and columns wrapped in vines. The interior walls are lined with gilt panels set with 17th- and 18th-century paintings from Guatemala, and the pulpit is one of the most richly carved in Mexico. Indians in town for the market bring flower offerings, light candles on the floor and pray in front of the most revered images. The **Museo Regional** (Tues–Sun, 9–2) in the convent next door contains an excellent display on San Cristóbal's history on the first floor, and the Pellizzi collection of local costumes and textiles on the second. The plaza in front of the convent has become a handicrafts market at which Indians make and sell textiles, toys and other crafts. Higher-quality crafts are woven and sold by Tzotzil and Tzeltal Mayas in the cooperative **San Jolobil** store across the street. The **municipal market**, which attracts colorfully dressed Indians from throughout the highlands, is one block further north. The market's sights, sounds and smells (phew!) give you a sensory overload.

A short ten-block walk east of the Santo Domingo church on Avda Comitán takes you to the **Casa Na Bolom**, a museum, library and guest house at 33 Vicente Guerrero. Founded by the Danish archeologist, Frans Blom, who died in 1963, and his wife Trudi, who is still active, the museum (visits by guided tour only, at 4.30) has an interesting collection of pre-Columbian artefacts and displays on the life and culture of the present-day Chiapan Maya, particularly the Lacandón. The library (Tues–Sat, 9–1) has a large collection of books on the region; reservations are necessary for the guest house. There is a great view of San Cristóbal from the **Templo de Guadalupe**, eight blocks east of the Zócalo. The **Convento del Carmen** nunnery, three blocks south of the square, has a distinctive tower (1680) in the form of an arch over the street. The **Casa de Cultura** next door has temporary exhibitions. When the conquistador, Diego de Mazariego, laid out the plan of San Cristóbal, he settled the various tribes—including the whites—into sepa-

Templo de Santo Domingo, San Cristóbal de las Casas

rate neighborhoods, each with its own church. Today, the ethnic boundaries are blurred, but the neighborhoods, 17 in all, still celebrate their patron saints in colorful festivals; May, August, November and December are the busiest months. The city-wide San Cristóbal festival runs July 17–25. The various **bus terminals** are on the Tuxtla Gutiérrez road, six blocks due south of the Zócalo.

THE INDIAN VILLAGES

The traditional Tzotzil and Tzeltal villages of the highlands have remained apart from the mainstream of Mexican culture both because of their isolation and of the zeal with which the Indians protect their customs and traditions. This area was also brutally exploited by the Spanish, and outsiders are still viewed with distrust. Visitors are required to respect their traditions by covering their legs, not wearing traditional Indian clothing and not taking photographs of people, festivals and especially inside churches. If you must take photos, you should get permission at the tourist office in San Cristóbal *and* in the towns themselves. According to local legend, a tourist couple who photographed the inside of the church in Chamula were killed for their transgression. If you have any questions about these customs, ask at Na Bolom.

Zinacantán, 12 kilometers (eight miles) northwest of San Cristóbal, is a Tztotzil town: the men wear pink striped jackets and wide brimmed hats with tassels, and the women wear blue rebozos and dark skirts. The 16th-century **Templo de San Lorenzo** in the center of town has a wooden roof over a simple barn-like interior—the plan of all the colonial churches in highland villages. The Tzotzil market town of **Chamula**, a few kilometers north, is famous for its **church**. There are no pews in the interior; worshippers kneel on the floor, light candles and chant prayers, while clouds of incense fill the air. Chamulans' religious beliefs are a mixture of Christian and pagan; they still celebrate (in a Christian way) holy days from the Mayan long count calendar, for example. Sunday is market day and Indians from throughout the highlands visit and sell crafts and textiles here. Carnival is the major festival, but there are many minor ones. Among the other traditional villages worth visiting in the highlands are **Tenejapa**, **Amatenango del Valle** and **Venustiano Carranza**.

PALENQUE

The beautiful Maya site of **Palenque** lies at the very base of the highlands, just above the floodplain of the Río Usumacinta in northern Chiapas. Almost all the hotels and restaurants are in the town of **Santo Domingo de Palenque**, eight kilometers (five miles) east. At the crossroads of the site road and Mexico 199, there is a spectacularly ugly sculpture of a Mayan giantess rising out of the ground. The parallel streets of Hidalgo and Juárez form Santo Domingo's main drag; the cheap restaurants, shops and the ADO and Trans-

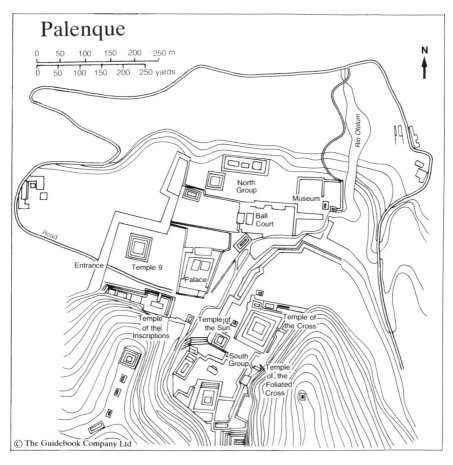

Palenque

0 50 100 150 200 250 m
0 50 100 150 200 250 yards

N

Rio Otolum

North Group

Museum

Ball Court

Road

Entrance

Temple 9

Palace

Temple of the Inscriptions

Temple of the Sun

Temple of the Cross

South Group

Temple of the Foliated Cross

© The Guidebook Company Ltd

portes Tuxtla **bus stations** are located here. Collective taxis run to the ruins from the stand at the corner of Calles Allende and Hidalgo. You can also book taxis to the ruins of Bonampak and the Aqua Azul cascades here. The **Zócalo**, at the east end of Juárez and Hidalgo, is the site of the **Palacio Municipal**, with the **tourism office** on the first floor, and the **Casa de Cultura** opposite.

With the jungle at its back and the flat floodplain at its feet, the Palenque has one of the most dramatic settings of any Mexican archeological site. Visitors to the ruins should arrive at the site early and wear a hat; at midday the sun is oppressively hot. Bring your own water, because no beverages are available inside the ruins. Lacandon Maya frequently sell arrows and other handmade objects at the site entrance.

The first structure on your right after you enter is a 20-meter (66-foot)-tall step-pyramid, on top of which stands the **Temple of the Inscriptions**. The three panels on the temple walls are covered with glyphs listing all the rulers of Palenque until Lord Pacal, the history of his reign and the ritual garments and jewelry he wore at his accession. In 1952, the Mexican archeologist, Alberto Ruz, discovered that one of the temple's stone floor slabs was removable and beneath it was a staircase filled with rubble. After clearing the stairs, he found a chamber with the skeletons of sacrificial victims on the floor and a stone slab blocking the entrance to another room. When that was finally removed, he looked into the funerary crypt of Lord Pacal, who ruled Palenque for 68 years in the seventh century and built this temple as his tomb. Pacal's sarcophagus was covered by a huge stone lid, carved with a relief depicting his fall into the gaping maw of the Underworld on top of the Sun Monster (*not* a UFO), while the cruciform World Tree seems to rise from his mid section. His corpse was covered by a jade mask and a trove of jade jewelry. You can imitate Pacal's trip and descend the slippery stone steps to the tomb: Pacal's skeleton and jewelry are now in Mexico City, but the sarcophagus lid—one of the most important works of Mayan artwork—is still there.

The **Palace** beyond and to the left of the Temple of the Inscriptions is the largest structure (91 by 73 meters, or 300 by 240 feet) in Palenque. A maze of tunnels, galleries and patios, the Palace's most unique structure is the four-story tower on the southwest corner. A staircase leads to the top, and you can decide for yourself if this was an observatory or merely a watchtower. The patio at the tower's base contains the **Oval Palace Tablet**, which shows Pacal's mother, Lady Zac-Kuk, handing him the royal headdress at the moment of his accession. The Palace's patio and gallery walls are lined with stucco reliefs depicting Maya lords; others depict captives in positions of submission. Bring a flashlight to explore all the nooks and crannies.

The three temples of the **North Group**—the **Temple of the Cross**, the **Temple of the Foliated Cross** and the **Temple of the Sun**—are built around a plaza on the edge of the jungle to the south of the Palace. Each of these temples sits on step-pyramids, and their mansard roofs are topped with combs. The first of these, and one of the best preserved of any Mayan temple, is the Temple of the Sun, with tablets depicting Lord Pacal and Chan-Bahlum. The shield in the center has the face of the Jaguar God of the Underworld, who was the god of war—researchers believe this temple was dedicated to war, not to the sun. The Temple of the Cross, the largest of this group, beyond and to the left, contains tablets of Pacal's son, Chan-Bahlum, wearing the full paraphernalia of royalty after his accession, and the cigar-smoking God L, a Lord of the Underworld, in an owl feather headdress. The central tablet, depicting Chan-Bahlum and Pacal with the cruciform World Tree, is now in Mexico City. The small Temple of the Foliated Cross against the jungle wall to the right, holds more tablets celebrating the succession of Chan-Bahlum. Here the

World Tree sprouts ears of corn, symbolizing the social world, while Chan-Bahlum receives the Perforator God from his dead father, symbolizing the ritual blood-letting necessary for human survival. A short walk into the cool jungle behind these temples leads to some smaller temples. Walking north from the Palace you come to a small **ball court** and a line of late, less interesting temples called the **North Group**. The **museum** down the path to the right contains some very well preserved sculptures and hieroglyphic tablets from the Palace, including the **Tablet of the Slaves**, which is translated in this chapter.

If Palenque's heat debilitates you, there are two spectacular waterfalls nearby with good swimming holes. **Misol-Ha**, 22 kilometers (14 miles) south of Palenque on Mexico 199 (the San Cristóbal road), has a 35-meter (115-foot) waterfall pouring into a large circular pool and a cave in the cliff-side for exploring. The **Agua Azul Cascades**, a further 39 kilometers (24 miles) south into the hills, are a long series of low waterfalls pouring into white limestone pools, which give the water a bright blue cast. The lower cascades are safer for swimming. Camping is possible here.

Eastern Chiapas

The eastern highlands gradually descend into the dense, green Lacandon rain forest, which is filled with wildlife and once inaccessible Maya cities. This is home to the Lacandon Indians, the last Maya tribe to remain beyond the pale of the modern world. The Mexican government is now trying to settle them in permanent villages. To reach the ruins of Bonampak and Yaxchilán, visitors must either charter a small plane in San Cristóbal or Palenque, or drive about four or five hours on the rough Frontier Highway from Palenque to the trail for Bonampak. A third possible route is via rafting expeditions on the Río Usumacinta (Guatemalan guerrillas occasionally detain and harangue such groups).

Bonampak is a small site, with a group of temples built around a plaza. Some stelae are arranged at the foot of the staircase. Unfortunately, the famous murals in the **Temple of the Frescoes** have badly deteriorated because of exposure and bungled preservation attempts (see, instead, the reconstruction in the museum in Mexico City). Dated from AD 790 to 792, they depict the glorification of Bonampak's Lord Chaan-Muan through scenes of battle, torture of captives, ritual dances and blood-letting. **Yaxchilán** is a much larger site, spectacularly situated on a hill in the middle of an oxbow of the Río Usumacinta. The main buildings are very well preserved; carved lintels, stelae and other sculptures are scattered throughout the ruins. Yaxchilán's rulers, like Shield Jaguar and his son Bird Jaguar in the eighth century, were enthusiasts of such Maya rituals as blood-letting and warfare; they left many monuments in glorification of their achievements. The Lacandon still perform Maya rituals at both these sites.

The Tablet of the Slaves at Palenque   *by Khristaan D Villela*

The Tablet of the Slaves, now in the Palenque site museum, was originally mounted above a throne in the building complex known as Group IV. This small residential complex lies immediately east of the site road just before it reaches the parking lot. During the Classic era (AD 400–800), Group IV was the dwelling and burial place of an aristocratic lineage that probably controlled various political and religious offices.

The image

The Tablet of the Slaves shows the accession as *ahaw*, or lineage head, of Chak Zotz'—'Great Bat'—who in fact never became the ruler of Palenque but was nevertheless very powerful. Aristocratic lineages played a critical role in Mayan politics, since kings held power by forging coalitions between the most powerful families of their cities.

Chak Zotz' sits on a throne made of two stripped and bound captives. Cloth or paper pulled through their ears shows that Chak Zotz' forced them to let blood. Chak Zotz' himself wears a simple loincloth and jade wristlets, ear flares, a necklace, a head band and other hair ornaments. He holds a small bag decorated with an owl and spear-thrower darts, while his parents sit on either side and present symbols of Maya rulership. On his left, his father offers a headdress (dubbed by some the 'Drum Major Headdress'), decorated with jade plaques, feathers and a little god with a tri-pointed head. The latter, called the Jester God by modern scholars, is actually named Sak Hunal—'White Headband'. This headband symbolized Maya rulership. On his right, his mother holds a flint blade atop a shield made from a flayed human face; Mayanists believe that, taken together, the flint and shield symbolize warfare. The Drum Major Headdress and the bag of Chak Zotz' also incorporate warfare imagery. Why so many references to war? From their own hieroglyphic records, we know that the ancient Maya required their leaders (both kings and lineage heads) to prove themselves in battle, both before their accession and as rulers.

The hieroglyphic text

Maya hieroglyphs are almost always read in pairs of columns from left to right and from top to bottom. In other words, we read from the top glyphs of the first two columns down to the bottom and then start again at the top of the next two columns to the right. Many hieroglyphs denote dates, which the ancient Maya

A monumental birthday card, the Tablet of the Slaves at Palenque, *depicts the accession of the Lord Pacal and his 60th birthday; Chak Zotz' on a throne of captives is flanked by his father with headdress and mother with flint blade and shield. Drawing by and courtesy of Linda Schele.*

recorded by using a highly sophisticated system called the Calendar Round. Their calendar included both what we would think of as days in a week, and numbered days in a 'year' of months. The day calendar, called the *Tzolkin*, alternated 20 named days (like our Monday, Tuesday, etc) with the numbers one through 13, yielding 260 different positions. Each *Tzolkin* combination also

continues

had a position in a 365-day calendar, called the *Haab*. In the *Haab*, 18 20-day months and one five-day period count consecutively (as our own months do: January 14, 15, etc). The *Haab* thus had 365 possible positions (18 x 20 + 5). Since particular combinations of *Haab* and *Tzolkin* positions can only repeat every 52 years (18,980 days), the Calendar Round was a reasonably accurate method of fixing dates. I have converted all Calendar Round positions in the Tablet of Slaves interpretation below to our own Gregorian calendar, using a correlation constant developed by Maya scholars early in this century.

The hieroglyphic text of the Tablet of the Slaves relates the milestones in the life of Chak Zotz' and links these to important historical and political events. The first two glyph blocks record the accession of Pakal the Great, who built the Temple of the Inscriptions, on July 29, AD 615. The following glyphs give the dates of the accessions of Pakal's sons, Chan Bahlum (he built the temples of the Cross Group) and K'an Hok' Chitam, who succeeded him as kings of Palenque. After these events, we read that Chak Zotz' was born on January 25, 671. Next, we jump forward 50 years to the accession of Chaacal III, a later Palenque king. To this event, Chak Zotz' appends his own accession as Group IV lineage head a year and a half later—on June 19, 723. This is the occasion illustrated by the relief of Chak Zotz' and his parents. Chak Zotz' then records three battles and the prisoners he captured. The closing hieroglyphs state that Chak Zotz' dedicated a building on March 8, 730. Mayanists believe that the verb in this sentence refers to a cache of precious objects that the Maya often buried at house dedication ceremonies and, moreover, that the building itself was actually the same structure that held the Tablet of the Slaves. Archeology supports this interpretation, because in the 1950s archeologists discovered a cache here. Chak Zotz' finishes his hieroglyphic statement with the celebration of his 60th birthday.

In the Tablet of the Slaves, Chak Zotz' publicly declared the origins of his claim to power. He ruled the lineage because his parents gave him the war headdress and the flint/shield emblem, and because he proved himself in battle and captured many prisoners. Finally, he lived to commission what some have called a giant birthday card: the Tablet of the Slaves.

(For further reading suggestions on the Maya, see Recommended Reading, p 325)

State of Tabasco

The steamy Gulf state of Tabasco was the site of La Venta, the largest Olmec city, which contained 18,000 inhabitants at its zenith between 800 and 500 BC. On an island on the Tonalá River delta 15 kilometers (nine miles) from the Gulf, archeologists found the remains of a 34-meter (112-foot)-tall ceremonial mound, four colossal heads, mosaic floors in the shape of jaguar masks and tombs made of basalt pillars, containing offerings of jade figurines arranged in circular ceremonial scenes. Between AD 200 and 900, Tabasco lay on the western border of the Classic Maya expansion. The only major site was Comalcalco, northwest of Villahermosa. After AD 900, the state was the home of the Chontal-speaking Putun Maya, who were known to the Aztecs as the Olmeca-Xicallanca. These aggressive traders penetrated as far as Oaxaca, Cholula and Cacaxtla in central Mexico; not much is known about their culture along the Gulf coast.

In 1518, Juan de Grijalva landed in Tabasco, and he was soon followed by Cortés, who landed his expedition at a Putun Maya town called Potonchán. The Spanish won a bloody victory against a large Maya army near a town up the Río Grijalva named Tabasco (now Villahermosa) and were given a peace offering of 20 Indian maidens. Among them was La Malinche, whose assistance proved crucial to the Spanish effort. Cortés passed through the region again in 1525 on his expedition to Honduras, but the state wasn't conquered until the next decade by Francisco de Montejo. Spanish colonization arrived slowly in Tabasco due to its isolation and lack of rich resources to exploit.

During the last three decades, huge oil deposits have been found underneath and offshore Tabasco; the state is now booming with petroleum-induced prosperity.

VILLAHERMOSA

Tabasco's capital, the steamy oil boom town of Villahermosa (pop 275,000), lies along the oxbows of the Río Grijalva on the coastal plain, about 45 kilometers (28 miles) from the Gulf. The Grijalva here is faintly reminiscent of the Nile in Cairo, with green water, floating weeds, ferries and even dinner cruises on air-conditioned boats. The riverfront downtown, centered on the **Plaza de la Constitución**, is a pleasantly chaotic area of pedestrian shopping arcades, cinemas and the cheaper hotels. The **Centro Cultural**, about a kilometer (0.62 miles) away, contains the state library and theater and the **CICOM (Centro de Investigaciónes de las Culturas Olmecas) Archeological Museum** (Tues–Sun, 9–8). The exhibition begins on the second floor with an overview of pre-Hispanic cultures. The first floor contains Olmec artefacts, primarily from La Venta, Maya ceramics from Comalcalco, and funerary urns from caves near Tapijulapa that are half-covered with stalagmites. The ground floor exhibitions include more stone sculptures from La Venta and pieces from the museum's Maya collection. There is a good bookstore next door.

The **Cathedral** on Paseo Tabasco has twin 75-meter (248-foot)-tall rocket-ship-like towers. The **Parque-Museo La Venta** on Blvd Ruíz Cortines, just east of Paseo Tabasco in the northwest part of town, possesses 31 major Olmec monuments from La Venta. Ask for a guidebook at the entrance, because the pieces are not labeled. Highlights include three colossal heads, two stylized jaguar-mask mosaic floors and a tomb made from basalt pillars. Deer, monkeys and other animals run free through the park, and there are also cages for jaguars and crocodiles. The park is built on the **Lagoon of the Illusions**; to the east there is a fancy playground, and to the west lies the **Parque Tomas Garrido Canabal**, which is worth a visit just to see the space-age design. The expensive hotels are in this neighborhood.

The Yucatán Peninsula

Introduction

The Yucatán Peninsula is a limestone shelf that juts out north from the main land mass of Mexico and divides the southern Gulf of Mexico from the Caribbean. The peninsula is almost perfectly flat until the low Puuc Hills rise in the south of Yucatán state. Dry scrub forest covers Yucatán along the coast, gradually turning into lusher rain forest as one moves inland. There are almost no lakes or streams here, because the limestone is so porous that rainwater runs underground immediately, causing a severe water shortage. However, underground streams carve out caves, which eventually collapse, creating the limestone sinkholes—called *cenotes*—that dot the landscape.

Mérida, the state capital, is a crowded colonial city with many hotels and restaurants catering to all levels of travellers. It is a fine place to begin sampling Yucatán's distinctive and spicy regional cuisine. Some of the most impressive Mayan ruins lie within a two-hour drive. The Puuc cities, particularly Uxmal, are notable for their ornate stone mosaic façades covered with Sky Serpent masks. Chichén Itzá, the origins of which are some-what controversial, contains many well-preserved carvings as well as the Pyramid of Kukulcán, which in turn holds a secret treasure chamber and various astronomical mysteries. Yucatán's many natural wonders include vast flamingo resting grounds along the coast and the Puuc's flora- and fauna-filled jungles. Finally, the beauty and simplicity of the traditional Yucatec Maya villages will leave a lasting impression.

The state of Quintana Roo presents the seeming paradox of typical Maya villages nestling inland, while huge, glittering resort cities rise like mirages along the blue waters of the Caribbean. Cancún, the most popular tourist destination in Mexico after Acapulco, presents a wide array of fantasies to even the most well-heeled visitor: ultra-modern hotels, theme restaurants and spage-age discos. The offshore islands of Cozumel and Isla Mujeres are more laid-back, being devoted to water sports like snorkelling and scuba diving. The reefs around Cozumel are some of the most famous dive spots in the world. To the south stand the Maya city of Tulum, dramatically perched on a cliff overlooking the Caribbean, and the enormous but barely excavated jungle city of Cobá. Smaller beach resorts dot the coast between Cancún and Tulum. In the jungles east of Quintana Roo's steamy capital, Chetumal, lie the rarely visited Maya ruins of Kohunlich and the Río Bec settlements.

The state of Campeche's low-key charms include Campeche City's attractive colonial center, which is ringed by fortifications, and numerous smaller Maya sites, of which Edzná is the most important.

Getting There

The main road to the state of Yucatán is Mexico 180, the Gulf highway, which connects the state with Campeche to the west and Quintana Roo to the east. Mexico 261 from the Campeche coast to Mérida is slower but more scenic, as it passes through the Puuc hills and by many archeological sites, including Uxmal and Kabah. East of Mérida, Mexico 180 is now being turned into a four-lane highway running through Chichén Itzá and Valladolid all the way to Cancún. In the Puuc town of Muna, Mexico 184 branches off from Mexico 261 and runs east to Felipe Carrillo Puerto in Quintana Roo. If you are not in a hurry, many of Yucatán's back roads are worth a detour, because they pass through traditional Maya villages where customs have not changed for centuries. A rugged vehicle—a VW Beetle at least—is recommended for dirt roads.

A very slow train without sleeping cars travels to Mérida from Mexico City via Campeche; it is supposed to take 36 hours, but often takes twice as long. A local train runs the Mérida–Valladolid route via Tixkokob and Izamal. Mérida's international airport is served by direct flights from Belize City, Cancún, Chichén Itzá, Cozumel, Guadalajara, Guatemala City, Havana, Houston, Mexico City, Miami, Minatitlán, Monterrey, New Orleans,

Yucatec Maya women making the best tortillas in the world,

Oaxaca, Philadelphia, Tuxtla Gutiérrez, Veracruz and Villahermosa. There is also a small airport at Chichén Itzá, which is served by scheduled flights from Cancún, Cozumel and Mérida.

Mexico 180, the highway that runs along the Gulf coast all the way from Matamoros on the US border, ends in Cancún, in the state of Quintana Roo. From here, Mexico 307 heads down the resort-heavy Caribbean coast, via the Maya ruins of Tulum and Felipe Carrillo Puerto to Chetumal on the Belize border. The huge archeological site of Coba lies 42 kilometers (26 miles) northwest of Tulum. Mexico 186 runs due west from Chetumal to Escarcega in Campeche, passing the small Río Bec-style ruins of Xpujil and

Becán. The resort of Isla Mujeres may be reached by car ferry from Puerto Juárez, just north of Cancún, or on one of the many passenger boats that run from Cancún. A slow (three to four hours) car ferry makes one roundtrip daily between Cozumel and Puerto Morelos; there are also two ferries, including a fast (30 minutes) catamaran waterjet, plying the route between Cozumel and Playa del Carmen. Cancún's international airport has direct flights from Belize City, Boston, Chetumal, Chichén Itzá, Cozumel, Dallas/Fort Worth, Denver, Detroit, Flores (Guatemala), Guadalajara, Guatemala City, Hartford, Houston, Los Angeles, Madrid, Memphis, Mérida, Mexico City, Miami, Minneapolis, New Orleans, New York, Oaxaca, Orange County, Paris, Raleigh/Durham, San Francisco, San José (Costa Rica), Tampa, Tuxtla Gutiérrez, Villahermosa and Washington D C. Cozumel's international airport is served by flights from Cancún, Chichén Itzá, Dallas/Fort Worth, Houston, Mérida, Miami, Oklahoma City and Orange County. There is also an airport in Chetumal, with flights from Cancún, Mexico City and Villahermosa.

The two main roads into the state of Campeche from the west are Mexico 180, the slower but more scenic coast route, and the inland Mexico 186, both of which begin in Villahermosa. At Escarcega, Mexico 261 heads north to Champotón, while Mexico 186 turns east through the jungle-covered and ruin-filled hills of southwest Campeche to Chetumal, in Quintana Roo. After passing through the state capital, the city of Campeche, Mexico 180 heads north to Mérida. The more scenic alternative route to Yucatán, Mexico 261, passes Maya sites like Hopelchén and the great cave at Bolonchén. The ruins of Edzná lie

Embroidering a huipil, *Yucatan*

about 40 kilometers (25 miles) due east of Campeche. The capital is on the Mexico City–Mérida train line, which also passes through Escarcega. Campeche's small airport is served by flights from Mexico City; there is a larger airport at Ciudad del Carmen.

State of Yucatán

The earliest signs of humanity in the state of Yucatán are a pile of bones of extinct mammals, including horses, found in the Loltún Caves and dated 11,000–7,500 BC. Beginning in the 5th century BC, a Maya village culture centered in the Peten jungles of Guatemala spread as far as Dzibilchaltún, in northern Yucatán. Chichén Itzá, Kabah and Acanceh also became population centers; a temple at the latter site was decorated with Teotihuacán-style reliefs, a testament to the long reach of that culture. After AD 600, the Puuc hills in southern Yucatán and northern Campeche gave their name to one of the most elaborate regional styles of the great Maya efflorescence. This style includes limestone veneer buildings, decorated along the upper stories with ornate stone mosaics and repeated sky-serpent faces. The Puuc reached its apogee about AD 750–800, but little is known about the history of Uxmal, the largest site, or Labná, Kabah and Sayil. What happened next in Yucatán is currently the subject of much debate among Mayanist scholars. The Puuc collapsed and, some time later, Chichén Itzá became the most important city in Yucatán—but why and when has not been decided. Both sides use the Maya history of Yucatán, the *Chilam Balam*, which unfortunately was not written according to modern historiographic principles, in order to back up their arguments.

According to the traditional view, a chief named Kukulcan ('Feathered Serpent') defeated the Maya in a great battle around AD 987, and made his new capital in the once-Puuc city of Chichén Itzá. This chief was Topiltzin Quetzalcoatl, who had been ejected from the Toltec throne at Tula. In their new capital, the Toltecs merged their religion, customs and architectural styles with the Maya, introducing *chac mools* and warrior-columns among other things. Others claim that the Toltecs never arrived in Yucatán and that the chiefs who both founded Chichén Itzá and presided over its most glorious era centuries later were descendants of the Itzá, a seafaring tribe that established settlements in the eighth century on the coast of what is now Quintana Roo. They see a continuous line of development, not an abrupt change when a new culture moved in. What they do not explain is the origin of the Toltec-type objects. A major stumbling block to a full resolution of the issue is the fact that few of these ancient cities, particularly Chichén Itzá, have been adequately excavated. After the abandonment of Chichén, probably in the 13th century, the center of power in northern Yucatán became Mayapán, a city of 12,000 inhabitants that was architecturally far inferior to its predecessors. Mayapán's ruling Cocome lineage controlled the surrounding cities through force and intimidation, until it was overthrown in the mid-15th century. Yucatán was then broken into 16 feuding city-states, who were unable to unite against the Spanish invasion.

The first European contact with the Maya came in 1502, when Columbus' last voyage encountered several large trading canoes in the Gulf of Mexico. Juan de Grijalva and Cortés briefly stopped in the region in 1518 and 1519 respectively, but it was not until 1527 that the conquistadors, led by Francisco de Montejo, tried to conquer it. He was driven back, but his son, de Montejo the Younger, landed in Campeche in 1531 and defeated the Cocomes at Mayapan, followed by the Cupules at Chichén Itzá. In 1542,

Mérida was founded at the site of T-hoo, a Maya city whose stones were used to build churches and mansions. The Franciscans were the first evangelists in Yucatán and built 30 convents across the peninsula. Bishop Diego de Landa destroyed 5,000 Maya idols, 197 sacred vases and 97 codices—nearly the entire written religion—in a huge bonfire at Maní, but later Spanish authorities forced him to 'atone' for his actions by writing his *Relación de las Cosas de Yucatán*, a primary source of information about Maya culture. Yucatán's Indians suffered greatly on the Spanish rice, vanilla, sugar cane and tobacco plantations; rebellions were frequent. In 1761, a convent-educated Indian named Jacinto Canek incited his people to kill whites and *mestizos*—the military responded by massacring Indians. The rebellion spread through the peninsula until Canek was captured and executed along with eight others; 200 of his followers were flogged and had one of their ears cut off. For much of the Colonial era, Yucatán was so isolated from the rest of Mexico that the main political currents passed it by.

After the ejection of the Spanish, Yucatecan politicians flirted with the idea of independence, particularly when the Republic of Texas seceded in 1839. During the 1846–48 invasion, Yucatán signed a treaty of neutrality with the US. In 1847, inspired by Mexico's political turmoil, the Maya of southeastern Yucatán decided to oust the whites from their land. They took up arms, killed hundreds and captured many important towns, including Valladolid, in the conflict called the War of the Castes. Within a year, they were on the outskirts of Mérida and the city of Campeche. Many whites fled and the local government was forced to ask for Mexico's help, acknowledging its sovereignty in return. The Indians were pushed back to the eastern jungles, now Quintana Roo, where they formed their own state, which lasted until 1901. The late 19th century was a time of unparalleled prosperity in Yucatán, fueled by a boom in the *henequén* industry, which produced rope for sailing ships and twine for the new automatic hay balers. Mérida became the most glittering state capital in the country, with electric lights before Mexico City and a bishop who drove around town in a bejeweled coach. The price of this boom was paid by Maya and Yaqui Indian laborers (forcibly moved here from Sonora), who were virtual slaves on the *henequén* plantations and were literally worked to death.

During the early years of the Revolution, Yucatán's reformist governor, José María Pino Suárez, became vice-president under Francisco Madero—and was assassinated with him in Mexico City. After the collapse of *henequén* and a brief boom in *chicle* (fueled by the US chewing gum craze), Yucatán's economy fell into a depression that lasted until tourists discovered the region's attractions in the 1960s. The Mérida area has recently begun to attract *maquiladoras*, and many new factories ring the city.

Mérida

Yucatán's state capital, Mérida (pop 662,000), retains much of its colonial charm, despite the booming economy and its downtown streets choked with cars and buses. Mérida's

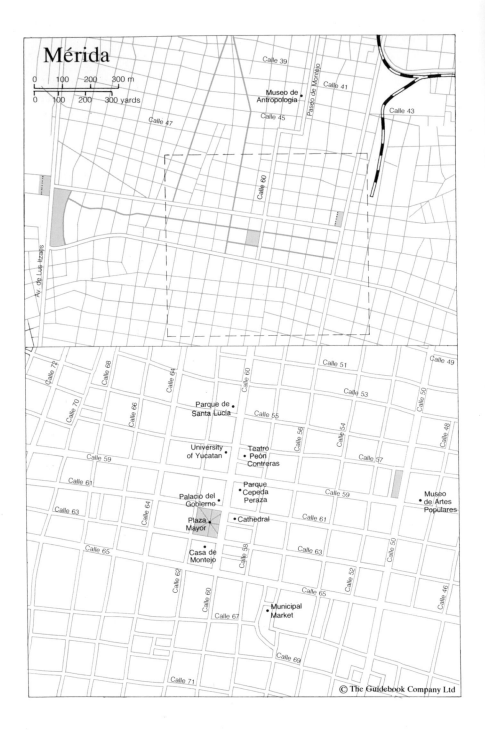

Mérida

0 | 100 | 200 | 300 m
0 | 100 | 200 | 300 yards

Calle 39

Museo de Antropología

Calle 41

Paseo de Montejo

Calle 43

Calle 45

Calle 47

Calle 60

Av. de Luis Itzaes

Calle 72

Calle 68

Calle 64

Calle 60

Calle 51

Calle 49

Calle 53

Calle 50

Calle 70

Calle 66

Parque de Santa Lucía

Calle 55

Calle 56

Calle 54

Calle 48

Calle 59

University of Yucatan

Teatro Peón Contreras

Calle 57

Calle 61

Parque Cepeda Peraza

Palacio del Gobierno

Calle 64

Calle 59

Museo de Artes Populares

Calle 63

Plaza Mayor

Cathedral

Calle 61

Calle 65

Casa de Montejo

Calle 58

Calle 63

Calle 50

Calle 62

Calle 60

Calle 65

Calle 52

Calle 46

Municipal Market

Calle 67

Calle 69

Calle 71

© The Guidebook Company Ltd

streets are numbered; the odd ones go east–west, and the even ones run north–south. The city's center is the **Plaza Mayor**, which is flanked by Calles 61, 63, 60 and 62 and contains the blessed relief of shade trees. In this and other parks you will find S-shaped *confidenciales*, the local type of love seat. Every Sunday at 1 pm the police orchestra and a local dance troupe perform the 'Mestiza Wedding Ceremony' in the plaza. The north side of the plaza is occupied by the portaled **Palacio del Gobierno** (1883–92), in front of which political demonstrations frequently take place. One branch of the **tourism office** is on the first floor. The stairway and the second floor meeting room are decorated with murals by Fernando Castro Pacheco, depicting Yucatán history. The fortress-like 16th-century **Cathedral**, on the east side of the plaza, was built with stones from the temples of the Maya town of T-hoo. The interior is so stark because in 1915 it was sacked and burned by a mob. A chapel to the left of the altar displays the miraculous image of the Christ of the Blisters, a small crucifix that was charred in a fire in the town of Ichmul. At the south side of the plaza a branch of Banamex occupies the **Casa de Montejo** (1549), the mansion constructed by Mérida's founder, Francisco de Montejo the Younger, and the city's oldest building. The Montejo coat of arms on the façade bluntly depicts the conquistadors' mission—two Spanish soldiers stand on the bodies of prostrate Indians. The west side of the plaza is flanked by the **Palacio Municipal** (1735), which contains a pleasant arcade. Just behind it on Calle 63 stands the **Casa de Artesanías**, where you can purchase high-quality crafts at reasonable prices. The small **Parque Cepeda Peraza** (previously the Parque Hidalgo), half a block north of the plaza on Calle 60, is surrounded by inexpensive hotels, two cinemas and outdoor cafés. The **Iglesia de Jesús** (1618) on the north side is undistinguished, but the convent in the rear has been converted into the **Pinacoteca del Estado**, the state art gallery with portraits of notables, and the **Gottdiener Museum**, featuring bronze sculptures of Maya Indians by a local artist (both museums open Tues–Sun, 8–8). Next door to the church stands the **Teatro Peon Contreras** (1908), a Porfiriato monument with frequent concerts and dance and theater performances. The larger branch of the **tourism office** occupies an office on the first floor of the theater. The main **University of Yucatán** building stands opposite; on Friday evenings at nine, the university troupe gives free folkloric ballet performances in the courtyard.

Calle 59 heads six blocks east to the Convent of La Mejorada, now the **Museo de Artes Populares** (Tues–Sat, 8–8), which contains exhibitions on Yucatecan crafts on the first floor, and artisanry of the rest of Mexico on the second. The **Los Almendros** restaurant, across the square to the west of the museum, is highly recommended; it serves the best regional cuisine in the city. Continuing north from the university, Calle 60 is lined with gift shops, hotels and restaurants. The **Parque de Santa Lucía**, between Calles 55 and 53, has a crafts market on Sundays. Thursday nights at 9 pm, an orchestra performs traditional Yucatecan songs in the park. At Calle 47, take a right and walk two blocks east to the **Paseo de Montejo**, Mérida's broad 'Champs Elysees', lined with 19th-century *henequén* millionaires' mansions. The **Museo de Antropología** (Tues–Sun, 8–8), at the corner of the Paseo and Calle 43, occupies one of the most ornate houses, the Palacio Cantón (1909–11), which was built by an Italian architect for the governor of Yucatán appointed by Porfírio Díaz. The museum's excellent collection begins on the first floor, with exhibitions on the Yucatán Peninsula's ecology and on pre-Hispanic cultures from the Loltún Caves finds to the Conquest. The second floor is devoted to temporary exhibitions, which frequently highlight the latest archeological discoveries in the state. The **Holiday Inn**, way out on the Paseo at the corner of Avda Colón, is Mérida's most luxurious hotel and the meeting place for Mérida's élite.

Returning downtown, Calle 65, which runs parallel to the Plaza Mayor and one block south, is the city's main shopping street. The massive and pungent **Municipal Market** sprawls behind the **post office building** on Calle 65, between Calles 58 and 56. This maze-like assortment of buildings attracts many Maya women in traditional dress, selling chillies and fruit. The **El Centenario Zoo and Park**, 15 blocks west of the Plaza Mayor on Calle 59 and Avda Itzaes, is a tacky amusement complex for children, presenting animals in small, dirty cages. The **train station** is at the corner of Calles 48 and 57, while the **central bus terminal** is on Calle 69, between Calles 70 and 72. The most popular crafts purchases in Mérida are hammocks, hats, *huipíls* (a traditional blouse worn by Maya women), *guayaberas* (the loose, ribbed shirt that is the uniform of Méridan businessmen) and baskets. Calle 65 near the market is the main street for hammock stores; the larger hammocks—150 strings and up—are better, and cotton is preferable to synthetics. For hats, try Sombrería El Becaleno, 483, Calle 65; for less expensive straw hats and for high-quality Panamas (*jipijapas*), La Casa de los Jipis, 526, Calle 56. The downtown *guayabera* stores include Camisería Canul, 496, Calle 59; Guayaberas Lol Tun, 523, Calle 59; Jack, 507A, Calle 59; and Genuina Yucateca, 520, Calle 58. You can find *huipils* and baskets at the Casa de las Artesanías behind the Palacio Municipal, in the market, and in gift shops along Calle 60. Yucatán's spicy and delicious cuisine is based on corn tortillas, fiery *habanero* peppers, pork, turkey, onions, seville oranges, limes and coriander. (For dishes see 'Food', p 38.) Mérida also has a large Lebanese population, and there are many good Middle Eastern restaurants here. A local brewery produces the excellent León and Montejo beers. The *Diario de Yucatán* newspaper is one the two best independent dailies in Mexico (the other is *El Norte* in Monterrey). Mérida's wrestling and boxing arena is on Calle 62, between Calles 69 and 71.

THE YUCATÁN BEACHES

The Paseo de Montejo turns into Mexico 261, which heads to the nearest Gulf coast beaches. At kilometer 17 (11 miles) from Mérida's center, a side road turns right and continues another seven kilometers (four miles) to the ruins of **Dzibilchaltún**. This large site is one of the oldest continually occupied Maya settlements, from 2000 BC to the Conquest, and may have had a population of 50,000 at its zenith. There is a small **museum** at the entrance. Directly ahead of the gate, you come to the clear waters of the **Xlacah cenote**, 44 meters (145 feet) deep, at the bottom of which divers have found thousands of ritual objects. The only restored building here is the **Temple of the Seven Dolls**, which received its name from primitive clay dolls found in front of the altar. This building had been covered with a larger temple, but when that collapsed, the Indians cleared it away and used the older structure for rituals. The temple has masks of the god Chac over each door and corner; it is unique in that it contains the only windows yet found in a Mayan temple. There are thousands more unexcavated buildings, mostly simple residences, in the surrounding bush. If it gets too hot, you can swim in the cenote.

The beachfront town of **Progresso**, 36 kilometers (22 miles) north of Mérida, becomes the city-dwellers' favorite playground during Easter Week and the summer holidays. It is built on a long sandbar between a lagoon and the Gulf, and the sights include a two-kilometer (1.2-mile)-long pier, as well as numerous seafood restaurants and bars. The beach is not the cleanest, but the sea floor slopes very gently into the deep, making it a good swimming place for children. The next town to the west is **Yucalpetén**, with many vacation homes and a handful of beach hotels. Many kilometers more beach are found heading east of Progresso on the paved road that stretches 79 kilometers (49 miles) to Dzilám de Bravo. In the opposite direction, a dirt track runs 44 kilometers (27 miles) west along the shore to the port of **Sisal** (you may also reach here on a paved road northeast of Mérida, via Hunucma). Beginning in 1811, this town was the main deepwater port for Yucatán and the *henequén* industry. In 1865, the Empress Carlota embarked from Sisal to Europe on her unsuccessful journey to drum up support for her husband's tottering empire. Today, it is a sleepy fishing village with two lighthouses, some seafood restaurants and lots of beach. The even smaller and more isolated port of **Celestún** lies due west of Mérida (via Umán and Kinchil), on the other side of a wide, swampy jungle. This village is situated on the southern corner of the **National Park of the Mexican Flamingo**, a preserve that is the winter resting spot for huge flocks of these birds and many other species. Guides can be hired in town.

UXMAL AND THE PUUC

At the town of Umán, Mexico 261 heads south from Mexico 180 into the beautiful Puuc region of Yucatán. **Yaxcopíl**, about 15 kilometers (nine miles) south of Uman, is an old Rejon family plantation that has been preserved as a **museum** (daily 9–5) of the *henequén* industry. Just beyond Muná rises the first ridge of the Puuc hills; from the top, there is a beautiful view into the state of Campeche.

The ruins of **Uxmal** (daily 8–5), the ancient Puuc capital during the Late Classic era (AD 600–900), lie 16 kilometers (ten miles) south of Muná on a flat, forest-covered plain. Little is known about who built this city and why they abandoned it, because it has never been systematically excavated. During the Post Classic period, Uxmal was occupied by the Xiu clan, who were no relation to the original inhabitants. One of the site's continuing mysteries is where their water came from—there are no springs, streams or lakes nearby. Archeologists believe the Maya stored water in large underground cisterns called *chultunes*. Next to the parking lot there is a tourist mall, which includes a small museum with a brief outline of Maya history along with a display of stone and ceramic objects.

Directly up the hill from the entrance stands the **House of the Magician**, an elliptical pyramid alleged to have been built overnight by a dwarf wizard. The west-facing doorway on the temple on top of this 39-meter (128-foot)-tall structure is carved in the shape of a monster mask. The pyramid's staircases are among the steepest of any in Mexico—a chain is provided for support—and should be avoided if you have a fear of heights. A tunnel halfway up leads inside, where you can see the façade of one of the three earlier temples on which the most recent was built. The **Nunnery Quadrangle**, just to the west of this pyramid, is one of the most beautiful Puuc structures. Four, multi-roomed buildings flank a rectangular courtyard and are covered with limestone veneer façades, decorated along the upper portions with stone mosaics. The mosaic motifs include representations of miniature Maya huts and Sky Serpent masks with long hooked noses, which also may be seen on nearly every other Puuc temple. To the south of this building, across a plaza containing the remains of a ball court, stands the **House of the Governor**, the largest complex in Uxmal. This was built by Lord Chac, one of the few Uxmal rulers who have been identified, and was probably an administrative center. The first building on the platform is the small, jewel-like **House of the Turtles**, so called because of the turtle motifs that cover the structure. The House of the Governor building, just to the south, is considered the acme of the Puuc style. This is actually three interconnected structures 100 meters (328 feet) in length, linked by an extended frieze made from 20,000 carved stones; these are arranged in geometric patterns and interspersed with Sky Serpent masks. Two doors topped with arrowhead-shaped arches lead into 24 rooms. The plaza in front of the House of the Governor contains a two-headed jaguar sculpture, possibly a throne. The 32-meter (105-foot)-tall **Great Pyramid**, just to the south, has only been partially restored. The **House of the Pigeons** to the west is so named because of its elaborate roofcomb. You can reach two small, half-ruined temples, the **House of the Old Woman** and the **Temple of the Phalli**, along a mosquito-infested path that heads south behind the House of the Governor. To the west of the Nunnery Quadrangle lie the weed-choked remains of the **Cemetery Group**, where stelae marked with skull symbols

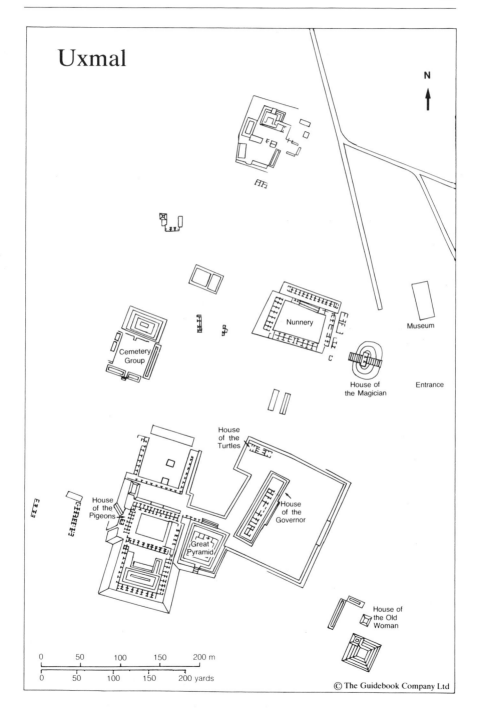

lie in front of a small temple. Sound and light shows lasting 45 minutes are performed at the site at 7 pm (Spanish) and 9 pm (English). There is no town at Uxmal, but you can eat at one of the three expensive hotels near the ruins.

A string of smaller Puuc sites runs through the hills southeast of Uxmal. At least a half-day should be set aside to explore them properly. The first of these is the largest, **Kabah**, 23 kilometers (14 miles) from Uxmal. The road bisects the ruins, and the entrance and the main sights are to the left if you are heading south. Directly in front of the gate stands the **Palace**, and to the left is the **Temple of the Columns**. To the right of the entrance stands the most remarkable structure in Kabah, the **Palace of the Masks**, also known as the Codz Pop, which is covered with seven tiers of 270 hook-nosed Sky Serpent masks. These noses may have originally held lanterns. The steps into the temple are also Sky Serpent noses. Across the road, most of the temples have returned to the bush after being excavated, but a path leads to the **Arch of Kabah**, which marks the beginning of the *sacbe*, or causeway, to Uxmal.

Five kilometers (three miles) south of Kabah, a road turns left through beautiful jungle-covered hills to the other Puuc sites. The first of these is **Sayil**, at five kilometers (three miles), whose most important building is the three-story **Palace**. This building once contained over 50 rooms and is covered with an ornate façade, displaying large Sky Serpent masks and figures of the mysterious 'Diving God'; a colonnade runs along the second story. A large ball court occupies the plaza in front of the Palace, and you can find the ruins of a temple called **El Mirador** about a quarter mile south. Behind El Mirador is a stela representing a man with enlarged genitalia. The next site, **Xlapak**, five kilometers (three miles) further, only has one restored building, a small structure with Sky Serpent masks and geometric stone mosaics on the façade. The last Puuc site on this tour is **Labna**, three kilometers (two miles) beyond Xlapak. The most imposing structure is the **Great Palace**, which is longer than the one in Sayil, but is decorated with a more austere façade, displaying few—if much larger—Sky Serpent masks. On the second floor are the remains of a *chultún*, thought to be a cistern for collecting water. A sculpture of a giant serpent with a man's head in his jaws hangs from the eastern end of the building. A causeway leads to the remains of the **El Mirador** pyramid with a large roofcomb, to the right of which stands the **Arch of Labná**, one of the finest in the Puuc, which was originally a gate between two courtyards. Above the doorways on either side of the arch are reliefs depicting traditional Maya huts.

The road continues 18 kilometers (11 miles) to the **Loltún Caves**, where the earliest evidence of human habitation on the peninsula has been found in the form of rough tools and a pile of extinct animal bones. The guided tours (Spanish only; at 9.30, 11, 12.30, 2 and 3) through the muddy caverns lead you past ancient petroglyphs and hand prints, crude stick figures and Mayan wall paintings, ending up in **El Catedral**, a huge

(above) *House of the Magician, Uxmal;*
(below) *double-headed jaguar throne inside the Nunnery Quadrangle*

cavern open to the sky with hanging vines and wheeling flocks of swallows. *Loltún* means 'rock-flower' in Mayan; archeologists believe that the caverns were a crucial source of water as well as a site of ritual. There is a good restaurant at the exit of the caves. The attractive colonial town of **Ticul** is the commercial center of the Puuc. The residents navigate the streets on large tricycles, some of which have been converted into taxis. The main industry here is manufacturing replicas of Mayan objects, which you may buy in the market or at the factories themselves. Ticul also contains the Yucatán Peninsula's finest regional cuisine restaurant, **Los Almendros**, at 196, Calle 23.

A paved road heads northeast from Ticul back to Mérida, via the traditional Mayan towns of Mamá, Tekít and Acanceh. About 17 kilometers north of Tekit, there is a turn off for the ruins of **Mayapán**, the most powerful town in northern Yucatán after the fall of Chichén Itzá. Covering 6.4 square kilometers (2.5 square miles) and containing a population of 12,000 at its height, Mayapán was not known for its architectural excellence. The main sight here is the **Pyramid of Kukulcán**, a small and poor replica of the large pyramid in Chichén Itzá.

Chichén Itzá and Valladolid

The main road to the ruins of Chichén Itzá, the colonial town of Valladolid and Cancún is Mexico 180. If you have time, the local road that runs parallel and to the north of 180 is much more scenic, passing through many traditional towns, including **Tixkokob**, which is known for its hammocks. The yellow-walled town of **Izamal** was built on the site of a Maya city and contains the unexcavated remains of the **Kinich-Kakmo**, once one of the tallest pyramids in Mexico, two and a half blocks north of the main plaza. On top of another pyramid mound the Franciscans built the **Convent-Fort of Saint Anthony of Padua** (finished 1549), with a large colonnaded courtyard. The image of the Virgin of Izamal inside is the patroness of Yucatán.

The most impressive archeological site in Yucatán is **Chichén Itzá** (daily 8–5), which lies on a scrub forest-covered plain 120 kilometers (74 miles) east of Mérida, on Mexico 180. The nearest town is **Pisté**, with less expensive hotels, restaurants and gift shops, a kilometer or two to the west. Mexico 180 does a wide loop around the ruins; the main site entrance lies on the old highway west of the ruins, and there is another to the southeast, next to the Hotel Hacienda Chichén. The main entrance is a large **tourist center** with a museum, restaurant, craft market and bookstore. The first structure you encounter inside the site is the fine **ball court**, at 83 meters (272 feet) by 30 meters (99 feet) the largest in Mexico. Two walls of eight meters (27 feet) run the length of the court and are covered with reliefs depicting ballplayers being decapitated as well as an assembly of nobles, one of whom, Captain Sun Disk, sits inside a representation of the sun. The small structure at the north end of the court is the **Temple of the Bearded Man**; another tem-

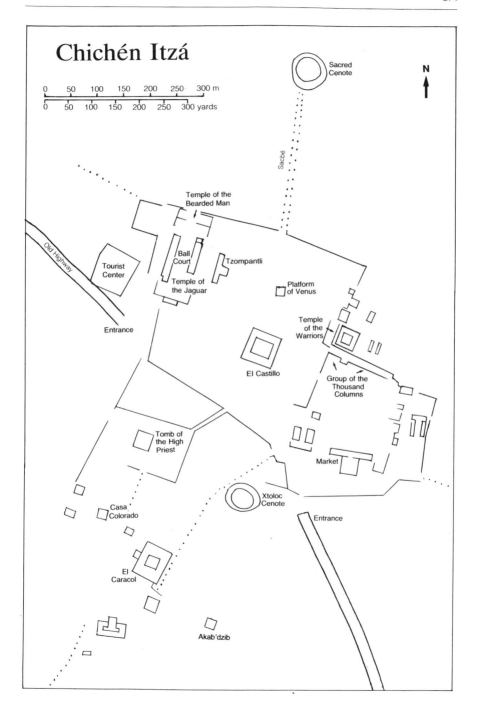

Chichén Itzá

0   50   100   150   200   250   300 m
0   50   100   150   200   250   300 yards

N

Sacred Cenote

Sacbé

Temple of the Bearded Man

Old Highway

Tourist Center

Ball Court

Tzompantli

Temple of the Jaguar

Platform of Venus

Entrance

Temple of the Warriors

El Castillo

Group of the Thousand Columns

Tomb of the High Priest

Market

Casa Colorado

Xtoloc Cenote

Entrance

El Caracol

Akab'dzib

(above) El Caracol and Chichén Viejo from the air; (below left) ballcourt relief, Chichén Itzá; (below right) feathered serpent columns atop the Temple of the Warriors

(above) El Castillo; *(below) view north from the Nunnery—El Caracol and El Castillo*

ple sits on top of the southeast corner of the ball court wall, the **Temple of the Jaguar**. The interior of the latter is covered with carvings, including more portraits of Captain Sun Disk, who may represent a warrior class, and a large mural of a crowded battle scene. The next structure to the east, the **Tzompantli**, is the most macabre on the site. It is a T-shaped platform carved all around with skulls that represent its original purpose— as a skull rack for the heads of sacrificial victims. The neighboring **Platform of Eagles and Jaguars** is surrounded by panels that show eagles and jaguars, perhaps representing warrior orders, with hearts in their claws. Beyond this platform in the middle of a large plaza is the most imposing edifice in Chichén Itzá, the great four-sided pyramid called **El Castillo**. This was apparently dedicated to the cult of Kukulcán, and the stairways are flanked by long Feathered Serpents. All of El Castillo's architectural features, such as the stairs, tiers and the panels along each side, may be added up to find calendrically significant totals. An entrance at the bottom of the pyramid (open 11–1) leads up to an older pyramid encased within, and a sanctuary that contains a *chac mool* as well as a throne in the shape of a brilliant red jaguar with eyes of jade and slivers of shell for teeth. Every year, on the vernal and autumnal equinoxes, thousands of people gather to see a serpent-like shadow undulate down the side of El Castillo; whether this was intended by the Mayas or is merely the result of the 20th-century restoration is not known. The **Platform of Venus**, just to the north, has four staircases flanked by the Feathered Serpent. A causeway leads north from here about a quarter of a kilometer through the forest to the **Sacred Cenote**, also known as the Well of Sacrifice, a circular limestone sinkhole 58 meters (190 feet) across and 40 meters (130 feet) deep; it is half-filled with water. According to Bishop Landa, the Mayas hurled offerings and human sacrifices into the cenote; many objects and over 50 skeletons have been retrieved by divers. One of these offerings was a crude rubber doll dressed in a skirt made of rayon, a fabric not invented until 1910. An open-air restaurant sits at the edge of the cenote.

Returning to the plaza, the complex to the east of El Castillo is the **Temple of the Warriors**, with four rows of square columns at the base. These columns are carved with figures of warriors, captives and priests striding in frozen procession to the main staircase. On top of the four-tiered platform, a *chac mool* for sacrificing the captives gazes over the plaza; behind him are two Feathered Serpent columns guarding the entrance to a two-roomed temple, which is filled with more carved square columns. This temple was built over an earlier structure, the **Temple of the Chac Mool**, in which was found a throne containing a cache of power-bestowing objects, including divination stones and a mirror surrounded by turquoise mosaics. An entrance leads to a room containing some faded murals of the older temple.

The plaza south of the Temple of the Warriors is flanked on the north with the **Group of the Thousand Columns** and opposite them sits the **Market**, actually thought to have been a palace. A path leads south from El Castillo to the **Chichén Viejo** ('Old Chichén') portion of the site, which is older and less restored than the 'New Chichén' just toured. The first structure on the right is the **Tomb of the High Priest**, a crumbling pyramid in which a skeleton and Chichén's earliest date glyph—June 20, AD 842—were found. The **Casa Colorada** ('Red House'), the next building on the right, is named for a red paint mural around the doorway and has a Puuc-style stone mosaic façade. Beyond and to the left **El Caracol** ('The Snail'), also known as the Observatory, is a circular two-story structure on top of a square platform. The walls are pierced with slits through which priests could view Venus, the sun, the moon and the stars from the spiral staircase inside. The path ends at three more Puuc-style buildings, the **Nunnery**, the **Temple of the Panels** and the **Akak'dzib**, which contains as-yet-untranslated hieroglyphic panels. A path behind the Caracol passes the **Xtoloc Cenote**, probably the main water source for the ancient city, and returns to the main plaza. The expensive hotels, including the colorfully dilapidated Hotel Hacienda Chichén, which was a base camp for American archeologists, are all south of the ruins.

The **Balankanché Caves**, about six kilometers (four miles) east of Chichén, were an important ritual site for the city's priests. You can only enter the steamy, electrically-lit caves on guided tours of six or more and only between 9 am and 4 pm. Discovered in 1959, they are a long series of caverns with many carvings leading to an underground pool. Around the pool and in a domed cavern with a huge fused stalagmite-stalactite, researchers have found over 100 ceramic incense burners in the shape of the rain god Tlaloc and 252 grinding stones. The priests apparently sealed the caves before they abandoned Chichén. There is a good museum next to the parking lot.

The large town of **Valladolid**, 40 kilometers (25 miles) east of Chichén, has a pleasant colonial **Plaza Principal**, flanked by two good and inexpensive hotels, regional restaurants and some crafts stores. The cannon in the plaza was used against the Indians during the bloody War of the Castes battles here. The 16th-century **Convent of San Bernardino** in the Sisal neighborhood is built over a cenote. A modern restaurant and disco have been built on the edge of the nearby Cenote Zaci, whose waters are 70 meters (230 feet) deep and contain blind cave fish. A road north of Valladolid leads 104 kilometers (64 miles) to the fishing port of **Río Lagartos**. To the east lies a large lagoon, now a park, which is a resting ground for migrating flamingos from April through June.

State of Quintana Roo

Until two decades ago, Quintana Roo was the most isolated part of Mexico. This was not always so. The Maya flowering that began between AD 250 and 600 came early to sites like Kohunlich, where there is also evidence of Olmec and Izapán influence. A region of low hills in the state's southwest was the center of the Río Bec culture, which predated the Puuc in Yucatán. Río Bec ceremonial centers, like Xpujil, are unique in that they include steep pyramid-like structures, with reliefs of staircases impossible to climb on the sides, topped by temples that cannot be reached because the pyramids are solid. The Indians apparently wanted the look of a Tikal-style pyramid without the trouble of building one. The enormous, and mostly unexcavated, site of Cobá to the north is notable for *sacbes*, raised causeways, which extend to Yaxuna, 100 kilometers (62 miles) due west. It seems that these were a means for Cobá's rulers to reinforce control over their domain. After the abandonment of Chichén Itzá, the Quintana Roo region was first ruled by Mayapán; when that collapsed, it became the Ecab city-state, governed from Tulum on the Caribbean coast. This scenic city, built on a cliff overlooking the sea, was evidently occupied after the arrival of the Spanish, because frescoes there show the Rain God riding a four-legged animal—a horse.

In 1511, a Spanish ship was wrecked on this coast, and all but two of the survivors were sacrificed. One married the Indian daughter of Chetumal's ruler, was tattooed with a chief's insignia, and refused to return with Cortés when he landed on the peninsula in 1519. (Indeed, he had advised the Mayas to slaughter Juan de Grijalva's expedition of the previous year.) The other became a slave and was ransomed by Cortés; he was crucial to the subsequent expedition, because he could communicate with Cortés' Indian consort, La Malinche, who knew both Nahuatl and Maya. Franciso de Montejo returned to the peninsula in 1527, founding a settlement at Chetumal that was soon abandoned. After a long, fierce campaign led by Montejo's son, Quintana Roo's coast was conquered and a military post was established at Bacalar. However, Spanish settlement was all but non-existent because of the region's isolation and the fear of English privateers from neighboring Belize, who did indeed destroy Bacalar in 1652 (it was rebuilt as a fort in 1726). Moreover, the inland forests were home to Maya tribes well beyond the reach of Spanish rule.

In 1853, during the War of the Castes, the Indian rebels were forced to retreat to a town called Chan Santa Cruz (now Felipe Carrillo Puerto). There they gathered in front of a particularly holy wooden cross and heard it speak (apparently with the help of a ventriloquist), revealing that the Indians would be immune from Mexican bullets. The rebels made Chan Santa Cruz their capital and formed a government called a Cruzob, based on traditional Maya principals; for the next 50 years they lived in an autonomous state in the forests of central Quintana Roo. They were supplied with weapons by the British in Belize, who hoped to extend their control in the area. This help ended in 1893, when England and Mexico signed a treaty defining the boundaries between Quintana Roo and Belize. In 1899, Porfirio Díaz appointed General Ignacio Bravo to end the Cru-

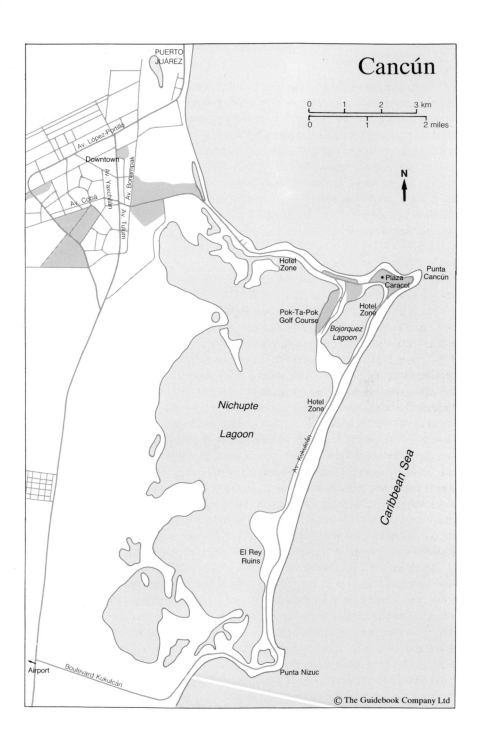

Cancún

PUERTO
JUÁREZ

0   1   2   3 km
0   1   2 miles

N

Av. López-Portillo

Downtown

Av. Bonampak

Av. Yaxchilán

Av. Cobá

Av. Tulum

Hotel
Zone

Plaza
Caracol

Punta
Cancún

Pok-Ta-Pok
Golf Course

Hotel
Zone

Bojorquez
Lagoon

Nichupte

Lagoon

Hotel
Zone

Av. Kukulcán

Caribbean Sea

El Rey
Ruins

Airport

Boulevard Kukulcán

Punta Nizuc

© The Guidebook Company Ltd

zob experiment. Bravo founded the state capital, Chetumal, as a military port, cutting off all supplies to the Maya from the outside world. When the Indians were sufficiently weakened by hunger, Bravo's troops methodically slaughtered them with efficient new cannons, finally capturing Chan Santa Cruz in 1901. Although a few roads were built, Quintana Roo remained isolated—it did not become a state until 1974.

The first tourist hotel was built in the early 1960s, on Isla Mujeres, and in 1968 planning began on Cancún. Within five years of the opening of the first hotel in 1971, Cancún had a population of 30,000. At the current rate of development, the entire Caribbean coast will be lined with hotels by the year 2000. It remains to be seen if the region's delicate ecosystem will survive.

CANCÚN

The ever-expanding resort of **Cancún** (pop 100, 000) is built on Quintana Roo's northeast coast overlooking the blue waters of the Caribbean. Size and glitz are the operating principles here, and the resort is beginning to have crowding problems that resemble Fort Lauderdale at the height of Spring Break. There is nothing older than 1970 in Cancún, except for some tiny vestiges of Mayan temples; for antiquity or colonial sights, you have to head west to Yucatán or south to Tulum and Coba. Cancún is divided into **downtown** and the **hotel zone**. The latter is a 33-kilometer (21-mile)-long sandbar that arcs south around the polluted **Nichupte Lagoon** and returns to the mainland near the **airport**. The hotel zone's main street is the four-lane **Avenida Kukulcán**, which is lined with condominiums, malls, discos and big resort hotels catering to tourists on package vacations. The first few kilometers of Kukulcán have fiberglass reproductions of Mesoamerican monuments, like an Olmec colossal head, placed in the median. The **Pok-Ta-Pok Golf Course** on the right has a small Mayan temple at the 12th hole. There are also Mayan structures, probably watchtowers, on the grounds of the Camino Real and Sheraton hotels. The Anthropology Museum near the Hotel Krystal was badly damaged by Hurricane Gilbert in 1988, and there are no signs that it will ever re-open. The **El Rey ruins**, Cancún's largest, lie to the west of Avda Kukulcán, about two-thirds of the way down the hotel zone. The highlight is a low pyramid surrounded by several platforms.

Returning to the north, downtown begins where Avda Kukulcán hits the mainland at Blvd Bonampak. The next major crossing is **Avda Tulum**, downtown's main street. The sculpture in the middle of the traffic circle commemorates the 1970s meeting of the Organization of American States that put Cancún on the map. Avda Tulum is lined with money exchanges, less glitzy restaurants, cinemas, the **bus station**, airline offices, nightclubs, municipal offices, the **crafts market**, supermarkets, gift shops and medium-priced hotels. Buses head out from here to the public beaches of **Playa Tortugas** and **Playa Chac Mool** in the hotel zone. **Avda Yaxchilán**, three blocks west, has an even heavier concentration of restaurants and bars. Avda Tulum heads north to **Avda López Portillo**, the main street of the Mexican workers' neighborhood and where you can find the cheapest hotels and the **market**. Hundreds of blocks of slums spread out over the swampy ground to the north. **Puerto Juárez**, just to the north of Cancún, has a few beachfront hotels and a passengers-only ferry to Isla Mujeres. The car ferry to the latter island leaves from **Punta Sam**, five kilometers (three miles) further north.

ISLA MUJERES

In the Caribbean ten kilometers (six miles) northeast of Cancún, Isla Mujeres (pop 5,000) is the polar opposite of the garish resort: low-key is the watchword here. Isla Mujeres is only eight kilometers (five miles) long and half a kilometer (0.31 miles) at its widest. It was named after stone sculptures of Mayan goddesses found in a temple here—perhaps indicating that it was dedicated to a cult of fertility—by Francisco de Córdoba in 1517. The island's isolation and protected harbor made it a perfect base for pirates and slavers. The pirate, Jean Lafitte, supposedly spent time here. Today, Isla Mujeres survives on tourism, fishing and as a base for the Seventh Naval Zone, which operates in the eastern Caribbean. In 1988, Isla Mujeres was heavily damaged by Hurricane Gilbert and dozens of residents died. The ferries from Puerto Juárez and Punta Sam dock at the pier on the north end of **Avda Gustavo Rueda Medina**, Isla Mujeres's main street, which runs along the western side of the island to the southern tip. Downtown Isla Mujeres spreads out before you. A two block walk east on Avda Morelos takes you to the **Zócalo**, around which are the **Palacio Municipal/police station**, the squat, concrete **Iglesia de la Inmaculada Concepcíon**, the island's only movie theater and a fiery sculpture of Miguel Hidalgo, the hero of the Insurgency. This plaza is particularly pleasant in the evening, when locals and tourists promenade. A half block further east the waves of the Caribbean crash against the rocky shore. Inexpensive and medium-priced hotels, gift shops and open air restaurants are scattered throughout the downtown area. Avda Guerrero heads three blocks north of the Zócalo to the **post office** and the **municipal market**. This street ends a block further on at **Playa Cocoteros**, also known as North Beach, Isla Mujeres's broadest and most protected beach. The more expensive resort hotels are built in this neighborhood.

The remainder of Isla Mujeres' sights lie south of downtown on Avda Rueda Medina; many visitors rent mopeds to reach them, and taxis are also available. The road passes the Navy base (photography prohibited), a small airport and a fish processing factory. In the scrub forest to the east lie the ruins of the **Hacienda Mundaca**, built by a slave trader in the 19th century. On the right are two small commercial beaches, **Playa Lancheros** and **Playa Indios**, with restaurants and changing rooms. Just beyond is **Playa El Garrafón**, an underwater park with a brilliant variety of tropical fish swimming over a protected reef. Unfortunately, the coral was killed by Hurricane Gilbert and has not grown back yet. On the beach you can rent snorkeling equipment and there is also a small museum, gift shop and changing room complex. El Garrafón gets crowded when the day-trippers from Cancún arrive in mid-morning. At the tip of Isla Mujeres stands the **Southern Lighthouse**, and nearby is the **Observatory**, a small Mayan temple completely flattened by Hurricane Gilbert and since rebuilt. The eastern shore of Isla Mujeres is too rough and rocky for swimming but is preferred by shell collectors. Although the underwater sights are not as spectacular as Cozumel's, the reefs and wrecks offshore are popular with scuba divers. Five kilometers (three miles) northeast of the island a local lobster fisherman discovered the **Cave of the Sleeping Sharks**, where strong currents allow sharks to rest while replenishing themselves with oxygen. A popular excursion is to **Contoy Island**, a bird sanctuary about 25 kilometers (16 miles) to the north.

COZUMEL

The island of Cozumel, a paradise for scuba divers and other outdoors enthusiasts, lies 18 kilometers (11 miles) off the Quintana Roo coast. A flat limestone plateau 53 kilometers (33 miles) long and 14 kilometers (nine miles) wide, Cozumel is covered in dense forest filled with tropical birds and mammals. Playa del Carmen, with a regular ferry service, is the nearest mainland settlement. During the pre-Hispanic era, Cozumel was a pilgrimage destination for Mayas worshipping Ix Chel, the Goddess of Medicine. The main communities were located at San Gervasio and San Miguel, and the island's population may have reached 40,000. After the arrival of the Spanish under Juan de Grijalva and Hernán Cortés in 1518 and 1519 respectively, the Indian population was decimated, not by warfare but by European diseases. By 1600, Cozumel was abandoned, and for 250 years the only visitors were pirates and fishermen. In the late 19th century, Indian refugees from the War of the Castes settled here. Cozumel finally came to the attention of the outside world during World War II, when the US Navy ran a dive school here. The divers returned as tourists after the war and spread the word, to Jacques Cousteau among others, that Cozumel had some of the most beautiful reefs in the world. Today, the island is a full-service vacation spot with both laid-back Isla Mujeres-style hotels and glitzy Cancún-style resorts.

San Miguel, also called 'Cozumel' and *El pueblo*, is the island's only town. The Playa del Carmen ferry docks at the pier right on San Miguel's **main plaza** (the car ferry from Puerto Morelos uses the cruise ship pier south of town). The plaza is surrounded by medium-priced hotels, restaurants and gift shops catering to the cruise ship trade. A small **tourist information booth** stands in the middle of the plaza. The town's principal streets are **Avda Melgar**, also known as the Malecón, which runs along the island's west coast, and **Avda Juárez**, which heads east from the plaza all the way to the opposite coast. Avda 5, a few blocks inland from the Malecón, is lined with gift shops selling, among other things, ceramics, silver and gold jewelry, Maya artefact reproductions, shells, novelty T-shirts, and liquor. The **Museo de Cozumel** (daily, 10–2, 4–8), three blocks north of the plaza on the Malecón, contains excellent displays on the island's underwater and land ecosystems on the first floor and on local Maya culture on the second. The Malecón continues north to the **airport**, which was built on top of Mayan ruins, and the **North Resort Zone**. South of San Miguel—you need a car or moped; bus service is erratic—Avda Melgar passes through the **South Resort Zone**, favored by divers, by the **international pier** at kilometer five (three miles), and reaches the **Parque Chankanaab** (daily 9–5) six kilometers (3.7 miles) further on. The park is built around a lagoon filled with exotic tropical fishes and with more reefs in the sea offshore. A botanical garden, a restaurant, four dive shops and two snack bars are also on the premises. The **Playa San Francisco**, seven kilometers (4.3 miles) down the road, has a popular dive reef and a broad beach with a restaurant and changing area. The agricultural settlement of **Cedral**, a few kilometers inland, possesses a small Maya temple in the center.

The road now turns east and heads to the opposite coast. Right where it hits the rocky east shore, a dirt track turns south and heads to another small Maya temple, called **El Caracol**, and the **South Lighthouse**. The paved road now runs north along the wave- and wind-swept east coast, which is more or less empty, except for a small restaurant and hotel called **The Naked Turtle**. The waters here are too rough for swimming. About halfway up the island, the road meets the eastern extension of Avda Juárez. Another dirt track continues north along the shore—offroad vehicles only—to some more small Maya temples and another lighthouse. A dirt road leads six kilometers (3.7 miles) north of the Avda Juárez extension—the turnoff is seven kilometers (4.3 miles) east of San Miguel— to the ruins of **San Gervasio**, the largest extant Maya site on the island. The largest structure is a 12-meter (40-foot)-high pyramid, and there are numerous smaller temples scattered through the forest. The paved road continues right back to the main plaza in San Miguel. Divers and those seeking to learn how to dive can find all their needs met at one of Cozumel's many dive shops and scuba schools. Unfortunately, the most spectacular underwater sights, like the **Palancar Reefs**, are very deep and require advanced training to visit safely.

THE EAST COAST

The broad white beaches of the Quintana Roo coast south of Cancún are lined with resorts and campgrounds. Offshore, divers, snorkelers and fishermen will find a barrier reef—the second largest in the world after Australia's—that stretches all the way to Belize. **Puerto Morelos**, 34 kilometers (21 miles) south of downtown Cancún on Mexico 307, is notable only for the car ferry (one roundtrip daily) to Cozumel. **Punta Bete**, a few kilometers down the coast, contains some pleasant but expensive resorts. The passenger ferries to Cozumel leave from **Playa del Carmen**, 32 kilometers (20 miles) south of

Puerto Morelos. A couple of decades ago, this small town began to attract international budget travelers, and many inexpensive hotels—some of them just glorified beach shacks—were built along the shore, particularly north of the pier. Tourism has boomed to such an extent that the beaches are littered and the town has lost its relaxed atmosphere. The center of town is the small **plaza** just above the pier. Downtown is sometimes congested with buses that haul passengers from the cruise ships anchored offshore to the ruins.

A few kilometers to the south you find the **Xcaret Lagoon**, a natural aquarium in a brackish, spring-fed cove surrounded by limestone walls. Aquarium fanciers may recognize popular freshwater tropical fish, including sailfin mollies. A small Mayan temple is perched above the cove. **Paamul**, further down the road, is a beautiful crescent-shaped beach that becomes a sea turtle nesting ground in July and August. The next stop on Mexico 307 is **Puerto Aventuras**, a big, new hotel/condominium complex that includes a golf course, tennis courts, a shopping center and a marina. The resort of **Akumal** to the south is one of the oldest in Quintana Roo. The wreck of a Spanish galLeón lies in the water offshore, and one of the divers who first explored it liked the area so much that he built a dive resort here in 1958. Good beaches stretch in either direction. The **Xelha Lagoon** south of Akumal is one of the largest and most fish-filled natural aquariums in Quintana Roo and attracts hundreds of tourists every day. There is a restaurant and a small museum at the entrance, and you can also rent snorkeling gear—a must—to see the fish, which have become blasé about human presence. Xelha is a national park, but there are rumors that a developer wants to turn it into an amusement park called 'Mexicoland'.

The walled city of **Tulum** is dramatically situated on a cliff overlooking the blue waters of the Caribbean, 129 kilometers (80 miles) south of Cancún. After the fall of Mayapán and the Cocome lineage, Tulum was the capital of the province of Ecab, which comprised most of present-day Quintana Roo. There is evidence that the site, which had a population of 500–600, thrived for decades after the Spanish Conquest. You enter the ruins through the central archway in a limestone wall that once was five meters (16 feet) high and 4.5 meters (15 feet) wide. The first structure is the **Casa de Chultún**, with a collapsed roof, and immediately afterward is the two-story **Temple of the Frescoes**, the most important building on the site. Three reliefs on the façade feature a winged upside-down figure, known as the 'Diving God' because archeologists have not yet deduced his real name. His image also appears at Cobá and Sayil. The interior contains frescoes depicting gods engaged in rites, perhaps for fertility, and one image of the Rain God on a four-legged animal—a horse. The north–south street in front of the temple was probably lined with dwellings for the nobility. The next complex toward the sea is built around the **Castillo**, a small pyramid that is the highest point in Tulum. Twenty-five steps

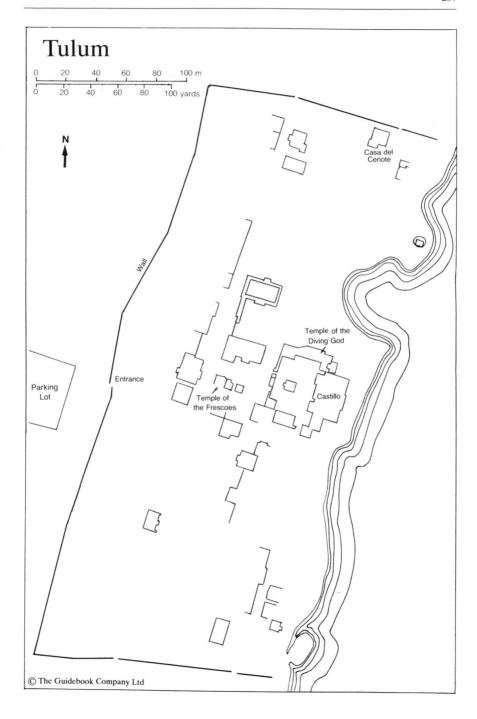

Tulum

0 20 40 60 80 100 m

0 20 40 60 80 100 yards

N

Wall

Casa del
Cenote

Temple of the
Diving God

Entrance

Parking
Lot

Temple of
the Frescoes

Castillo

© The Guidebook Company Ltd

(above) Maya city of Tulúm on the edge of the Caribbean; (below) El Castillo on top of Tulúm's cliffs

lead up to a excellent view of the Caribbean and of the site. Just to the north stands the **Temple of the Diving God**, with another image of that divinity over the entrance and some badly preserved murals inside. A path leads to a small cove at the north end of the site, and, against the city wall, the **Casa del Cenote**, which was built over the well that supplied the community with water. The modern town of Tulum is a kilometer or two down the road south. The only lodgings in the immediate area are very inexpensive beach hotels built on a side road, east off Mexico 307. This road heads down a long sandbar to the fishing resort of **Boca Paila** and the tiny village of **Punta Allen**, 57 kilometers (35 miles) to the south.

From the town of Tulum, a paved road runs west through the jungle 42 kilometers (26 miles) to the enormous Maya site of **Cobá**. This was probably the largest city in the northern Yucatán Peninsula; its ruins cover 70 square kilometers (27 square miles). During the Late Classic era, Cobá rivalled the Puuc cities to the east (AD 600–900). It cemented its control over the territory by building 16 *sacbes*—perfectly straight raised masonry causeways—reaching as far as 100 kilometers (62 miles). As Chichén Itzá began to flourish, Cobá declined; it underwent a brief revival in the Post Classic era before being abandoned completely. The city was built around five lakes, rare on the peninsula, which were obviously the reason for its location. Very little of Cobá's vast extent has been excavated, and a visit is always an adventure (bring mosquito repellent and watch out for snakes).

The site entrance is just beyond the village of Cobá, on the other side of a lake that occasionally floods the road during the rainy season. The **Cobá Group** complex of structures inside the gate is overgrown with jungle, but it is possible to recognize a ball court and several temples. In the center of this group stands the 24-meter (80 foot)-tall pyramid called the **Castillo**, which you can climb. A small Tulum-style temple sits on top, perhaps indicating that city's control over Cobá. From the top you have a breathtaking view of the jungle and scattered temples rising above the treetops. Some stelae lie at the base of this pyramid, and more temples, including one with fragments of Tulum-type murals, are found along a path to the south. Another important complex, the **Nohoch Mul**, lies 2.4 kilometers (1.5 miles) east of the Castillo on a jungle path. Aside from the ruins, one of the most remarkable things about Cobá is the abundance of wildlife, including butterflies and brightly colored parrots. If you find the natural world too much, you can visit the luxurious Club Med-run **Villa Arqueológica**, providing fine French cuisine in the heart of Cobá town.

Returning to Mexico 307, the dusty crossroads town of **Felipe Carrillo Puerto**, 95 kilometers (59 miles) south of Tulum, was until 1901 the Mayan insurgent capital of Chan Santa Cruz. There is a small museum at the site of the famous Talking Cross, five blocks east of the gas station. **Bacalar**, 107 kilometers (66 miles) further down, contains the **Fort of San Felipe de Bacalar** (begun 1726), built as protection against pirates. The fort is now a **museum** of Mayan and colonial history through the War of the Castes. The **Cenote Azul**, just to the south, is a limestone sinkhole 182 meters (600 feet) across and filled with bright blue water. The cenote's walls sink straight down to a depth of 60 meters (200 feet) and large schools of fish, mostly cichlids, swim along the edge. You can swim, snorkel or scuba dive in the cenote or just admire the view from an excellent but expensive restaurant. Over the ridge to the east lies the **Bacalar Lagoon**, which is also popular for swimming and fishing.

The last town in this corner of Mexico is the steamy state capital and port city of **Chetumal** (pop 120,000). Belize is just on the other side of the Río Hondo. The city's atmosphere is a mix of Mexican and Caribbean, and the architecture is Caribbean-style tin-roofed houses with wooden clapboards and porches. Chetumal has a seamy reputation because of the bars and other businesses catering to seamen's amusement, but most travelers will find these relatively low-key. Chetumal's main street is **Avda Héroes**, which slopes down a hill to the Bay of Chetumal. The **Plaza de la República** at the corner of Avda Héroes and the bayside Malecón contains **Palacio del Gobierno**, with the **tourism office** on the first floor, and the **state theater**. Most of the town's hotels are on Avda Heroes heading uphill, and the **market** stands at the corner of Heroes and Avda Efrain Aguilar. The downtown streets are lined with stores selling electronics and other imported goods at a lower tax rate than the rest of Mexico. Blvd Bahía, also known as the Malecón, heads east and north from downtown to the small town of **Calderitas**, with good fishing and swimming in Calderitas Bay. The **bus station** for Belize, Cancún and Villahermosa is at Avdas Insurgentes and Belice north of town. A Mexican army checkpoint frequently searches for drugs at the turn-off for Belize.

Several interesting Maya sites lie west of Chetumal on Mexico 186, the Villahermosa road. **Kohunlich**, about 50 kilometers (31 miles) west and then eight kilometers (five miles) down a road to the south, contains one great attraction: the **Temple of the Masks**. The staircase of this pyramid is lined with 1.5-meter (five-foot)-high stucco masks, some in an excellent state of preservation. The masks represent gods, including the Sun God, and a thatched roof has been built to protect them. The site has not been excavated; archeologists believe that it was built during the Late Preclassic era (300 BC–AD 250) and that the pyramid may contain a royal tomb. The lush jungle surrounding the ruins is filled with wildlife and orchids.

The Río Bec sites of **Xpujil**, **Becán** and **Chicana** lie 120 kilometers (74 miles) west of Chetumal, just before the Campeche border. Xpujil's main structure is the **Palace**, a large platform with three Río Bec-style false pyramids arranged around a series of rooms; one of the towers has a narrow staircase that climbs to the top. Becán is surrounded by a moat that contains a complex of several temples. Chicana, the smallest of the sites, has two partially restored temples with intricate decoration, including a doorway carved in the shape of a serpent's mouth. More ruins, including Río Bec itself, lie in the jungles to the south and are only accessible by horse or four-wheel drive vehicle during the dry season.

State of Campeche

The state of Campeche has always been a major trade conduit between the Yucatán peninsula and the rest of Mexico. Between 800 BC and AD 250, the Chicanel Culture spread throughout the Maya region, and major settlements were built at Edzná, Jaina Island, and Santa Rosa Xtampak. During the Classic era, El Hormiguero and Calakmul were centers of the Río Bec style in eastern Campeche. To the north were the Chene Culture sites of Hochob, Santa Rosa Xtampak and Dzibiltún. Campeche was also on the southern boundary of the Puuc region, and much of Edzná, the state's most impressive archeological site, was built in this style. Jaina Island, just off the west coast, may have been a burial ground for Puuc nobility. Inside the many tombs here archeologists have found beautiful ceramic figurines, many of which are probably portraits of the dead. After the Maya collapse, many wandering tribes—including the Xius, Itzas and perhaps the Toltecs—passed through Campeche on their way to settle in Yucatán. The Campeche coast was a base of the Chontal-speaking Putún Maya, the great traders who settled in Cacaxtla and other sites in central Mexico.

In 1517, Francisco de Córdoba landed in Campeche and was mortally wounded in a great battle with the Putún Maya. After the failure of his father to conquer the peninsula, Francisco de Montejo the Younger landed here in 1537, defeated the Putun and founded settlements at Champotón and Ah Kin Pech (now the city of Campeche). In the Colonial era, the territory prospered because of its sugar cane and cattle estates and because, at least until 1811, the city was the sole port for the entire peninsula. Spanish shipping was the quarry of English privateers based in the nearby Laguna de Términos, and Campeche was girdled with fortifications for its protection. The Indian rebellion led by Canek and the ensuing War of the Castes also spread to Campeche, but not as seriously as in Yucatán. In this century, Campeche underwent a slow decline, until oil was discovered in the Gulf and the economy began to expand again.

CAMPECHE

The state capital, Campeche (pop 220,000), consists of a colonial core girdled by a series of *baluartes*, 'bulwarks', surrounded by a prosperous and modern city beyond. All the main sights are handily located in a seven by nine block area within the fortifications. The **Plaza Principal**, one block from the Gulf, is flanked by the **Catedral de la Con-**

cepción (1540–45), the oldest church on the Yucatán Peninsula. The portalled building on the south side of the plaza is the 19th-century **Palacio Municipal**. On the Gulf side of the plaza you come to a remnant of the old city wall, which contains the **Archeological Museum** (Tues–Sat, 8–8), with a small collection of Maya sculptures from around the state. Between the old wall and the waterfront Avda Ruíz Cortines lie a number of government buildings and expensive hotels. Two blocks southwest of the Archeological Museum stands the modern **Palacio del Gobierno** and the **tourism office** across the square. The **Baluarte de San Carlos** at the corner of Calles 8 and 65, just west of the Palacio del Gobierno, contains a **fortifications museum** (Tues–Sat, 9–1, 4–8; Sun, 9–1). The **Avda Circuito** circumnavigates the old city walls, and a stroll along it will take you to the **Baluarte of Santa Rosa** (containing the historical library), **San Juan**, **San Francisco**, **San Pedro** and finally to **Santiago** at the northeast corner of the fortifications. The **Museo Regional** (Mon–Sat, 9–8; Sun, 9–1) at Calle 59, between Calles 14 and 16 near the main plaza, contains exhibitions and artefacts from the Mayan and colonial eras. South of downtown on the coastal u Ruiz Cortines, a famously ugly sculpture of a concrete giant clutching a torch struggles to rise out of the ground. The **central bus station** is on Avda Gobernadores, four blocks west of the Baluarte de San Pedro, while the **railway station** is another kilometer further out on the same avenue. Campeche is famous for its seafood, particularly shrimp, but finding a good restaurant downtown is difficult. According to residents, the seaside Ramada Inn has the best restaurant and also attracts crowds of local politicians.

Edzná

A 60-kilometer (37-mile) drive east of Campeche will take you to the Puuc-influenced Mayan ruins of **Edzná**, the most impressive in the state. The highlight is the unique **Temple of the Five Stories**, a tiered pyramid 20 meters (66 feet) high, which contains entrances to rows of rooms on each story. The temple on top is capped with an ornate roofcomb. No other structure in Mexico combines the features of a pyramid-temple with a palace; smaller structures and a ball court lie at the foot of this temple. Aerial photographs have revealed an extensive drainage system around the site that may have been used for irrigation.

Smaller archeological sites, like **Hopelchén** and **Hochob**, lie off Mexico 261, which heads northeast into the Puuc Hills of Yucatán. Just before the border you can visit the **Bolonchén Caves**, which were an important source of water for the Mayas. In the 19th century, the explorer, Frederick Catherwood, sketched the dramatic scene of dozens of Indians with large jugs of water on their back climbing up a huge ladder to the top of the Bolonchén Caves—an illustration of the peninsula's desperate lack of water.

Edzná's unique Temple of the Five Stories, a combination pyramid and temple;

Legend of the Suns

Thus it is told, it is said: there have already
been four manifestations and this one is the fifth age.

So the old ones knew this, that in the year 1-Rabbit
heaven and earth were founded. And they knew this,
that when heaven and earth were founded
there had already been four kinds of men, four kinds of manifestations,
Also they knew that each of these had existed in a Sun, an age.

And they said of the first men, their god made them,
fashioned them of ashes. This they attributed to the god Quetzalcóatl,
whose sign is 7-Wind, he made them, he invented them.
The first Sun or age which was founded, its sign was 4-Water,
it was called the Sun of Water. Then it happened
that water carried away everything. The people were changed into fish.

Then the second Sun or age was founded. Its sign was 4-Tiger.
It was called the Sun of Tiger. Then it happened
that the sky was crushed, the Sun did not follow its course.
When the Sun arrived at midday, immediately it was night
and when it became dark, tigers ate the people. In this Sun giants lived.
The old ones said they greeted each other thus: 'Do not fall down',
for whoever falls, he falls forever.

Then the third Sun was founded. Its sign was 4-Rain-of-Fire.
It happened then that fire rained down, those who lived there
were burned. And then sand rained down. And they say
that then it rained down the little stones we see,
that the tezontle stone boiled and the big rocks became red.
Its sign was 4-Wind, when the fourth Sun was founded.
It was called the Sun of Wind. Then everything was carried away
by the wind. People were turned into monkeys. They were scattered
over the mountains, and the monkey-men lived there.

The fifth Sun, 4-Movement its sign. It is called the Sun of Movement
because it moves, follows its course. And the old ones go about saying,
now there will be earthquakes, there will be hunger, and thus
we will perish. In the year 13-Reed, they say it came into existence,
the sun which now exists was born. That was when there was light,
when dawn came, the Sun of Movement which now exists,
4-Movement is its sign. This is the fifth Sun which was founded,
in it there will be earthquakes, in it there will be hunger.

This Sun, its name 4-Movement, this is our Sun, in which we now live,
and this is its sign, where the Sun fell in fire on the divine hearth,
there in Teotihuacán.
Also this was the Sun of our prince of Tula, of Quetzalcóatl.

From *Anales de Cuauhtitlán*, 'Manuscript of 1558',
translated by G Lobanov and M León-Portilla

Hotels

Mexico offers a wide selection of hotels, ranging from beach shacks with hammocks strung between the poles to ultramodern resorts containing every possible facility. Hotels are regulated by the government's Secretariat of Tourism (SECTUR), and room rates must be posted at the front desk and in every room. Any complaints should be brought to the local SECTUR office. Hotels are inspected twice a year and then rated depending on the type and quality of services offered. The ratings are Gran Turismo (the best), Five- to One-star and Special Category, which is reserved for inns and small hotels in historic buildings. There are also many motels built on the outskirts of Mexican cities; the majority of these cater to guests that do not spend more than an hour or two. You can recognize an hourly motel by the high wall around it, and by the fact that each room has a car port across which guests can draw a curtain to shield their license plates from prying eyes. At a crunch, these motels are usually acceptable, except for the constant comings and goings all night long.

PRICE RANGE OF HOTELS (US DOLLARS)

Gran Turismo	$125 and up
*****	$ 65-125
****	$ 35-65
***	$ 18-35
**	$ 10-28
*	$ 4-10

Mexico City

■ GRAN TURISMO
Camino Real
Mariano Escobeda 700, tel 203-2121, 716 rooms.
Dramatic Ricardo Legoretta structure with three restaurants, five bars, nightclub, disco, two pools, tennis courts, health club, shopping arcade, next to Chapultepec Park.

■*****
Crowne Plaza (Holiday Inn)
Paseo de la Reforma 80, tel 705-1515, 625 rooms.
Four restaurants, seven bars, nightclub, many top entertainers performing nightly, centrally located halfway between Chapultepec and Alameda Parks.

María Isabel Sheraton
Paseo de la Reforma 325, tel 207-3933, 754 rooms.
Three restaurants, two bars, nightclub, pool, tennis courts, health club, shopping arcade, at the Angel de Independencia monument.

Nikko
Campos Eliseos 204, tel 203-4020, 770 rooms.
Four restaurants, two bars, disco, health club, tennis courts, pool, health club, non-smokers floors, on Chapultepec Park.

Sevilla Palace
Paseo de la Reforma 105, tel 566-8877,

400 rooms.
Ultra-modern with restaurants, bars, pool, health club, shopping arcade.

Stouffer President
Campos Eliseos 218, tel 250-7700, 809 rooms.
Six restaurants, three bars, disco, nightclub, next to Chapultepec Park.

Fiesta Americana Aeropuerto
Fundidora de Monterrey 89, tel 762-0199, 480 rooms.
Two restaurants, three bars, nightclub, shopping arcade, health club, next to airport passenger terminal.

Krystal Zona Rosa
Liverpool 155, tel 211-0092, 335 rooms.
Two restaurants, three bars, nightclub, pool, Zona Rosa.

■ ****

Calinda Geneve (Quality Inn)
Londres 130, tel 211-0071, 343 rooms.
Two restaurants, three bars, Zona Rosa.

Maria Cristina
Lerma 31, tel 566-9688, 146 rooms.
Colonial style, restaurant, bar, quiet neighborhood near Reforma.

Gran Hotel (Howard Johnsons)
6 de Septiembre 82, tel 510-4040, 124 rooms.
Turn of the century building with magnificent Art Nouveau lobby, two restaurants, bar.

Hotel de Cortés
Hidalgo 85, tel 585-0322, 27 rooms.
Built in 1780 as a hospital by Augustinian friars, baroque façade, patio with fountain, two restaurants, bar, noisy, on Alameda.

■ ***

Vasco de Quiroga
Londres 15, tel 546-2614, 50 rooms.
Colonial style, restaurant/bar, near Zona Rosa.

Cancún
Donato Guerra 24 at Reforma, tel 566-6083.
Bar, restaurant, good location.

Mayaland
Antonio Caso 23.

Jardín Amazonas
Rio Amazonas 73, tel 533-5950.
Restaurant, bar, pool, near Reforma.

■ Guest House
Casa González
Corner Rio Lerma and Rio Sena, tel 514-3302.

■ Special Class
Majestic (Best Western)
Madero 73, tel 521-8600, 85 rooms.
1925 neo-colonial building with rooftop bar and restaurant, and magnificent view of the Zócalo.

Around Mexico City

CUERNAVACA

■ *****
Racquet Club
Francisco Villa 100, tel 13-6122.
Restaurant, bar, pool, tennis courts, colonial buildings in quiet neighborhood north of downtown.

■ ****
Hostería del Sol
Bartolomé de las Casas 107, tel 12-1227.
Restaurant, bar, pool, colonial building.

■ **
Papagayo
Motolínia 13, tel 14-1711.

■ Special Class
Las Mañanitas
Ricardo Linares 107, tel 14-1466.
Beautiful and famous colonial building, restaurant and gardens.

PACHUCA

■ **
Noriega
Matamoros 305, tel 25000.

PUEBLA

■ *****
El Mesón del Angel
Hermanos Serdán 807, tel 48-2100.
Two restaurants, bar, two pools, health club, northwest of downtown.

■ ***
Royalty
Portal Hidalgo 8, tel 42-0202, 44 rooms.
Restaurant, bar, cafeteria, parking, on main square.

Palacio San Leonardo
2 Oriente 211, tel 46-0555, 75 rooms.
Restaurant, bar, neo-colonial building.

■ **
Imperial
4 Oriente 212, tel 42-4980, 63 rooms.
Restaurant, parking, downtown.

Gran Hotel San Agustín
3 Poniente 531, tel 32-5089, 74 rooms.
Restaurant, cafeteria, kiddie pool.

TAXCO

■ *****
Monte Taxco
Tel 21300, 156 rooms.
Restaurant, bar, tennis courts, golf course, cable car, above town.

■ ****
De La Borda
Cerro de Pedregal 2, tel 20025.
Pool, just outside town.

Hacienda del Solar
Paraje del Solar, tel 20223.

■ ***
Agua Escondida
Guillermo Spratling 4, tel 20726.

Los Arcos
Juan Ruíz de Alarcón 2, tel 21836.

Posada de los Castillo
Juan Ruíz de Alarcón 3, tel 21396.

The Colonial States

QUERÉTARO
■ *****
Holiday Inn
Carretera Constitución 13 Sur, tel 60202.
West of downtown.

■ ****
Amberes
Corregidora Sur 188, tel 28604.
Near bus station.

■ ***
Impala
Colón 1, tel 22570.
Near bus station.

■ **
Hidalgo
Madero 11 Pte, tel 20081.
Downtown.

GUANAJUATO
■ ****
Castillo Santa Cecilia
One kilometer north on Valenciana road,
tel 20485.
Castle.

Parador San Javier
Plaza San Javier (on Valenciana road), tel
20626, 120 rooms.
Two restaurants, cafeteria, bar, disco,
bullring, gardens.

Posada Santa Fé
Plaza Principal, tel 20084, 50 rooms.
Since 1862, excellent restaurant, bar,
jacuzzis, in the center.

■ ***
San Diego
Jardín Unión 1, tel 21300.
Central.

El Insurgente
Avda Juárez 226, tel 23192.

■ **
Mineral de Rayas
Calle Alhondiga 7, tel 21967.

SAN MIGUEL DE ALLENDE

■ ****
Posada de la Aldea
Calle Ancha de San Antonio, tel 21022.
Pool, gardens, colonial.

■ ***
Mansión del Bosque
Aldama 65, tel 20277.

Posada de las Monjas
Canal 37, tel 20171.
Ex-convent.

Mesón de San Antonio
Mesones 80, tel 20580.

■ **

Posada Carmina
Cuna de Allende 7, tel 20458.

LEÓN
■ *****

Fiesta Americana
Blvd López Mateos 1102, tel 13-6040,
211 rooms.
Two restaurants, bar, pool, health club,
on top of shopping mall, convention
facilities.

AGUASCALIENTES
■ ****

Francia
Plaza Principal 113 Oriente, tel 56080.
Restaurant, historic building, central.

■ **

Señorial
Corner of Colón and Montoro, tel 51473.
On main square.

SAN LUIS POTOSÍ
■ ****

Panorama Venustiano
Carranza 315, tel 21777, 127 rooms.
Restaurant, bar, disco, pool.

■ ***

María Cristina
Juan Sarabia 100, tel 29408.

Nápoles
Juan Sarabia 120, tel 12-8418.

ZACATECAS
■ ****

Paraiso Radisson
Miguel Hidalgo 703, tel 26183.
Restaurant, bar, on main square.

Gallery Best Western
Blvd Lopez Mateos, tel 23311.

■ ***

Posada de los Condes
Juárez 18-A, tel 21093.
Cafeteria.

Posada de la Moneda
Hidalgo 413, tel 20881.

GUADALAJARA

■ GRAN TURISMO
Crowne Plaza (Holiday Inn)
López Mateos Sur 2500, tel 31-5566, 300
rooms.
Restaurant, cafeteria, bar, disco, pool,
convention facilities, near malls southwest
of downtown.

■ *****

Fiesta Americana
Aurelio Aceves 225, tel 25-3434, 396
rooms.
Three restaurants, four bars, tennis courts,
pool, meeting rooms.

Hyatt Regency
López Mateos and Moctezuma, tel 22-
7788, 347 rooms.
Restaurant, cafeteria, bar, pool, shopping
center, ice skating rink.

Jalisco charreada—*Mexican rodeo*

■ ****

De Mendoza
V Carranza 16, tel 13-4646, 110 rooms.
Restaurant, nightclub, pool, parking,
central.

Fénix
Corona 160, tel 14-5714, 262 rooms.
Restaurant, two bars, nightclub, parking,
central.

De Los Reyes
Calz Independencia Sur 164, tel 13-0076,
171 rooms.
Restaurant, bar, nightclub, pool, central.

■ ***

Nueva Galicia
Corona 610, tel 14-8780.
Restaurant, bar, parking.

Colón
Avda Revolucion Pte 12, tel 13-3390, 78
rooms.

URUAPAN
■ ****

Mansion del Cupatitzio
West of town on Guadalajara road, tel
30333.
Restaurant, pool.

■ ***

Plaza
Ocampo 64, tel 69334.

MORELIA
■ *****

Calinda Quality Inn
Avda de las Camelinas 3466, tel 41427.

Restaurant, bar, pool, out by southeast of downtown.

■ ****

Virrey de Mendoza
Portal Matamoros 16, tel 20633.
Colonial building with courtyard, central.

Alameda
Madero Pte and Guillermo Prieto, tel 22023.
Restaurant, bar, colonial building.

■ ***

Casino
Portal Hidalgo 229, tel 31003.
Restaurant, near Cathedral.

■ **

Concordia
Gómez Fárias 327, tel 23052.
Restaurant, downtown.

PÁTZCUARO
■ *****

Posada de Don Vasco
Lázaro Cárdenas 450, tel 20227.
Motor inn.

■ ***

Mesón del Gallo
Dr Coss 20, tel 21474.
Restaurant, pool.

Los Escudos
Portal Hidalgo 73, tel 20138.
On main square.

The Pacific States

LOS MOCHIS
■ ****

Santa Anita
Leyva and Melgar, tel 57046.

MAZATLÁN
■ Gran Turismo
El Cid Mega Resort
Camarón Sabalo, tel 33333, 1,100 rooms.
Six pools, 17 tennis courts, two golf courses, shopping center, etc.

■ *****

Camino Real
Punta de Sabalo, tel 31111, 170 rooms.
Two restaurants, two bars, tennis courts, beach.

Playa Mazatlán
Rodolfo Loaiza, tel 34455, 425 rooms.
Restaurant, bar, two pools, beach.

■ ****

El Quijote Inn
Camarón Sabalo, tel 41134, 67 rooms.
Restaurant, pool, kitchenettes, beach.

Hacienda
Avda del Mar and Flamingos, tel 27000, 95 rooms.
Restaurants, bars, pool.

■ ***

Belmar
Paseo de Olas Altas 166, tel 20799, 250 rooms.

Restaurant, bar, pool, beach.

TEPIC
■ ****
Fray Junípero Serra
Lerdo 23, tel 22525.

■ ***
San Jorge
Lerdo 124, tel 21324.

SAN BLAS
■ ****
Marino Inn
tel 50340. Restaurant, pool.

■ ***
Las Brisas
tel 50112.

PUERTO VALLARTA
■ Gran Turismo
Camino Real
Playa Las Estacas, tel 30123, 250 rooms.
Pool, private beach, three restaurants, two
bars, tennis court, shopping arcade.

Sheraton Buganvilias
North of downtown, tel 30404, 670
rooms.

■ *****
Fiesta Americana Puerto Vallarta
North, tel 22010, 291 rooms.

Holiday Inn
North, tel 21700, 460 rooms.

Krystal Vallarta
North, US tel (800) 231-9860, 500 rooms.
Beach, two pools, tennis courts, six restaurants, three bars, miniature bullring for
guests.

■ ****
Buenaventura
Mexico 1301, tel 23742, 210.
In town.

Playa los Arcos
Olas Altas 380, tel 21175, 146 rooms.
Town.

■ ***
Posada Río Cuale
Serdán 242, tel 20450, 22 rooms.
Downtown.

COLIMA
■ ****
America
Morelos 162, tel 29596, 55 rooms.
Restaurant, bar, parking.

■ **
Ceballos
Portal Medillín 12, tel 24444, 70 rooms.
Cafeteria, on main square.

MANZANILLO
■ Gran Turismo
Las Hadas
Peninsula de Santiago, tel 30000, 220
rooms.

Moorish fantasy with restaurants, bars, nightclub, pools, golf course, tennis, beach.

■ ****

La Posada
Lázaro Cárdenas 201, tel 31899, 24 rooms.
Restaurant, bar, pool.

IXTAPA
■ **Gran Turismo**
Westin Resort
Playa Vista Hermosa, tel 32121, 428 rooms.
Four restaurants, bar, disco, two pools, tennis, beach.

■ *****
Stouffer Presidente
Blvd Ixtapa, tel 30018, 401 rooms.
Restaurants, bars, two pools, tennis courts, beach.

Omni Ixtapa
Blvd Ixtapa, tel 30303, 281 rooms.
Restaurants, bars, pool, health club, beach.

ZIHUATENEJO
■ **Special Class**
Villa del Sol
Playa la Ropa, tel 42239, 30 rooms.
Bungalows, restaurant, pool, tennis, beach.

■ ***
Avila

Cemetery vigil during the Day of the Dead, Janitzio Island

Juan N Alvarez 7, tel 42010, 25 rooms.
Restaurant, bar, on town beach.

■ **

Zihua Inn
Los Magos and Palapas, tel 43868, 30
rooms.
Pool.

ACAPULCO

■ **Gran Turismo**
Acapulco Princess
Playa Revolcadero, tel 43100, 1020
rooms.
Everything.

Fiesta Americana Condesa
Costera Miguel Alemán 1220, tel 42828,
500 rooms.
Three restaurants, two bars, nightclub,
pool, meeting facilities.

■ *****

La Palapa (Best Western)
Fragata Yucatán 210, tel 45363, 376
rooms.
Three restaurants, three bars, pool, health
club, private beach.

■ ****

Caleta
Cerro de San Martín, tel 39940, 250
rooms.
Four restaurants, two bars, two pools,
private beach.

■ ***

Maralisa
Costera, tel 56677, 90 rooms.

Tropicana (Best Western)
Costera 510, tel 41100, 140 rooms.

Posada del Sol
Old Acapulco, tel 41010, 240 rooms.

The North

GUAYMAS

■ ***

Playa de Cortés
Bahía de Bacochibampo, tel 20121.
North of town.

HERMOSILLO

■ *****

Holiday Inn
Blvd Eusebio Kino 369, tel 15112.

CIUDAD JUÁREZ

■ ****

Calinda Quality Inn
Calz Hermanos Escobar 3515, tel 13-7250.

CHIHUAHUA

■ ****

San Francisco
Victoria 409, tel 16-7550.
Behind Cathedral.

■ ***

El Campanario
Blvd Díaz Ordáz and Libertad, tel 15-4545.

Victoria
Juárez and Colón, tel 12-8893.

COPPER CANYON
■ ****

Rancho La Estancia
32 kilometers (20 miles) from Cuauhtemoc, tel 16-1657, 40 rooms.

■ ***

Cabañas Cañón del Cobre
20 kilometers (12 miles) from Creel, tel
15-8214, 23 rooms.

Motel Parador de la Montaña
Creel, tel 15-5408, 50 rooms.

Cabañas Divisadero Barrancas
Divisadero Barranca station, tel 12-3362,
34 rooms.
On the lip of the canyon.

Mansión Tarahumara
South of Divisadero, tel 12-7943, 15
rooms.
Looks like a castle.

SALTILLO
■ *****

Camino Real
Blvd Los Fundadores 2000, tel 52525.
Restaurant, pool, elegant motel-style
south of town.

■ ****

San Jorge
Manuel Acuña 240 Norte, tel 30600.
Downtown.

TORREÓN
■ ****

Rio Nazas
Morelos 732 Pte, tel 16-1212.

MONTERREY
■ *****

Gran Hotel Ancira
Hidalgo 498 Oriente, tel 43-2060.
Restaurant, bar, boutiques, historic build-
ing, central.

Crowne Plaza (Holiday Inn)
Constituyentes 300 Oriente, tel 44-9300.

■ ****

Río
Corner Morelos and Zaragoza, tel 43-5120.
Restaurant, bar, pool.

■ ***

Colonial
Hidalgo 475 Oriente, tel 43-6791.
Restaurant, cafeteria, nightclub.

Quinta Avenida
Madero 243 Oriente, tel 75-6565, 70
rooms.
Restaurant, parking.

El Paso Autel
Zaragoza 130 Norte, tel 40-0690, 65
rooms.
Restaurant, cafeteria, bar, pool.

DURANGO
■ ***

Casablanca
20 de Noviembre 811, tel 13599.

■ **

Posada Durán
20 de Noviembre 506 Pte, tel 12412.

Baja California

TIJUANA
■ *****

Fiesta Americana
Blvd Agua Caliente 4500, tel 81-7000,
422 rooms.
Four restaurants, four bars, disco, on top
of shopping mall, pool, privileges at golf
club next door.

■ ****

Lucerna
Héroes and Rodríguez, tel 84-1000.

Conquistador
Blvd Agua Caliente 700, tel 86-4801.

Caesar
Revolución 827, tel 88-0449. Central.

■ ***

Paris
Calle Quinta 1939, tel 85-3023.

MEXICALI
■ ****

Lucerna
Blvd Benito Juárez 2151, tel 66-1000.
Three restaurants, two bars, nightclub,
pool, gift shop, convention rooms.

■ ***

Castel Calafia
Justo Sierra 1495, tel 64-0222.

Del Norte
Melgar and Madero, tel 54-0575.
Next to border crossing.

Rock carved by the elements, Sierra Madre Occidental

ENSENADA
■ *****

San Nicolás Resort Hotel
López Mateos and Guadalupe, tel 61901.

■ ****

Villa Marina
Blancarte and López Mateos, tel 83321.

■ ***

Mision Santa Isabel
López Mateos and Castillo, tel 83616.

LORETO
■ ****

Presidente Nopolo
Blvd Mision de Loreto, tel 30700.
South of town.

■ **

Misión
Malecón, tel 30048.
Restaurant, pool.

LA PAZ
■ ****

Los Arcos
Alvaro Obregon 498, tel 22744.
Restaurant, bar, pool, on Malecón.

■ ***

Perla
Alvaro Obregón and La Paz, tel 20777.
Restaurant, bar, nightclub.

CABO SAN LUCAS
■ Gran Turismo
Hacienda
Playa El Medano, tel 30122, 112 suites.

Restaurant, bar, pool, dive shop, own beach.

Hotel Cabo San Lucas
4.5 kilometers (three miles) east of Cabo San Lucas, California tel (213) 655-2323, 77 rooms.
Restaurants, bars, pool, beach, dive shop, luxurious.

■ ****

Mar de Cortéz
Lázaro Cárdenas and Guerrero, tel 30032, 72 rooms.
Restaurant, bar, pool, downtown.

■ **

Casa Blanca
Revolución and Madero, tel 30262.

The South

VERACRUZ
■ *****

Emporio
Paseo del Malecón, tel 32-0020, 202 rooms.
Restaurant, bar, cafeteria, three pools, on harbor downtown.

■ ****

Mocambo
Calz Ruiz Cortines, tel 37-1531.
Restaurant, bar, pools, tennis, on beach east of town.

■ ***
Colonial
Miguel Lerdo 117, tel 32-0193.
On main square.

Hostal de Cortes
Avila Camacho and Bartolomé de las
Casas, tel 32-0065.

■ **
Amparo
Aquiles Serdán 482, tel 32-2738.

JALAPA
■ ****
Xalapa
Victoria and Bustamante, tel 82222.
Restaurant, pool.

■ ***
María Victoria
Zaragoza 6, tel 73530.

SAN ANDRES TUXTLA
■ ***
Del Parque
Madero 5, tel 20198.
Restaurant, cafeteria, bar, on main square.

SANTIAGO TUXTLA
■ ***
Castellanos
Main square, tel 70200.

PAPANTLA
■ ***
El Tajín
Dr Núñez 104, tel 21064.

OAXACA
■ *****
Presidente
5 de Mayo 300, tel 60611.
Restored 17th-century convent, restaurant,
bar, folklorica dance performances, pool.

■ ****
Calesa Real
García Vigil 306, tel 65544, 77 rooms.
Restaurant, bar, pool, two blocks from
main square.

■ ***
Marqués del Valle
Portal de Clavería, tel 63295, 95 rooms.
On the plaza.

Senorial
Portal de Flores 6, tel 63933.
Restaurant, pool, main plaza.

■ **
Mesón del Rey
Trujano 212, tel 60023.
Central.

Francia
20 de Noviembre 212, tel 64811.

Ruiz
Bustamante 103, tel 63660.

PUERTO ANGEL
■ ***
Angel del Mar
Playa del Panteón, tel 6.
On hill overlooking bay.

Puerto Escondido
■ ****

Posada Real (Best Western)
North of town, tel 20133, 100 rooms.
Two restaurants, three bars, pools, beach club.

■ ***

Paraiso Escondido
Union 10, tel 20444.
Pool, in town.

Huatulco
■ *****

Royal Maeva
Tangolunda Bay, 300 rooms.
Restaurants, bars, pools, tennis.

Sheraton
Tangolunda Bay, tel 10055, 346 rooms.

■ ****

Posada Binniguenda
Santa Cruz Bay, tel 40080, 100 rooms.
Restaurants, bar, pool.

Tehuantepec
■ ***

Calli
On highway west of town, tel 50085.

Tuxtla Gutiérrez
■ ****

Bonampak
Blvd B Dominguez 180, tel 32050, 118 rooms.
Restaurant, cafeteria, bar, pool, tennis.

■ ***

Gran Hotel Humberto
Central Poniente 180, tel 22044.

San Cristóbal de las Casas
■ ****

Diego de Mazariegos
María Adelina Flores 2 and 5 de Febrero 1, tel 81825, 80 rooms.
Restaurant, bar, courtyards, fireplaces.

■ ***

Ciudad Real
Plaza 31 de Marzo 10, tel 80187, 31 rooms.

Español
10 de Marzo 15, tel 80045.

Santa Clara
Insurgentes 1 and Plaza Central, tel 81140, 40 rooms.
Restaurant, bar, pool, Diego de Mazariego's mansion completed in 1531.

■ **

Rincón del Arco
Ejército Nacional 66, tel 81313.

Palacio de Moctezuma
Benito Juárez 16, tel 80352.

Palenque
■ ****

Misión
East end of town, tel 50241.
Tour groups.

■ ***
La Cañada
Calle Merle Greene 13, tel 50102.
Owner is an expert on the ruins.

Chan-Kah
Km 31 ruins highway, tel 50018.
Nearest to ruins.

VILLAHERMOSA
■ *****
Exelaris Hyatt
Avda Juárez 106, tel 34444.

■ ****
Villahermosa Villa
Blvd Ruiz Cortines and Paseo Tabasco, tel 50000.

The Yucatán Peninsula

MÉRIDA
■ *****
Holiday Inn
Colón 498 and Paseo Montejo, tel 25-6877.
Restaurants, bars, disco, tennis, pool, where the local élite meet.

■ ****
Los Aluxes
Calle 60 No 144, tel 24-2199, 109 rooms.
Restaurant, cafeteria, bar.

El Castellano
Calle 57 No 512, tel 23-0100, 170 rooms.
Restaurant, bar, pool.

Casa de Balam
Calle 60 No 488, tel 21-9212.

■ ***
Caribe
Parque Hidalgo, tel 24-9022, 56 rooms.
Restaurant, bar, small pool.

■ **
Gran Hotel
Calle 60 No 496, tel 21-7620.
19th-century atmosphere.

Reforma
Calle 59 No 508, tel 24-7920.
Pool.

UXMAL
■ ****
Hacienda
Tel 24-7142.
Restaurant, gardens, pool.

Villa Arqueológica
Tel 24-7953.
Restaurant, pool, tennis.

CHICHÉN ITZÁ
■ ****
Hacienda
Km 120 Carretera Mérida-Puerto Juárez.
Charming seediness.

Mayaland
Km 120 Carretera Mérida-Puerto Juárez.

Villa Arqueológica
Tel 62830.

■ ***
Pirámide Inn
Piste.

■ **
Dolores Alba
East of the ruins.

VALLADOLID
■ ***
Méson del Marqués
Calle 39 No 203, tel 62073.
Main square.

CANCÚN
■ Gran Turismo
Fiesta Americana Coral Beach
Beach, US tel (800) FIESTA-1.

Presidente
Beach, US tel (800) HOTELS-1.

Krystal
Beach, US tel (800) 231-9860.

■ *****
Cancún Puerta Al Sol
Beach, US tel (800) 346-8225.

Cancún Beach Club
Beach, US tel (800) 346-8225.

Meliá Turquesa
Beach, US tel (800) 336-3542.

■ ****
Club Las Velas
Lagoon, US tel (800) 223-9815.

Plaza Las Glorias
Lagoon, US tel (800) 342-2644.

Kin Ha
Beach, US tel (800) 521-2980.

■ ***
America
Brisa and Tulum, tel 41500, 168 rooms.
At entrance to hotel zone.

Soberanis
Coba 5, tel 41858, 60 rooms.

■ **
Antillano
Tulum and Claveles 1, tel 41244, 48
rooms.
Downtown.

ISLA MUJERES
■ ****
Posada del Mar
Rueda Medina 15, tel 20212.

■ ***
Berny
Juárez and Abasolo, tel 20025.

■ **
Caracol
Matmoros 5, tel 20150.

María José
Madero 25, tel 20130.

COZUMEL
■ *****
El Cozumeleno
South of town, tel 20149, 98 rooms.

Fiesta Americana Sol Caribe
Playa Paraiso, tel 20700, 321 rooms.
Three restaurants, two bars, private
beach, meeting rooms.

■ ****
La Ceiba
South, tel 20815, 113 rooms.

Villa del Rey
Downtown, tel 21600, 43 rooms.

■ ***
Casa del Mar
South, tel 21944, 110 rooms.

Paraiso Caribe
Downtown, tel 20740, 36 rooms.

Soberanis
Downtown, tel 20246, 12 rooms.

CHETUMAL
■ ****
Continental Caribe
Héroes 171, tel 21100.

■ **
El Márquez
Lázaro Cárdenas 121, tel 22888.

Real Azteca
Belice 186, tel 2066, 26 rooms.
Above the Chez Farouk restaurant.

CAMPECHE
■ ****
Ramada Inn
Ruiz Cortines 51, tel 62233, 119 rooms.
Restaurant, cafeteria, bar, disco, pools,
central.

■ **
Colonial
Calle 14 No 122, tel 62222.
Colonial house with courtyard.

Lopez
Calle 12 No 189, tel 63344.
Art Deco style.

Restaurants

MEXICO CITY

■ MEXICAN
Café de Tacuba
Tacuba 28, tel 512-8482.

Círculo del Sureste
Lucerna 12, tel 535-2704. Yucatecan.

Focolare
Hamburgo 87, tel 511-2679.

Fonda del Recuerdo
Bahía de las Palmas 39, tel 254-8107.

Fonda Santa Anita
Londres 38, tel 514-4720.

Fonda del Refugio
Liverpool 166, tel 528-5823.

Hostería de Santo Domingo
Belisario Domínguez 72, tel 510-1434.

■ CONTINENTAL
Bellinghausen
Londres 95, tel 511-1056.

Cícero
Londres 195, tel 525-6530.

Delmonico's
Londres 87, tel 514-7003.

Prendes
16 de Setiembre 10-C, tel 747-0082.

San Angel Inn
Palmas 50, tel 548-6746.

■ FRENCH
Champs Elysées
Amberes 1, tel 514-0450.

Les Moustaches
Rio Sena 88, tel 533-3390.

L'Estoril
Genova 75, 511-3421.

Normandie
Niza 5, tel 533-0906.

Rivoli
Hamburgo 123, tel 525-6862.

■ ITALIAN
Alfredo's
Genova 74, tel 511-3864.

La Pergola
Londres 107, tel 511-3049.

■ SPANISH
Casino Español
Isabel la Católica 31, 2nd floor, tel 585-1093.

Circulo Vasco
16 de Setiembre 57, 1st floor, tel 518-2908.

Mesón del Cid
Humboldt 1, tel 512-7629.

■ SEAFOOD
Danubio
Uruguay 3, tel 521-0976.

Nuevo Acapulco
López 9, tel 521-1982.

Around Mexico City
■ CUERNAVACA
Las Mananitas
Ricardo Linares 107.
Posh continental.

■ PACHUCA
Casino Español
Matamoros 207, 2nd floor.
Spanish-Mexican, great decor.

■ PUEBLA
Fonda Santa Clara
3 Poniente 307.
Local specialties.

La Bola Roja
17 Sur 1305.
Local.

La Poblanita
10 Norte 1404-B.
Local.

The Colonial States
■ QUERÉTARO
Mesón Santa Rosa
Pasteur 17.
Regional specialties.

Antique car museum, Colima

Fonda del Refugio
Jardín Corregidora 26.
Mexican.

Flor de Queretaro
Juárez Norte 5.
Regional.

■ SAN MIGUEL DE ALLENDE
Mama Mía
Umarán 8, tel 22063.
Pizza and more.

Mesón de la Bugambilia
Mesones 53, tel 20785.
Continental.

■ GUANAJUATO
Café El Retiro
Sopena 12.

Posada Santa Fé
Jardín Unión.
Regional.

Rincón de la Plata
Juárez and Alones.
Mexican.

■ AGUASCALIENTES
Mitla
Madero 220.
Mexican.

■ SAN LUIS POTOSÍ
Café Tokio
Los Bravos 510.
Mexican.

La Lonja
Madero and Aldama.
Regional, elegant.

La Parroquia
V Carranza 301.
Mexican and continental, café.

■ ZACATECAS
Café Acrópolis
Hidalgo and Plazuela Candelario Huizar.

La Cuija
Basement of the old market.
Regional, continental, local wine.

■ GUADALAJARA
Caporales
López Mateos Sur 5290.
Mexican with show.

Carnes Asadas Pipiolo
All over town. Roast meat

Carnes Asadas Tolsa
Enrique Díaz de León 510.
Roast meat.

Copa de Leche
Juárez 414.
Huge café.

Gemma
López Mateos Sur 1800, also Plaza Sol,
Plaza Patria.
Luncheonettes.

La Gorda
General Coronado 543.
Mexican.

La Rinconada
Morelos 86.
Mexican.

Los Otates
Americas 28.
Regional.

■ PÁTZCUARO
El Patio
Plaza Vasco de Quiroga.
Mexican, local specialties.

El Munjo
Plaza Vasco de Quiroga.
Same.

THE PACIFIC STATES
■ MAZATLÁN
Doney
Mariano Escobedo 610.
Downtown Mexican.

El Marinero
Olas Altas.
Seafood.

Shrimp Bucket
Olas Altas 11 (Hotel la Siesta).
Local institution.

■ PUERTO VALLARTA
El Dorado
Playa del Sol.
Seafood.

Moby Dick
31 de Octubre 128.
Seafood.

Ostión Feliz
Libertad 177.
Oysters and seafood.

■ COLIMA
Los Naranjos
Gabina Barreda 34.
Regional.

■ MANZANILLO
Willy's
South Beach and Las Brisas, tel 31794.
French.

■ IXTAPA
Villa de la Selva
Paseo de la Rosa beyond Westin, tel 30372.
International.

■ ZIHUATENEJO
Coconuts
Paseo Agustín Ramirez 1, tel 42518.
International.

■ ACAPULCO
Goyo's
5 de Mayo and 2 de April.
Mexican.

(above) Panning for silver, Chihuahua; (middle) maguey plants turning into tequila, Jalisco; (bottom left) firm friends; (bottom right) hot air ballooning, Jalisco

(above left) Iguana vendor, Juchitán de Zaragoza; (above right) lizards eye their fate, Guerrero; (below) market herbalist, Mexico City

Hard Times
Blvd Costera across from Calinda Quality
Inn.
Tex-Mex.

Normandie
Malaspina and Blvd Costera, tel 51916.
French.

Pinzona 65
Pinzona 65.
Seafood and continental.

THE NORTH
■ GUAYMAS
Del Mar
Serdán 206.
Seafood, steaks, bar.

■ CHIHUAHUA
La Calesa
Juárez and Colón.
Steaks.

La Parrilla
Victoria 450.
Steaks.

■ SALTILLO
El Tapanco
Allende Sur 225.
Mexican.

■ MONTERREY
El Cabritero
Zaragoza and Arreola, tel 42-8376.
Goat specialties.

Regio
González and Vancouver, tel 46-8650.

Regional.

El Tío
Hidalgo and Mexico in Quinta Calderón,
tel 46-0291.
Regional.

■ ENSENEDA
El Rey Sol
López Mateos 1000, tel 81733.
International.

Mariscos Casa Mar
Macheros and Blvd Costera 499.
Seafood.

■ LORETO
Cesar's
Zapata and Juárez.
Seafood.

■ LA PAZ
El Taste
Obregón and Juárez.
Steak and seafood.

THE SOUTH
■ VERACRUZ
La Parroquia
Independencia 105-7.
Mexican and international, institution.

■ JALAPA
Café La Parroquia
Zaragoza 18.
Mexican and international.

Casona del Beatrice
Zaragoza, a few doors down.
Mexican.

■ OAXACA
El Asador Vasco
West side of main square, 2nd floor.
Spanish and international.

Flor de Oaxaca
López 311.

La Catedral
García Vigil and Morelos. Regional.

Los Arcos
Hotel Calesa Real, main square. Regional.

■ TUXTLA GUTIÉRREZ
Las Pichanchas
Avda Central 837, tel 25351. Regional.

■ SAN CRISTÓBAL DE LAS CASAS
El Mural
20 de Noviembre 8.
International.

Madre Tierra
Insurgentes 19.
International.

Plaza
Main plaza, 2nd floor.
International.

YUCATÁN PENINSULA
■ MÉRIDA
Cedros de Líbano
Calle 59 No 529.
Lebanese.

El Patio Continental
Calle 64 No 482, tel 21-2298.
Lebanese, regional and continental.

Express
Calle 60 between 59 and 61.
Café.

Los Almendros
Plaza de Mejorada, tel 12851.
Excellent regional.

Soberanis
Calle 60 No 443, tel 39872.
Seafood.

Yannig
Avda P Ponce No 105 at Calle 21, tel 27-0339.
French.

■ CANCÚN
Los Almendros
Avdas Bonampak and Sayil, tel 40807.
Yucatecan specialties.

■ ISLA MUJERES
Gomar
Hidalgo 5.
Regional and seafood.

■ COZUMEL
La Misión
Juárez and 10 Norte.
Mexican seafood.

Las Palmeras
Main pier.
Mexican and international.

Morgan's
Main square.
Steak and seafood.

Glossary of Language

Spanish is a relatively simple and regular language, and all visitors should pick up at least a few common phrases. Many people in the resort areas speak English, but they always appreciate it when you attempt to communicate in their language. The main difference between Mexican Spanish and the Spanish of Spain is that the former is spoken more slowly and without the Spaniards' lisp. Also, Mexicans have adopted many indian and American words into their language, such as *tianguis* for 'market' and *el lunch*.

The pronunciation of Mexican Spanish is almost totally regular. The letter 'j' is pronounced like 'h' in 'hat'. In Mexico, 'll' is pronounced like the 'i' in 'machine'. The letter 'x' is normally pronounced like 'h' in 'hat', but may also be pronounced as an 's', 'sh' or 'ks'.

Other letters

a	as in 'father'
b	between vowels, almost like a 'v'
c	before 'a', 'o' and 'u', like a 'k'; all other times like 's'
ch	as in 'church'
e	as in 'set'
g	before 'h' and 'i', like 'h' in 'hat'
h	always silent
i	as in 'machine'
ñ	like 'ny' of 'canyon'
q	like 'k'
rr	rolled
y	like 'i' in 'machine'
z	like 's' in 'sass'

Common expressions

yes	*sí*
no	*no*
good morning	*buenos días*
good afternoon	*buenas tardes*
goodbye	*adios*
see you later	*Hasta luego*
thank you	*gracias*
please	*por favor*
My name is	*Mi nombre es.../Me llamo*
What is your name?	*¿Come se llama?*
How do you do?	*¿Como está usted?*
Fine, and you?	*Bien, ¿y usted?*
I don't understand	*No entiendo*
Do you speak English?	*¿Habla usted inglés?*
I don't speak Spanish	*No hablo español*
Pardon me	*Perdóneme*
Excuse me	*Con permiso*
Where is..?	*¿Dónde está..?*
What is..?	*¿Qué es..?*
I want...	*Quiero...*
How much is..?	*¿Cuánto cuesta..?*
Is there..?	*¿Hay..?*
Do you have..?	*¿Tiene..?*
I am lost	*Estoy perdido*
I do not feel well	*No me siento bien*
The check, please	*La cuenta, por favor*
Help!	*¡Socorro!*

Days

Monday	*lunes*	thirteen	*trece*
Tuesday	*martes*	fourteen	*catorce*
Wednesday	*miércoles*	fifteen	*quince*
Thursday	*jueves*	sixteen	*dieciséis*
Friday	*viernes*	seventeen	*diecisiete*
Saturday	*sábado*	eighteen	*dieciocho*
Sunday	*domingo*	nineteen	*diecinueve*
		twenty	*veinte*
		twenty one	*veintuno*

Time

thirty — *treinta*

What time is it?	*¿Qué hora es?*	thirty one	*treinta y uno*
morning	*mañana*	fourty	*cuarenta*
today	*hoy*	fifty	*cincuenta*
yesterday	*ayer*	sixty	*sesenta*
tomorrow	*mañana*	seventy	*setenta*
week	*semana*	eighty	*ochenta*
month	*mes*	ninety	*noventa*
early	*temprano*	one hundred	*cien*
late	*tarde*	one hundred and one	*ciento uno*
later	*después*	five hundred	*quinientos*
		one thousand	*mil*

Numbers

one million — *un millón*

one	*uno/una*		
two	*dos*	**Directions**	
three	*tres*	here	*aquí*
four	*quatro*	there	*allí/allá*
five	*cinco*	near	*cerca*
six	*seis*	far	*lejos*
seven	*siete*	left	*izquierda*
eight	*ocho*	right	*derecha*
nine	*nueve*	straight	*derecho*
ten	*diez*	at the corner	*a la esquina*
eleven	*once*	behind	*detrás*
twelve	*doce*	at the back	*al fondo*

city block	cuadra	plate	plato
next	próximo/próxima	bowl	tazón
entry	entrada	bread	pan
exit	salida	butter	mantequilla
closed	cerrado	sugar	azúcar
open	abierto	milk	leche
pull	tire	cream	crema
push	empuje	ice	hielo
		without ice	sin hielo

Hotel

room	cuarto	salt	sal
bed	cama	eggs	huevos
key	llave	tea	té
soap	jabón	beer	cerveza
towel	toalla	soda	refresco
purified water	agua purificada	coffee	café
hot	caliente	mineral water	agua mineral
cold	frío	bill	cuenta
blanket	manta	change	cambio
pillow	almohada		

Locations

bill	cuenta	bank	banco
pool	piscina	money exchange	casa de cambio
credit card	tarjeta de crédito	airport	aeropuerto
		bus station	central camionera

Restaurant

table	mesa	train station	estación de ferrocar-
waiter	mesero		riles
waitress	mesera	ticket office	taquilla
breakfast	desayuno	post office	correos
lunch	comida	ferry terminal	embarcadero
dinner	cena	bathroom	sanitario, lavabo,
fork	tenedor		baño
knife	cuchillo	hospital	hospital
spoon	cuchara	gas station	gasolinera
napkin	servilleta		
glass	vaso		
wine glass	copa		
cup	taza		

Recommended Reading

Bazant, Jan, *A Concise History of Mexico, from Hidalgo to Cárdenas* (Cambridge Univ Press, Cambridge, 1977)

Coe, Michael et al, *Atlas of Ancient America* (Facts on File, New York, 1986)

Coe, Michael, *The Maya* (Thames & Hudson, London, 1987)

Davies, Nigel, *The Aztecs* (Macmillan, London, 1973)

Díaz, Bernal, *The Conquest of New Spain* (Penguin, London, 1963)

Kandell, Jonathan, *La Capital* (Random House, New York, 1988)

Leon-Portilla, Miguel, *Pre-Columbian Literatures of Mexico* (Univ of Oklahoma Press, 1969)

Leonard, Irving A, *Baroque Times in Old Mexico* (Univ of Michigan Press, Ann Arbor, 1959)

Lewis, Oscar, *The Children of Sanchez* (Random House, New York, 1961)

Lewis, Oscar, *Five Families* (Basic Books, New York, 1959)

Meyer, Michael C & Sherman, William L, *The Course of Mexican History* (Oxford Univ Press, New York, 1979)

Miller, Mary Ellen, *The Art of Mesoamerica, from Olmec to Aztec* (Thames & Hudson, London, 1986)

Morley, Sylvanus & Brainerd, George W, *The Ancient Maya* (Stanford Univ Press, Standford, 1946)

Oster, Patrick, *The Mexicans* (William Morrow, New York, 1989)

Paz, Octavio, *The Labryinth of Solitude* (Grove Press, New York, 1961)

Quirk, Robert E, *The Mexican Revolution, 1914–15* (Indiana Univ Press, 1960)

Riding, Alan, *Distant Neighbors* (Knopf, New York, 1984)

Schele, Linda & Miller, Mary E, *The Blood of Kings: Dynasty and Ritual in Maya Art* (George Braziller, New York, 1986)

Schele, Linda & Freidel, David, *A Forest of Kings: The Untold Story of the Ancient Maya* (William Morrow, New York, 1990)

Simpson, Lesley Bird, *Many Mexicos* (Univ of California Press, Berkeley, 1941)

Soustelle, Jacques, *Daily Life of the Aztecs* (Weidenfeld & Nicolson, London 1961)

Stephens, John L, *Incidents of Travel in Central America, Chiapas and Yucatán* (Dover Publications, New York, 1969)

Stephens, John L, *Incidents of Travel in Yucatán* (Dover Publications, New York, 1963)

Tedlock, Dennis, *Popol Vuh* (Simon & Schuster, New York, 1985)

Toussaint, Manuel, *Colonial Art in Mexico* (Univ of Texas Press, Austin, 1967)

Wolf, Eric, *Sons of the Shaking Earth* (Univ of Chicago Press, Chicago, 1959)

Index

Portrait of a Lady, Tomb Culture burial offering, Guadalajara Regional Museum

342